PETER ROY

NOBODY'S SPEAR CARRIER

A LIFE

Editor: Robert Flemming

Copyright © 2025 Peter Roy

All rights reserved. No part of this publication may be reproduced or transmitted in any form or by any means, electronic or mechanical including photocopying, recording or any information storage or retrieval system, without prior permission in writing from the publishers.

The right of Peter Roy to be identified as the author of this work has been asserted by him in accordance with the Copyright, Designs and Patents Act 1988

First published in the United Kingdom in 2025 by
The Cloister House Press

ISBN 978-1-913460-70-9

Dedicated to

IVAN JOHN BALL
(Managing Director Theatre Projects)

Simply the Best

Contents

1	Burgess, Burgess & Co	1
2	The Food Trade Protection Society	23
3	The Pall Mall Safe Deposit Company	37
4	Beginnings 1939-1956	43
5	Wilson Wright & Co	84
6	Journeyman	154
7	Conway's Group Ltd	167
8	Empire Catering	230
9	Napper Stinton Woolley	232
10	Theatre Projects	256
11	Hanging The Shingle Out	331
12	Barnett Williams Partnership	416
	Afterword	426

1 Burgess, Burgess & Co

'Money does not buy you happiness, but lack of money buys you misery.'

Daniel Kahneman

For a long, long time, I had imagined the day when I could leave the world of children behind and step into the workplace of adults. To be free from the bullies, sneaks, show-offs, spitters, wind-breakers, cheats and the myriad of awful characters that shared my school days. Not only the kids but the teachers as well. And it should have been a momentous day.

It all started in May 1956 when I was called to see the Careers Master. To be honest, I was surprised that the school boasted such a worthy. And more so when it turned out to be the Head of Geography, Mr Smith, in a different guise.

'Top subject, mathematics I see Roy. Might be in luck. A possible opportunity that came to my attention recently might suit your talents. Firm of accountants in the West End has an apprenticeship on offer for a promising lad. Interested I should think.'

'Yes Sir, Thank you.'

'I'll arrange an interview. Let you have the details later.'

An apprenticeship in the West End: the notion was appealing and came as a relief. Living in East London provided a dearth of options. One major employer was the London Docks but that was a closed shop; without relatives already working there, you had no chance. There were other big employers like Tate & Lyle, power stations, public transport services and thousands of small businesses where there might be openings. But they weren't offering anything as far as I knew. Smith hadn't offered anything in the East End but he had come up with the better off West End. But there was one little question in my mind: what's an accountant?

Two days later, I set off for my interview with one Mr D J Sate, a partner at Burgess, Burgess & Co of 26 Craven Street London WC2 with my father in tow. Mr Smith had informed me that this was compulsory and I had no choice. I was horrified as I'd ceased to rely on my parents for help or support a long time ago. By the time I was ten, I was earning little bits of money by running errands, distributing leaflets and mail drops, repairing bicycles and painting walls. At fourteen, I worked in scrap yards during the school holidays. Mainly that entailed sorting out and de-nailing aluminium panels, then collecting different classes of metals together for resale to merchants. It was hard and dirty work but you met some colourful people for sure. For around 18 months, I'd been helping the local chimney sweep from 8.30 to noon every Saturday morning. That brought in £1 plus a share of the tips but I was planning to discontinue once I'd found full time employment.

Number 26 Craven Street was a rather fine 18th century terrace house with partly glazed wooden doors. Sitting in Mr Sate's rather grand office in front of his desk, I was naturally a little nervous that my father would mess things up somehow. He sat on a chair beside me looking bored and leaden.

'We live in bountiful times gentlemen! You will actually be paid a salary during your apprenticeship, Roy. Before the war, your parents would have had to pay us to have you here: that would have been a lump sum for the whole apprenticeship or an annual fee. Assuming we are agreed,' he continued, directing his comments to my father, 'there will be a six month trial period and if all goes well, Articles will be signed to last five years. The remuneration' he said proudly, 'would be £4 per week.'

Remuneration. It seemed to be a very big word for such a small sum. So, no giving up the Saturday job just yet. My mind was racing – how could I survive on £4 a week? Fares alone would take it down to £3.50, leaving a budget of 50 pence a day to live on. To put that into context, a packet of cigarettes cost around 25 pence. It seemed that the grinding poverty of my formative years was to simply grind on.

Although I was a pretty naïve kid, I knew that average wages were in the order of £12 per week. A road worker was paid upwards of £15 and a nurse maybe £10 but what was on the table was less than the minimum wage. (Later I found out that apprentices were not included in the relevant legislation.) My fellow school leavers were signing up to be draughtsmen, designers, printers, copywriters and juniors in a wide range of offices. The average going rate was around £8; my pal David Mercer went into the Co-op's accounts office in Whitechapel and was paid £8.50 per week plus overtime.

So bring the chimney sweep back and, with a little ducking and diving, maybe find an extra quid here and there. Learn to study the pavements and look for small change while walking.

Mr Sate was a smallish man, wearing an expensive suit and he told a grand tale.

'Yes, becoming an accountant is a hard path to walk but when you qualify, the tap's turned fully on and the money flows. Your services will be in high demand and the world's your oyster. Then you too can have a quality suit, an office, a house, car and a pretty girl on your arm.'

'But until then,' I thought, 'I'll have nothing, or even less than nothing!'

My father sat there silently, asking nothing, saying nothing. He was no businessman and his abysmal record of being incapable of holding down a job spoke volumes. I knew that I could have represented myself far better than he ever could but I was invisible in this transaction. Alone, I'm certain that I could have realized a higher pay offer. Not much maybe, but in the circumstances, every penny would really count.

After half an hour we left with the agreement that I would start my apprenticeship with Burgess, Burgess and Co in August. Not with my agreement, I wasn't asked; that was something between the grown-ups. Even then I knew it would end in tears.

We took the tube home from Embankment station to Plaistow. Our borough was neighboured to the west by the more famous West Ham, whose football team's home ground was at Upton Park to our east. Confused? Rather than being at the Bow/Bethnal Green cockney-land east end, we were further out towards Essex. But we were still solid working class. An interesting historical side note: in 1892 West Ham was represented by Keir Hardie, the first Labour Member of Parliament.

On arrival in Plaistow, my father retired to the pub for a couple of pints of Indian Pale Ale and a game or two of dominoes. After all, it was a Monday and therefore his day off. I returned home to find my mother waiting and I dutifully gave her a summary of what had occurred. What came next was an absolute shock.

'Well, whatever you earn, I want half of it on the table every

Friday. We've paid for you for over 16 years; now it's time for you to start paying back.'

Now I know it's the traditional image of a mother to be warm, generous and caring but I didn't get that version. Here we had a real piece of work. At a stroke, she'd shot to pieces my plans to survive. My daily cash had been reduced to 20 pence. Something would turn up – it always did. Clearly my destiny was to become a latter day Mr Micawber. After all, Mr Sate had mentioned that the practice was committed to reviewing salaries every September. Therefore, surely it was logical that if I proved my worth over the previous twelve months, I would see a pay increase of some substance.

Tipped off that the local council had a grant scheme for poor families that provided a gift of £5 towards their first work clothing, I presented myself at the Town Hall. At first they denied that that any such scheme existed but my perseverance paid off. In the end, the official grudgingly admitted that perhaps something might be done. After completing a mountain of paperwork and passing a means test, I was issued with a voucher that enabled me to buy an off-the-peg suit. Otherwise I would have had to wear my school blazer and flannels.

When school ended and summer arrived, I went on a cycling holiday to Devon and Cornwall. After that I found casual work to build up a fighting fund to tide me over the first few weeks. It was the best I could do to prepare for what was to come.

*****

At 8.45am on Monday 13 August 1956, I exited Embankment station, crossed the road and entered Craven Street. This narrow thoroughfare that ran uphill to end at The Strand was bounded by four storey buildings on either side, giving the impression that the sun never penetrated the shadows. Henry James, the American author – who became British during World War One to demonstrate his support – described Craven Street as 'packed to blackness with accumulations of suffered experience'. How right he was!

Reaching Number 26, I walked in and headed for Mr Sate's office on the first floor, knocked and waited. After a long pause I heard a muffled voice say: 'come in'. I found Mr Sate sitting behind his desk and in addition, another man sitting at a desk to his left.

'Who are you and what do you want?' Sate asked curtly.

'I'm Peter Roy. I've come to start work today.'

'Ah, I'd forgotten all about you.'

Walking over to Sate's desk, I offered my hand to be shaken, noticing that the desk was entirely empty apart from a day-per-page diary open at 13/14 August. The only entry for the 13th was my name at the top of the page, which proved that his unfriendly words were a lie. I didn't understand. Why was it important to him to make me feel unwelcome and feel worthless? Why did he want our relationship (whatever that would turn out to be) to begin with a pointless lie?

Ignoring my hand, he gestured to the new face in the room.

'This is Mr Hodgson.'

A limp handshake was offered but without any eye contact.

Leonard William Hodgson. Of a similar age to Sate, he was in his late twenties but taller with very apparent premature balding. In contrast to Sate's unencumbered desk, Hodgson's was a battlefield of papers; clearly he was struggling with his task.

'I'll show you where you'll be working Roy. Follow me.'

We walked out onto the landing, Sate to the fore with me following and Hodgson trailing behind. Down the corridor, he opened a door to the right that led into a small drab room, sparsely furnished with bits of old furniture. The sole window looked out onto a vast brick wall which I later identified as being the western side of Charing Cross station. Far below, I could see Hungerford Lane running parallel to Craven Street before dog-legging under the railway tracks and coming out at Villiers Street. It was the habitat of the homeless, down and outs and general penniless derelicts. I wondered how long it would be before I joined them.

Pulling a telephone directory from a shelf, Sate dropped it on the desk and opened it at the first page of listings.

'Little test for you. I want you to cast the telephone number columns.'

'Cast Mr Sate?'

'You might say add-up. But in accounting terms, it is cast or tot.'

I didn't respond to this revelation but thought hard. We seemed to be in the twilight zone.

'And' Sate added, 'we know the correct totals, so you had better get it right.'

Lie number two. Of course they hadn't added up, cast or totted the bleeding telephone numbers. Two qualified accountants wasting their time and expertise? I didn't think so. What in God's name had I signed up for? I could hear them giggling like schoolgirls as they went back to their office. Then I realised the sickening truth: I might have left school but not my schooldays. They were still with me, albeit that I was better dressed and had more cash on my hip. A hateful cast of characters were there right now, in front and forever.

There was no way that I was going to add up all the telephone numbers. I added half of one column doubled it and then added similar numbers plucked out of the air. Working a column every twenty minutes, when the two stooges returned at noon I had several pages under my belt.

'Not bad,' Sate said with a snide grin. 'In fact, pretty close.' (As if he bloody knew!) 'We're off for lunch. I'll start you on some real work at two.'

Off they went, giggling down the corridor. At least somebody was getting some pleasure out of the charade. No lunch for this boy. I'd briefly thought about taking something from the kitchen before I left home but as mother's tongue could kill at 50 paces, I quickly dismissed the notion. It had already sunk in that for the foreseeable future, I would be a one meal a day guy. Without lunch to consume, there was time to explore.

The ground floor was occupied by a legal firm while the third floor offices simply had a brass plaque bearing the name Fielding & Co. But no indication of their speciality. The top floor was much more interesting. The front office housed the agent for a swing band called Ivy Benson and her All Girls Band and it turned out that he was a really decent sort. I think he really looked after Ivy Benson and her ladies, a very successful band at the time. At the back of the office I discovered a kitchenette and, without permission, made myself a brew.

Sate and Hodgson returned a fraction before two. It was left to Hodgson to reveal some of the accountant's arcane arts.

'The cornerstone of our work is the system of double entry bookkeeping. We don't know for certain where or when it was invented but general consensus holds that it's at least a thousand years old. The golden rule is that every transaction gives rise to two entries: one on the debit (left) side and one on the credit (right) side, thus ensuring that the books balance at all times. The debit side is always near the window.'

That last one-liner really cracked them both up, almost howling with laughter. Having taught me the golden rules of accountancy and automatically assumed I would remember every word, Hodgson plonked a bag in front of me.

'Client's a shopkeeper and those are his accounts.'

Apparently said shopkeeper used a patented book named Simplex where transactions were only recorded a single time.

'Um what do I do?'

'Just copy what they did last year.'

It was a phrase that would bring me grief some ten years later. And that was more or less the extent of my training; then they left me to it. I studied the file that together with this year's book started to make sense. The task was to summarise the entries on a sheet of analysis paper, tot them up and take through to produce a profit and loss account. Of course, it wasn't quite as simple or as quick as that but eventually I did get the sense of it all.

In the course of the afternoon, there was a call for tea which task fell to me as the office junior. Up two flights of stairs, I made it my mission to produce the most barely bloody drinkable possible but despite my worst efforts, Sate and Hodgson drank whatever was put before them. The chai wallah's role was mine, if not for life at least until an even more junior person was recruited.

At 5 o'clock I headed for the tube and home. That evening not a word was said nor a question asked. Life is what it is, not as it should be. The following day, I made a conscious decision to get to work 20 minutes early. Not through any sense of enthusiasm but to brew myself a strong, sweet mug of tea that I could enjoy before the wheels started turning. The bosses double act duly arrived and apart from a brace of brusque good mornings, no pleasantries were ever exchanged. Sate spent most of his time out and about dealing with the matter of keeping the workload moving.

I was of course learning on the job and as I finished one task, there was always another lined up behind, waiting for my attention. It was Hodgson's pleasure to set unfeasible time limits for the completion of each job which gave him ample opportunity to complain. Opportunities which he never failed to take. I continued to provide dishwater tea and coffee; they continued to drink the stuff.

Friday afternoon. At three o'clock the door of my room opened and in walked a small rotund elderly man who introduced himself as Mr Burgess. This Burgess was the only version that I met and nobody ever told me what had happened to the other Burgess. A large cigar was firmly clamped between his lips and was never removed. Therefore when he spoke, a cloud of smoke and ash poured out the sides of his mouth rendering him both hard to see and understand. He handed me my first wage packet without any polite, friendly 'welcome aboard' or similar. I was beginning to think that the profession was very short on social skills.

When he left the office, I was just returning from an errand. I watched him climb into a chauffer driven limo, cigar to the fore, and waft off into the afternoon traffic. Food for thought.

That evening mother welcomed me back home with her hand out and half my measly pay was gone. More food for thought. Saturday morning I was back on the brushes but the afternoon was enjoyed playing football.

*****

My passion was for cycling and from my earlier cash generation efforts, I managed to acquire a Hetchins racing bicycle. I hand assembled it myself and that bike was my pride and joy. For day-to-day transport, I had an old Claud Butler.

Seeking to improve my financial lot, I considered the possibility of riding a bike to work. I could leave my business gear in the office cupboard, saving some wear and tear on that; ride back and forth in proper cycling gear that I already had. As the crow flies, it was approximately eight miles each way; the logical route in would be either along Barking Road or Romford Road into the City and then along the Embankment.

Even back in 1956 these corridors were heavily congested, so I looked for a series of rat runs to make the journey safer and just more comfortable. So over to Stratford Broadway, onto Carpenter's Road (aka The Valley of Stinks), cut through to Old Ford Road and onto Bethnal Green Road. Then pass north of Liverpool Street Station, along Clerkenwell Road/Theobalds in Holborn, past Covent Garden and finally The Strand. Convoluted perhaps but it made complete sense at the time and only added about a mile each way.

At lunchtime on Monday, I looked for a spot to keep the bicycle during the course of the day. I dismissed the entrance hall immediately, sure that the other users of the building would be up in arms about a bike in the lobby. Outside the building was not an option either as there was nowhere it could be locked away safely and out of the way. The top floor utility room might be possible but again, a shout might go up and there were a hell of a lot of stairs to climb with a bike on your shoulder, even a lightweight one.

Realistically, the only place I could think of where nobody was likely to object was outside the window on the half landing. The ground floor had a small extension that offered a flat roof of three yards by two yards; a bicycle could be squeezed through the window and parked there. It was a long drop to Hungerford Lane but needs must.

I decided to give it a try. Naturally if the weather was crazy I'd revert to the tube but otherwise there were financial savings to be made and I'd get a daily workout to boot. It would mean leaving home earlier and work later. In late August and September the plan worked well but as winter set in a rethink would be needed.

Foyles, the massive bookshop on Charing Cross Road, bought second hand books as long as they were in reasonable condition and for a time they were a great help to me as I filtered some out of my small collection. They were always decent people and gave very reasonable prices. There was no doubt in my mind that they were most sympathetic to people like me who were in dire straits.

Lack of cash was never a problem at school, just a nuisance but setting off to work in the morning with empty pockets was terrifying. I was becoming obsessed with finding ways to get from one day to the next. I went to bed thinking of money and woke up with the exact same thoughts. Mine was truly a nickel and dime existence.

One morning I was despatched to our Harlesden office to help out.

The limo was waiting for me outside Harlesden station not, as the driver explained, for my benefit but to save the firm's time. The office turned out to be the front room of 5a St Mary's, a small terraced house and home to one Mr Burgess of Burgess, Burgess and Co. He was there with the omnipresent cigar. It gave the lie to the big public front he presented. I churned through a pile of paperwork without even being offered a cup of tea, finished at five and had to walk back to the station. No limo to save my time and effort.

In September I asked permission to arrive a couple of hours late as the results of my end of school examinations were being posted on the school noticeboard. Otherwise I would have to wait for a few more days for them to arrive in the post. Sate agreed but with the proviso that I made up the time. Brimming with generosity that fellow.

My results were good. I passed all six of the Certificates of General Education that I'd taken and was naturally pleased. Arriving in the office at around eleven, I informed Sate and Hodgson of the good news which was received with profound indifference. Sate's only response to my presence was to say that they were waiting for their tea.

Apart from my brief sojourn in beautiful Harlesden, all of my work had been carried out in the Craven Street office. However, towards the end of October, it was decided that it was time to introduce me to the wonderful world of auditing. My introduction to audit-life was to take place at a Savile Row tailor's that was situated not on Savile Row but Cork Street.

'I will be going straight there on Monday morning. Meet me there at nine and don't be late.'

On arrival I naturally walked into the shop to be met by two men with tape measures hanging around their necks. It was perfectly clear that neither was impressed by the scruffy youth in the cheap suit in front of them. Not a potential customer by a long chalk.

'And how may I assist you young man?' one asked in a condescending tone.

'I'm from Burgess, Burgess and Co, here to do the audit.'

'In that case please would you mind going back out of the shop and entering by the side entrance.'

Of course I complied, walking back through the door and onto the street. I walked past the shop window, turned down the alley to the side and located the side door marked as the 'Tradesman's Entrance'. Opening the door and entering, I found myself in the same spot that I had vacated two minutes earlier, with the same two men waiting for me.

'I'll show you to your audit area.'

He led me through various workrooms to a rear office where a desk and two chairs had been placed. Hodgson arrived a few minutes later and we ploughed though the various areas of bookkeeping for three days, then taking everything back to the office to pull it together and produce the results. For me the best part of each day was lunchtime; Hodgson would head for a trough while I simply wandered around the area, loving every minute. I gazed in shops, strolled through arcades, took in the smells wafting from restaurants and admired the beautiful people. This was definitely something to aim for.

From the sublime to the vile. Immediately after we had finished in Mayfair we went to Cricklewood, the black hole of transport and dump extraordinaire. This time it was a sweatshop on the High Street that produced small leather goods such as handbags, wallets and purses. We soon discovered that although the books had been written up, nothing had been added up and nothing balanced. There were hundreds of small sales to retail shops and market traders resulting in approximately twelve pages for each month together with all the customers' accounts. In those days we didn't even own a hand cranked adding machine, which meant the jobs were all hand and mind. The arduous tasks were shared out and work began. When 12 o'clock arrived, Hodgson uttered the first words to date that were even remotely of a social nature: he suggested going for lunch. His tone gave the impression that lunch was to be his treat but my instincts and previous experience suggested otherwise.

The lunch venue was a nearby greasy spoon where he found a table, then ordered steak and kidney pie with two types of vegetables plus a pudding. Guessing the probable outcome, I asked for a bowl of tomato soup and bread. At the end of the meal, he went to the counter, paid and left. Following his example, I headed for the counter.

'Did my friend pay for my soup and bread?' I asked.

'No mate, here's your bill.'

My intuition had been one hundred per cent correct. Fortunately I had just enough but my weekly budget was shredded.

After almost two days we started to bring the accounting towards balance but I was not surprised that there were anomalies everywhere. Although I didn't think they were significant in the context of the whole and we needed to work towards an audit cost that this little outfit could bear. Fortunately I kept my thoughts to myself as Hodgson's decision was to recheck everything, this time him going over my work and vice versa. If a mistake were found it would have to be checked for a third time. I had a vision of us as the Flying Dutchmen of accounting, sailing along in bleeding Cricklewood until the end of time. Hodgson finally had little choice but to write off the differences and call it a day.

I was never privy to how the fees for the job worked out; that was way above my pay grade. But even then I realised that what we had done wasn't an academic exercise. Practical decisions had to be taken to cut the cloth to fit, especially in Cricklewood.

*****

Christmas, Boxing Day 1956 and New Year 1957 came and went. Brief public holidays allowed in the forest of working days, far removed from the leisurely two week break common today. The office was always a bleak place but the absence of any normal exchange of seasonal wishes added an additional level of gloom.

The New Year offered nothing in the way of casual work and saw me riding into work as broke as usual, geared up for more fun and laughter. Or rather the total lack of it. But 1957 brought changes of another sort.

Sate had disappeared and Hodgson had taken his place at his desk. Tradesmen appeared to rearrange the main office, dividing it into two parts; a front office was created as a smaller area to be tenanted (as I found out later) by a secretary while the larger portion retained its original use. Then a Mr Mansel arrived who, Hodgson informed me, was the new manager.

A nasty piece of work, I thought on first sight and that was borne out a few days later. He told me that he'd changed his name from Mansel to Mandel. When I forgot and used the wrong one, the man threw all his toys out of the pram. Fortunately we were never forced to work together and after four weeks he was gone. His replacement's tenure was even shorter: Carter lasted a mere two weeks before he shuffled off. Not that I was given any information about this ebb and flow. At the end of it all, the line-up of the firm settled down to four people: Burgess, Hodgson, Miss Miller (the new secretary) and me.

As an aside, years later Sate reappeared on the horizon as a director of Ladbrokes, the turf accountants. I applied for an advertised vacancy and received a letter inviting me to an interview. Seeing his name on the letterhead, I declined their offer. One experience working for that bastard was enough to last a lifetime.

Cycling in and out every day was starting to wear thin; it was dark when I left in the morning and dark when I got home. I made my biggest possible sacrifice and sold my beloved Hetchins, subsequently purchasing a BSA Bantam 125cc two-stroke motorbike that was super fuel-efficient. This made my journey much, much easier, more comfortable and more convenient with motorcycle parking close to the office. Plus tea-making arrangements were amended as Miss Miller made tea for Hodgson and I'm sure he appreciated the improvements. Of course, I continued to make my own and the pecking order principle had settled.

With the failed exercises of middle management installation, I was back to tackling all of the smaller jobs and routine work on the major stuff. I was also entrusted with carrying out audits on my own. Hodgson sometimes came in towards the end to oversee the final adjustments and prepare the tax calculations that for me was a completely unknown area.

My first solo mission was to a happy place. The client company manufactured mannequins in a basement in Savile Row. Everybody was on first name terms and they chatted, gossiped, laughed while they worked but none of that impinged getting the job done. It stood in total contrast to the funereal atmosphere of my Craven Street office environment. In all the time I worked there I never learned any personal details about my colleagues: whether anyone was married, had children or even where they lived. Apart from Burgess, of course.

The client's secretary-cum-bookkeeper was a lovely freckled girl named Sally. I discovered that she lived on the inaptly named

Paradise Row off Bethnal Green Road which was more or less on my route. If I spotted her on my way in I would give her a lift to work on my motorbike; something that became a regular habit, not organised or formal, just casual. We did take a couple of rides into the Essex countryside and I'm sure she wondered why we never stopped at a country pub. Sadly that was simply due to a complete lack of funds on my part.

Hodgson's plan to install a manager at Craven Street had been an unmitigated failure. That led to my role being expanded as my ability and confidence grew. The work involved was not so much mathematics as simple arithmetic. Thus by following basic rules coupled with the application of a little common sense any task could be completed. If a question required an answer, a call to the client would usually provide a solution. I even started to provide rudimentary tax calculations to accompany the finished accounts.

April brought better weather that made the travelling easier. But little else changed much until 14 August when I was called into Hodgson's office, more or less at the end of my first year with the practice.

'All in all, we're quite pleased with your progress Roy. Therefore Burgess, Burgess and Co is prepared to offer you Articles which as you know is a five year apprenticeship to train to become a qualified accountant. Of course that also means job security and in the long term, a well paid career.'

The training element was an exaggeration as the reality was that one learned by doing the work. Mentoring didn't come into the equation. There were three examinations to be passed to qualify as an accountant at which point, the dogsbody metamorphoses into a somebody.

I brought up the subject of money, emphasising how useful I had become and bearing in mind that I was the sole member of staff they had apart from the secretary bird. Hodgson hated talking about money and would only offer the reassurance that there would be a salary review in September which would take everything into account. So was I suckered in and he must have rubbed his hands to the bone in celebration that a very simple Simon was in his employ.

There was an inordinate amount of delay in getting the contract signed, mainly due to my father's intransigence. The fish shop in

Plaistow was shut on Sunday and Monday, which were his two days off and as far as he was concerned, that time was inviolable. Hodgson insisted that he attend the signing; my father's response was to say that if it was that important, they should come to him. And there was no way on earth that Hodgson would visit a fish shop in Plaistow to get the job done. So all was in limbo.

My father also maintained that anything to do with children was women's work; his total lack of interest in our lives bore testament to this way of thinking. The impasse was finally cleared after Hodgson sent him a frank and honest man-to-man letter. It might be said that my father simply dissociated himself from the family that he'd jointly created. But I think he was just a bum and a loser of the first order. A man of his time.

Always the optimist, I put my trust in the belief that employment was two-way street: that the bosses would do their best for their employees in return for them doing their very best for the firm. I was soon to find out that that trust was misplaced.

Out of the box, I had to sign up to a correspondence course and buy a truckload of books. I assumed that as an apprentice I would get, and therefore asked for, financial assistance. That was rejected out of hand and so my Claud Butler cycle had to be sold.

During my summer holiday, I managed to get a few days work at the scrap yard and noticed an MG J1 parked in one corner.

'Get it running son and you can have it for the scrap price.'

I managed to get the engine to turn but all efforts to fire it up failed, including towing it for a distance. Time was committed and spent, a grand effort made with plenty of advice freely given but to no avail.

Post holiday, everything returned to the daily routine. I rode to work on the BSA Bantam, churned out the 'paper bag' jobs, went to clients on audit and handed sets of accounts to Hodgson. On Friday I received my pay accompanied by the usual dose of passive smoking and on Saturday joined the chimney sweep on his morning rounds.

To my mind, everything was on hold until the promised salary review at the end of September. My hope was for an increase to at least six pounds which would be well behind that of my compatriots but enough to live on. Just. After all, I was producing all that the ill-fated managers were hired to do and they were paid over ten pounds per week.

So it came to pass that on Friday 27 September 1957 I heard the familiar cough ascending the stairs to enter the main office. Half an hour later, it moved into my back room. I was on the telephone to a client, making arrangements for their audit. Burgess quietly put my wage packet on the corner of the table and buggered off. Finishing my call, I picked up the small envelope and saw that I had indeed received a pay rise: fifty pence per week or ten pence per day, translating to a fraction over one penny per hour.

I couldn't believe that they valued me so little after all my efforts and progress. That all I was worth was an extra penny per hour! My first thought was to roar into Hodgson's office and let fly. But I knew only too well that that's what he was expecting. So I decided to leave the confrontation until Monday.

I waited for Miss Miller to make his tea and went into the room.

'What do you want?'

But he knew exactly why I was there and wanted.

'My pay rise wasn't what I expected Mr Hodgson, after all the work I've done and the progress I've made. It really was very disappointing.'

'Roy, what you have is a rise of twelve per cent which by most people's judgement would be deemed very generous.'

'Twelve per cent of almost nothing is almost nothing! I was led to believe that my increase would reflect the quality and volume of the work I am doing and my overall progress. I don't believe that a rise of fifty pence a week is just reward.'

'You were not led by me to expect anything of the sort. This has all been explained to you clearly several times in the past. You are articled and as such paid a stipend. It is expected that your parents would provide funding to meet your expenses and I, for one, am tired of these discussions.'

'My parents live on the breadline and expect me to help them.'

'Well maybe you're in the wrong profession. There will no more increases until next September.'

'What another fifty pence per week maybe, to take me up to a full five pounds?'

'Damn your insolence boy,' Hodgson snarled. 'No more on this. Get out.'

Here we had a man who had never known the taste of hunger or the cold of poverty. He was content that an impoverished staffer supported his income and business. A young man who was forced to subsidize his pay by pushing brooms up chimneys, slaving in scrap yards and selling everything that he owned and that wasn't much.

I was in an impossible situation and knew that it was out of the question to continue with accountancy under the circumstances. On the other hand, I was now a year behind my fellow school leavers and moving into another line of business would mean starting from the bottom again.

*****

Christmas came to Bleak House. I managed to pull several double shifts over the holiday period at a petrol station in Manor Park. Back then the attendant was not sitting behind bulletproof glass or steel bars. Far from it, he was expected to run outside to the customer, put the required amount of petrol in the car and clean the windscreen. If asked, he would even have to check oil and water levels, tyre pressures and top up as necessary. Given that it was a holiday period, there were plenty of happy people about, a few tips and nobody drove off without paying. The money would have come out of my pocket if that had happened!

Then back to the grindstone. 1958. Happy New Year? I actually got through to August before the wheels fell off. Without warning, my job with the chimney sweep disappeared. At the end of my last Saturday morning with him, he told me I was no longer needed but gave no explanation. Maybe it was a result of the 1956 Clean Air Act as people moved away from using coal or anthracite in fireplaces. But it was more likely that it was linked to an accident that had happened two weeks earlier.

Cleaning the chimney of a first floor flat in a terrace house conversion, we dislodged a brick that dropped down the parallel chimney into the flat below. As luck would have it, a newly married couple were in the midst of consuming the wedding breakfast together with family and friends. Allegedly, it's lucky to see a sweep on your big day but that's not exactly how the collected diners perceived the unfortunate incident. It really was a bad business and we were lucky to escape unscathed.

I did the rounds but couldn't track down any Saturday or Sunday jobs. And my expectations for the famous annual salary increase were not optimistic. Once again my ragged finances were at the fore.

At around the same time Hodgson put me in charge of the petty cash. I was astounded. He'd always busted my chops when I'd put in a claim for travel expenses and he knew full well that my financial situation was beyond desperate. On a Wednesday morning only a few weeks later, he informed me that Miss Miller was to take over the role. Unfortunate in the least since I had borrowed one pound from the tin against an IOU! I explained my dilemma to Miss Miller but added that I would be able to repay the money on Friday. One look at the sneer-cross-smirk on her face told me what would happen next and she didn't disappoint. There was no doubt in my mind that we were moving towards the endgame.

It was not only the money. A couple of quid a week would have made a huge difference to me with no effect whatsoever on the firm's finances and they knew it. Burgess had smoked his way through two pounds by the time he was lighting his third Havana of the day! It was about the lack of money but it was also about the dismal atmosphere that prevailed and the lack of respect. There was never ever a word of appreciation for efforts made or a job well done. Occasionally there'd be a grunt acknowledging the completion of a job. If you were lucky. Deep down, I knew that the only person who could, or would, bring about change was me. And now was as good a time as any.

Less than twenty seconds. That was the interval between Miss Miller leaving the room and the summons to attend Hodgson's office. Since she'd been with the firm I'd always been friendly and helpful, simply a decent, good workmate. She could have easily kept her mouth shut until Friday, let me repay the miserable pound and nobody would have been the wiser. But no, she was in like a greyhound out of the traps to squeal like a pig. I just didn't bloody care any more. Ready for a showdown I went in, leaving the door open so she could hear the direct consequences of her action. Hodgson's fake fury made him look ludicrous and even more so when he spoke.

'Miss Miller has reported to me that you have stolen some money from petty cash.'

'Incorrect. I took an advance on my wages to settle an IOU.'

'An IOU has no standing here. Who authorised it?'

'You put me in charge, so I authorised it.'

'I'm calling the police right now.'

I've known fourteen year old girls tougher than this cream puff. Girls who would kick you in the nuts or stick a thumb in your eye without need for any particular reason. Walking over to the visitor's chair, I sat down, grabbed the phone and dialled Whitehall 1212 as fast as I could. Probably one of the most famous numbers in the country. Simultaneously, Hodgson was shouting.

'No one asked you sit down. What the hell are you doing with the phone?'

My call was answered immediately.

'Scotland Yard,' said the disembodied voice.

I placed the phone on Hodgson's desk. He looked at it as though it was a freshly minted dog turd.

'Pick it up. It's the police.'

You have to have a damn good reason for phoning Scotland Yard. I sat back to listen as out dear leader squirmed in his chair, trying to explain that there had been a misunderstanding. And apologising. They only allowed him to hang up when he'd identified himself and given them the office address. When he looked back at me, my feet were up on his desk giving a fine view of the holes in the soles of my shoes, going through to the cardboard backing.

'Take your feet off my desk,' he squeaked indignantly. 'What do you think you're doing?'

'I look forward to the police coming here. We could talk, among other things, about slavery and Dickensian working conditions.'

'Get out,' he hissed.

I slowly replaced my feet on the ground and strolled out of the room. As I passed Miss Miller, I broke into a rendition of a song popular at the time, the Ink Spots' Whispering Grass.

Why do you whisper, green grass

Why tell the trees what ain't so

Whispering Grass, the trees don't have to know

Within half an hour, two gentlemen from Scotland Yard arrived to qustion Hodgson about the unnecessary waste of time. And rake him over the coals for the same. They didn't need to speak to me. I think I'd been mistaken for the slow boy. Given all the movement in the past, from place to place, home to home and school to school, a lot of stuff had taught me lessons. I'd been through mountains of character testing, attempts at bullying and I'd learned how to handle myself the hard way.

When Friday came, I repaid the pound. Not a word was spoken. On Saturday, I was out with friends while they shopped for new clothes. My mind was made up, I would resign on Monday. Two years wasted; too bad.

On Monday morning, I waited until Miss Miller had served Hodgson his tea, together with a plate of biscuits on this occasion. With a bit of luck, he would choke on one.

Greeted with the customary – what do you want – I approached his desk and dropped the envelope in front of him.

'What's this?'

'Clearly it's a letter, for you.'

I started to walk away.

'Yes, but what is it, this letter?'

I half turned to look back at him.

'It's my letter of resignation Mr Hodgson. I'm leaving on Friday 19 September. Or earlier if you prefer.'

'Don't be absurd. You have signed articles. You can't just resign like that.'

'I can and I have. I'm withdrawing my signature. You could say I'm unsigning. I may not have learned much but I do know that nobody can be forced to do work that they don't want to do. So unless you send two big lads to bring me in every morning, that's it, the end. Put simply, I'm not going to put up with all this crap and be paid a pittance any more. Like Boff, I'm off.'

There was no further discussion and life went on much as it had before, at least for a few days.

Being an apprentice meant that I was not required to undertake National Service until my term was completed. After that, in theory I would be called to serve Queen and country for two years. However it was fairly common knowledge that conscription was to end on 31 December 1960. In any event nobody born after 1 October 1939 would be conscripted and that included me. Anyway, we'd moved house so many times that it would have taken a lot of determined effort to track me down and hand me call-up papers. If they had, I'd have probably been rejected anyway since I only had one working eye. Although, if that were ignored, my time with the Air Cadets would have guaranteed my admission to the RAF, which was definitely preferable to the Army or Navy.

On my final day, the usual wheezing could be heard ascending the stairs and I heard him enter the room. I could smell and hear him standing behind my left shoulder. I didn't need to see him to know that the usual cigar was clamped between his lips. Positive proof came when he coughed and an inch of ash fell onto the only suit I owned.

'I hope you enjoy your time in the army,' he said.

The man was an ignorant buffoon. I regretted all the work I'd done to keep putting those bloody cigars in his mouth and the limo at his disposal. A suite of ripostes instantly came to mind but immediately evaporated; it wasn't worth my breath. Standing up, I stood over him for a few seconds and simply left.

Ironically, if I had been called up I'd have been better off financially. Given £1.40 a week, food, accommodation and transport all found, there would have been no worries on how to get from one day to the next. I would have been in a better place. Although it would be a daunting task to find a worse place to be than Burgess, Burgess & Co.

*****

What happened to the Burgess people?

I have no information on Burgess himself but I'd hazard a guess that cancer probably killed both him and his chauffeur. As for Sate, he died aged 81 on 6 September 2008 in Ruislip.

In the 60s Hodgson rebadged the business Hodgson Burgess & Co and moved it to Canterbury in Kent where it is now a leading firm. When he died in 2019, someone wrote an obituary which included the observation that he had been 'a very nice man'. Not my recollection of the man at all. To me he was always totally inflexible and lacked any empathy whatsoever. His view of poverty was that it was something which you unfortunately saw from your car as you roared past on the way to the golf club.

At that time, the reality was that there was little difference between protectionism at the docks and the elitism of the accountancy and legal professions. Entry to the first required family ties whereas the second two called for family money to subsidise the pitiful pay. Stockbroking was based on a similar model to the docks in so far as family ties were key. However this needed to be backed up by family money and the correct school tie. I cannot recall ever seeing a job advert for a vacancy on the Stock Exchange or with a firm of stockbrokers.

If it had been difficult for me, I cannot imagine the obstacles that a female aspirant would have faced. Despite women's contributions to the war effort, there was an inbred, stubborn belief that a woman's role in life was firmly harnessed to the home. Any changes to that stone-age mentality would be a slow and painful process over a long, long time.

The one lesson I did take away from all of this was that as an employer you have a great measure of responsibility for your employees. The responsibility to provide a decent and safe working environment. To ask of them only what is reasonable to expect and show them human respect. And above all, pay them a decent wage for the job in hand. When all that is in place, you can expect their loyalty and their best efforts.

Many times in the future, I was to come across bad behaviour on both sides: employers justifying underpaying people with poor excuses and employees cheating their bosses by swinging the lead. A sad state of affairs all round.

2 The Food Trade Protection Society

'Hell is – other people.'

Jean-Paul Sartre – 'No Exit'

Monday 22 September 1958 provided me with a new experience: a visit to the Labour Exchange (aka the Dole Office) in Stratford, East London. Searching for work, I chatted to the counter clerk for a while and told him what I'd been doing.

Looking hopeful he asked: 'I think I might have something for you. Are you any good on the phone?'

'Sure, I was on the phone a lot with the last lot. Doesn't bother me. What's the job?'

'Slot's for a telephone credit ratings person with a firm in the High Street. Nine to five, £7.50 per week.'

It wasn't fantastic but being local would save time, money and hassle.

'Sounds good. Can you arrange an interview.'

'Surely. Be back in a sec.'

And disappeared through the open door behind him. He took less than two minutes.

'They can see you now Mr Roy.'

'Thank you, that's brilliant.'

The offices were on the first, second and third floors above a shop. A receptionist led me to the Company Secretary's office to the rear of the first floor. There, one Mr Merton introduced himself with a smile, invited me to sit and we had a pleasant conversation for an hour or so. Somewhere along the road, he explained what the business was about.

'Basically, there are two sections to the business. Firstly we have subscribers who pay for a number of credit rating enquiries and with most of them, their first contact is with the telephone guys. If we have a report on hand, that can be given verbally there and then; a written report follows in the post. If no report exists, we send a request out to one of our local agents who act as necessary and sends his report to the office. When we receive that, we can contact the customer. As the name implies, it's all food related. The other section involves debt collection but that's a totally separate entity.'

Finally, he offered me a job with a start date of 1 October. When I asked if I could start earlier, he told me that it was company practice to start new employees on the first day of any one month.

'Sorry but it makes record keeping easier.'

I didn't press my luck. Once back on the street, I dropped into a pub a few doors away and ordered a shandy. Using the pub's payphone, I called the scrapyard and, praise be, I was in luck. A few days cutting up vehicles was all mine. But the situation with the scrapyard begs a little background.

Frank Kirby was one of our neighbours, a very thin man of around thirty. There was little notable about Frank other than that in one way he was unique: he was dead. At least officially. He never spoke of the events that enabled this situation but I gleaned some of the details from other local lads.

Conscripted into the army, he was duly sent to war to fight and in 1944 he found himself in a very bad place. He was in France, the weather was freezing and lots of Germans wanted to shoot him. Deciding that enough was enough, he slipped away from the front line, making his way on foot to the coast and somehow managed to cross the English Channel back to Blighty. Meanwhile at the front, his regiment could find no trace of Private Frank Kirby and so he was listed as 'missing in action, presumed dead'.

He did not get the warm reception that he'd expected when he arrived back in Plaistow. His 'widow' had been allocated a council flat plus a wealth of benefits. If news of his return had reached the ears of the authorities, she'd have lost the lot plus her very much alive husband. Frank would have been arrested and spent the subsequent eight years or more in a military prison.

Ever a pragmatic lot, the East Enders might not have approved of him scarpering away from the fight but could imagine themselves facing a similar situation. Fight or flight? No one knows how they would react if they were in danger of losing life or limb. Very few gave their lives for the country, someone else usually gave it on their behalf.

Nobody snitched but Frank had to live very carefully and kept a very low profile. He had no papers, no driving licence, no National Insurance number or National Health number. His total lack of teeth was a direct result of the last absence. But he was a very capable mechanic and naturally lived within a cash economy.

Although there was an age difference, we got on well and one day he asked me to go with him to look a damaged Ford in Barking. He'd recently acquired a Ford himself that was the same model. His car had suffered a rear end crash while the other one we were going to see had serious frontal damage. Frank's plan was to cut both in half and use the two undamaged halves to create a complete undamaged car.

'Called cut and shut,' he told me. 'You wouldn't want to buy one but people want cars and I'm not going to be telling.'

In the 21st century, it's highly illegal but as Frank said, people wanted a car, any car, and they were in high demand. When we arrived, we were confronted with a horrible scene with plenty of evidence to exacerbate that effect. Syringes littered the footwells and blood was everywhere but nothing deterred Frank. To his delight, he spotted treasure: a pair of false teeth lay amongst the footwell detritus. Without even a cursory wipe, Frank grabbed them and slotted them into his mouth. They gave him a bizarre equine look reminiscent of Fernandel, a French comedy actor of the day, perhaps most famous then for his portrayal of the Italian priest Don Camillo.

The vehicle was dead (sorry) right for his needs, so a deal was done and we headed for home. Frank insisted on stopping at a café for lunch and ordered steak, something he'd been unable to chew for a very long time. The teeth worked so the teeth stayed. His long suffering wife and the rest of us just had to adapt to the new look.

But I digress. Well before the saga of the teeth, when I was still at school, Frank sought my help. With the promise of ten bob, I was up for it whatever it was. It turned out that Frank had borrowed a costermonger's barrow and loaded it up with scrap metal from his yard. While empty, it was a simple one man job to push along the road but fully loaded with iron and steel, it was a different kettle of fish. It was cash hard earned. Just a mile struggling through the streets with that juggernaut took us both to the end of our respective ropes.

Our arrival caused a lot of mirth but we had a brew while we recovered. I simply asked the bossman if there was ever any casual work. Impressed with this kid's efforts, he suggested that I phone in from time to time. So I did. My pay was a lot less than the regulars but they were all older, bigger and stronger. I tackled every job I was given without complaint and never got knocked back. Over the next few years, until I moved away from the area, Frank helped me out with various cars and motorbikes. Equally I sent a fair amount of mechanical work over to him.

Our association does however have an eerie footnote. Years after I lost touch, I was driving a 1935 Ford 10 along Huron Road in Balham with two mates on board and I'd just told them the tale of Frank and the false teeth. I had jerry-rigged a radio in the car and the DJ was rambling on in the background. Then there was a pause. Silence.

'I wonder what happened to Frank Kirby?' I mused.

A few seconds later a voice spoke, coming from the radio.

'I wonder what happened to Frank Kirby?'

The hairs on the back of my neck stood up. We were totally freaked out. I pulled over to take a break and calm down. Weird or what?

Looking back, it is amazing that so many cars were torched. Today many of them would be sought after vehicles, restored at great expense to concours condition. The recent Suez crisis, coupled with fuel rationing had taken the appeal off the big stuff. I personally helped to pull apart an Armstrong-Siddely, a Lanchester and a host of pre-war Yank tanks.

On the given date, I duly arrived at the Food Trade Protection Society (FTPS) and was taken up to the front room on the second floor. Along the window side of the room stretched a full width bench, carrying a batch of telephones. I joined Bob and Harry manning the enquiries counter. The former was a stocky guy in his mid-20s, the latter in his 50s, slim and well worn. Four desks lined the back wall, two occupied by a couple of tired old geezers called Paul and Herbert, the remaining pair by Pam and Florence, their female assistants.

I hit it off with Pam straight away and we could have become good friends but (there is always a but) she was married to a real stinker. An unemployed Irishman, he was permanently morose and ill tempered. When I did meet him it was clear that he was a highly jealous bloke with a very short fuse. Simply off the wall, Florence was the spitting image of Popeye's girlfriend Olive Oil complete with ankle length skirt. I kept our contact to the minimum.

This gang of four sent out reports to clients and mail out to our battery of local agents for information when we had no current report to hand, together with requisite postal order. Floor to ceiling shelving clung to the walls, carrying all the report files. An identical room on the floor below was home to the typists and similar shelving also adorned its walls bearing more credit rating paperwork.

The debt recovery department and the directors' offices were somewhere else in the building. There was never any contact between those worthies and us but whether by design or accident, I know not.

At this stage of the game, my only ambition was to secure a spot with a decent wage. I had done just that with FTPS but it was clear from the start that it would be a dead end job. Any expansion of the firm's activities would be organic and progression limited by those above. Which in my case was everybody either retiring or dying. And after many years of waiting, to reach a desk where you stuffed report requests and postal orders into envelopes was hardly reaching for the stars. But for the moment it would do.

All that was needed was a decent telephone manner and the energy to chase around the racks on two floors seeking files. A weekly side task was to go through the London Gazette for County Court judgements that related to our industry and copy those to our own records.

The files were A5 size with cardboard backs, growing in both density and number. There was no process for thinning them out and as the racking was running at 120% capacity an overhaul was sorely needed. Or more shelves built. But where?

The typing pool comprised around 12 women at any one time. The standout for beauty was a young girl called Virginia who came from the west coast of Ireland. She had glossy red hair, green eyes and was an absolute stunner. The downside was that she was a Roman Candle, living with a very religious aunt and uncle making any prospect of romance a total non-starter. A scrawny teenager called Tina showed an interest in me, or possibly my motorbike. My guess was that any liaison with her would be reported back to the others in lurid detail so I kept well clear.

Christmas came and apparently it was customary to exchange presents with one's immediate co-workers and have a drink at the pub. A big step up from my last place of work, for sure. I moved into 1959 with a much improved condition.

The combination of an extra few pounds a week without the burden of travelling to the West End meant more personal time and, most important, the end of the exhausting chase for cash. If an opportunity arose I would consider it of course but my every moment was no longer consumed with finding the means to keep afloat.

It was about this time that a group of us discovered an art cinema in Leyton which showed foreign films, a rarity in those days. Kurosawa's Seven Samurai was a real eye opener for us, as were the works of Henri-Georges Clouzot. Without a doubt, that was the beginning of my deep and long term interest in films outside the mainstream.

Even a girlfriend called Mary appeared on the scene but I suspect that once again my motorbike was the real attraction.

Frankly, I felt as though I'd managed to escape from under a filthy rock and was suddenly able to live life as an ordinary bloke. I had a routine job, a few quid in my pocket and time to enjoy life. The days of oppression were a distant memory. Of course, there were no prospects whatsoever but for the moment I'd decided to put aspirations on the back burner. Tomorrow is another day.

*****

One Saturday at noon I called round to a friend's house to go together to our match. Football was a sort of escape from home: he was the eldest of eleven children and there was no television to amuse. Television was still in its infancy and unavailable to the working man. He looked rather solemn in the doorway.

'Can you come in for a minute. Me and me dad, we sort of need some help.'

'What sort?'

'You'll see, it's a bit of lifting we need.'

I followed him into the front room to find his father standing by a double bed on which lay the dead body of the grandfather. Not a sight that I'd anticipated.

'Has the doctor been?' I asked.

'No not yet' the man responded, 'but we need a hand to get him off the bed.'

'Where're you going to put him?'

'On the floor.'

'Jesus, why not just leave him where he is?'

'Because the bed's been promised to some of the kids and they're keen to move in.'

Between the three of us, we hauled the poor bugger off the bed and dumped him on the deck. Before the dust had settled, three kids came tearing past and leapt onto their new sleeping quarters.

Perhaps it was a sign of the times, so soon after World War II, that death had become so matter of fact and almost casual. In many ways we were desensitised to life and the loss of life.

Another Saturday, I was visiting a motorcycle shop on the Romford Road in Stratford Broadway when my ears picked up the wonderful sounds of two single cylinder bikes heading my way from the west. Moving outside onto the pavement, I listened to the approaching noise changing tones as the riders changed through the gears. Finally I was rewarded with the breathtaking sight of two BSA Gold Star Clubman DB34s rolling side by side towards me. Magnificent. That started a lifetime ambition to own such a machine – that was never achieved! When I reached the point of actually being able to afford one, the youthful bravado was long gone.

My friend Ben had been a great help when I moved from bicycles to motorbikes. His mode of transport was a 1934 BSA three-wheeled car powered by a Hotchkiss 900cc engine similar to that of a Morgan. Instead of the power unit being exposed out at the front, Ben's engine was enclosed under a conventional bonnet. Hand-painted a bilious brown with upholstery made from gunny sacking, the look was pretty basic. But I can state from personal experience that it had a fair turn of speed, although with only one wheel at the back its roadholding ability left much to be desired.

He'd pulled over when he'd spotted me cleaning my bike and we were just chatting. A guy about my age was approaching us with an entourage of much younger kids and obviously knew who I was.

'I'm George. Pam's brother.'

'Who's Pam?'

'You work with her.'

'Got you. That Pam. Good to meet you George, this is Ben.'

A round of handshakes.

'Who are these guys?' I asked.

'They're my gang.'

'You're kidding! They're a bit young and pimply.'

'They're all solid, trust me.'

There was zero chance of my trusting him on anything. Big red warning flags were flying around my mind: crazy man on the loose.

'I hear you've been bad mouthing me,' he continued, a harder tone creeping into his voice.

'What the hell are you talking about? Until you arrived with your gang ten seconds ago, I didn't know you from a hole in the ground. Didn't even know Pam had a brother.'

'So it wasn't you then?'

'Not this boy. No way José.'

Seemingly satisfied, he nodded and strolled off with his gang fanned out behind him. Curve balls keep flying. I never mentioned the meeting to Pam and she never spoke of him. But since then I often spotted him with his rat pack all over town. I guessed he thought of himself as some kind of gangster or aspired to be a sort of Kray brothers type. But he must have done something to impress the kids enough to keep them onside; after all they weren't old enough to go into a pub.

Back at work, several enquiries came in on a fellow named M J Oxenberry with as many addresses spread across the Home Counties. Who knows whether the name was real or an alias but our local agents reported that he was connected to some large warehouses with little or no trading activities. Even at my junior level, it smelled like a long firm operation, designed down the line to defraud customers and suppliers. My seniors felt that there was no real evidence but advised our clients to proceed with caution.

A couple of months later, the debt collection forms started rolling in and it soon became clear that business premises had been abandoned or burned to the ground. We should have been bolder but that was not the style here in credit reference.

In June, my best friend John Ringshaw tipped me off that a small car sales yard in his neighbourhood had a Singer sports car up for sale at thirty quid. Immediately I thought of the Singer Nine, a diminutive two-seater which would be an ideal car for me.

With Frank Kirby to advise, the three of us headed over to Forest Gate where a surprise awaited: no Singer Nine but a much larger Singer 1.5 four-seater. More a tourer than a sports car, it fired up with a strong sound, no smoke and we drove around for twenty minutes without any sign of problem. At the drop of the asking price from thirty to twenty five pounds, I became a motorist.

The following week, I sold my trusty BSA Bantam, scratched up the rest of the money and I was on the road. Of course I still had to find the money to pay for the road tax and insurance, but all in all it was a good deal. In addition, my future travels would be spent sitting in the dry rather than battling the elements.

By a lucky coincidence, a small extra income stream kicked off at about the same time. It had been evident for a long time that the state of the filing was costing the business actual cash losses. Our records might indicate that we had a current file to match an enquiry but when that file could not be found there was no alternative other than sending out a request for a fresh report together with payment. Time and time again we were forced to pay for something we already had but couldn't find. Care had to be taken in broaching the subject, so I approached Bob and Harry over a drink.

'Here's the plan,' I said. 'If we stayed back one evening a week, we could go through the files, shelf by shelf. Clear out the dead stuff, eliminate all the duplication and recover. In maybe six months we'll have built a fresh and accessible set of records. Whaddya think?'

'I like it,' said Bob.

'Especially since it would be overtime,' added Harry.

'It has merit,' they more or less chorused.

Harry took the scheme to Herbert, the room's titular head, who took it from there to the powers that be, whoever they were. News came back that the plan had been given the green light and that two hours overtime each per week would be approved. Tuesday was chosen as the night for our endeavours and we were all surprised at how quickly real results showed. And of course, that extra little thickness in the wage packet was appreciated.

Most days I drove into work even though it was only a fifteen minute walk. At weekends, subject to petrol money, I'd take a run into the Essex countryside. But the thought at the back of my mind was always that the job really was a road to nowhere. Something always turns up and something did. But not always the right thing at the right time.

On Sunday 22 November 1959 I had a car accident. I was almost stationary when the other fellow headed towards at me as though he was Queen Boudicca of the Iceni in her chariot. The unpleasantness increased by a factor of ten with the arrival of the Old Bill.

On Monday morning I phoned FTPS, got through to Herbert and explained what had happened. I told him that I had a lot off running around to do which included taking papers to the police and recovering my car from the crash site. He didn't say much but I felt that I had done all I could in the circumstances.

My first port of call was to West Ham police station where I was generally harassed for an hour. As I left I bumped into Jill, one of the firm's typists, who was heading in late after a dentists' appointment and filled her in, so to speak.

Then on to find Frank and a tow truck. When we got to the wounded Singer and Frank investigated, he confirmed my fears. A curved part of the chassis called the dumb iron to which the front springs were attached was smashed and beyond economic repair. This was the age of dubious insurance companies: given my youth, my premium was relatively low and the reason for that was that the company was based in the Netherlands Antilles and adverse to paying claims whatever the situation. The fifties and sixties became notorious for the sheer number of dodgy insurance companies in the market place. Perhaps the most infamous was Fire, Auto and Marine run by the international fraudster Emil Savundra. When the company crashed in 1966, it left some 400,000 British motorists without cover and out of pocket.

The police had made a great song and dance about the immediate removal of the car and there was only one decision that could be made. Thus my Singer went on its final and ignominious journey to the scrapyard.

I never saw another 1500cc Singer in all the years of going to car shows and museums. Recent research has revealed that only 77 were made but only 12 surviving and I've seen it described as 'one of the 1930s' rarest and most desirable sports cars'. And saw an auction estimate for a restored car of between £70,000 to £80,000. Lost for words, I feel that I owe an apology. But to whom? Perhaps the car itself.

On Tuesday I returned to the phones and the filing, to find a very quiet atmosphere in the room. I put it down to a postal worker having been caught intercepting our postal orders. When Friday arrived, my payday came with a shock: my packet was one days' pay short. When I approached Herbert about it, he avoided eye contact and brushed me off saying: 'You'll have to see Mr Merton'.

Four days had passed without a word. The decent thing would have been to sit down with me and discuss the situation. I could have been given the opportunity to take the time out of my holiday entitlement and thus provide me with an intact week's wages. Why was nothing said? It was obvious that 'their way' would lead to a confrontation. Maybe that was the cunning plan. Finally. The long walk to Merton's office allowed me time to calm down and prepare. I was expected.

'Mr Merton, I'm sorry to trouble you but my wages are a day short this week.'

'That is because you were not in on Monday, so we can't pay you for that day. You were seen.'

'Seen? So what? I phoned in first thing on Monday morning, spoke to Herbert and explained the reasons for me being unable to be here.'

From his expression it was obvious that he hadn't been told about my call.

'Look Mr Merton, I've been here for over a year, had no time off and have never been late. It was I who suggested the total overhaul of the filing system which has actually saved the company money on duplicating report requests.'

'You didn't suggest anything,' he retorted. 'That plan came from Herbert.'

I was astounded.

'You really believe that? Herbert couldn't plan his way out of a paper bag!'

'I am not going to listen to you talking badly of senior staff. I …'

I cut him off sharply.

'One week's notice as of now. Leaving on Friday 4th and please check with Bob and Harry where the filing idea came from. Herbert a man of innovation? Well bugger me.'

Mr Merton didn't deserve my rudeness but I was angry. To think that that half-dead old codger had claimed someone else's scheme as his own and not shared the fact that I had notified the firm of the reasons for my absence seriously pissed me off.

Back at the front office, I was not inclined to talk immediately and left the air frosty. I answered a few client calls, but as it was Friday afternoon activities were slowing down. I picked my moment, waiting until the room was perfectly quiet and everybody was present.

'Hey Herbert,' I called across the room, 'your proposal that we overhaul the filing system has gone down really well. It's so much easier to access everything. I'd have never have thought of it.'

Bob and Harry looked shocked and all eyes turned toward Herbert. He stood up, slightly red faced and glared at me.

'Yeah well mate,' I continued, 'very well done.'

He left the room.

On Saturday, after a game of soccer, I went for coffee with some of the team. After I'd regaled them with the events of the week, one of the players told me that a neighbour had a motorbike stored in his shed that he wanted to offload. So it was arranged that we would take a look the following morning.

We had to pull out a large amount of rubbish but finally revealed a 1953 Francis-Barnett Falcon 197cc, filthy dirty but complete. The engine hadn't seized so it looked doable. We settled on a price of ten quid which was less than the break-up value. I used a foot pump to inflate the tyres, fitted a new spark plug, filled up the petrol tank, oiled and generally cleaned it up and it fired up on the first kick. Mobile again.

On Monday I reported for duty and entered the room of unhappy campers. At lunchtime I went back to the Labour Exchange and got the same staffer as before.

'Hello. Guessing Food Trades didn't work out?'

'Up to a point but it seems I wore out my welcome.'

'There is something right up your street but it is up west. Eight pounds a week. Interested?'

'Maybe. Doing what?'

'Assistant to the Company Secretary at the Pall Mall Safety Deposit near Piccadilly. Apparently he's run off his feet.'

'Yeah.'

Back to the back room and out in under five minutes.

'Interview on Wednesday at 9am. Man's a Mr Lewis.'

'Thanks for that.'

I dropped a note in the FTPS office for Mr Merton saying that I would be on the missing list for Wednesday morning and fully understood that I wouldn't be paid for the time lost. The interview with Mr Lewis went well and he offered me the post with Pall Mall Safety Deposit (PMSD) to start on Monday 7 December.

When Friday came, I left quietly. I didn't want to prolong the departure with drinks at the pub. So on the stroke of 5pm, I waved a cheery farewell to the room's denizens and patted Herbert's shoulder as I passed.

'Goodbye everyone,' I called from the doorway, 'it's been fun.'

What had to be done was done; without much grace or charm but it was over. That was the last I saw of any of the FTPS staff and I would have liked to stay in touch with the lovely Pam. Given the paranoid morose husband and the crazy idiot brother, I decided it wasn't worth the potential hassle. A couple of years on, I heard that the company had been taken over by Dunn and Bradstreet but that turned out to be false.

More recent research led me to an Eddie Parker in Wickford, Essex. According to Eddie, the owners had been the Sunderland family but they had sold it in1983 to John Beetwell and Fred Roberts. Eddie took over the business in 2011 and continues to operate it from his Wickford offices but the actual company FTPS is currently non-trading.

My reality at the time was that there was no employment that would offer the same opportunities that could be found in the City or West End. The commuting was simply a price that had to be paid.

*****

In the main the social whirl was the kids from school with the addition of new faces that appeared and stuck and others that disappeared again. Naturally the soccer team provided a good base for blokes to knock about with on and off the field. Our results were very mixed but we were bringing together the skills that would form the basis for our terrific 1960/61 season. If matches were cancelled, a game could often be arranged with a team short of a man or two. That called for a temporary change of name to that of a registered player with that particular league. Then there were other guys from outside the area who I'd met during my cycling days. Those included Colin Woodward and David Stubbs with whom I subsequently remained firm friends for many years.

For female interest, it was just the local girls, sisters of mates or neighbours. Given the fact that that we were all living at home there weren't any serious romances. Certainly there was no rush on anyone's part to make heavy-duty commitments or get buried by financial debts.

3 The Pall Mall Safe Deposit Company

'It is not enough to be industrious; so are the ants. What are you industrious about?'

Henry David Thoreau

The company was based in a fine building on St Albans Street which runs parallel to the Haymarket and Lower Regent Street, south of Jermyn Street.

On my arrival, Mr Lewis led me to my office at the rear of the ground floor. On the way, we passed the office of the company's CEO, a Mr Llewellyn. (Fortunately, I never met, saw or had any dealings with the gentleman.) Affixed to the opaque glass pane in the door was an A4 sheet of paper with the following instructions to any lowly employee seeking entry:

KNOCK SOFTLY

WAIT

UNTIL YOU ARE CALLED

ENTER QUIETLY

STAND SILENTLY

DO NOT SPEAK UNTIL

INVITED TO DO SO

My first thought was: what a silly pompous man and wondered what I had let myself in for. My second was that there was no additional note in respect of the penalty for failing to carry out the instructions to the letter. Perhaps a public flogging might have been in order. I knew that I had to find a way to add some personal observations without getting caught.

On reaching my office, I was introduced to Bridget McSweeney with whom I would be sharing the said space. So that was to be our office. Before he left, I asked Lewis for some work.

'I'll get to it later,' he said on his way out.

Which left me with Bridget who had a warm Irish welcome prepared.

'You English?'

'Yes.'

'I hate all you bloody English, every one of yer and yer bloody country.'

'If you feel like that, why live here?'

''Cos there's no work in the auld country. So I have to live and work with you English feckers to keep body and soul together.'

It transpired that all her angst went back to her childhood in Cork. She could clearly remember the time during the Irish War of Independence when Tomás Mac Curtain the Lord Mayor of Cork, was assassinated by the Royal Irish Constabulary on 20 March 1920. On 11-12 December of the same year, the centre of Cork was burned to the ground by the Black and Tans together with British forces.

Mac Curtain was the second mayor of Cork to be killed by the English. In 1491 when John Atwater was Lord Mayor, Perkin Warbeck arrived in Cork. A pretender to the British crown, he raised a rebellion against Henry VII with Atwater at his side and in 1497 invaded England with his troops. Atwater was captured by Tudor forces and held in the Tower of London for two years. In 1499 he was tried for treason and sentenced to be hanged, drawn and quartered.

Back to the Bridget and her memories. The Black and Tans was a 10,000 strong force recruited into the Royal Irish Constabulary as reinforcements during the Irish War of Independence. In the main the recruits were unemployed British soldiers who had fought in World War I. They were assembled in such a rush that there were no uniforms available; in their absence the men were issued with khaki trousers and either dark blue or green tunics. In the course of time the Black and Tans (or simply Tans) became the generic name for all the different groups formed to fight against the Irish. Terrible atrocities were perpetrated on all sides; for a young girl of ten, it would have been a horrendous and terrifying period to live through.

But as I kept telling Bridget, I wasn't there, it wasn't my fault and none of it was my responsibility! She didn't quite see it that way: the sins of the fathers mattered then and forever. Every English man (and probably English woman) should carry the burden of the hundreds of years of oppressing the Irish people.

Every day of my short stay with the Pall Mall Safe Deposit company (PMSD), I received an earful about the ongoing troubles in Ireland after the War of Independence, after the partition of Ireland, the continuing British rule and oppression by the British. At the end of my stay I could have taken an exam on the subject and I'd have passed with flying colours.

I never actually discovered what she did for the business. She always had papers to shuffle and walked around the place in a purposeful manner but I had a gut feeling that she'd been employed a long time ago and slowly slipped off the radar. That she'd been forgotten and, having no actual work to do, simply become part of the scenery.

Everybody was allowed two coffee breaks per day and I was keen to escape for my 15 minutes of peace. Away from the tales of blood, guts, murder and mayhem.

But back to day one. After lunch I again approached Lewis in respect of work and again was brushed off. This did not bode well. By the end of the first week, I had not done one single stroke of work and was naturally perturbed by this unhealthy state of affairs.

Lewis was a strange anomalous phenomenon and one that I would come across many times in my career. Appointed along the Peter Principle to the point of incompetency, he been promoted to a level in the business where he simply couldn't cope. He couldn't manage, he couldn't delegate and could be constantly seen rushing around the office like a blue-arsed fly. Clerical work as practiced by accountants and administrators is not difficult and for the most part, requires very little creativity. It merely involves pulling together facts and figures into a comprehensive record. It helps to have a little dose of obsessive compulsive disorder (OCD) but this is not a strict job requirement.

Of course, my worry as his theoretical assistant was his inability to trust someone else with any of his workload. There was I ready, willing and able to work but having to spend my days on idle thoughts or fending off attacks from my virulent co-worker. But in the second week, I was finally given a task.

The actual safe deposit boxes did exist and were kept in the basement with a cold storage area. The latter was used for fur coats and various beasties preserved by the arts of taxidermists. Three guards were stationed down there to supervise all activities.

My job was simplicity itself. All I had to do was invoice customers for using the facilities. Start with the previous billing, go through the custodian's records, draft up a set of invoices for typing and then check everything before posting them out. It was work that could have been done in half a day but I managed to stretch the work to a full day.

And that was it! During my twelve weeks at PMSD that was the only mission with which I was entrusted. It was truly a waste of their money and my talents, such as they were.

Additional sources of the firm's income derived from a substantial travel agency business with a bureau de change and letting offices to other businesses. Away from Pall Mall in North Kensington, they had a massive furniture depository that was also used to store antique cars and works of art.

Just before Christmas, one of the tenants, Cavendish Travel asked me if I would like a day's work on the following Sunday to help them get out a mail shot. I jumped at the opportunity but once the job was completed, it was an up hill struggle to get paid. It took six weeks before they finally paid the few quid promised. Christmas itself was uneventful. A few staff went out for drinks but I hardly knew anyone and Bridget was a non-starter as far as any outside activities were concerned. It was obvious that the matter of idle hands would have to be brought to a head earlier rather than later. I was not to know that salvation was just around the corner.

I don't know how but I staggered through January 1960 asking Lewis every day, twice a day, if I could help him in any way. His response was invariably negative as he continued to rush around the place looking like a man with the weight of the world on his shoulders.

Wednesday 3 February started off much like any other day. Bridget kicked off with the tale of Archbishop Oliver Plunkett who was accused of fomenting revolt against the British, imprisoned in Dublin Castle and subsequently hanged, drawn and quartered in London. All carried out by my ancestors, of course. Then she moved on to the Wexford martyrs who were convicted of high reason and suffered the same fate as the Archbishop. And after lunch we re-enacted the Battle of the Boyne.

A little after three, a smartly dressed man entered the room and introduced himself as Michael Berger. He explained that he needed to check the records that I'd been allowed to maintain. Fortunately Bridget was on the missing list. We started to chat and in the course of conversation, I told about my ridiculous position as an assistant not allowed to assist, trying not to sound as though I was complaining.

'We need staff you know. We'd need permission from PMSD, probably from Mr Lewis, to allow us to poach you. I take it you'd be interested.'

'Very interested,' I said eagerly.

'Leave it with me. I'll do a little checking, arrange an interview with one of the partners.'

A few days later, he phoned and told me to call Bill Smith at Wilson Wright & Co. I made the call the following Monday.

'I'll have a word with Mr Llewellyn and Mr Lewis but I've talked to Michael and he doesn't think there'll be a problem.'

He called again on Tuesday morning.

'Permission has been duly given. I spoke to Mr Llewellyn who had no idea who you were and Mr Lewis said that he hadn't really been impressed with your work. Which according to Michael is hardly surprising since he wasn't giving you any work! You're free to leave and we're free to take you on, subject to interview naturally.'

On Friday 12 February I phoned Mr Smith with regard to an interview as he had suggested. The interview was to be with him at 9.30am on Wednesday, 17 February. On Tuesday, 15 February I handed my resignation letter in to PMSD, giving notice that I would leave on 26 February. Perhaps it was a little reckless as there was no certainty that I would be offered a slot at Wilson Wright. However the truth of the matter was that I would have been happier washing dishes than sitting on my thumbs day after day, having to listen to Bridget's tales of yore.

The practice was located in a rather fine old building above the National Provincial Bank at 1 Hatton Garden at the heart of the UK's most famous jewellery district. Mr Smith was an Anglo-Indian guy, very friendly but clearly professional and our meeting went well.

'There are three partners of which I am one, as you know. Harold Gould is the most senior partner, essentially the owner of practice, and Ralph Temple. Then we currently have twelve accounting staff and four or five secretaries.'

Cutting to the chase, I was offered a job with a start date of 29 February at £8.50 per week. Most importantly I would be back doing work that I understood and enjoyed. My last days at PMSD dragged by with nothing changing apart from the fact that I stopped asking for something to do as it seemed a pointless exercise.

Friday, 26 February 1960 was my very last day. When Bridget arrived, I was already at my desk and before she could launch into a tirade, I held a finger to my lips.

'Today is my last day Mrs McSweeney and I would like it to be day without rancour. I would like to be able to say that I have enjoyed my time here but I haven't for a number of reasons. Let's say you forget that I'm a bloody Englishman and I'll forget that you're a bloody Taig. So let's just get through the next few hours and then go our separate ways. But be assured Mrs McSweeney, I will never forget you even though I would like to.'

My little speech took the wind from her sails and she hadn't known that I'd resigned. Spreading the gossip would keep her pretty busy, leaving me to finish reading The Count of Monte Cristo. There was no doubt in my mind that Bridget was suffering from long-term post-traumatic stress disorder (then called shell shock), exacerbated by living in the enemy's capital city and that her unhappy life stretched out before her with no hope of redemption. I really did empathise but she couldn't take that on board and for twelve weeks I shared her cuckoo's nest.

It goes without saying that I didn't keep in touch with any of my co-workers after leaving. The only good thoughts that I have about the place are that my stay was short and by luck led me to far better things.

As a coda, the depository building in North Kensington has now been converted to house offices, studios and workshops while the travel agency now operates from premises in Golders Green.

4 Beginnings 1939-1956

'Some of us have great stories, pretty stories, that take place at lakes with boats and friends and noodle salad. Just not in this car.'

Jack Nicholson in 'As Good As It Gets'

I have never been able to able to use the word 'family' in connection with my blood relatives. Mainly due to the wonderful world of advertising, it conjures up images of love, security and solidarity. With my mob, the expression 'fear and loathing' springs to mind.

Logically this chapter should have been the first and without it much of the story will not make sense. But in another way, it's appropriate that it is a flashback, to give some more clarity to the first three. The main difficulty is that over the years I have taken every effort not to look back on this period and I have never discussed these events with anyone. I know that to extract the memories and set them down on paper will be akin to drawing my own teeth with a pair of pliers. However, needs must.

The earliest paperwork I have is a Certificate of Baptism for my father Frederick, dated July 1894 and issued in Durban, Natal Province. I believe that his parents, Alexander and Emily were Swedish. I also have a photograph dated 1896 that shows a group of people standing outside the Volksrust Hotel. Amongst the group is a child that I was told is my father aged around two.

Volksrust was at the edge of the Boer's territory in the Anglo-Boer War 1899-1902 and the Roy clan left what is now South Africa in about 1905. Whether they backed the wrong side in the conflict as is rumoured, I will never know. Apparently they headed off to join the Alaskan Gold Rush and ended up in Pontefract, Yorkshire. My mother was born in Yorkshire in 1899.

My parents were married in Pontefract in 1918 and the wedding photograph shows father wearing an army uniform. Two soldiers called Frederick Roy appear in The National Archives and one of them died in France in 1915 which leaves one that presumably was my father. He was in the army from 1914 to 1920 and it would be logical to think that he fought in World War I. Curiously he was a gunner in two separate regiments, initially with the Royal Garrison Artillery Regiment and then with the Royal Warwickshire Regiment.

Not that he necessarily distinguished himself as his medal card simply implies that he received a service medal. But he did manage to survive.

Back in Blighty in 1920ish, the couple moved to Manchester. It was there in the suburb of Chorlton-cum-Hardy that they enjoyed some sort of purple patch, never to be achieved again. Jeffery was born in 1922, Anita in1926 and Freda in 1931. By the time it was my turn at the end of December 1939, they had all relocated to a set of rooms above the fish and chips shop at 312 High Street, Chatham, Kent.

The premises were far too inadequate to merit the description of flat or apartment. The overcrowding led to a move to a terraced house overlooking the railway station. It might have been on Lumsden Terrace or close by with the usual layout for that time, including a back scullery where the tin bath was hung ready for its weekly outing. And of course, an outside toilet. My father still managed the chippy in Chatham five days a week.

I discovered at a very early age that my mother was a real piece of work and invariably wore a truly miserable look on her face. We were poor but then everyone around us was poor; it was just a matter of degree. It seemed to me that in her heart she believed that she'd been born to have a better life but I was never privy as to why she thought that.

My first memory as a child, perhaps in early 1942, was brother Jeffery heading off to war. Conscripted into the Royal Artillery, he immediately informed the military authorities that he was unwilling to fight the Germans as he was a Germanophile. A fact that was absolutely true and he spoke the language fluently. Always willing to accommodate the foibles of an individual recruit, they excused him from the European and African campaigns, sending him to Burma instead. Be careful what you wish for. I was only two and a half but clearly remember the trauma in the house when he said his goodbyes and set off in his brand new uniform on an open-ended trip to the East.

A few months later, big sister Anita joined the Land Army and it was rumoured that she'd lied about her age. Towards the end of the war, she volunteered for the Royal Air Force, returning home briefly in 1948. Another early memory was of V1 flying bombs over Chatham. (People called them doodlebugs or buzz bombs because of the sounds they made.) One came down in the next street taking out several houses and a piece of shrapnel smashed through my sister's bedroom window and landed on her bed. Not that any of it woke her up. That night hysteria reigned all around me.

In England there has always been rivalry and dislike between the north and the south. The southerners tended to be snobbish, referring to everywhere north of Watford Gap as 'primeval swampland' and 'the barbaric north'. Northerners on the other hand said that all southerners were 'poofters and perverts'. From a very early age I really felt I was the odd one out in this mob as they all came from Pontefract and Manchester. That was where they'd enjoyed their happier days and somehow I epitomised the reasons for their current hard times.

Like most kids, I started school at about five and think that it might have been St John's in New Street. But after just a few months, I was moved to another school a little further away. My only memories are of massive disorganisation and confusion. Teachers were coming and going due to call-ups and evacuations and many children were being relocated elsewhere in the country. After all, Chatham had a naval dockyard and it was a short journey to mainland Europe. When the war with Japan came to an end in 1945, I clearly recall travelling to London with my parents and Freda to join the multitude outside Buckingham Palace to celebrate. How could you forget?

Our settled life was over soon afterwards as we moved to 118 Westmead Road, Carshalton where my parents were to manage a fish and chips shop, living behind and above. Amazingly the premises still exists, works in the same trade and by all accounts produces excellent food. My third new school was a small church junior called St Barnabas. That closed when the principal/owner died and I was moved to a local authority unit.

Something strange happened about this time, around 1947/48: we seemed to have money to spare. Up to then, even when I was a little kid, we were living our lives on a shoestring. We had to make do with second-hand clothing and treats were rare or non-existent. The war had left the country in a sorry state, rationing was to stay in force for years to come and it was really tough going for everyone. Christmas 1948 brought a bonanza of gifts, my mother stuck me in music lessons and then the really disastrous move of putting me in a private school. It was also about the time that they realised that I was almost blind in one eye.

The source of our short-lived financial relief is still a mystery to me. One day my father took me to meet a man at a dock somewhere in London. I'd never seen such a wonderful suit and this gentleman patted me on the head and gave me half a crown! No one had ever put cash in my hand and I thought I would burst with the excitement of it all. The only quick cash at the time was through the black market, dealing with dodgy ration books or outright criminal activity and that was rife. All the unemployed men recently discharged from the services had been trained to be violent killers and to handle weaponry like guns and knives. Now they were adapting those skills and putting them to the test. The only other possibility was having a relative die and leaving you a few bob.

Anita did return briefly before taking the opportunity offered by the £10 migration scheme to Australia. On the boat she met an Irishman called Tom Armstrong, married him soon after they landed and became a Roman Candle. Like many converts, she took the faith on board big time; I do hope that all has worked out for her in the afterlife.

The piano lessons were totally wasted on me and it was obvious from the beginning that I was absolutely talentless. My teacher struggled with his frustration but persevered because, to put it bluntly, he desperately needed the money. During one lesson when I suddenly needed a piss, he led me out of the front room and down the stairs to the basement en route to the outside dunny. A young woman with four very young children was living there in abject poverty. Pupils must have been in short supply and the teacher really needed to find another line of work to lift the family out of its extreme penury. Even though I did feel very sorry for them, after six or seven weeks I told my mother that piano lessons were a waste of her money and my time.

'Whatever I might become in the future, I can guarantee that it's not going to be a musician,' I said.

The business of the private school reflected my mother's deep-seated notion that she/us deserved better than her/our circumstances dictated. The school was a large old building on Ringstead Road and consisted of just two classes for children: one for children up to the age of eleven and the other for those over eleven. But the ages of children within in each class varied over a span of five or six years making it difficult for the younger ones to keep up and pretty hard for the older kids to stay interested.

Being just over eight, I slotted in the lower age group and our teacher was a French lady. It was a big class with maybe 35 kids that she found hard to control. Being deemed a disruptive pupil and a bad influence on the others, I was 'promoted' to the big kids' class where I was three years younger than the youngest. I did not have the faintest idea of what was going on, so simply freewheeled, doing very little work and not participating in anything. The form teacher here also had a large mob to control but directed most of his efforts and time to the 16 year olds who had examinations around the corner. We came to an unspoken understanding: if I didn't cause him grief, he would leave me be. But not for long, as it turned out.

Father had lost his job again and we were on the move again. This time it was not far: Wallington. It was obvious that the premises had been empty for some time and a lot of effort was required to bring the house up to a liveable standard and get the shop ready for business. It was the usual arrangement with the eatery at the front with the residence above and behind. But what struck me as strange was that it was the only retail outlet in sight, surrounded on all sides by streets of terraced housing. Normally a fish and chips shop would form part of a retail parade or at least a group of business outlets. This was a stand-alone.

Rising alongside the building was a tall chimney that had previously been used for smoking fish. Soon after he'd opened the shop up for business, my father fired up old smoky and suddenly all the neighbours who thus far had been invisible, rushed out to complain. It was an ugly scene and certain to become uglier if he persisted and repeated the offence.

My sixth school was a nearby local authority junior. Having been a new boy many times, I expected attempts at bullying which I'd previously coped with by befriending the toughest looking kids. This time it came from an unexpected source in the shape of the teacher Miss Moset. Given the information provided by my previous alma mater, she abused me all day, every day in respect of the fact that I had come from a fee-paying school as though it was my fault, my choosing and it was a crime. The other kids were too young and uncaring to have the faintest idea what she was banging on about but she simply wouldn't let it rest. After three months, I told the old folks that I wouldn't be going back there any more. It's bad enough not learning anything but to be continually singled out for abuse for no good reason was a big step too far. Mother went to see Miss Moset who naturally denied everything, implied that I'd made it all up and was lying. Absurd and untrue.

Thus I moved to junior school mark seven with my reputation as a troublemaker probably preceding me and I wasn't even nine. But it didn't matter because father had lost his job again and announced that we were heading north to Askern near Doncaster. What awaited a London boy among our friends up north, I wondered. I had come to the conclusion that we'd been on the road to nowhere and just about to reach skid row. This whole business lark seemed to be a total puzzle. The fish and chips my parents cooked were pretty good from what I'd tasted and there had never been fallouts with shop owners or customers. Yet here we were after only a few months, packing up and on the move again. It was worse than being a Romany didicoi, traveller or gypsy; at least their homes moved with them and they had regular stopping places.

Communications were very basic by comparison to today's technology and access to information. There were newspapers and magazines with advertisements for job vacancies in the house but I never saw them being read. Old copies lying around were used for wrapping paper. Radios were commonplace but few people had a phone and even fewer had a television. So where did the next job appointment come from? And why would anyone give my father a chance once they learned of his history of short tenures?

I had little doubt that my education was screwed. When we got to Askern, getting me into school would not be a priority, in fact probably way down the list with the result that the gaps between desks got ever wider. I read anything I could get my hand on, determined to teach myself as much as I could. There were no signs of stability on the horizon, in fact quite the opposite.

*****

Askern was a few miles from Doncaster and seemed a million miles from London. In Victorian times it had been a pleasant village enjoying several spas but in the early 1900s coal was discovered and a massive mine developed. Around it grew a town to house and service the miners and their families. The mine's dominant features were the massive slag heaps and the winding gear. The street echoed to the sound of the knocker-up in the early mornings, banging a rod against the miners' windows due for the first shift.

The fateful day soon arrived and we loaded up the removal van before leaving for King's Cross to catch the train to Doncaster. As we headed out of London, I felt we had crossed the Rubicon but when we got off the bus in Askern, I realised that we had crossed the Styx as well and landed in Hades.

Don't get me wrong, Chatham, Carshalton and Wallington were hardly modern versions of Shangri-La but here we had industrial heartland at its worst. In addition, I couldn't understand the Yorkshire dialect and the locals couldn't comprehend my melodic southern tones. I came to the conclusion that I must have done something really bad in a previous life and my punishment was being meted out, here and now.

In contrast to our last place, the premises were truly excellent and the living room had a beautiful waxed wooden floor that my mother immediately had covered with linoleum. Why? Because it annoyed her. Actually everything and everybody annoyed my mother. When Hitler sent his troops into Poland, it was not for the reasons he'd stated, he did it to annoy my mother. Any decisions made by anybody, anywhere were designed to upset her equilibrium which they invariably did.

The removals van arrived the next day and backed up to the shop door to unload. At which point a bizarre phenomenon occurred. People seemed to come from far and wide to watch our belongings being taken from van to house, to the point that we were forced to push through the throng to get the job done. It was blatant, in your face nosiness at a level I'd never seen before and it didn't bode well for a future happy life in the town.

On the other hand, the owners seemed really nice people. As well as handing over premises that had clearly been looked after, they gave me a large Meccano set which, although a little old and rusty, was a fantastic unexpected gift. Maybe things weren't going to be so bad. Oh yes they were!

Mother took me to the local junior school, handed me over and I fitted right into the scenery. The kids were all sons or daughters of miners and just as scruffy as me. Of course there was no such thing as a uniform, quite a few wore rags and some didn't even have shoes. That's how bad it was. After school many went down to the tailings to search for any useable lumps of coal that might have slipped through. Given my last school experience, I expected to be picked on by the teachers for being different but it didn't happen. I was allowed time and space to settle in.

A school inspector came to the school on one occasion, eliciting a great deal of kowtows from the staff. When he arrived in our classroom, he asked us to stand if we liked school. Stupid patronising bastard! I encouraged the kids around me to stay seated but they ignored me and stood up as one. None of these future tough miners boasted an ounce of mischief. Spotting me quickly, the inspector instructed the form to sit down and me to stand.

'You didn't stand boy. Don't you like school?'

'Not much. It's a stupid waste of time if you ask me.'

My accent took him by surprise and he turned to the teacher for help.

'He's only been with us for a couple of weeks. Still finding his feet, as it were. And he's from London.'

'Ah, of course.'

Those few words appeared to fully satisfy the man and his inspection took him elsewhere. My act of defiance was unique, had never been seen before and would never be seen again. To challenge authority openly and in front of the whole class, you'd have to be unhinged and doing so could have terrible consequences. After that, nobody had any thought of crossing me; crazy folk should be given a wide berth. Which suited me to a tee.

True to say most of those didn't need any education as their future lives were predestined. The boys would follow in their fathers' footsteps and go down the pit. As for the girls, they'd get factory jobs in Doncaster, get married and have kids of their own. I'm not being judgemental or derogatory; those were the simple facts of life.

From Monday to Friday we'd sit at our desks, usually told to turn to a page in our books and read. And a few would do so but others would quietly chat to each or simply look out of the windows while some boys would make spit balls to fire at the girls. When break times came, we'd go outside and hang around until it was time to go back to the classroom.

Generally speaking, my father was a man of few words but one Saturday morning, an amazing thing happened.

'Would you like a puppy Peter?'

'No he wouldn't!' my mother interjected.

Ignoring her my father continued.

'A customer's dog's just had puppies and he needs to find homes for them. If you want one, you can have it for free.'

Thirty minutes later we were walking home with my new best friend. Mother was not pleased, had plenty to say and none of it was pleasant but we kept the little guy. Undoubtedly he helped make up for a lot of the misery of living in the bloody place.

I walked him before I went to school, then in the evening before 'tea' (as it was called then) with longer runs over the weekends, all the time working hard to train him in the basics. Mother invariably put on a gala performance at the occurrence of any little accidents but we persevered and after a while he settled.

One walk I often took, before and after he arrived, was to walk east along Moss Road out of town, past a couple of farms until I reached the main LNER railway line between London and Edinburgh. A wait would often be rewarded by the sight and sounds of a Pacific Class locomotive, hopefully an A4, roaring through pulling a dozen carriages with a blur of all those lucky passengers.

Since it was a Monday and in the middle of a school holiday, my father suggested that we took that walk together with the dog. Little more than a country lane, Moss Road was usually devoid of traffic but not that day. On that fateful walk we were on our way back when a farm utility vehicle ran over the dog. I rushed to the back of the truck hoping beyond hope that it had just passed over my little mate. But no such luck, sadly the poor little fellow had been crushed. His body went into a sack and the farmer took it away. I was totally distraught. When father broke the news to mother when we got home, she was beside herself with joy. I'll never forget her words.

'Thank God. That filthy creature is gone for good.'

It was very, very rare to see my mother be anything other than miserable. It had come at a very high cost.

Avoiding repetition is one of the arts of telling a story but it has to be said, my father lost his job again and we were off – again. Where to? Aberdeen or Belfast? Another foul coal mining town? No, praise be, this time my prayers and dreams had been answered: we were heading for Peckham, South London. Hallelujah!

No crowd appeared to watch us load up the van and there were no fond farewells. Mother took up her beloved lino, I packed my Meccano set, Freda gave her notice to the stocking factory in Doncaster and we were on our way back to my spiritual homeland.

*****

Peckham – gateway to the south. There were plenty of bombsites and railway tracks for kids to mess about on, surrounded by the familiar sounds of everyday metropolitan life. The shop and living quarters at 114 Queen's Road was laid out in the usual way but featured a unique element in the fact that it was next to a funeral directors' parlour. If someone fell off their perch in the chips shop, they wouldn't have to go far.

Another new school but I started to find my feet and fit in with normal day to day life. It was not to last. About three weeks in, I was walking back home along Queen's Road, minding my own business when I sensed I was being followed. Stopping outside a shop window, I saw the reflections of two large lads from school which was not good news. They were bullies who I'd actually seen pushing smaller kids around and nicking their stuff. I could have sprinted for home but that would only have postponed the inevitable and might have made my punishment worse. Anyway, Queen's was a main road with plenty of people around. So nothing terrible could really happen, could it? Passing me on either side, they stopped, turned and blocked my progress.

'Hello new boy.'

'What do you two want?'

'Oh! Straight to the point,' said Dumb, 'we like that. What we want from you is a bob (5p in decimal money) every Friday without fail as insurance.'

I didn't need to ask what risk I was insuring against.

'I don't have any money. Never have any money.'

'Don't believe you,' said Dumber.

With that they were all over me like a cheap overcoat, pushing, shoving and trying to get their big hands into my pockets. Then disaster struck as my glasses fell off, hit the ground and broke in two. In an instant I had a vision of my mother giving me hell for making her life even more miserable than usual. Without a thought, I went berserk.

Seeing their gleeful grins, I watched the sudden change of countenance as I stuck my finger in the taller boy's eye, digging the nail in deeper. Then piling into the other with my fists and feet flying, I propelled him backwards until he tripped. Falling on top of him, I grabbed his head with both hands and slammed it down on the concrete several times. Four meaty hands pulled me off. I picked up my broken specs and walked off without a backward glance.

Up to that moment, I had always avoided playground fights and if one threatened, usually found the words to calm the situation. The raging ball of anger that must have grown over the years finally exploded and Dumb and Dumber found themselves on the receiving end.

Mother didn't let me down, switching on her monologue of misery just for me. I didn't tell her what had happened; the least said the better, I thought. A temporary fix to my glasses with a Band-Aid would have to do until some future date. The following morning when I arrived at school, a teacher blocked my entry.

'You can't come in Roy. Go home and come back at 10 o'clock accompanied by one of your parents to see the Headmaster.'

'Why?'

'Just do it.'

Here we go again: father would be preparing the shop, so it would have to be mother. Happy days. The same teacher was waiting for us when we arrived and led us to the Head's office. We were greeted without the customary handshake and told to sit.

'Roy. It has been reported to me that you attacked two other pupils yesterday afternoon without any reason. What do have to say for yourself?'

Mother's jaw dropped.

'That the report you have? That I'm walking along the road and then, without rhyme or reason, I attack two much bigger boys who are simply standing quietly on the pavement.'

'That is about the size of it, yes.'

'And that makes sense to you?'

'Young man, I am giving you the opportunity to tell me your version of the events.'

'I'd like to say that Peter ...'

The Head cut her off, holding his hand up to stop her.

'I need to hear what your son believes happened not theorising from a parent who was not present.'

Mother was dying to say her piece but the Head was having none of it and I liked him for that.

'They demanded money from me. Said I had to pay them one bob every Friday or else. When I said I didn't have any money, they called me a liar and attacked, trying to search my pockets. And they broke my glasses so I defended myself, that's all.'

'Do you have any evidence of this? Or witnesses?'

'Look at my glasses, Sir. That's evidence enough.'

'There is no bullying at this school. I am certain of it and therefore I am going to have to ask you to find another school.'

'I'm being expelled?'

'No you are not, not at all. But clearly you are not fitting in here and I do believe there will be reprisals if you remain. From what I have been told, your action may have blinded one boy's eye and the other may have concussion. I am not saying that I disbelieve your version but I do believe my decision is the best for the school.'

'For the best you say?'

There was no way I was going to beg for another chance from an idiot who believed that Dumb and Dumber might be a couple of cleanskins. I stood, turned and left without another word. Mother followed me out and we walked home in silence. The course of events had rendered her speechless; that had to be a first.

A few weeks later another school did accept me; ten schools

before the age of ten must be some sort of record. I think this one was off Peckham Rye. I caught a break there with the class teacher, Mr Clarke. Horrified by my chequered educational history, he asked me to stay behind after school for a chat. I explained that the root cause of the problems was directly linked to my father's employment: any job involved a shop and accommodation, meaning that when he lost his job, we lost our home. It was as simple as that.

'Post war, there was a lot of internal migration, people moving from place to place has been far greater than in settled times. But your travels are off the scales. What concerns me is that your eleven plus exams are not that far away; they set you on a course for the future and you're totally unprepared.

'I'm prepared to give you my time outside school hours if, in turn, you make every effort to fill the many gaps and catch up. What do you think Peter Roy?'

'Thank you very much Sir,' I said gratefully. 'I promise I'll do my best.'

Of course, what he couldn't do was compensate for the lack of continuity, stability and structure in my life; that would come back to haunt me in the future.

He was as good as his word and looking back, I owe him a massive debt of gratitude. Without his help I would have certainly failed my exams. As it turned out, I passed with flying colours and had offers from three local grammar schools, all judged to be up on a level with the best in South East London for pupils passing exams.

My father appeared to have little interest in everyday life and took no part in anything beyond running the business, enjoying a few pints and a game of dominoes. Therefore the decision was my mother's to make: her choice of school and her decision.

As mentioned previously, she firmly believed that she had been born to have a better life, despite living down among the dead men as we did. We were so poor that we couldn't even afford a radio. As was the fashion, she smoked but not the usual working class brands like Wills Woodbines, Players Weights or Gold Flake. Instead she chose the upmarket brand Du Maurier; even at that age, I resented what little money we had going up in expensive smoke while I was kitted out in second hand clothes and shoes. Today it is common knowledge that smoking can lead to cancer, chronic obstructive pulmonary disease (COPD), damaged eyesight and cause gum disease. Not back then. Movie stars idolised across the world puffed their way through the films and their admirers followed in their footsteps. Politicians, doctors, bankers, lawyers and more smoked and because all these illustrious people had the habit, smoking was obviously a good thing and the proles followed suit.

My mother's mindset naturally included me, so she chose the pre-eminent establishment for my further education, Haberdashers' Aske's Hatcham Boys Grammar School. Set up in 1875 from a bequest originally left by Robert Aske to the Worshipful Company of Haberdashers, the school sat on the top of Telegraph Hill in New Cross Gate. Mother and I had to attend an interview with the headmaster and it was a fair walk uphill. She complained every step of the way. On arrival at the head's office, my mother was ushered in while I was asked to wait outside. It would have been better to have opened the door, thrown in a stink bomb, closed the door and walked away. In my opinion.

To my surprise, ten minutes later I was invited to join them and asked what occupation was I aiming for once I left school. Unprepared to field questions, I blurted out the words 'engine driver'. Like all boys, I was mad about steam locomotion but this was not really the banker, doctor, stockbroker, solicitor, 'following in my father's footsteps' answer that was expected. On the other hand, given my experiences over the years there was no way that the words 'fish and chips shop manager' was going to escape my lips. I anticipated rejection but a few days later a letter of invitation to join the school dropped through the letterbox.

The first job was to obtain the compulsory school uniform. Bypassing the expensive recommended drapers, my mother took me down to the open-air market at Peckham Rye where she found a well-worn blazer and short trousers that assured that I'd stand out from the crowd on day one. Haberdashers' main sports game was Rugby Union for which I would need boots. The second-hand pair that my mother found looked as though they'd last seen service at the battle of the Somme. She also bought some studs that my father was given to hammer into the soles of the boots. Which he did, until the studs penetrated through the soles to the other side, requiring several cardboard inserts to dull the sharp points.

The journey to school called for a new bicycle as I had outgrown the model I had by several years. The only way I could raise the money was to work. I ran errands, painted walls, creosoted fences, cleaned anything that stood still and scraped together ten quid, enough to buy a Raleigh out of the shop window. At last I had one new item to my name.

So the day arrived. I cycled up Pepys Road and parked my bike in the church grounds next to the school. My suppositions about my fellow first formers proved to be correct. They all wore brand new uniforms and looked as though they came from middle class families. For them, education was simply a stepping-stone to pre-ordained success.

Assembled in the yard, we were addressed by the headmaster in somewhat sombre tones. At the back it was nigh on impossible to understand exactly what he was saying but we got the gist of what he said. Apparently on the previous Saturday during a school rugger game, somebody had broken his neck. We stood in silence in honour of the deceased unnamed player: perhaps a Haberdashers' pupil, a kid from another school or even an old boy, we were not told. Personally I didn't feel it augured well.

Each of us new boys were then divided into pre-assigned forms and, horror of horrors, I was put into the 'A' class, among South-East London's best and brightest. The more I saw, the more I was reminded of the 1830s Rugby School as depicted in Tom Brown's Schooldays by Thomas Hughes.

Firstly there was the school motto: serve and obey. In whose fortune cookie did they find that gem? Or perhaps some mad army type dreamed it up before sending the cannon fodder into battle. Secondly it was immediately obvious that bullying was institutionalised: prefects were expected to deal with pupils as they saw fit without any adult supervision or guidance. Then there was a tuck shop that stocked sticky buns, sweets and the like with red-faced old biddies on hand to serve. But I don't think obey.

Why was the school organised on a house system? As far as I knew, houses were normally found in boarding schools where the pupils were grouped in named buildings, each with a housemaster and matron. During term times, houses competed against each other for a cup; this was intended to give pupils a sense of belonging and replace the missing family life. At Haberdashers, pupils were allocated to the various houses and identifiable by the colour of the button on their caps. But there were no boarders, housemasters, matrons, dormitories or competitions! The cup was awarded on the basis of the cumulative numbers of gold stars and black marks awarded to pupils that to my mind was as artificial as it could get. I didn't know that I was to embark on a course that would bring a reign of chaos to the stupid system.

My final gripe was that the main school sport was rugby union. I had always enjoyed soccer that is played with a round ball whereas rugby is played with an oval ball in a totally different way and has its own set of rules. About which I did not have a clue!

I quickly realised that I was distinctly disadvantaged in the A form, surrounded by kids who had a solid grounding and, more importantly, were brimming with confidence. I tackled the work diligently and religiously handed in my completed homework that was handed out daily. But I felt that I was at the top of a slippery slope and I was right.

The only other element missing from the Tom Brown comparison was that no fagging system existed, then a norm in elite boarding schools. Essentially younger pupils were required to act as personal servants (or fags) to Seniors in the sixth form. Fags were commonly mistreated, beaten and in many instances, sexually abused. Fagging no longer legitimately exists in public schools; Eton banned the practice in July 1980 and other schools followed.

My opening brush with authority arose in my very first week in the art class. My knowledge on all things artistic was zero, I'd never seen an artist's brush let alone held one but here I was with the rest of the A form awaiting an art lesson surrounded by the paraphernalia of water colours and oils. The young teacher began by going through the range of colours and asking pupils to name them.

'What would you call this one?' he asked on pupil.

'Erm, blue Sir?'

'Almost correct but not quite. It's actually cobalt blue.'

Working his way around the room he finally appeared in front of me and waved a tube of paint. Easy peasy lemon squeezy.

'Yeller, Sir.'

'What did you say?' he asked incredulously.

'Yeller.'

'Again.'

'Yeller.'

'What in God's name are you saying? I have no idea what yeller means.'

'It means, yeller Sir.'

When it finally dawned on him, he was apoplectic with anger.

'You idiotic vile boy, the colour is YELLOW,' he shouted, emphasising the second syllable. 'Yell-ow, ye-llow. In the King's English as spoken by normal people, this colour is called yellow.'

From there the lesson went to hell in a handcart. I can't speak for my peers but I certainly learned nothing else in the remaining time. When it finally came to an end, I waited for the form to file out wanting to be the last to leave. He glowered at me when I paused on my way out.

'Thank you Sir; for putting me right Sir. I won't forget it Sir.'

The words in themselves sounded polite enough but were spoken in such a way that he and the boys nearby would know that I was taking the piss.

'You insolent boy,' he shouted, 'get out, get out!'

I readied myself for the blow but it never came. I kept a low profile in future art lessons and he ignored me. A winning formula.

Week two presented another test in the shape of sport. Rugby was completely foreign to me and I'd never watched it so didn't have any idea of how it was played. I did know that it was easy to get hurt and in extreme cases killed. The sports master divided us into teams but since all thirty kids wore the same uniform that made it all rather confusing. My immediate problem lay in my boots: as the cardboard insoles compressed, the stud nail points were becoming more pronounced and it hurt.

In low-level ball games, the players chase the ball in a mob, kicking and rushing. At the other end of the spectrum, the players make the ball do the work broadly in team position. These eleven and twelve year olds charged after the ball with a lot of shouting and abundant body contact. Nobody could really remember who was on which side or who was going which way. When the ball came to me, I couldn't avoid it so threw it away and apparently gave away a penalty. I resolved to do as the professionals do and keep away from the craziness.

I was sitting on a bench in the changing rooms when I spotted the coach heading my way and not looking pleased. He was about to crack into me when he spotted my bloody socks and that stopped him in his tracks. Instead of firing off a bollocking he dropped down on to one knee so he was down to my head height.

'Rugby isn't your sport is it lad?'

'No Sir, I like soccer.'

'I could see you were struggling.'

I played the missing eye card.

'I'm blind in one eye …'

He interrupted me, the expression of shock clearly registering on his face. Given the combination of my bloody feet and semi-blindness, I sensed that I might be about to be given some slack.

'You should have told me. Look lad, I think you and rugby should remain strangers. As of now, you have my permission to excuse yourself from both training and playing. Take yourself to the library and work on your own. I do want you out there for other sports but rugby's definitely out. Two bits of advice: wash your feet and get rid of those boots.'

'Thank you Sir.'

Without another word, he rose, patted my shoulder, turned and started shouting at some other boys. My fears of being forced to be a rugger bugger were over.

Unsurprisingly, none of my fellow first formers attracted much attention. My first real trouble hit as soon as week four and started with a single word. Arriving for the outdoor assembly, I shuffled into line and looked at the kid next to me.

'Cold,' I said, shivering.

A prefect was onto my case in an instant.

'Who spoke?'

'Me.'

'No talking in assembly. You know the rules.'

'Assembly hasn't started yet.'

'Don't get cheeky with me. What's your name?'

Looking at the face of a born bully, I was glad that fagging didn't exist at Haberdashers.

'One hundred lines on …' The self-styled Harry Flashman paused while the wheels and cogs of his brain found a crackerjack subject. 'On Harry Roy.'

I had absolutely no idea who he was talking about. The headmaster addressed us as usual, prayers were spoken and we were dismissed. The rest of the day was spent struggling how to write 100 lines on a person I knew nothing about. In desperation, after I'd finished my homework that evening, I wrote the name Harry Roy over and over again on a piece of paper until I'd completed the task. The following morning I arrived early and sought out the prefect to give him my work.

'That's rubbish. One hours' detention after school.'

'That's not fair. I've written the lines.'

'Detention.'

Over the course of the day, I positively seethed with anger at the inequity of the punishment. I'd done my best and to be punished a second time was not right. So I skipped detention and went home as usual but I knew there'd be hell to pay in the morning. My class had not even started when the summons came.

'Roy, headmaster wants to see you. Now.'

From what I'd seen of the headmaster, he seemed a very decent, reasonable man and I liked him. However, although he was responsible for the wellbeing of the staff and boys, maybe a thousand souls in all, he was also responsible for maintaining the long traditions of the grammar school. I knocked on his study door.

'Come.'

Opening the door, I walked into the room and stood in front of his desk.

'It has been reported to me that you failed to attend your detention yesterday. What do you have to say for yourself?'

'The report is correct, Sir but it wasn't fair.'

'Please explain why you did not attend Roy. You must have known there would be repercussions?'

'Because I was being punished twice for the same offence Sir. I was given the lines for speaking during assembly. Later I wrote them all out and gave them to the prefect on time. And that should have been it Sir.'

'As I understand it, you were asked to write a hundred lines about Harry Roy but what you did was to write his name down over and over again.'

'Yes Sir but I've never heard of him. Who is Harry Roy?'

'Everybody's heard of the man. He's a hugely popular and well-known dance bandleader. Come on Roy, you must have heard of him, he's on the radio all the time.'

'We don't have a radio Sir.'

'Don't have a radio? That's extraordinary. Why not? Is it some sort of religious belief that forbids listening to the radio?'

'No Sir. We don't have enough money to buy one. Mother says it's because we're living on the breadline.'

'Listen to me boy. We have neither the time nor resources to discuss and sit in judgement on every slight, whether real or perceived. We have a school to run. In future you will obey all instructions given to you by your teachers and the prefects, without question. I suggest that it is in your best interests to follow that guiding rule at all times. '

'My best interests Sir. Yes, thank you Sir.'

'After school today, you will report for your period of detention. To ensure that you do attend, I will send two prefects to be your escorts. Learn the lesson boy. I do not want to see you in my study again. Do I make myself clear?'

'Yes Sir, I understand.'

For some reason I had developed the habit of pausing briefly before saying the word Sir, which confused a lot of people. Either I was always being polite and respectful or seriously taking the mickey.

The prefects were ready and waiting for me at the door when it was home time. They pretty much frogmarched me to detention and to my amazement, stayed there for the full hour to make certain that I didn't use a loo visit to escape. They were just as much imprisoned as me and were definitely not happy about it, making it clear that they'd be watching me like hawks for the slightest future misdemeanour. There was nothing more I could do than what I'd done already. In drawing attention to the first prefect's stupidity, I'd wasted the head's time, the prefects' time and made some enemies. That was achievement enough for a 48-hour period.

I managed to reach the end of term without any further confrontations but I was not doing well academically. When it was announced that we would be learning a language in the New Year, I was horrified. (I think it was going to be German or Latin.) I need not have worried. On the first day back after the holidays, we were told our form position and I was second from bottom. It wasn't much of a surprise but still upsetting and I was dropped to form B.

Three were chosen from each class, to be transferred upwards or downwards. Together with my two downward moving classmates, I gathered my gear and we left to find our new home.

Trios of boys wandered the corridors, half in despair and half in triumph, some bragged while others cried. For me it was another upheaval, an internal migration to be handled like so many others in my life. My belief was that they could do anything to you apart from kill you. In later years I discovered that I'd been lucky not to have been born in Japan where teachers do occasionally kill children with impunity. In the late 1990s a teacher intentionally closed electronic gates on a pupil for being late. She was crushed and lost her life as a punishment. No police action was taken. Part of the culture, I presume.

During my travels through the English educational system between 1945 and 1956, I came across teachers some of whom were good, some bad but mostly indifferent. One that I met at Haberdashers was without doubt, certifiably insane and I was just about to meet him. We shuffled in through the opened door to a classroom housing two dozen stony faced boys and a short man on the stout side. He naturally warmly welcomed us to his class.

'Oh good, here come the failures. I've lost my three best boys to form A and I get its rejects. Lucky me.'

It wasn't the words that struck me as much as the sound that they made on issue. It was a rasping croak as if his vocal chords were wrapped in barbed wire. His nickname was as predictable as it was unimaginative – Froggie. Waving his arm at the four rows of pupils, he continued the welcome speech.

'My best boys sit at the back, so you take those seats in the front row,' he added, pointing at them.

I couldn't resist piping up.

'Excuse me Sir. If we were at the bottom of form A, shouldn't we be at the top of form B?'

His face changed to the colour of an aubergine and looked as though it would explode or that he might even hit me.

'Sit down you arrogant little boy and shut up.'

We were roughly the same height and I objected to being called little.

'I will be watching you.'

That was kind of him, he'd joined the prefects in keeping watch over me. What harm could befall? All jokes apart, this was serious. His voice was almost unintelligible and I genuinely couldn't understand much of what he said. If he did have knowledge to impart, little if any was likely to sink into my memory bank. It's possible that he had dysphonia, a condition where the muscles around the larynx (or voice box) constrict it so tightly the sufferer's speaking is badly affected. On he might even have had throat cancer.

Every boy in the form was terrified of Froggie to the point that it was an utterly soulless group. There was absolutely no interrelationship between teacher and pupils. Nobody spoke unless invited and then with reticence. Froggie addressed pupils variously as: beautiful boys, the back row, imbeciles or morons – the majority. He had special alternatives in reserve for the three of us who'd come down from A and the three who'd moved from C: we were retards and failures, individually and collectively.

I don't know whether there were others who found him as unintelligible as I did; perhaps comprehension improved with time and acquaintance. But no one could have enjoyed being forced to endure the torrents of abusive language on a daily basis. In all my previous experience, a small silly incident such as someone involuntarily farting or howling after closing a desk lid on his finger would elicit a burst of laughter followed by the teacher's admonishment. Not in Froggie's form. One boy who'd been told to distribute a pile of books to the class, managed to trip and fall sprawling in aisle, volumes flying everywhere. Not a sound other than our teacher screaming abuse at the poor bugger on the nature of his parentage and his distinct lack of prospects. Abandon hope, all who enter here.

By this time, my absence from rugby had expanded unnoticed to incorporate all sports. Since I loved reading, I spent a lot of time in the library, which is where I came up with a mad plan. The idea was to annoy Froggie so much that he would send me out of the room allowing me to skive off with a book and escape the insanity of it all.

My desk was in the centre of the front row that was physically closest to the ogre. I yawned, scratched, picked my nose, closed my eyes, coughed and made a real drama of wiping off the spittle that rained down on us front row retards with a big blue handkerchief. No one else dared but I just didn't care.

The plan failed but I did make a small gain. It didn't take long before Mr Aubergine reappeared, spewing out a stream of invective on the subject of my incessant fidgeting. Before waiting for a response, he ordered me to the empty desk at the end of the row thus taking me away from the Mississippi flood.

Outside of school, Peckham suited me well enough as it offered a range of diversions to be enjoyed. On several occasions I went to the local speedway track, a few games at Millwall Football Club and watched the odd Saturday morning picture at the cinema. Of course, having the bicycle meant that I could venture further afield.

As it happened I didn't need to worry about being at Haberdashers much longer as my father got the sack and were off on our travels again. I decided not to tell anyone at school and continue as normal. At lunchtime on my final day, the same two prefects who'd been my prison warders for detention cornered me. The bigger one did the talking.

'Listen, you little piece of dung, you have single-handedly

wrecked any chance of our winning the House Cup this year. And I care about that a lot because I'm the Senior Boy of our House.'

'What have I done?'

'Black marks is what you've done. What the hell is wrong with you? Failing to complete lines, ducking detention, speaking back, insolence, homework in late, being in the library without permission, failure to supply a sick note. The list is endless.'

'I am sorry about all that. And I will try harder.'

'Roy don't try, just do as you're told and as is expected. I suggest you pull your socks up as far as your bloody neck and I will be watching you!'

With that they left me alone. I shrugged, knowing they wouldn't have to watch me for long – maybe a couple of hours. When the bell went, I gathered up my stuff and headed for the front door. On the way, I dropped a letter on the headmaster's secretary's desk informing him of my immediate departure. Call me paranoid but I glanced through a window towards the gate and spotted the senior boy of my now ex-house and three other prefects. I guessed that there was a fair chance that they were waiting for me and pain would be involved. Fortunately I knew the way out through the back of the buildings that led to the churchyard where my bicycle was parked. Out of bounds, of course, but once the bird has flown … Gone and free.

Our next destination was to be East Ham, north of the River Thames in East London. It could have been worse.

But before that leap you, might be wondering what happened to the quasi-public school. Did it catch up with the 20th century? It did, it actually did. In 1979 it morphed into a comprehensive school and since 2005 has held Academy status. An Academy does not have to follow the National Curriculum, may set its own term times and receives its funding directly from the government.

In reality, I was only there for a few weeks but sometimes that felt endless. Much of the silliness and stupidities have stuck with me over the years, embedded in my memory. But one of the appalling aspects was the employment of a man whose method of teaching included shouting and hurling abuse at twelve year olds in a voice far less comprehensible than that of Kermit the Frog. My memory suggests that his name might have been Green but perhaps that's just a mischievous thought.

I recently bought a copy of a book on the place entitled – Serve and Obey: The Story of the Haberdashers' Aske's Boys School – in the hope that it might provide a few details to enable me to put names to titles and check my memories of the geography of the place. Unfortunately, the work was not a history of the school that I attended but its brother school now based in Elstree. However a couple of paragraphs caught my eye.

'The good out-of-class discipline being sustained by sixth formers who enjoyed "Sixth Form Powers and Privileges" (being excused roll call for assembly, giving lines, using the main entrance but wearing the white-banded cap).

'Strict classroom discipline was intended to produce the best possible examination results and that only a minority of masters used the cane to keep order ... no master made any boy more important than another, demonstrating the high standard of fairness that prevailed at all times.'

My eyes were drawn to the photograph of senior boys walking between the open school gates. Not that I could have met any of the individuals portrayed but I knew their faces well. All from the same mould as the seniors from my time at Haberdashers, they were smug, self-satisfied and assured. They were secure in the knowledge that their fathers had successful careers that they could follow if they chose. They lived in proper houses that weren't going to disappear overnight and didn't have to worry about money as there was more than enough to allow them to coast through school, university and through life itself. There were also several photographs of the drama group; they depicted too many pretty young boys dressed as girls for my liking.

*****

Our new home at 365 High Street North, East Ham had unusual features. One was that it backed onto Plashet Jewish Cemetery that ensured the neighbourhood was nice and quiet apart from a couple of ceremonies each year. The other one was that halfway up the staircase between the ground floor shop and our first floor living quarters was a doorway. This entrance led to a self-contained flat in a rear extension tenanted by a woman in her 20s and her Border Collie.

It was a rather strange arrangement but not ours to change.

After a few weeks settling in, I went for an interview at East Ham Boys' Grammar School, next to the Town Hall. Sorry to say that my mother had to accompany me once again. The trouble with teachers, I believe, is that they spend so much time with children that they start to think and act like their wards. When he heard that I'd been in Form A at Haberdashers and only recently been demoted to B, the headmaster and his mate decided that I should join Form C in their illustrious establishment. I was not going to complain, as it would keep me away from the hothouses of the higher forms. Their decision was obviously a source of considerable mirth and it would have been no different if I'd been to Eton or Harrow.

Their next decision was just as inane: my joining the school in mid-term would cause too much disruption and therefore I would be allowed to start at the beginning of the next term. What utter nonsense! Who or what would I be disrupting? One new kid turning up on a Monday morning would hardly be a great event. There'd be a five-minute flutter of interest and that would be the extent of the disruption. I didn't argue as delaying my re-entry to the human zoo suited me down to the ground. My mother was told that I would be expected to be wearing a new school uniform when I arrived. Fat chance of that I thought, she'd be making a mental note to find the nearest flea market.

The next few weeks were pure magic. As our mid-floor neighbour worked full time, she gave me a key to her flat and I was allowed and encouraged to take her lovely dog out for walks whenever I liked. The rest of the time, I either read or rode my bicycle into the Essex countryside. Happy days.

Sadly those halcyon days came to an end with the beginning of the new school term. I duly presented myself at East Ham Boys' Grammar School with my inappropriate school uniform and the headmaster was seriously unimpressed.

'I demand to know the reason for your deplorable state of dress. Why are you not wearing a new school uniform?'

'My mother said to tell anyone who enquired about my not wearing a new uniform that, in her opinion, there was plenty of wear in left in what I've got.'

There was no money for new clothes or even second-hand ones.

To make them wearable, I'd pulled the studs out of my boots, cut off the sharp points and replaced them. Then relined the inner soles with some thick rubber scavenged from an old inner tube. Needs must.

It was obvious that the head's initial reaction was to send me home with a flea in my ear. Then seeing the sheer hopelessness of the situation, he shook his head and walked me to the door of classroom 1C where he called the teacher to have a quiet word in his shell like. I was then ushered into the room and taken to a vacant desk. Naturally, all of the kids followed me with their eyes as I walked through their midst.

'The new boy's name is Peter Roy. You will note that he is wearing his previous school's uniform rather than ours. As he has not had time to source a new uniform as yet he will be wearing this one for the time being.'

Approximately 20 seconds of disruption before the classes' collective eyes turned back to face the front. Level C was only one above level D, which is where they dump the most moronic dullards. As I'd anticipated, 1C was an absolute breeze and a million miles from 1A or even 1B at Haberdashers.

East Ham Boys' Grammar was a down to earth place with none of Haberdashers' pretentions to being a quasi public school. East Ham itself was a solid working class area and the school reflected that in how it operated. There were prefects but their powers were limited, essentially providing assistance to the teachers in keeping order but they had no licence to terrorise kids for their own cruel amusement. There was no tuck shop or any other nonsensical trappings of England's famous fee-paying elite schools.

I started breaking the rules from the outset. First form pupils were not allowed to get to school by bicycle but I cycled in rather walk as it was a long way. A prefect noted my two-wheeled arrival, glanced at my foreign uniform and decided to leave well alone. I liked that.

Within a couple of days, I'd joined a local library but the books weren't in great condition. On my second visit, a librarian called me to the counter.

'We found your library card on the floor an hour ago and you still haven't found a book?' she said, putting my card on the counter in front of me. 'What were you looking for that's so hard to find?'

'A clean one,' I replied and left without taking the card.

The public swimming pool was next to the library and we were taken there to be taught how to swim. There was little if any formal teaching, more a case of learning by doing. Basically the kids were thrown into the water and after that a lot of boisterous behaviour followed. The one thing I did learn was how to avoid getting drowned by a bunch of tykes. The pool boasted a small café where you could buy a lovely slice of buttered toast for one old penny. After swimming that was an absolute necessity to eliminate the taste of chlorine.

It didn't take long before it all fell into a comfortable routine. Once I'd removed the Haberdasher badge from my blazer, the only difference then lay in the colour and the new boy novelty aura soon wore off. They played soccer, cricket and practised athletics that really involved a lot of running and jumping. The latter two were really not of interest, particularly in winter.

Tuition was given at a steady pace and the homework manageable. Bullies existed as they do everywhere but in the main I avoided their attention. At break time a tennis ball usually appeared and led to an impromptu game of soccer. Finally a wild shot hit a teacher on the back of the head and that resulted in a blanket ban on all ball games. For a while, this was circumnavigated by the use of a simulacrum of string and rags but the games degenerated into a hacking contest at close quarters. Slowly the tennis ball reappeared and the ban forgotten in the mists of time.

I never went out of my way to acquire friends as I knew that I wouldn't be around long enough to reap the benefits. However I did get on with a lad called David Knight who was super bright, destined for university and beyond. I always regretted losing touch but am sure that with such great parents supporting him, he would have had a very successful career and life.

The long summer break of 1952 arrived and my prime concern was the pursuit of odd jobs. Fortuitously a couple of house painting jobs came my way and although the pay was scandalous, at least it was money. As usual, needs must. Then it was back to school to form 2C and life continued.

The term kicked off with some good news. A kid named John MacDonald had been treated to a beautiful new pair of soccer boots by his parents and sold me his old ones cheap. Not a big deal maybe but after a year with the old cripplers it was a luxury to have a pair that not only fitted and had been worn in but had no spikes poking through. Notwithstanding my poor eyesight, I enjoyed the game and wasn't too bad at it although too often I was given the goalkeeper's job. I didn't feel that was my best position but at least it meant less running around.

The school year of 1952-53 went by without any significant events. I rode in every day come rain or shine and, unlike Haberdashers, didn't come to the attention of any of the teachers or prefects. I simply performed as well as I could and without any drama. The one thing I could not control was my natural growth and it was a constant struggle to get mother to provide replacement clothes.

One ongoing relief was that learning a foreign language was not on the curriculum that was limited to the basics plus sports. Nor did the school award any time for religious education, which I would have resented even then. I have always considered that one's beliefs are a private matter. Given that Christianity is the official religion of the United Kingdom, upheld by the monarch and his government, I believe that children should not be force-fed religious education.

After a year at East Ham Boys' Grammar School, I think that I was more settled than I'd ever been before. I'd made a few friends and we knocked about together as kids do. On most days I took the collie out for a long walk that was for mutual benefit. As for the weekends, they were filled with cycling, soccer practice, watching the local football team West Ham or going to the cinema.

There were two cinemas on Barking Road, Granada and Odeon, and their programmes were much more extensive than today. In addition to the main feature there would also be a B film that would usually be shorter and often a western. But before the films, there would be a variety show with dancing girls, a magician, singers and a comedian. One of the funniest I saw was a mini-circus that had a solo elephant as one of its stars. As soon as it was brought onto the stage, it decided to take an enormous and very liquid dump in several places; it brought the house down. Following the elephant's increasingly messy footprints was small man carrying a small shovel and a very small bucket. Running on and off stage, over and over again, it was a valiant effort to clear the mess that continued to be trampled by elephant and trainer. It was a hilarious spectacle, worth double the admission fee on its own.

It was probably in the early part of my second year when I managed to break my nose for the first time. Whether it was an accident or I had some help in the matter, I have no idea. My attempt to get over the vaulting horse in the gym went badly wrong when I hit the deck on the other side. The PE teacher was not amused by the amount of blood spreading across his floor.

'Get yourself out of the gym and go home. Get your mother to sort it out.'

Was I offered first aid or ambulance? Was a health and safety report mentioned? No, bugger all. Knowing how my dear mother would react, I rode to the local hospital where they stemmed the bleeding and patched me up as best they could. Mother's eventual wrath could not be avoided but at least it was delayed.

My parents suddenly decided that we should emigrate to Australia for a better life, spurred on by letters and parcels sent by Anita. Although it was a pleasant surprise to open a box of tinned goods or various gifts, I resented the fact that we were so poor that my sister had to buy things and post them to us to bring a little cheer. It just didn't seem right. In any event we put ourselves forward for assisted passage, going over to Australia House in Aldwych for interviews and medical examinations. My parents never told me the outcome. Had we been rejected? Or had we been accepted but they changed their minds and chose not to go?

Shortly afterwards we were on the move when father lost his job. But this time it was only to the next borough to the west, Plaistow. At school I gave my form teacher a note with my change of address that he shoved into a pocket without a glance. For the next few days I expected to be called to see the headmaster to be told to find another school but nothing happened. It occurred to me that maybe, just maybe I could ride this out; I'd done my bit but maybe the teacher hadn't done his. Why not just continue to turn up for school? The ride would only be a couple of miles longer, so I decided to give it a go and it worked.

Every day I rode in as though nothing had changed, making sure that I was always on time and never on the missing list, careful not to draw unwanted attention. It was necessary to be circumspect in matters of house and home, and avoid visiting other pupils' homes in case they expected a reciprocal invitation.

A strange incident took place in Woolworths one day on the High Street. Drawn in by the book sale sign in the window, my friend and I walked in towards the counter, quickly taking in the heap of paperbacks on display. Before we could look at any of them, a store security officer placed his hands firmly on our shoulders, marching us out of the store and into the street. As soon as he walked back inside, I turned and flew in past him to grab a couple of books from the heap while holding my money in the air. I saw him heading towards me at a fast trot but held my ground, guessing that he couldn't throw me out while the sales assistant was taking my money and wrapping the books. Having called the man's bluff, I gleefully left clutching my purchases and once on the street, had the chance to see what I had bought: unreadable rubbish!

There were some after school activities on offer, so I joined the chess club and the stamp collecting club but dropped them after a couple of visits. As we approached the annual prize-giving day, our form was chosen to sing a song for the occasion. Since I couldn't sing for nuts and very little time had been allocated for practice, I decided to keep a very, very low profile. In the evening I made sure that my form teacher knew I was present and correct by greeting him with a bold handshake. The class trooped onto the stage with me bringing up the rear, only to divert into the toilets. I waited until the singing finished and heard the sounds of my classmates walking by outside. At which point I slipped out of the loo and caught up with the merry band of singers. And the teacher was waiting.

'I didn't see you on stage Roy.'

'I was there Sir. I mean, I'm here with the others.'

'Clearly you're with them now. But I didn't see you with them on the stage.'

'You must remember, I spoke to you before we went on stage and here I am coming off.'

'If I find you playing tricks, there'll be trouble.'

'Not me Sir. No tricks Sir.'

He'd forgotten about my change of address, so maybe he wasn't the sharpest knife in the drawer. With a bit of luck he'd forget about the invisible singer as well.

In the summer holidays of 1953, I took my first long distance railway journey on my own. I went to stay with my mother's sister Anne and her husband Sam for a week in Sheffield. I'm not sure what they were meant to do with me but I remember Sam taking me to Sheffield United's opening match of the season and taking me fishing a couple of times. Then aged thirteen, it seemed to be quite the adventure but nothing compared with kids travelling today who get handed over to airlines and flown half way round the world. I was lucky to get some casual work during the other weeks that brought in enough money to buy a second-hand Claud Butler to replace the Raleigh I was outgrowing. Then back to school, form 3C and school life continued. It was not to last.

In early October all boys were instructed to complete a card with their personal details as the school's administration department was upgrading its filing system. How to dodge the bullet? Giving my old address might buy some time but if, or more likely when, I was caught out in a lie, the repercussions could be severe. I could have been sent to a comprehensive school to finish my education. Accordingly I filled in my card truthfully.

Nothing happened for two weeks until eight names were read out during morning assembly. The named boys were required to attend the headmasters' office and my name was on the list. As we filed in and stood like ducks in row, we all knew what was coming. So many, I thought and it transpired that a couple of boys were even further out than me.

'I think you all know why you are here. You have concealed, wittingly or unwittingly, that you no longer live in this borough and therefore you are not entitled to attend East Ham Boys' Grammar School. This is your last day here; you have already cost East Ham's ratepayers quite enough already. You will clear your desks immediately, go home and find a school to which you have the right to attend. Dismissed.'

In my father's opinion (who normally didn't get involved), it was a pack of lies and that in reality I'd been expelled. That really helped the situation! In mother's opinion, everything I did was to spite her and bring her misery. She lit a cigarette to calm her nerves. Naturally no one was interested in my opinion. It was a shame that you couldn't choose your parents when you were born.

The nearest suitable school was Stratford Grammar. With mother in tow as usual I was interviewed by the headmaster Mr Simms and accepted, joining form 4BU (equivalent to previous 3C).

East Ham Boys' Grammar became Langdon Comprehensive and in 1971 merged with two other schools on the same site, forming today's Langdon School with some 1750 pupils.

By the time I switched schools, we had already been living at 65 Stratford Road in Plaistow for several months. The premises were pretty much standard, flanked on one side by a newsagent's and a ladies fashion outlet on the other with a run of the mill pub on the next corner. What did surprise me was the number of remaining bombsites and the general neglected, run-down feel to the place; it was definitely a step down from East Ham.

The newsagent's was run by a chap called Mr Probert who seemed to be a decent bloke. (At some point he gave me a fishing rod that I assumed meant it was mine, until he asked for it back at a later date.) Sadly his son had recently been killed while delivering newspapers to street sellers. They were supplied by van that had a team of two, a driver and a cannonball. The latter's job was to leap from the van with a bundle of newspapers and throw it across the pavement to the vendor. For some bizarre reason, cannonballs tackled the job as if they were life-or-death deliveries. And sometimes it was. Probert's lad had jumped out of the van with a bundle of papers only to smack into a piece of hard street furniture and goodnight Vienna. Was it worth it? Of course not! Losing your life delivering papers is just dumb.

*****

In November 1953, I started school at Stratford Grammar dressed in the wrong blazer of course. French, crafts and divinity were all new subjects to me and naturally I floundered. I could barely hide my resentment at the time given to religious education. The lessons basically consisted of readings from the bible and I was forced to take my turn. Initially I said I was Jewish because Jews were excused but that didn't work. Nor did my subsequent claim that I was an agnostic.

The good news was that Stratford Grammar was co-educational that made it far better than all-boys establishments in my opinion. It was the first time in my educational history that I'd ever met a West

Indian girl or indeed, anyone from the West Indies. Certainly the place had a much better atmosphere than I'd encountered elsewhere.

Although the average age in my class was 14, a couple of the lads were close to six feet tall. Classical stereotyping would automatically mark them as bullying material. In actuality, Dave Mason and Ted Rouse were both really straightforward blokes and we quickly made friends. The bullies of our year were a couple of very bright lads in 3A and to be avoided at all costs.

It was here that I encountered my second truly certifiable teacher, Mr St John who was head of science. A science laboratory is a potentially dangerous environment full of acids, alkalis, self-combusting materials, Bunsen burners and lots more. The addition of a bunch of pupils endeavouring to blow things up, stink the place out or burn it down made the lab pure hell. While many of the kids tried to wind him up to the point of madness, the majority just sat it out, especially the girls to avoid being burned by acid or flame, hit by shards of exploding glass or gassed by toxic fumes. Over and above that, avoiding the long black cane that St John thrashed about.

It was a short first term and for what it was worth, I finished fifth in the class. Shortly before we broke up for the year-end holidays, our form teacher Mr Roberts asked the boys to stay behind and we were joined by Mr Evans, another teacher.

'Now you are all over 14 I would like you to consider joining the school's Air Training Corps as you are now eligible. The ATC meets after school every Friday for about two hours when you would be given the basic training that could lead to a career in the Royal Air Force.

'You will be provided with a uniform and have the opportunity to attend an air force camp once a year. When your time comes to do National Service, your can choose the RAF over the army or navy.'

Initially it didn't obviously appeal but I hung back while a lad that I rode home with signed up. During the course of the ensuing conversation between my mate and Mr Evans, I heard that the kit included a greatcoat. That was a game changer. I was about as likely to get a greatcoat as much as a one-legged man had in winning an arse-kicking contest and I was in like a flash. No only did I envision the extra warmth while out and about but an additional bed cover for the hard winter months.

It turned out to be a good choice as it was interesting and informative. I did feel a bit of a twerp wearing the itchy serge uniform at school on Fridays but I wasn't alone and nobody else gave a damn.

My first term of 1954 was disastrous: in a class of 29 I came 24th and in geography I was fourth from last. Mr Roberts told me it was 'shocking' and Mr Simms expressed the opinion that I was 'weak'. I have no idea what happened. Maybe the trauma of my confusing past was creeping up on me or maybe I spent too much time looking at the girls.

The summer of 1954 brought two adventures but the remainder of the time I spent chasing down paying jobs.

I decided to cycle up to Sheffield on my own, to visit my aunt and uncle. Having joined the Youth Hostel Association, I was able to plan a route each day that would end with a hot meal and a bed at very cheap prices. Fortunately the weather was fine all the time and I saw some wonderful countryside.

The week-long ATC camp was just outside Aberdeen in Scotland and since everything was paid for, all I needed was pocket money. We caught the 10pm sleeper out of King's Cross but travelled sitting down in 3rd class, arriving at Waverley Station in Edinburgh early the following morning. From there, we took another train to Aberdeen where we found several RAF transports waiting to take us on to Dyce RAF base (now Aberdeen Airport).

With a dozen or so other cadet squadrons also gathered there, we were allocated our barracks for living and sleeping. They all looked derelict and I guessed that they'd last been used for the previous year's intake. In true military fashion, we were instructed to render them spotless but given no materials to do so. A few other lads and I went scavenging, returning with a large can of white paint and brushes as well as cleaning materials. The four officers (our trainers) turned a blind eye to our initiative. After a massive effort sprucing up the barracks, we were given bedding and taken to the canteen for a meal that seemed to consist primarily of powdered egg. How our fighting forces were expected to live on rations like that was beyond me. Morning started with uproar when our NCOs – who had a separate room at one end of the hut – discovered they'd been robbed overnight. No cadets were to have breakfast until the thief, or thieves, had been found. Logically the cadets of our squadron 962 were prime suspects but despite a thorough search, no cash or watches were discovered. Suspicion then fell on all the other cadets. When I had the temerity to ask our officer why serving RAF personnel weren't included in the dragnet, I was told in no uncertain terms that airmen don't steal. The phrase, looking through rose tinted spectacles comes to mind. Personnel working and/or living on the base would know the lie of the land so how could they be exempt? But they were.

We were marched to the parade ground, lined up, stood to attention and told we would remain there until the culprit stepped forward. When we boarded the train at King's Cross, I'd noticed a lad from another London squadron and was surprised he'd been allowed to take part. His uniform was so filthy that it looked as though he'd slept in the gutter and he just looked dodgy. That was borne out later post rifle shooting when he displayed a small heap of live rounds that he'd nicked.

We'd been standing on the parade ground for over two hours when Mr Evans approached.

'Are you all right Roy?'

'Yes Sir but hungry.'

I was determined I would stick it out to the bitter end. Then one boy fainted, then another and another. After a quick confab among the officers, the cadets were stood down and the parade ground emptied without getting the desired result. We were allowed to have lunch and the canteen served up a mountain of powdered egg polluted by mystery ingredients.

One of the strangest things on the base was that the water flowing from the taps was dark red. At first I thought it was rust contamination due to a lack of use over a long period. But it persisted and we came to the conclusion that the water was coloured by iron and it wasn't doing any harm when we used it for washing.

The highpoint of the busy week was actually flying. There were two 15-minute flights in a Chipmunk and then a half hour flight in an Avro Anson. I was the last to board and since the only seat left was the co-pilot's, on this occasion it was mine.

Rifle shooting was a trial for me and not a simple task. The weapons used were standard issue Enfield 303 bolt-action rifles that were designed for right-handed marksmen. Thanks to my useless right eye, I was forced to shoot left-handed which proved to be almost impossible. Needless to say, I did not achieve a marksman's badge.

Regular RAF officers carried out daily barrack inspection that primarily involved a great deal of bawling and screaming. This was generally directed at the cadets' inability to fold their bedding or lay out kit to the officers' liking. The room did have a stove but we couldn't use it because it would have made a mess, although we did have a supply of coal. Since we couldn't use that either, we painted it white.

One morning, we boarded covered trucks and were driven into the countryside. When we finally stopped, our squadron was ordered out, issued an Ordnance Survey map, a compass and a reference point. And told to get there, just before they drove off. A lesson in early orienteering?

'What I think we should do is find the rendezvous location on the map and then look at a rough five mile circle around it,' I suggested.

And was promptly and universally voted to be 'in charge'. From experience gained with cycling, it didn't take too long to ascertain where we'd been dropped and work out a route. We set off at a trot, confirming our position as we went and were the first to arrive, much to our officers' pride. A couple of squadrons weren't so fortunate, were declared missing after a few hours and had to be recovered.

In between the activities noted there was an awful lot of marching and drilling on the parade ground. On Sunday morning we marched to church following a piper playing his bagpipes on the way. We were entitled to use the NAAFI but the RAF guys made it very clear that we wouldn't be welcome, so it wasn't worth bothering. All in all, joining the ATC had been a good idea despite my earlier doubts.

Returning to school for the start of the autumn term 1954, the form voted in a new form captain and to my utter amazement, I was elected. I could only think of one explanation: that I had no fear in speaking up for what I believed was right, not only for me but also on behalf of other pupils. It was not an honour that I'd sought or even wanted.

A pattern settled in as it always does. That term we were blessed with an exceptional history teacher but it's embarrassing to have to admit that I can't remember his name. I still struggled with the subjects to which I'd arrived late but generally survived without too much drama. One lad lost the top of his finger in woodwork which dulled any enthusiasm I might have had for the subject. My protests against divinity lessons continued and occasionally I joined the two Jewish boys in the library. If my absence was noted it would be reported to the Deputy Head and I would receive two strokes of the cane across my hand. It was a small price to pay for evading the tedious bible readings. Music lessons were introduced but discontinued without fanfare.

By 1955 my father was still holding onto his job and I could see that I might possibly see out the rest of my education at Stratford Grammar School. Twenty per cent of the class didn't return in the new year as most would shortly be 15, if they weren't already and many saw no point in furthering their education. They were committed to working with their families in small businesses, on market stalls or down in the docks. By the end of the term another ten per cent had disappeared. When the 1954/55 academic year came to an end, I was top of the class but I was in 4C and there were some 60 kids in 4A and 4B above us.

The onset of the summer holidays saw me cycling in Wales and staying in youth hostels with my best pal John Ringshaw and his friend Michael Travis. Along the road we met Colin Woodward and David Stubbs. We rode back to London in their company and they stayed good friends for many years.

The ATC took us to Wales as well, to Hawarden RAF base which was just over the border from Chester in England. We were put on a train to Liverpool, met by RAF transports and driven through some desperate parts of the city on our way to the camp. I thought the East End of London was impoverished but this was much worse.

In the days of the Battle of Britain, Hawarden had been an important airfield but later became a scrapyard of planes. In early 1959 it was demilitarised and became simply Hawarden Airport. Our barracks were in good shape, only needing a quick tidy up. Sadly no flights were on offer but otherwise the activities were much the same as they had been at Dyce. Marching, parade drills, class lessons, orienteering and shooting both .22 and .303 rifles were all aspects of the week. Not forgetting the correct presentation of kit at all times.

Returning to school, now in form U5M (5C) for what was to be my final year, I knew that it was vital that I did well. The standard requirement necessary to get a decent job was to achieve five General Certificate of Education passes including maths and English; it was time to knuckle down. The maths teacher told me that I would be taking lessons with the top form as maths was my best subject. I was not well received by the elite of 5A but I had acquired a reputation of being a rough boy by this time and they left me alone.

Pupil attrition continued. Two big lads decided that it was better to shelter in the art room from the heavy downpour rather than get wet on the edges of the playground. When two prefects took issue with them, the pair demolished them and had to leave school. Two girls who misbehaved during a history lesson were sent to see the head and never returned and form D simply disappeared.

The annual compulsory visit to the school dentist identified the need for extractions. I was required to come with a parent who could escort me home after the blast of gas. My mother took the opportunity of the captive audience, the receptionist, to bang on about the hard life she'd suffered. Since the waiting room was packed with other kids from school, including many from my class, I tried to stop her moaning but to no avail. I have no doubt that the butchers employed there ruined my teeth. It took many years and a lot of money to repair the damage inflicted.

To my great relief, my father didn't lose his job and my ragged-arsed education duly finished in June 1956.

The summer of that year was to be the last long break before joining the rat race. John, Michael and I took our bikes down to Devon and Cornwall but it was difficult finding YHA accommodation. After spending a couple of nights in barns, we cut the trip short and headed home early.

Although I could have stayed on with the ATC, I knew fitting it in every Friday night would be difficult once I'd started work. However I did take up the offer of a third and final stay at an RAF base, this time at Watton in Norfolk. Bombers were based there during World War II but now part of it is a housing estate. The week took the same general pattern of the previous two but did have flying highlights. This time we had two long flights in a Dakota to South West England. At the end I promised to return my uniform and my beloved greatcoat, as soon as it was convenient.

We had a lovely tabby cat that I regarded as mine, although nobody can really own a cat. Although she was great mouser, she was fed on scraps from the fish shop and didn't have a bad life. Fortunately she was never ill because there was no chance of my parents paying vet's bills. From time to time she would produce a litter of kittens but finding homes for them was never a problem.

When I got back from RAF Watton on 4 August, she was nowhere to be seen. When I asked my mother where the cat was, I received an immediate and very nasty answer.

'I drowned the filthy animal in that while you were away' she said viciously, pointing her finger at a galvanised bucket.'

No question about it, my mother was a real stinker. One week later, my school days were a thing of the past and what a torrid, chaotic and bloody hard 12 years they had been. The worst part for me was never knowing what was happening or why. I could deal with not being interested in what you were learning or how you were coping because that seemed normal.

Being uprooted over and over again, without a clue as to why it was happening was hard. It made me feel as though I was inconsequential and therefore, lacking in worth. I did realise that 99% of kids in the world were probably worse off than me, especially given the vast numbers of civilian losses during the war. But that was no help or comfort.

What mattered to me were the kids with whom I interacted on a daily basis. They weren't moving from place to place every few months, constantly being the new boy. The odd boy who has to establish himself, time and time again, in an echo of Lord of the Flies. That is the kid's everyday existence. I think it was Charles Dickens who apparently said that his childhood years were the best time of his life. Lucky Charlie. Mine were not, simple as that. My last connection with Stratford Grammar was to attend the Speech Day on 25 October 1956 at which I was awarded a minor prize.

*****

When we had returned to London from Yorkshire we found that my sister Freda had secured a job with a shipping agent based in Leadenhall Street in the City. No doubt she had hoped for Mr Right to arrive and take her away from it all but no suitor ever stepped up to the mark. Maybe she settled for Mr Wrong in an attempt to distance herself from our disparate version of family life.

Sister Anita was now firmly established on the Mornington Peninsula in Victoria. The garage was providing a decent living and she'd had a son who they named Roy Armstrong. Apparently she went to church every day, perhaps to pray for us all.

Brother Jeffery had returned from Burma in 1946 and like many others who fought in that campaign, he suffered with recurring bouts of malaria. He found work with a massive jeweller and pawnbroker called Robertson's on Edgware Road in London and lodged close to the shop.

In 1950 he began to run the Ted Heath Fan Club in Denmark Street. Ted Heath was the bandleader of what has been described as the 'best ever British swing band' and the fan club was a serious support base. At the risk of upsetting the band's many fans, I have to disclose that all of the autographed photographs sent out to adoring fans were actually signed by Jeffery. The facsimiles were authentic enough to fool even the experts. At the end of the year, he married a singer, Eve Catt and set up home with her mother in Streatham. At some point in the 50s he was employed by Dun and Bradstreet and stayed there until retirement. They had one daughter, Karen.

With hindsight, I regarded myself as an autodidact with my learning frequently interrupted by having to attend yet another school. I simply loved to read, devouring every book that came my way, even a census report in Yorkshire! Schools were jungles in which I learned real life survival skills. Very few teachers had the ability and imagination to bring their subjects to life and hold their students' attention for long. I pitied those disadvantaged kids who were unable to stand up for themselves since they were never given an iota of support. And I suspect that little has changed.

5 Wilson Wright & Co

'When you side with a man, you stay with him. And if you can't do that you're like some animal, you're finished.'

Pike Bishop played by William Holden in The Wild Bunch (1969)

On Monday 29 February 1960, I travelled by tube to Chancery Lane, walked a block to Hatton Garden passing the Gamages Department store (1878-1972) and headed into the door at the side of the National Provincial Bank on the corner.

My new employer's main suite of rooms was on the second floor, comprising the Principal's office, another for the managers, a reception and secretarial room plus an area for the juniors. Further rooms for the partners and managers were dotted along the corridor intermingled with small businesses. The men's toilets were on the top floor: one for senior staff that boasted soft loo paper and soap; the second toilets were designated for all other ranks, therefore having bleeding hard paper but no soap. Beyond those lay the janitor's apartment.

Bill Smith and Michael Berger were waiting for me and I was immediately thrown in at the deep end. I was told that I was going out with Michael and two very young boys on audit. I was amazed as I was pretty much an unknown quantity.

The client was Michael Dunne a leading professional photographer whose studio was on Kensington High Street. Having introduced ourselves, we were squeezed into a small mezzanine area with two accounts staff; Mary was in her 30s but Arlene was still in her teens. Michael stayed for half an hour to make sure that we had everything we needed and then returned to the office. Although the books were written up, nothing was cast or balanced – the bane of an accountant's life. So the first three days were a real slog and it wasn't until Thursday that the accounts started to come together. At least we had something to show Michael when he dropped in that day although I was not sure whether he was pleased or simply relieved. The studio was a distraction but it was a nice place to work and the journey was no big deal.

By Friday we were on the home straight. I told the younger of my two assistants to report to the office on Monday, knowing I would get the job completed by the Wednesday with the help of the other assistant: John was a Belfast lad and a pleasure to work with. But on Tuesday we hit a snag, one which I hadn't encountered before and haven't since. The system used for preparing wages in Britain was common to all companies and businesses. Using tables supplied by the Inland Revenue, income tax and national insurance contributions were deducted from each employee's gross pay. At the end of the month, the total of all the money deducted over that period would be sent to the Tax Office. Admittedly I only had a couple of years' experience and those as a junior, but as far as I knew there was no other way. At Michael Dunne's the payroll was withdrawn gross from the bank in cash and the net pay given to the employees. The deductions had been calculated but where was the government's cut? I asked Mary and she replied immediately.

'The tax and national insurance cash is put into the safe and physically taken to the collector once a month. That ensures that we're always able to pay on time.'

At first it seemed to make sense and I admired her foresight in taking steps to protect the studio from falling behind with its payments. However I quickly established that the company was six months in arrears.

'Mary, it looks as though you haven't paid the Man for some time. Can you show me the money.'

She opened the safe but apart from the petty cash that we'd already dealt with, the cupboard was bare.

'Mary, there's nothing there.'

'Someone must have taken it, we're not here every minute that the studio is open.'

On my first job for Wilson Wright, not only was there money missing but the bailiffs could come through the doors at any moment. I also knew that Michael's confidence in me might be dented when I related the story. John and I went to his office the next day and laid out our stall. His reaction was just as I had expected.

'I can't believe it, that's insane. I have never heard of anyone withdrawing the gross payroll in cash. Are you both absolutely sure about this?'

'Michael, I'm very much aware that this is my first job for you and I didn't want it to be true. At first I didn't really believe it myself but John and I have checked this several times. There's no record of payments made and the cash that should be in the safe just isn't there. I haven't checked with the tax office because I knew that would raise a big red flag. But there is a real danger of debt collectors calling.'

'I'm going to have to check this out for myself before I speak to Michael Dunne. But if you're wrong Peter,' he said, looking rather stern, 'I think your stay here will be a very short one. You have in effect accused Mary of embezzlement and if you've made a mistake, it would be very serious for this firm and for you. And don't forget that I recommended you and therefore it would reflect on my judgement. Since you were the junior on the job John, if this is a mistake it will not affect your position.'

Suddenly I was having real doubts and knew that if I was wrong, I'd be back on the streets in a flash. John and I sat in the general office while Michael took the papers down to Bill's office. We were finally called down to his office to find the two men sitting grim faced.

'I've been through this carefully with Michael and we agree, the arithmetic is as you say. I too have never come across any company that draws gross wages from the bank and pays the taxes in cash. Apart from anything else, there's a massive security issue. Michael has talked to the Revenue in confidence and payment is indeed six months in arrears. So it all depends on what's in the safe.'

'There's nothing in the safe apart from some petty cash. John's my witness.'

'He's right Mr Smith, there was no pile of cash in there, just air,' he said, backing me up.

Solid lad, willing to put his neck on the block as well.

Bill phoned Michael Dunne and arranged a meeting for Michael Berger and I at the studio at 8am on Friday. The job itself had finished so there was no necessity for John to be there as well. Although he had been there when the safe was opened, there was nothing new or different that he could contribute.

Michael and I arrived at the stroke of eight, Michael Dunne some ten minutes later. He didn't look cheerful as when a non-creative calls for a meeting with a creative, the latter automatically expects bad news. And it had arrived as well. He took us up to the office.

'I obviously have no idea what this is about but I can see from your faces that it's not good news. Spit it out and let's deal with it.'

I'd already decided to only speak if asked to do so, which might not be easy. I was on very thin ice with both Michael Berger and the firm so I'd keep it buttoned and answer any questions with short, clear untechnical answers and pray that I hadn't made a monumental cock-up. It was possible for Mary to have replaced the cash if she had the wit and wherewithal. But that seemed highly unlikely.

Michael Berger explained the situation in respect of the outstanding debt to the tax office and that it appeared that the money was missing. He added that I had asked Mary to explain but that her only response was to suggest that an outside party had stolen the money. We opened the safe. It was empty apart from the small amount of petty cash.

When Mary arrived at 9.30am Michael Dunne saw her alone. Naturally he was devastated by the breach of trust and there was not to be a second chance. She was gone and very lucky that Mr Dunne did not intend on taking the matter to court. Obviously he would have to look for a new bookkeeper but he was in the middle of a big campaign that would take him out of the country for at least two weeks. He dreaded the idea. There was no way he could find someone immediately. Or could he? And he looked across at me.

'Peter you've been an absolute star here. Could you possibly hold the fort for a month or so until I have the time to sort things out? Maybe come in a couple of evenings a week to keep on top of things. Could Arlene manage the day to day stuff?'

'Definitely. Arlene's very capable and yes, I could come in on Tuesday and Thursday evenings if it's OK with Mr Berger, of course.'

He agreed and I was over the moon. A new job plus a second job all secured in such a short time was nothing short of magic. I had just had my twentieth birthday and my luck had changed. Ironically my arrangement with the studio was to last longer than my employment with Wilson Wright.

When I reported in on 14 March, I had already been in the job for two weeks but it felt like my first day. The previous two weeks had been almost surreal.

A formidable woman called Mrs Trew managed the front office with four secretaries in her charge. Beryl who was one of the girls was a stunning redhead who put the others in the shade. They certainly earned their keep using massive manual typewriters to type up the accounts in multiple formats. Woe betide anyone who produced drafts with errors that would trigger a total retype. Without Tippex or photocopiers it was all old style and just one step up from hand written presentation.

It was clear from the outset that the firm was very cosmopolitan. As previously mentioned, Bill Smith was Anglo-Indian and there were guys from India, Sri Lanka, Turkey, Greece, Cyprus, Nigeria and Ireland. But seven or eight Londoners formed the core. At any one time half or more were out on audit so I introduced myself around as the occasions arose.

I found a spot in the junior's office and a tall guy in his twenties approached. Introducing himself one of the managers, Brian handed me an old favourite, the paper bag job. So called as it always indicated the client was a small trader who kept his own records, compact enough that they could be delivered in a carrier bag. This was the test I was expecting. There was no way of knowing that the man would prove to be my future nemesis.

I'd cut my teeth on one man band operations, got stuck in and in between meeting some new faces, finished it off before lunch. I took the result in to Brian who was based in an office between reception and Mr Gould's corner suite. Whilst waiting for my test result, I chatted with Eital from Sri Lanka.

'Have you met Mr Gould yet?' he asked.

'No, not yet.'

'Oh, he's a lovely man and always has time for the staff, although he leaves much of the day to day stuff to Mr Smith and Mr Temple.'

'I haven't met Mr Temple either.'

'You will. He's very clever.'

Our conversation was interrupted by Brian's return. He told me that he'd been impressed with the work and that I could be reclassified from Junior to Semi-Senior. Sorry to say, there was no mention of additional money but I thought it wise to wait until my feet were firmly under the table. He handed me a similar job to the first and that formed the pattern for the next few weeks.

I met Mr Gould the next morning and he was, as Eilat advertised, quite charming. For a few minutes we chatted about my past experiences and touched on my baptism of fire at Michael Dunne's studio. I thanked him for the opportunity of a new start.

Towards the end of the week, I was summoned into Mr Temple's room opposite reception, and he was brusque to say the least. Tall, imposing and definitely a no nonsense type, chit-chat was certainly not on the agenda. I was to head out to help with client audit for a day or two. The staff had got bogged down with reconciling the bank and fallen behind schedule. A fresh pair of hands was needed and I'd been volunteered. After that I was to take myself over to Market Activation in Dover Street. I was heading into a manic period.

My work at the Michael Dunne Studio had as I'd suspected, fallen into a routine. On Tuesdays and Thursdays I'd arrive at around 5.30pm and spend some time with Arlene to catch up with any news. Then I'd work until around 8.30pm getting everything up to date and processing the payroll so that Arlene could pay the wages out on Friday. If Michael was working late in the studio, more often than not we'd be treated to a Wimpy cheeseburger.

Wednesday evening was for soccer practice and Friday, weight training at the home of a friend of John Ringshaw, Phil the Barber. So cinema night was usually spent at The State in Leytonstone on Monday or Sunday that left Saturday for a visit to the pub after either playing or watching soccer. I still had the Falcon motorcycle but as the money situation was easier, I travelled around town on the tube, avoiding the unpleasantness of arriving on site like a drowned rat. The curveball arrived just when everything had settled into a solid routine.

I was sent down to Fleet Street with Eital and John to help with a 'pure audit', where everything was totalled and balanced. So it was up to us to check the systems, summarize everything and keep an eye out for any dark dirty deeds like false invoicing or dead men on the payroll. The bookkeeper and her assistants were all very nice, we had the boardroom to work in with tea and coffee to hand. So what could go wrong?

We arrived at 9.30 and set up shop, each of us taking a section of the work. At 10am a raw recruit on his first day joined us. His name is lost in the mists of time but I remember he came from Pakistan. Welcoming him on board, we explained that as everything was reconciled we only needed to carry out routine checking, and gave him a daybook to verify the additions.

We burrowed into our tasks until around 11.30 when the new man announced that the first page did not agree and produced a mass of working papers to back up his words. It took me a few minutes to work out what he had done. I kid you not, he had converted each line of currency into rupees, added these up and reconverted the total back to pounds, shillings and pence. I had a sick feeling that this wasn't going to work out and took the team back to base. I told Mr Temple what had occurred; he was incredulous but the other guys confirmed the tale.

'With respect Mr Temple, I do think whoever interviewed the guy should have checked a little more carefully. It really is disruptive to waste time on having to deal with totally unqualified people.'

'Your opinion has not been asked for and that's the end of it.'

The Pakistani was not seen again. So it was back to Fleet Street where worse was to follow. We made terrific progress until the Friday when Eital went into the accounts office and asked for the petty cash records. He returned looking very distressed.

'What's wrong Eital? You look shocked.'

'They tell me I can't have the petty cash records and that only Mr Gould is allowed to see them.'

'That's crazy. Why would the senior partner deal with petty cash?'

I went to see the bookkeeper to ensure that Eital had not misunderstood but no he had not. Mr Gould would apparently audit the petty cash.

I was furious. With that final piece of the jigsaw, we could have finished everything in the week and a set of figures could have been on Mr Temple's desk that afternoon. There was nothing more to be done so we thanked the staff and headed out. When we entered the lift, we were joined by the Managing Director, Mr Joplin, who was also the Chairman's son. And he asked how we were.

'Well, we have finished the audit apart from the petty cash. For some reason we're not allowed to see the records, which frankly I find unacceptable. Apparently only Mr Gould is allowed to deal with it.'

He scowled and pushed past us out onto the street. Mr Temple was waiting our return, clearly in a foul mood.

'What the hell did you say to Mr Joplin?'

I repeated verbatim and added that the whole job would be finished if not for this petty cash nonsense.

'Mr Joplin is very angry and so am I.'

'Did you know about this special arrangement Mr Temple?'

'Yes, of course I did, we all know.'

'We are new boys and we didn't know. Was it beyond the wit of someone to inform us, to warn us before we were sent down there and save all this embarrassment? We are just foot soldiers and you sent us into a minefield.'

I knew I was risking the chop but in all fairness I knew I was right, and I think he knew it too. For us the matter ended there. Temple apologised to both Joplin, father and son, and no doubt placed me at the top of his shit list. One day in the next week, I took some papers into Mr Gould's office in his absence. There on his desk was the infamous petty cash book and I couldn't resist a peek. It was little more than a cursory glance but, given the nature of the business, the claims looked pretty unreal. The staff must have realised that it is rare for a Chairman of a company to take on a minor accounting task and a disgruntled employee could have whipped up a storm if they had a mind to

In confidence I only told the two boys, no one else. They deserved to know the truth, I owed them that much. I realised that I needed to lower my profile and settle down to producing great finished products. Simple as that. If a problem arose just pass it up the line to a higher pay grade to sort out.

In May, I was sent over to M T Birkin at 7 Stephen Buildings, Gresse Street, Tottenham Court Road. The business was in the rag trade and if you were unkind, you could describe it as a sweatshop. Mr Birkin was a survivor of the concentration camps and had the tattooed number on his arm to prove it. He was a truly decent man and employed many who would be otherwise unemployable, making ladies coats for the lower end of the market.

I realised that there was not going to be a big audit fee and a realistic approach to the job was essential. Speed was of the essence. That's not to say that I skimped on the customary checks. The sad fact of the matter was that even if someone had a mind to nick some money, there was none to be had.

The bookkeeper was a girl about my age and we hit it off, which helped. The guy who was employed as a general factotum had a terrible case of the shakes and the tea arrived half in the cup and half in the saucer. Polishing it off in four days, I handed it in keeping my time record to the minimum.

Only a month later Mr Gould summoned me to his office. Agitated by the low wages, the garment union had got tough on M T Birkin. Activists waving banners that said 'Birkin is Black' were picketing the building. Mr Birkin was so upset that he had decided to close up and I was needed to work out the final pay for the staff.

It was a sad business. I pushed my way through the throng and met with Mr Birkin. Having completed the calculations and with the books under my arm I left to the noise of booing and abuse. Mr Birkin asked for a moment's quiet and faced the union's representative.

'You can all go home now, the business is shut for good.'

'You can't do that!' said the union guy. 'What about the workers?'

'I can and I have. And the workers aren't workers any more.'

He was crying and given his background, the world must have seemed an unrelentingly horrible place. I asked him if he'd like a drink but he said no; we shook hands and parted ways. Walking away, I looked back at the mob still hanging around the doorway and I could make out the shaker; where was he going to find another job, I asked myself. I could have understood if the boss had been making a fortune off the toil of his workers, but he wasn't. He took the lowest wage in the company and some weeks if times were really tough, he took nothing.

A major change took place in June 1960. Mother was too old and tired to continue helping out at the shop and we moved to 55 Eastern Road, only a couple of streets away. Father stayed on to manage the shop while another family moved into the living quarters to help him run the place.

Our new home was a corner house and a barber occupied what would have been the front room. That meant that the downstairs rear provided our daily living quarters with bedrooms on the first floor. The toilet was out at the back as usual in a large yard that substituted for a garden. And since we had no bathroom the tin bath continued its lifetime of service. The walk to Plaistow Station was similar so the move had little effect.

With a decent living wage coming in, I bought a 1949 MG TC, a rakish two-seater sports car for £100. My friend Colin Woodward owned a MG TD and now the soccer season was over we spent time together over weekends. I quickly realized that my pride and joy was a bit rough around the edges, so I embarked on a rebuild working Saturdays and Sundays until the end of summer, then just Sundays. The taking apart was the easy bit but acquiring new parts burned up all available funds. Colin was a real star, putting in a mass of time; also Bob Montgomery and a couple of other lads.

We had barely started when a bloke stopped by and told us that he had an old MG in his garden.

'If you can pull it out, you can have it for free, it's been there for years.'

We walked round to his place and there was a MG M type 1929 complete with a small tree growing through it. Still a gift horse and all that, it must be worth something if only for parts.

Frank brought round a Ford Pilot and some chains. We chopped the tree down and with no small effort, pulled the thing out onto the road. Then towed it to the yard where my TC was in a thousand pieces and parked it on the street. The Old Bill came knocking in less than twenty minutes and pumped with aggression, demanded that I got my new motor off the public highway or else.

As the yard was full, we had no other choice than to dismantle the thing and carry the parts into the rear. I'd have preferred to have got it running and sold as was but it was not to be. Advertising the bits and pieces in Exchange and Mart, I shifted everything apart from the chassis and got over £100 which was a huge help on the TC project.

The studio gig was not only a nice little earner but also a real pleasure. When I arrived, usually around 5.30pm, there was always someone there, either working late taking photographs, Jim the Print beavering away in his lab or people just chewing the fat. Arlene had taken on a young assistant and as I'd suspected, I was in for the long haul.

Michael was a lovely man to work for but being a creative guy he could be short with people who weren't performing up to scratch. In the main if you did what you were asked all was very well. He had several photographers there learning the craft and I remember Des Waring, Paul Orssich and Jamie Granger (son of Stewart).

He was married to Lord Rennell's daughter Mary and they had five children. Working for top fashion magazines and advertising agencies, he was always madly busy. My role was not to bother him with anything that I could handle and I think that accounted for my eventual longevity with the studio.

By the very nature of the business, there was a constant stream of beautiful people passing through. One model heavily in demand was Paulene Stone who decorated the cover of Vogue. She had a daughter with Laurence Harvey named Domino who became a bounty hunter in California. I can remember a very young Carol Dilworth coming in for her first photographs taken by Des Waring.

Around this time a new guy joined Wilson Wright and we hit it off straight away even though we were chalk and cheese. Max Thorne was another East Ender, about ten years older than me, quiet where I was noisy and unflappable where I would flap. But sorry to say very careful with money whereas my motto was spend, enjoy, then go and find some more. We remained close friends up to his death.

In August Mr Temple gathered a number of staff together and we headed for Harrow Stores at Burnt Oak. Tesco was taking over this group of supermarkets or was in the throes of doing so. I was given a few tasks to complete but it didn't last as I was allocated what must have been, without a shadow of doubt, the worst job on the books.

New Art Productions was a button factory located at The Hyde NW9 and public transport provision was dire. A long walk to a station and a spotty bus service combined to make it a long day out. But what was in store was not an audit of just a few days but a seemingly lifetime sentence. I had to go there every Thursday, rain or shine, to bring the accounting up to date and prepare the wages for the Friday payday.

The factory was huge, staffed 100% by women from Greece, Turkey and Cyprus all working on machines that emitted a fearsome noise. This was added to by the sounds of splintering buttons coming off like shrapnel, ready to tear into anybody walking past. All the walls were covered with metal sheeting.

The offices at the front consisted of two executive units for Mr Saunders the owner and Mr Kennedy the manager. Shirley the bookkeeper occupied a third room. Between these spaces was an area where we set up camp. Between the offices and the factory floor was a huge steel door.

Kennedy was back and forth every few minutes and would let the door swing shut on its heavy-duty spring on each trip. The combined noise of the machinery, missiles and the door was bad enough. Complemented by the two men screaming abuse at each other for at least fifty per cent of the time made it without any doubt the most awful working environment. On top of all this, on Thursday evening I then had to get over to the studio to prepare the payroll.

I could have used the motorcycle but the tube proved reliable. On rare occasions Shirley would offer a lift to Kingsbury tube station but generally I hoofed it, watching out for a bus to come along, a rare thing, to save me a little time.

The one and only positive was that there was a staff canteen. We would run the gauntlet of button shards and get a hot meal at a decent cost. A big downer was when one of the women was murdered by her husband in a jealous rage outside the factory. But not on a Thursday praise be. My first visit was on 18 August 1960.

Max came to see me in the office one morning and asked if we could have a private chat, as he had come up against something that worried him. We took an early lunch, grabbing a couple of sandwiches from the café in Greville Street and found a seat in an open space behind Leather Lane.

He told me that he had been sent on his first outside audit for the firm with an assistant to a client based in Victoria House, Kingsway. The work had gone as normal and as they approached the finish he had asked the bookkeeper for the petty cash records, only to be refused and told that only Mr Gould was allowed to check those. Déjà vu.

'I have never heard of such a thing, the boss dealing with petty cash. What do you think I should do about it?'

'Nothing. Finish the job with a slot open for the petty cash to drop into and hand it in as normal. I came across exactly the same thing and made a big fuss and it nearly cost me my job.'

'What about a tax audit?'

'Look, Max, they're the big cheeses and we are just expendable. I've made a record of what took place and put it safely away. I suggest you do the same.'

A year later Max was on the same audit and happened upon the secret book.

'You were right, it's a Micky Mouse thing.'

At least if any shit hit the fan further down the pike, we had covered our bases. Sad, shabby and sordid. I thought that we accountants should be better than this and cleverer.

The remainder of 1960 passed without any more dramas. My salary went up a little and I went onto monthly pay. The studio was kicking in a further few quid a month and at long last I was able to live a decent life with a few bob on the hip. I had been chasing a girl called Brenda for some time without success and a few other girls had been temporarily attached, but nothing serious. With two jobs, rebuilding the MG and my involvement in a soccer team, there was little time left over for serious courtship. Not to mention that I was still stuck at home.

Temple took a team of us up to Golders Green for the audit of Grove Lodge Garages and Max Williams Limited, both owned by Mr Williams and run by his two sons-in-law. The first business was a large petrol station group and the second, a chauffeur driven car operation that was highly profitable. That was mainly due to their retention by the Nigerian Embassy who would regularly call for a vehicle and then keep them waiting outside for more than twelve hours, all charged at full rate. The firm also had a group of clients around Vauxhall, so a lot time was spent down there. Not the best part of London, but not the worst either.

The firm threw a Christmas party but no bonuses appeared. I spent some time chatting to Bill Smith who had a different take to the festival season than I did. A family man, he had the traditional holiday with seasonal food and presents, the whole nine yards. I knew what to expect from my lot: mother would have cooked up a lunch, father would arrive fresh from the pub and it would go downhill from there. I was truly sick of it, bored and really wished they could try and get their act together. Maybe this was their idea of parenting. I had no way of knowing but 1961 would sort all of that out.

In early January I was called to Temple's office and found the man standing at his desk looking down on a set of client's accounts that seemed to have notations all over them. My instant thought was that mistakes had slipped through that the client had picked up. I was wrong. Temple beckoned me over

'This is your handwriting, isn't it?'

Moving around the desk in order to see what was actually written, it was obvious that the papers had been intercepted and foul abuse added before being forwarded on. It was pretty rough stuff and I could understand the anger.

'No Sir, it's not my handwriting. I've never seen this before, not a client that I've worked on.'

'This is your writing. Own up and that will be the end of it.'

Well if you believe that, you would be very gullible. If I am fault I am always ready with a peccavi and I have been known to take the blame for others but not here.

'Sir that is not my writing and I am adamant. Are you talking to everybody?'

'No, only you.'

'That's totally unfair. Something down and dirty happens and I'm automatically the guilty party. Where is any possible motive?'

'To cause trouble, it's as simple as that.'

'You have the wrong man, simple as that. And I'm insulted that no one else will be spoken to, now may I go back to my work if there's nothing else to add?'

A few days later, Temple was working on a consolidation that only he was clever enough to deal with and his desk was buried with sheets of calculations when he went to lunch. Even though it was pretty cool he had left his window open much to the delight of two pigeons who flew into the warmth and crapped over the carpet, furniture and especially Temple's vast spread of working papers. When he returned he was, to say the least, apoplectic and it was a hell of a job herding the birds out the way they had come in. Not wishing to be on the cleaning squad, I took the opportunity to slip out on an errand and be scarce for a couple of hours. Short-term karma maybe?

I think it was around this time that Mr Temple left; one day he was there and the next he was gone. As usual, we the rank and file, weren't told anything but it was no secret that he had joined Tesco as Chief Financial Officer. It was later reported that when the time came to carry out the weekly shop, he would drive to a distant Tesco and become a mystery shopper, much to his wife's annoyance. It maybe true or maybe an urban legend from my short time working with the man it would not surprise me.

Changes resulted. Boreham moved into the vacated office as Senior Manager. He came to see me to let me know that in future he was Mr Boreham to me but whatever he wanted to be called did not change what he was. I was able to move into his old space between Mr Gould and reception; Max joined me and we shared a huge double partner's desk. It was all rather nice and an improvement over jostling for a space in the general office.

Yet another strange incident occurred and yet again, the finger pointed at me. Boreham called me in to his new abode.

'You are aware of the two Margolis brothers?'

'I've heard the name, but never worked on them.'

'You know they hate each other, haven't spoken in years.'

'No, as I say I've never touched their jobs. What's all this about?'

'Well, we sent each one his accounts last week. They've received each other's figures and are both furious, as you can imagine.'

'So what's this all to do with me?'

'Did you change the envelopes over to cause mischief?'

'Of course not! It must be a simple mix up with the address labels by the girls, innocent but unfortunate.'

'Are you sure it wasn't you?'

'Are you asking all the staff about this?'

'No, only you.'

Without a word, I turned away and walked out. I should have gone to Mr Gould to complain, as many other people would have done, but I preferred to deal with problems myself and not tell tales.

*****

One evening I approached home to find father waiting on the doorstep which was very unusual.

'Your mother's died.'

I followed him up the staircase and into the front bedroom. He was right, she was as dead as a dodo.

Convention dictates that at times like these you are expected to weep and wail, generally falling apart. If one was of a Latino persuasion, throw yourself to the ground tearing chunks from your hair as you go. If Portuguese, you would also initially check the deceased's pockets. I felt absolutely nothing, not a single emotion. Whatever bond there had been at birth had been eradicated by years of unmitigated misery. I knew I really should care but the fact of the matter was that I didn't – not one iota.

As Freda had arrived, I left to get the doctor to come to see mother's body and make out the death certificate as soon as possible. She'd kept up with some penny insurance policies so there was enough cash to see her off. In the morning, on my way to Plaistow tube station I called into the local undertaker to get the process moving.

It all got sorted and we dispatched her in East London Cemetery. As it was a difficult place to reach without transport, I had taken my motorbike and after the service rode straight to work, making up the time lost over the next few days.

There was no wake, no ham sandwiches in the parlour, no hot tea, no nothing. Nobody suggested anything and I suspect it would have fallen on stony ground anyway. She was gone and as far as I remember, never spoken of again.

*****

As a kid the only two sports to catch my interest were cycling and soccer; running, jumping and chucking things had never appealed. And although I'd been determined to keep getting out on the bike, the reality was that the arrival of my first car changed all that for obvious reasons.

It was in the summer of 1959 when a few of the lads from East Ham Grammar started to pull together a team for 1959/60 season. The plan was to enter the Manor Park, Forest Gate & District Football League and I was invited and brought in a few boys ex-Stratford Grammar. A classics scholar among us suggested the name Juventus, which we were told was Latin for youth. Our first manager was Mr Rennell who ran a local public house and the father of Donald. He was nicknamed Emil after the long-distance Czech runner Emil Zatopek as the kid was never seen walking, always running all over the place.

Our first season was pretty poor and not having proper kit, we just turned out in white t-shirts. Our home pitch was at West Ham Memorial Grounds, used by Thames Ironworks (later called West Ham FC) up until around 1905. It was a terrible locale with a cemetery running along one side and an unofficial swamp at the north end. It was overlooked by a massive block of apartments that the local council used as a dumping ground for its most undesirable tenants.

The changing room/toilet block was disgusting and the assorted old codgers employed to look after the joint just sat around smoking and drinking tea. Often we would arrive to find a filthy burning mattress on the pitch and heaps of general rubbish strewn around.

At the end of our first season there was a groundswell of discontent. The manager never failed to select his son, who in truth wasn't much cop, and we felt that a better job could be done if we ran it ourselves. A meeting was called and I told Mr Rennell, rather dramatically, that the train had just arrived at a station and this was where he got off. David Mercer was appointed Secretary and I was appointed Captain. It seemed to me that other people had more confidence in me than I had.

We clubbed together to get a set of kit: red and white stripe top with black shorts, acquired a set of nets and three of the latest footballs. I bought a new pair of kangaroo leather boots for five guineas, no less. Our pool of players had grown and included a couple that I thought were good enough to get a trial with a league club.

The 1960/61 season was to be wonderful. Our two star players were Jack Harris and John Ringshaw. Jack was a talented all-rounder and a natural ballplayer. John could bend it like Beckham fifteen years before the great David (and fellow East Ender) was born. He took all our corner kicks and could place the ball so accurately that it would run along the underside of the crossbar and more often than not go directly into the net without human intervention. It was almost impossible for the goalkeeper to deal with it, especially with a bunch of hooligans pushing and shoving him around.

Juventus won its first ten games, scoring 56 goals and only letting in six. By the end of the season the sheet was 17 won, 4 lost with 1 draw; scored 95 against 29 and we were top of the table. East Ham Town Hall, Friday 12 May 1961 Dave Mercer and I took to the stage to be presented with the Winner's Shield and the player's medals; mine is still on display in my office. Officially, I was right back and I can still remember each of the three goals I scored in that magical season.

*****

My father was ill. Although he was still working, he was suffering from a great deal of pain that the useless doctor diagnosed as a hernia. It was obvious that it was much more serious than that. I marched round to the doctor's surgery and demanded he come and take another look. He did and immediately sent my father to hospital. It was cancer and in those days that was a sentence of death.

Reluctantly I visited him in hospital and it was clearly all over bar the shouting. He was doped to the eyeballs with morphine that had overwhelmed his thinking processes as well the pain. I sat there unable to say anything worth saying and left knowing that it was the last time I would see him alive. The next morning he was dead.

Once again some penny insurances came to light, the funeral was arranged and he would be buried next to mother. My guess was that that was the last place he would want to be but he'd chosen her 'until death do they part' and now even beyond that milestone. A man of impeccably poor judgement, to my way of thinking.

At the interment I tipped the gravediggers my last two quid but when I reached my motorcycle to head off to work, I found a ten-shilling note in a jacket pocket. A sign of better things to come, maybe. The Falcon had given amazing service, but I needed transport until the MG was finished, so acquired an Excelsior Consort motor bike in exchange for the Francis Barnett and a small wad of notes. It was only 98cc but went like stink, as they say.

Reality soon struck home: there was no way on God's earth that I could share a house with my sister, no way. I had to get out of the place, took holiday time that was due and piled into completing the job of putting the car back together. Colin was a massive help and although the paint job was not up to muster, it would have to do. Everything worked and it was back on the road. It was time to turn mother's picture to the wall and walk away.

Meanwhile life continued at Wilson Wright. I was still stuck with having to trek to Hendon for a day's earbashing every Thursday but other than that the work was varied and for the most part, the staff convivial. Michael Berger had left and Martin Wesson arrived as a senior man. Tony Hawthorne and Len Gurrie were two names that stood out and my friend Max was always good company. One young lad taken on was a Turk by the name of Mehet who was, without doubt, a scallywag. One day he phoned in to tell Mr Gould that his mother had died; he was naturally very sympathetic and told Mehet to 'take as much time off as you need'.

On his return everybody crowded around with handshakes, offering kind words and sympathy. It came as something of a surprise to us when, on a later occasion, his mother called Mr Gould to tell him that Mehet had a cold and would be unable to come in for a couple of days. Mr Gould expressed surprise at hearing her voice, as he had it on good authority that she was dead. What happened to the boy at home I can only imagine but to our amazement no rebuke was issued on his return and life for him simply continued as before.

Dave Mercer came up with a possible solution to my hunt for accommodation after our match on the Saturday. We had played a game over in East Ham and several of us stopped at a pub for a shandy. During the course of conversation Dave mentioned that his mother was thinking of taking a lodger and I asked if I could come over for a chat. It was manna from heaven. When Freda started talking up the new regime that she had in mind, I told her outright that it wasn't going to work for either of us.

Dave's mother was happy with me and we agreed a start date, so that I could give my sister notice, as it were. I called the local orphanage and they were pleased to take away my homemade Subbuteo table and the various accessories. The rest of my stuff fitted into a couple of cardboard suitcases and a duffle bag. Piling these into the TC, I headed east to 111 Sheridan Road, East Ham.

My room was at the back and I was thrilled to discover a bathroom actually indoors. That was a first. No more filling a tin tub once a week with water boiled on the stove and taking turns. Here everybody could have his or her own fresh bath at the turn of a tap. The toilet was out at the back but that was the accepted norm.

It soon became obvious the Mrs Mercer had realized that she had made a mistake and couldn't settle with a stranger in her house. I don't think it was personal; I think her feelings would have been the same with anybody. I told Dave that I'd picked up on the vibes and would be off as soon as I could organise something else.

Help can come from the strangest places and in this instance it came from young Mehet. His aunt and uncle had a bedsit to let with its own kitchenette and bathroom, over at New Cross. I knew that such a move would have drastic repercussions. At a stroke I would lose the social life and activities I'd built with friends. Getting across to east London after running two jobs and then at the end of the day homing south to New Cross just wouldn't be practical. But needs must as Mrs Mercer wasn't happy and ergo, David was getting impatient.

My new accommodation was a little unusual. The one big room was at the front of the house on the first floor front with a bathroom opposite that included a toilet. On the landing there was an oven with a large cupboard with a counter top. It would work. The rent was reasonable so I agreed to move in mid-November.

As I'd expected, weight training and soccer went out of the window. I continued to play for Juventus but not for long. The club had been promoted to the first division but the three best players had been poached by other clubs in the summer. Our first two games were away matches which we won 5-0 and 4-0.

When we arrived at West Ham Memorial Grounds for our first home match 1961/62 we discovered that our nets had been stolen but the groundkeepers knew nothing. The pitch was covered in horse droppings and not having a spade resulted in running a messy, smelly obstacle course and we lost nil to four. Of the next six games we won two and lost four. Without the midweek training, I was finding it all a hard ask and told the team to leave me out. I just couldn't crack the mustard so that was the end of it, no way back.

Most evenings I returned late and if I hadn't eaten out, simply put a can of soup on the stove. It was supplied by gas and there was a coin meter taking half-a-crown coins (12.5p). Every time I went to use it I had to find a coin. I tested it for leaks but it was sound as a bell and beyond comprehension that heating soup would use up so much gas.

I had only been there a few weeks when the Meadway Manufacturing audit came up. It was a plastics factory and happy days, it was in Lewisham only a ten minute walk away. I took a couple of the east London lads on a Monday and we got to work. I had the misfortune to spill some coffee on my shirt so decided to pop home to change. When I reached the landing, I was confronted by the extraordinary sight of very elderly Turkish woman standing by the oven with the biggest cook pot you have ever seen. It was filled with meatballs in tomato sauce and the gas rings were going full blast. Needless to say she spoke no English but words were unnecessary as my mystery was solved.

Unknowingly I had been helping with the overheads of a local café to the tune of 75p a week. When your weekly wage is around £10 that's unsustainable. When I returned that evening, I could smell gas and resolved that in future, I would either grab a takeaway or simply make a sandwich for my evening meal.

I always liked to think that the young guys liked working with me as I took the time to not only show them what needed to be done but why and what we needed to look out for.

One of the oldest tricks used by fraudsters was so send strange invoices for payment. One such case happened at Selfridges where a clerk had been operating such a scheme was able to continue even after he was fired. He'd slip into the accounts department on Saturday and pop his paperwork into the appropriate 'to be processed' stack. Large value sales invoices created just before the year end cut off was a way for management to inflate profits or eradicate losses. It wasn't just a question of ticking stuff off the audit programme, it was a matter of common sense and keeping your wits about you. Fraud is rare and sometimes hard to find but in time you can get a second sense that all is not what it should be. I'm not saying that auditing is fun but it really doesn't have to be a soulless slog that sorry to say, many never learn.

By the Friday morning it was all coming together. Mr Travis the clubfooted bookkeeper was very competent and his books in good shape. He was very proud of his family and told us on many occasions that he was strictly a 9 to 5 man, five days a week.

At 11am I asked him for the last item on our list the petty cash book. He told me that he was just finishing the annual summary and it would be ready in about fifteen minutes. At least we didn't have to call in Mr Gould to check the thing. So I told the guys that we should have it all wrapped up by noon and that we could head on back to the office, grabbing lunch on the way. We sat back and shot the breeze for a few minutes when the phone rang, it was Boreham.

'Get back to the office immediately.'

'Hang on a second, we should be all done in an hour, can't it wait till then?'

'No, get back now.'

I went next door to the MD, Mr Dreyfuss, told him of the mysterious recall and explained that we were waiting for Mr Travis to give us the petty cash stuff. Once we had that we'd have been out of there by lunchtime.

'You've been called back to the office because I complained that you have been sitting around chatting for twenty minutes.'

'We've been talking because we have nothing to do.'

'I didn't know that, I'll call Boreham now and explain the situation.'

'May I ask a question? How long did the audit take last year?'

'About two weeks. Why?'

'We'll be done today.'

He didn't say anything, just picked up the phone as I left the room.

When the petty cash came through, we tied everything up and

went to have lunch. While we were eating, I told the others what had occurred but without further comment. Once back in Hatton garden, I checked over our work and took it into Boreham, placing it on his desk without a word, then turned and walked out. I had no way of knowing but much, much worse was to come only two weeks later.

It was a Saturday morning when I awoke to a heavy-duty smell of burning. After checking it wasn't coming from inside the house, I opened the curtains to see thick black smoke. Dressing quickly, I headed down to the street and followed my nose. Ten minutes later I could see the fire engines and getting closer, I could not believe my eyes, the plastics factory was in flames. The second surprise was seeing Mr Travis tucked into a doorway ten yards away and Mr 9 to 5 five days a week Travis was clutching the account books under his arm.

I slipped past the Old Bill and reaching him, put a reassuring hand on this arm.

'Mr Travis, what the hell are you doing here on a Saturday morning?'

'I was called in and had only been here a few minutes when the building went up. I escaped over the small stream at the back of the factory.'

'Come on Mr Travis, you are in shock, let's get a brandy in you.'

The pub wasn't open but I knew the landlord. I steered him off the street and the landlord pointed out that they were not yet open. I shook the publican's hand passing a couple of quid inside the handshake.

'Look, he's just been rescued from the blaze and needs a large one, me too.'

'On the house,' he said loudly, as if the licence geezers were hiding in the cellar.

We sat at a corner table and drank. I repeated the dance with the landlord, although mine was a single.

'What's happening, Mr Travis?' I said, as if I didn't know.

'Well, I was told to come in as I told you. The fire started in the storeroom which is chock-a-block with packing materials, cardboard, foam, all that stuff and in no time there was smoke and a whoosh and the whole place was ablaze. I could have died in there.'

He talked about the old fashioned (even then) three bar electric fire and what could have happened. Being neither an electrician nor an arsonist none of it made much sense and I was never very adept at boozing in the morning. All I knew for sure was that it wasn't spontaneous combustion.

He settled down and after an hour I walked him to the railway station still clutching his books of account. He was terrified about losing his job, especially as he believed that his disability would mean that many doors were closed to him.

On Monday morning I got the call to attend Mr Boreham.

'I don't know whether you've heard but Meadway had a fire at the weekend.'

'I was there, I live just around the corner.'

'Right, they are sending over the insurance claims and I want you to deal with it.'

'Sorry, no can do.'

'It's not a request, I am telling you to deal with the insurance claims.'

'No, you are asking me to voluntarily become an accessory to arson and insurance fraud.'

'What nonsense are you talking about?'

'I was there and so was Mr Travis. You remember the guy who never works late or at weekends? He'd rescued the books from the flames. We had a chat over some drinks and I can guarantee that accident doesn't come into it.'

'I'm not interested in any of that.'

'Well I'm sorry but I am not going near this job. There are plenty of guys out there so give it to one of them.'

'You are forbidden to speak to anyone about this matter.'

'Of course, mum's the word.'

He wasn't happy with me but he was never happy with me. No matter how hard I tried or how the high quality of my work or how diligent I was in taking younger staff forward, my card was marked.

I think he knew perfectly well that I didn't respect him but in my book respect is earned not automatic. He was out of his time I thought and would have made a crackerjack workhouse overseer, absolutely crackerjack. His two favourite catchphrases – 'I am not interested in any of that' and 'you are forbidden to speak' – were to ring in my ears over and over again during the coming years. The irony of it all was not lost on me.

Chatting was a serious offence meriting a report to the bosses but torching a building with a human inside is just business. Double standards or what? I made sure that none of the aftermath came anywhere near me, recording what had happened and what I knew of the events. Should anyone try and shove me up the barrel, I'd covered my arse.

*****

Top of the agenda was to find a new home. Without soccer on Saturday I had the time needed to sort things out and saw an advert in a newsagent's window for a bedsit in Balham. It was a small back bedroom with a tiny kitchenette and a bathroom across the landing. The rent was reasonable and the mother/daughter combo seemed pleasant enough. The whole house looked like it was in the middle of being renovated but as I was out all day, that didn't matter. Colin helped me shift my stuff from Mornington Road to Ravenswood Road and I started to settle. But it was fairly obvious that someone was going through my stuff while I wasn't there and that the house was actually in a desperate condition. So back to the message boards and luckily I quickly found a bedsit at 42 Huron Road a few streets away.

Again it was a back bedroom with a tiny cooking space and a shared bathroom on a lower landing. The front room was not let but the attic was occupied by two boners from Smithfield Market.

I gave notice but when I returned to the house on the Saturday to move my stuff, I found that I was locked out. However the back door was open and I waded through a flooded basement to get access. It was all pretty fraught but I loaded my stuff into the MG and got away.

Mehet never mentioned my departure from his aunt and uncle's place. He continued to get away with gross liberties at the firm but never received the tongue-lashing frequently dished out to those less favoured. He tore around the town in an Austin A35 sans a silencer and going through the Blackwall Tunnel with him was a memorable experience.

He invited me to join him and a few friends for a drink at a pub off Borough High Street and I agreed. I'd expected a bunch of young Turkish blokes but it turned out to be a mixed bunch of boys and girls and was a terrific evening

One girl really caught my eye and when Mehet offered me a lift home, he suggested dropping her off at her block of flats near the Elephant and Castle. I was most impressed and asked Mehet for her phone number. Patricia was to become my first serious girlfriend; she was pretty and clever and the moment I saw her I was smitten.

Mehet provided the requested phone number and I made the call, arranging to take her out in the MG on the Sunday for a pub lunch in the country. It went well and I could not have been happier. She was three years younger than me and, strange as it may seem, was also born in Chatham. Her father was a Norwegian sailor, passing through on the night, so her mother had brought her up without any support. Life must have been tough for them both. They lived in a public housing unit in Langridge House that was actually a very smart apartment in a well-kept block.

So 1962 saw me in a much better place. I had a secure home to live in and a lovely new girlfriend. I had a job that I enjoyed, (apart from you know who) and a second spot that was providing a solid income. In no time at all I'd lost touch with the East End mob but was soon making friends in my new location.

The two guys in the attic rooms were wild, maybe because their days were spent chopping up the bodies of animals day after day. They gambled on the horses, spent a small fortune on tipsters and sometimes did win a lot. When that happened, they talked about it loudly but they also lost regularly which wasn't talked about. When they won eight hundred quid they rushed off to buy a Renault Dauphine from the worst car dealer in Tooting; it broke down before they got it home, less than a mile away.

The worst dealer was also the toughest dealer and unless they were prepared for a brutal physical encounter with the guy, they were shafted. Coming from the meat market they were no pushovers in everyday life but they were out of his league. They fiddled about with the car for a few weeks then cut their losses and scrapped it. I suspected that it had been used as a minicab for most of its life and the milometer had been massively wound back.

A local lad introduced himself the day I moved in, attracted by the car. Rod stopped to chat and was more interested than I'd realized. Within a couple of weeks he turned up with a MG TC he had bought for himself. I went to see his sign-writing shop and met his neighbour Sid who ran a brake and clutch workshop. All was moving along nicely.

Freda called me to tell me that she was following her big sister and was booked to sail to Australia. I was welcome to borrow her radiogram but if she came back to England she'd want it back.

Soon after I moved in, the landlady told me that she needed an operation and was going up to the Midlands to stay with her sister until she recovered. She asked if I could pay my rent into her bank account that was all fine for me. But it was an open invitation to the meaties upstairs to dodge the column and live life unconstrained. It did not look good. I shouldn't have worried as things weren't too bad, except for the evening they allowed their place to be used for an abortion. Not good, in fact just plain horrible.

When I look back over the list of clients it is depressing how few still exist, yet the accountants and lawyers are still plugging on year after year.

One job I remember coming in was Michael Gerson, a North London business which was/is I think in removals and storage. Somewhere in the back of my mind are fine arts but that could well be a false memory. Not only are they still extant but signed up with the same auditors.

Speaking of operations, Mrs Trew the queen of secretaries and typists announced she had to go into hospital for a hysterectomy. She had put it off as long as she could but it had to be now. On her first day on the ward, the powers that be sent her a card; not the get-well card she might have expected but the marching orders P45 kind.

I thought that this really stunk and I was not alone. But any protest would not only have been futile but have attracted a shit storm down on the protester. I couldn't understand their motive but the fact was that all the girls were treated in a strange way, as if they were lesser mortals in a society dominated by men. Female auditors were as rare as hen's teeth of course. I think if management could have found them, they would have engaged male typists and not had any women in the place at all.

One geezer I never got along with was a Cypriot named Avrum. In my opinion he had come down through a long line of lead-swingers but in the management's eyes he was a sacred cow and untouchable. When he left, Boreham told me to check his desk was clear and to complete any unfinished work. I couldn't get the drawers open and figured he had locked it up, taking the key just to screw us over. Ian Keller gave me a hand and when we finally managed to prise the top drawer open, we found it stuffed to the gills with uncompleted clients' tax returns.

The next drawer was the same, so I made an executive decision and shut the drawers, telling Ian not only to make himself scarce but that he was never there. Passing Boreham in the corridor, I casually remarked that the desk was locked and they would need a locksmith to open it.

Tragedy struck at the studio when Jim the Print was killed in a car crash on his way home. He was loved by everyone and missed by everyone and his replacement Steve had a hard act to follow.

A few months later I was preparing the month end cheque run and a couple of large invoices from Kodak were missing. I phoned their accounts department for duplicates, expecting them to arrive in a few days. When they didn't I collected them personally and was surprised to discover they were for two grand's worth of laboratory equipment. There was no evidence of the purchase either physically or on paper and I knew nothing about the equipment. Steve was confronted and admitted the theft but how did he think he could get away with it?

He had arrived early in the morning to get to the post and removed the invoices but it could only be a matter of time, and a short time at that, before all was revealed. Michael was furious that yet again, he was dealing with dishonesty. On this occasion the police were called, Steve's house raided, the gear found and Steve set off on the road to prison.

On a brighter note, I brought Max in to help me as the place was jumping. In addition to the two evenings sometimes it was necessary to put in a Saturday morning to keep on top of the work. For Wilson Wright it was a gift, as at audit time they not only had a full set of records to check, but even the tax calculations were complete. I can't recall any words of appreciation and more of Boreham's bizarreness was heading down the pike in my direction.

A Nigerian guy turned up at the firm and was introduced as David Dafinone. His clothes struck everyone immediately. The suit was definitely from Savile Row, the shirt from Jermyn Street and the shoes from Lobbs. If he had a hat it would be from Lock & Co of James Street. There was more money hanging off his carcass than I earned in a year and he made the partners look like they dressed in clothes from charity shops.

We were told that he would be with us for a few weeks while studying for his exams and that was all. Why couldn't he work from home? He commandeered a desk in the general office, came and went as he wished and spoke to no one. The wonderful display of tailored elegance continued to be paraded with a different outfit seemingly worn on each and every visit. This remittance man had a mighty stipend coming from the folks back home. In the early days I'd wish him a good morning when I ran into him but as he blanked me, I didn't even bother with that for long.

The time came to head off to Forest Gate for my second year of auditing Universal Radio run by Jo and Francis Stone. Jo was an east European Jew who had made his way to England, adopting an orphaned French boy called Francis on the way. He set up his company with a couple of shops and by sheer hard graft built up the business to some twenty stores in the Greater London area. Now Francis was running the show with one other director.

The problem was that Francis was funny about letting us have sight of the completion papers pertaining to any new stores and they were essential to do a proper analysis. My answer to this was to wait for the two chiefs to head off on a store inspection, pop into his office and with a gash key open the cabinet, whip out the file and make super quick notes. Francis was never the wiser but was puzzled when I told him he had paid two and a half grand's worth of rates twice. Then I told him it was a hunch but he didn't believe me.

The previous year it had been a very local job for me but now I was south of the Thames, it was a bit of a hike. A chance however to give my favourite East End boys a lie in. I walked into the general office and Dafinone was at his spot as usual and half a dozen juniors were available.

'Right, Monday morning we have the firm's worst client and I need two volunteers.' Before anyone could speak, I continued: 'Ian and John, you'll do, nine thirty Forest Gate and no hangovers.'

The three of us enjoyed some light repartee, as you do, and I returned to my office. Then the phone rang – his master's voice. This was going to be a poor end to a good week for certain.

'I've received a very serious complaint about you.'

'Is there any other kind?'

'Don't be facetious.'

'Look, I've been in the office all week so I can't imagine what bloody nonsense this is but trot it out and get on with it.'

'You are forbidden to speak to anyone about this. Mr Dafinone has told me you are not fit to be an accountant because you speak of clients irreverently.'

'You know what? I'm amazed that you didn't send him away with a flea in his ear and that you're bothering me with it!'

'His family is very distinguished and highly regarded in Nigeria.'

'What the hell has his family got to do with anything? I have never spoken to the man or had anything to do with him. I don't even know what he is doing here. He doesn't know anything about me?'

'What happened in the general office just now?'

'I simply told a couple of the lads they were with me on Monday for an audit in Forest Gate. We had a few laughs, the London sense of humour, a bit of fun. Do you remember that? Maybe they don't do humour in Nigeria. Look, I haven't any more time to waste on this, I've got some work to do.'

I left the office and later told Dafinone to mind his own business; as far as I was concerned, that was definitely with prejudice.

Fifty years later a few truths about the wealthy and distinguished Mr David Dafinone has been revealed. The Nigerian online media group Urhobo Today published the true story of how the man conducted himself during his time in Britain.

While at the University of Hull, he lived with Helen Joan MacKay with whom he had a daughter Elizabeth. But when he met Cynthia and she got pregnant, Dafinone dumped Joan and Elizabeth, leaving them to a life of poverty. Many years later our man stumped up a thousand quid to help with education.

As Urhobo Today observed in the piece: 'David was a wealthy man from a young age. He could have taken care of them.'

But he didn't. So now we have the measure of the man. One who makes a commitment to a woman and when it suits, just walks away from all responsibility without a backward glance. And do that when he had the financial muscle to stand up and do the right thing. There is a phrase that comes to mind and it sure don't include the word distinguished: moral turpitude.

The Universal Radio audit went off all right but as usual involved breaking and entering into the filing cabinet to get the facts, all the facts. The business financed its own hire purchase that made a great contribution to the profits. On the other side of the coin two or three stores were in very poor areas and the insurance companies would not cover them; understandably since they were frequently ram-raided. Personally I would have cut my losses but Francis persevered and would restock them only to be hit again and again.

My brother was having it tough. His wife had decided that the butcher in Purley was more to her liking. She simply decamped, leaving her ten year-old daughter to return after school to an empty house, not knowing what had happened until Jeff got back from work to find the 'Dear John' letter. Now he had to bring the kid up as a single dad and that's no easy task.

Although it was my habit to arrive at the office around eight, David Cohen our business neighbour was always there closer to seven. An elderly diamond dealer who would seem to pat the pockets of his waistcoat to check his stock, he was a familiar sight around the Garden. His equally ancient assistant would arrive before me and when I bailed up, I could see the door to their rooms open and hear the voices inside.

One morning I found the place crawling with police and they were very interested in who I was and why I was there. Pretty sharp thinking I thought as if I was one of the robbers, I'd be going down the stairs not coming up clutching a sausage sandwich.

Two guys dressed as window cleaners had walked in through open front door and then the Cohen's open office door. Then to their delight they were looking at an open safe door. Threats of violence were all that was needed to get a result. They tied up the two oldies and made off with a tasty haul of stones. Nobody was ever caught and I doubt that the insurance company would have shown any interest in paying the claim. The Old Bill asked for a statement but I declined on the grounds that they were on site before me and therefore I had nothing to contribute.

The MG had been running like a dream but I was offered an unusual early MG TC. It had been modified for use in trials with a double volume petrol tank, the wings and running boards replaced with cycle wings and the bonnet remodelled to enable the side panels to be removed to allow for improved cooling. I not sure how legal that was, allowing hands to be thrust into the moving parts of the engine area but I was never pulled for it. It came cheap at forty quid so I snapped it up and cleared my existing car for a hundred quid. Max asked me to find him a runabout, so I sourced an A40 for thirty pounds and he was a happy bunny.

Brother Jeff called to tell me that his neighbour wanted to sell his Ford Ten. It was new when his now deceased father bought it in 1936; they wanted ten pounds and it all worked. Couldn't be passed up, so I did the deal. The MG special sold at a profit but the Ford was old-fashioned even compared to the two MGs. It started and stopped but without much sparkle in between.

*****

One nagging worry was that I wasn't doing anything that was leading to a professional qualification. I knew that I could make a decent living with accountancy but without the letters after your name, the respect and the big bucks would never come my way. I had to formulate a plan and sharpish. By the end of the year I had a plan.

I had shown my worth at the firm and got along with the majority of the staff. The one real problem that existed were the occasional outbursts but I felt I could control that situation by simply standing up for myself. It was not a pleasant task but I was keeping a record of each outburst so that, in the event of a confrontation, I could produce a history with explanations.

I decided to approach Mr Gould with a proposition: if he would sign me on as an Articled Clerk for the remainder of the five year period, (which I had calculated as four years and four days) but on a proper salary level, I would guarantee to work on exactly as I was currently. Any study leave would come from my holiday allowance and I would expect no concessions.

A second decision was to acquire a more up to date vehicle that could be driven daily. At the time parking controls existing in Holborn did not apply a mile north around the Gray's Inn Road. By driving in early I could park there, walk to the office via the café and arrive at 8am as I did now.

Today the Christmas and New Year holidays usually evolve into a two-week break for most white-collar workers but not back in 1962. New Year's Eve was a Monday but we worked and it snowed heavily all day. With Philip Da Costa in charge, a group of us descended on Ralph Hilton Transport in Vauxhall for their annual audit.

Ralph Hilton was a hard man of the old school. He had started with a horse and cart bringing produce down from the London markets and had expanded to some twenty trucks run out of a yard off the Albert Embankment. He was not a man to be crossed.

According to the plan for the week, I was only meant be involved there on Monday and Wednesday, moving to the button factory Thursday and back to Hatton Garden on Friday. Mid-morning a red Aston Martin DB4 roared into the yard and out stepped the driver Charlie Richardson and his brother Eddie with Frankie Fraser. They got a warm welcome from Mr Hilton and his main men. I knew the Richardsons from my Peckham days (they attended the same school only they were a year or two older) and Mr Fraser from my time in the scrap business.

A little later there was a kerfuffle when the yard's general factotum, a West Indian named Winston couldn't be found. When he was discovered sleeping in the back of a lorry he was hauled out by Lurch the yardmaster, carried out to the main road and thrown into the traffic.

We pen pushers were in awe of what was happening but kept our heads firmly down to avoid catching anyone's eye. Unfortunately, I'd caught the eye of one of the office girls who slipped me her address and phone number. An older woman followed me as I walked out of the yard and quietly advised me to forget the invitation. Apparently a man standing very close by paid for the girl's flat and he had a fearsome temper. Here was one complaint I didn't need and I was relieved to see the end of my second day.

Selected to head up the audit of a new client, I met with a couple of the lads at Green Park on Monday 14 January to walk up to 4 Hill Street off Berkeley Square. The beautiful house was home to Alan Grossman Advertising Limited and gave me my introduction to the wonderful world of advertising.

The accounts department was in the basement complete with a full bathroom. The club footed accountant Mr Parsons and his staff shared the space with Mr Grossman's beautiful Boxer. I began taking her to Green Park for a lunchtime walk where she would have loved to be let free to run but I didn't dare. If I lost her, there would be hell to pay and Boreham would certainly have thrown all his toys out of the pram.

It was a vibrant atmosphere to work in and I was attracted to the industry immediately. The agency was newly established and cash flow was tight. Mr Parsons produced daily accounts, which in itself was amazing and it was important to finish as soon as possible. Accordingly I asked if I could come in on Saturday to push things along and was informed that the building would be open with some staff working. When I arrived the street was blocked off by a crane manoeuvring a huge custom-made piece of furniture through one of the windows in Mr Grossman's office on the first floor. I was to discover that this item would run wall to wall and carry the TV, audio equipment and all the awards that were surely in the pipeline. Clearly cost was no object. I made good friends with a number of the staff including Mr and Mrs Barnes, who I met socially from time to time.

We finished the job quickly and the result was tight. With the cost of an establishment in Mayfair, the loss of any single client would be catastrophic and it folded later in the year. I heard that Mr Grossman had moved to Mexico and wondered whatever happened to the Boxer. But my appetite for the advertising business had been duly wetted. It seemed a crazy industry and I knew that I would fit right in.

A weakness that I am aware of is the willingness to help. For some distorted reason I am flattered when asked and put myself forward without ever thinking of the possible consequences. Time and time again I have paid for my good deeds.

Brian Boreham and then Martin Wesson, both asked me if I could source them a decent car. I took a look at a number of vehicles: Rover 65, Ford Anglia 1955, Jaguar, Triumph Herald and a couple of Austins before asking Frank to check out a 1957 Singer Gazelle in smart two-tone grey and a blue Vauxhall Victor. I brought them to show BB and MW and they agreed to buy. Note all this running around and I didn't ask a cent in commission. What a fool I was to getting involved.

From that moment on, every problem or fault that appeared in the cars was laid at my door. I was expected to jump to it as an unpaid car recovery service, roving mechanic and apologetic.

This was years before Red Robbo led 523 days of strike action against British Leyland, effectively killing the car manufacturer. But it was a well-known fact that vehicles made in England were badly designed and made, apart from the very top end. In addition drivers needed to have basic mechanical knowledge to keep on motoring. A tool kit, a few spares and a tin of lighter fluid were essentials even in new cars. Soon the Japanese would arrive and show us how it should be done but not yet.

When Mr Gould asked my advice on buying a Rolls Royce, I politely declined to get involved for all the obvious reasons. Although I did suggest he looked at a Bristol as an alternative. He did acquire a Roller and one dark night out in Essex the throttle jammed open and gave him the ride of a lifetime. Thank God I had not been involved.

It was time to put my plan into action. I asked to meet Mr Gould and enquired if he would take me on as an Articled Clerk to finish my apprenticeship but with a proper regular wage. I would take my study leave in my holidays and ask no privileges of him or the firm. To my relief he agreed, so I must have proved my worth to the business. I also asked him to introduce me to the bank downstairs and that was the start of a long relationship.

On Friday 8 March 1963 I signed Articles and by my calculation had a few days over four years to go. I had to take up the correspondence course knowing full well that I would never complete it from A to Z with all the constraints on my time. What I needed to do was to read everything and try to understand the common sense of it all. The accountancy stuff was a given but the law and all that jazz needed digestion. Past examination papers were key components and were available. I sensed they could take you into the mindset of the guys setting the tests, indicate what was expected and what the regular lines of questions were. The bank was happy to have me as a customer and arranged a two hundred pound loan.

I quickly found a blue Austin Healey Sprite for sale in Kenley just around the corner from brother Jeff's house and agreed with Mr Brown at Welcomes Farm to buy it for two hundred and forty five pounds. An economical two-seater sports car affectionately known as frogeye due to the high headlight positioning, it proved to be a great little runabout. Max was so impressed he bought a white version. The Ford Ten sold easily and the Excelsior was finally passed on, signifying the end of my motorcycle days.

There was no doubt the Austin Healey made it much more convenient to get around the town especially when carrying books and papers. No more battling with public transport and walking miles now riding from door to door in comfort. I was still stuck with New Art every Thursday but it was no longer a logistical nightmare getting there and then on over to the studio. Now I could hammer down Edgware Road to Kilburn and use the rat runs to get down to Kensington that made it a piece of cake.

A big audit fell to me to manage and I was allotted almost every clerk available. BB Evans was a large department store in Kilburn High Street that was so old fashioned it still used the pneumatic tubes vacuum system to send cash between sales staff and the cashier department. However it was by far the biggest audit I had been on, let alone been in my charge. Sorry to say, my crew were selected for me. I had to deal with the Greek guy not wanting to work with the Turk, the Pakistani not talking to the Indian and neither liking the Sri Lankan (although he was worth both of them put together and more). The two Irish boys coming from opposite sides of the border were ready to bring the Troubles right up to my doorstep. But praise be, the Nigerian was non-partisan.

The solution was to split them into three teams and spread them around the building. One real benefit was that we were allowed to use the firm's canteen but even there, table sharing was out of the question for some of this happy band.

One vital part of the work was dealing with gift vouchers. Every year the store produced a new issue and all unissued vouchers from the previous year were destroyed. We had to be present to witness their destruction and that involved a trip to the confidential disposal yard to watch them thrown into the furnace. A profitable business as always, 10% to 15% were never claimed, lost or forgotten and a grand example of money for nothing.

There was no doubt that the age of the department store was manifestly, slowly coming to an end. A Victorian institution, many of the famous names would disappear over the next forty years. A behemoth such as BB Evans stood no chance and closed its doors for the final time in the early 70s. A tatty row of shops has taken its place and in my opinion, Kilburn High Street remains an unattractive area.

My relationship with Patricia was going well. We would get together for a meal during the week and usually on Saturday evening, then take a run out into the countryside on Sunday. I had the greatest respect for her mother for bringing up her daughter single-handedly. It wouldn't have been a cakewalk at a time when many people showed great hostility towards single parents. Not to mention the father having disappeared into the land of the fjords never to be seen again. But I didn't find her at all likeable and I'm sure the feeling was mutual.

Invariably attired in a plastic hospital cleaner's apron and with a cigarette clamped between her lips, she was about as rough as guts as you could get and opposed to anyone who threatened to steal her girl away. Like most poor people at that time her financial lifeline was the door-to-door tallyman who today has been replaced by online websites I imagine.

Two audits allocated to me were next-door neighbours in Latimer Road, near the famous Portobello Road. Leonard Whiting Limited manufactured plastic parts for the motor vehicle industry and was run by a Mr Whiting. He was a terrific bloke who drove a Jaguar, raced high-powered speedboats and always showed a real appreciation for what we did. Which was a rare thing indeed.

I think Messrs Buchanan and Barrett controlled Greville Tinners next door. I'm unsure because it was a soulless business and nobody spoke to us in a social respect. We went in, did the job and went away, no more no less. Both were straightforward as the bookkeepers were both top notch. It was the usual check of systems, summarise and bring together the figures into a result. At the end Mr Whiting, bless him, even gave us cash to have lunch on him. Buchanan and Barrett didn't even give us the soldier's farewell.

It was on Friday 9 May 1963 heading to Latimer Road that the steering of my Sprite failed. The wheel would turn but wasn't connected to the front wheels. I managed to get into the kerb and by trial and error found that if I pushed the steering wheel forward with all my might I could force a connection.

Knowing that there was an Austin-Healey repair shop at 1 Reece Mews, Kensington but not being a member of a recovery service, I drove very gingerly over there to get help. Thankfully I was informed that this was a common fault and easily fixed.

Reece Mews was an interesting place. Francis Bacon lived at number seven, Lionel Bart on the opposite side and at the far end was a Morgan dealer. But what really caught my eye was an outfit halfway down where a small bunch of young guys were having a great time by all appearances. Boothby Gordon Motors, TVR sales and service. I knew I had to find out more. The car couldn't be fixed until Monday so a weekend on shank's pony ensued.

When I was running the MG cars I would go to a motor race meeting from time to time, usually Silverstone or Biggin Hill. There I had seen the early TVR cars and loved their unorthodox styling and quick pace due in part to the lightweight fiberglass body. The current model was the Grantura mark III that succeeded, and this is stating the bleeding obvious, the mark I, mark II and mark IIa.

I decided to pimp up the Sprite by replacing the original metal bonnet with a fiberglass unit manufactured by Arkley. It would be a straight swop but the headlights would sit in the more conventional position at the end of the wings giving a modern appearance. Rod helped me respray the whole car in a gunmetal grey with a red pinstripe in his signwriting workshop and the finished result was pretty good. I also built a fake transmission tunnel cover with additional instruments that added to 'the look'.

That spring and summer seemed to be spent down at Vauxhall. I was spared the high energy atmosphere of Ralph Hilton but recall meeting Boreham at the station there to walk over to Leonard Ripley Printing. Why he needed to be present to introduce me and the crew was beyond me but there he was. These guys produced posters and had machines that could deal with the massive sizes utilised on billboard advertising. The accountant was a real professional and the company a serious endeavour having been in business since 1936.

Our next client was just around the corner. Vauxhall Glass was a balls-to-the-wall job, new and finding its feet. It sold glassware to restaurants, hotels, pubs and clubs, handling a vast amount of small sales to a long list of customers. But they could only afford a part-time bookkeeper. It would be pointless working towards balancing everything to the penny as the fees would have been horrific. So we ploughed in hard, concentrating on ensuring that the balance sheet reflected the true position of the business. I got in early and left late but didn't stick them with the overtime; my silent contribution to their future perhaps. There were a couple of other jobs to be done in the area and one down in Stockwell, a mile or two south.

There was a dearth of places to eat, just one small greasy spoon cafe and the infamous Vauxhall Tavern. This massive boozer catered for a single type of clientele into which I definitely didn't fit, so to be avoided at all costs.

In accounting you see the best and worst in people. The boss of one of Max's audits died at nine in the morning in the London Clinic and his newly minted widow phoned Mr Gould telling him that she was on her way over. I was working with Max in the antechamber to our chief's office when she arrived. Mr Gould rushed out to greet her brimming with sympathy, only to be brushed aside by the woman and her entourage, to wit her lawyer, accountant and gigolo.

As a gesture of her true love for him, the latter had been given an Austin Metropolitan. This vehicle was a miniature copy of a Yank tank built 1953-1962 mainly for the North American market although a few seemed to have escaped to the UK. Pininfarina had a small hand somewhere in the design but refused to allow their name to be associated with it. I thought it an awful looking thing back then and even more so today although apparently there is a cult following. If I was a twenty-five year old bloke squiring a sixty something old broiler around I would expect an E-type at the very least.

The meeting was to establish what money was to be expected for the sale of her husband's majority share in his business. The shouting and screaming was off the scale but when Mr Gould called for backup, Max and I took our work down to my room away from it all. And the poor geezer wasn't even cold yet. Some of the scenarios we enjoyed were beyond the imagination of the brightest and most inventive scriptwriters.

Another client had coughed his last and I was instructed to visit the home and close off his records. An émigré from Eastern Europe, he was a master carpenter named Vincent Franks. Nothing unusual there except his original name in the old country was Vincent Frankenstein, I kid you not. He was persuaded soon after his arrival that retention of his family name would guarantee a lifetime of hurtful comments, a great deal of disbelief and might for example, lead to difficult moments with the police.

The address I had was Sutherland Avenue in Maida Vale and I thought I knew the location. An A to Z was required because but I didn't and had to stop to pick one up. Mrs Franks was waiting for me and I set to work but by one o'clock I realized that it was a two day job. I packed everything into two boxes, squashed them into the car and headed for the office. Arriving just before 2pm I popped into Boreham's office to update him. He was primed for action.

'What time did you get to the client's house?'

Oh Jesus, here we go again!

'Don't know. I haven't got a watch.'

Mrs Franks hadn't told me that she had called the office to complain that I hadn't arrived. Before he could continue, I launched into one. I'd had a gutful.

'Look, I worked like a dog until one without being offered a cup of tea or even a glass of water with Mrs Frankenstein hanging around like Hamlet's ghost. Then I packed two boxes of stuff into the car but the nearest parking space I could find was Smithfield Market. So I had to walk back to the office with the two boxes and I'm cream-crackered. I'm going for a sandwich and a beer, or even two, so with respect, can you save the time-keeping lecture until I'm fed and watered.'

I didn't wait for his permission and left, going directly down to The Mitre Tavern for a very late lunch. I heard no more on the subject. Maybe he had reflected that just a few weeks earlier he had insisted that the meeting at Vauxhall was at 8.30am and life is all about quid pro quo; probably not.

By July 1963 I really needed a holiday. I arranged for Max to cover the studio for me and drove down to Cornwall with Patricia on

Tuesday 6 August. We loosely based ourselves in the Lizard but even though it was peak holiday season, the place wasn't crowded and there was plenty to explore. Patricia however never seemed able to relax. Maybe it was me or maybe she hadn't been apart from mother before and missed the daily routine back in the Elephant and Castle. After ten days we took the long lazy road back through Exmoor and Cheddar. No dramas and the car ran without trouble throughout.

On returning to the coalface, I was delighted to learn that I'd been taken off Thursday button factory duty at long last. Instead I was to attend Mr Gould's father's rag trade business in Whitechapel every Friday. The big issue was that I had to make the cheques out for the suppliers and they had to be spot on as there could be no forgiveness for any error. Every trader had a time/discount arrangement and those were sacrosanct. I cannot imagine the angst if a balls-up was made.

On 7 September my friend Colin married Eileen and I was the best man.

My room at Huron Road was working out well for me but as I suspected, the two guys upstairs were taking advantage of the landlady's absence and had skipped payment of the rent. Their gambling had taken hold and it was either feast or famine. I had to turn them down on numerous occasions when asked for a loan.

It all came to a head when the owner returned without warning. She was waiting for me in the hall and although my area was in good order, she was very unhappy at the general state of the place and especially with the condoms floating in the toilet. She asked whether they were mine. No they weren't and no prizes for guessing who were the culprits. Actually it didn't matter as she'd decided to sell the house and gave us notice to leave within the month.

After that she became difficult and unpleasant. The building filled with workmen and then debt collectors started visiting the meat market lads on a daily basis. The aggravation was so heavy that they decamped in the middle of the night, leaving me as the sole tenant. I decided to grab the first place that came along and then after the year's end, take my time to find a decent self-contained flat.

I found a tiny room in a tiny house that was available at 230 Franciscan Road, Tooting. It was so small that the sofa bed when pulled out blocked the door from opening. However, it was clean, the young couple were nice folk and it would serve as a stopgap.

On 2 October I gave notice, paying the rent until the end of the week and moved out on the Saturday. The landlady turned nasty and pushed for more money but I refused on the grounds that she had effectively thrown me out. And that all the time she'd been away I had voluntarily kept the common parts and the bathroom clean without recompense. She threatened to write to my employer and I said write away. End of story.

Where was I when the news of J F Kennedy's death came through on 22 November 1963? I was with Patricia and her mother at their apartment wondering how I was going to bring this relationship, whatever it was, to an end. I felt it would be best to get Christmas and New Year out of the way before dropping the bomb. There was no doubt that Pat and her mother were inseparable. I would always be the third wheel, having to deal on a daily basis with the pink plastic cleaner's apron topped with the ever present fag on the lip. Shame, Pat was a lovely girl but the die was cast.

And so it came to pass. I didn't want a scene in a restaurant or in the apartment, so I picked her up from work, drove her home and explained as decently as I could that living with Dracula's mother wasn't the future I had in mind. Dirty job done, not well, but done. In 1968 she married Albert J Pearce in Southwark and lived in Waterloo, under a mile away from the Elephant and Castle so it all worked out well, I guess.

One weird set of events came to light during my research. I couldn't track down Mr Pearce in later years but Patricia Elizabeth Pearce (60) married Johnson Folorunso Adegun (30) in Southwark in 2005. Then I discovered the wedding of Patricia Elizabeth Cannon, (60) to Johnson Folorunso Adegun (30) in Southwark, also in 2005. Mr Adegun comes from Nigeria. Must be a story there.

When I moved to Tooting I had signed up with a local GP, Dr Joslyn and had been told it was a walk in and take your turn operation rather than by appointment. My throat was giving me hell and I thought it might be the return of tonsillitis. I drove from Acton to the surgery only to be informed that the system had been changed and that all consultations were now by appointment only. The earliest free spot was two days away at 12.10, nothing sooner.

Once again, I drove across from West London and arrived early only to be faced with a mob about thirty strong piled up against the surgery's doors. When these were opened, the crowd fought their way in grabbing the seating like an obscene game of musical chairs. It was standing room only by the time I got in but I had nothing to worry about, I had an appointment.

Walking up to the receptionist I said: 'Good morning, I have an appointment at 12.10, my name is ...'

She cut me off.

'All the appointments are at 12.10, so just sit and wait your turn.'

'There are no seats left.'

'Then stand.'

'What sort of an organisation makes thirty appointments, all at the same time?'

'It works for us, just go and wait.'

By 1pm no one had been seen, in fact no movement of any kind had taken place, so I headed to the old biddy again.

'Excuse me but what's happening here? Has the doctor died and gone to that big surgery in the sky?'

'Enough of your cheek. I have told you, you have to wait.'

'No I don't and tell Dr Joslyn that she'll be hearing from the Medical Council.'

Funny enough, after all that my throat felt better. It was a miracle. I did write to the MC and in due course received the explanation that the doctor had been dealing with an emergency with a baby. My response was that I didn't believe a word and that the whole setup was a disgrace. If a delay arose why couldn't the harridan behind the jump not inform the mug punters waiting to show their filthy diseases to someone else.

There was no doubt in my mind that many of the older medical professionals still resented the changes to their lives that came with the advent of the National Health Service. They treated their patients with little more than contempt. To have completed all the training and examinations and then be stuck with a practice in darkest Tooting with the great unwashed pouring through the door wouldn't be my idea of Shangri-La.

As we moved into 1964, the Intermediate exams that I planned to sit in May were top of my list. As I'd forecast, I had not kept up with the correspondence course papers but had read as much as I could and worked hard on the previous year's tests. Max had been taken ill in the midst of an audit and I was sent to cover. When I walked into the place I suspected foul play on his behalf.

The Coleherne Pub in Old Brompton Road was famous for its 'leather bar' and, like the Vauxhall Tavern, infamous for its clientele. At one time the owners had tried to keep one bar straight and the other bar for the leather boys but this hadn't worked and the whole place was gays from wall to wall.

To get to the offices on the first floor, you were forced to negotiate the crush of bodies and when you did reach the desk allocated, you found an elderly dog asleep underneath. This creature broke wind with great force every ten minutes so exactly that you could set your watch by it and I complained to the bookkeeper.

'The dog will be here when you're long gone and forgotten.'

Fortunately, Max had done all the donkeywork and I had a huge incentive to close it all up in two days and escape, which I did.

The fee of ten guineas for the upcoming examination was paid and two weeks holiday arranged. On the Monday of the first week I awoke with terrible lower back pain and could not even get out of bed. The property owners had both headed off to work so there was no help available. All I could do was lie there and try to work out how or why.

Could it be the put-you-up bed that I slept on or did it go back to an accident years ago in the scrap yard? I couldn't afford to wait eight hours, so eased myself out of the bed onto all fours and turned the contraption back into a settee in order to get the door open. With the aid of an umbrella I reached the bathroom, ran a bath, climbed in and brought it up to the highest temperature I could stand. I kept it like that for an hour before getting out, dressed with great difficulty and struggled down to the car.

I drove over to see my new doctor, Dr Todd. On arrival I had to ask two guys to help lift me out of the car and headed into the surgery doubled up. After a long wait I struggled into the doctor's consulting room.

'What can I do for you Mr Roy?'

I thought it was obvious but explained the morning's events.

'You are a malingerer! There's nothing wrong with you, all you are after is a sick note.'

'No, I don't need a sick note. I'm on study leave.'

'A malingerer, I can't help you.'

I struggled out convinced that the Health Service was not serving the public in the manner that it was designed to do. Painkillers from the chemist plus a couple of hot baths and I could manage to get about but had lost a day. On Tuesday I was able to knuckle down and hone up on my studies. For any future medical needs I would have to go privately.

When three handsome gentlemen visited the office for a meeting with Bill Smith, it got all the female staff extremely excited and probably two or three of the males I suspect. All three had been in groups or bands in the past but two were on the cusp of international fame and fortune as solo artists.

Tom Woodward had taken Tom Jones as his stage name while Gerry Dorsey had transformed into Engelbert Humperdinck and both their careers were on the launch pad. The third man was Gordon Mills, a singer/songwriter, who managed the pair and was the organiser of a new enterprise. Once premises had been acquired in Park Lane, they went stratospheric. Our very own Bill Smith quickly joined them to control the vast sums of money pouring into the coffers.

I was sorry to see Mr Smith leave. He was always polite and made a point of thanking you for your effort, a real pleasure to work for and you gave of your best. This left us with Boreham effectively in charge as Mr Gould tended not to be hands on controlling the workflow which task he left to his subordinates. This did not bode well for me.

My last job for Mr Smith was to head to the home of Spike Milligan in Hampstead, with instructions to complete his tax return. I had no idea what to expect but the reality was that Spike (he didn't like Mr Milligan) was very well organised and the actual task, a piece of cake. The only odd quirk was his reminder at regular intervals not to forget to include his payment to a bird protection charity. I could live with that, no problem. If only all our clients were as affable and organized.

The accountancy exams were to be held in a hall off Holborn Circus, the roof of which I could see from my office window. Lucky me. I could adapt my daily routine: go up to town early, have breakfast, read and then, instead of working, stroll over the road to sit the tests. Magic.

I felt that I had done okay, being very happy with some papers but a little apprehensive on others. In the event, I needn't have worried. Not only did I pass, I came 61st out of 2,191 candidates that meant per se, that I must have been close to a prize in at least one paper. Mr Gould presented me with a Parker pen set.

Doing well was, of course a good thing but it lulled me into a relaxed state where the exams were there for the taking as and when I felt the need. I should have signed up for the next stage but didn't and let it slide.

The same audits came around as in previous years and I tried to get reliable young guys allocated to my jobs. Many times it was insisted that new blood be introduced which slowed down the processes but everybody had to start somewhere; sometimes they took to the work like a duck to water, sometimes they simply sunk without trace.

One of our senior men Tony Hawthorne was poached by Artesania Limited (one of our clients) to be their Chief Financial Officer. The company ran Casa Pupo, a shop in Pimlico selling Spanish and Portuguese carpets and ceramics and the business was taking off.

Tony called me and asked me to come over to discuss a problem. He had an accounts team of five or six but confessed that they couldn't keep pace with the workload and badly needed help. I thought at first that he was about to offer me a job but he asked if I could work there on Saturdays to troubleshoot. We agreed an hourly rate and I started on 8 August.

He was not wrong. The biggest problem was that many customers in the area were accustomed to having an account opened at every store they frequented, even if the purchase was a one-off and they no intention of becoming a regular customer. The sales ledger was accordingly huge and growing like Topsy.

In addition their original shop was now exclusively devoted to tiles. The new corner establishment was being extended with all the associated cost controls. Then there were suppliers to be dealt with, paid and a lot of shop staff to look after. Tony treated me to a fine meal and I needed it as after a ten-hour shift, I had barely scratched the surface.

Casa Pupo was established in the early 60s by Geoffrey Dobson and Jose 'Pupo' Casasus. Apparently Jose's brother Doro was also involved but I never came across him personally. Geoffrey was a very elegant man, a lawyer with a background in advertising and undoubtedly very well connected. Pupo was the artistic one and their creation was perfect for the location and period. By the time I came on the scene they were expanding across the country and into Europe. Shops had been opened in Brighton, Harrogate, Glasgow and other cities. All were successful although I doubted that some areas would sustain interest long into the future.

Geoffrey's personal assistant was a man named John McCulloch who was always smiling. It wasn't a nice smile but rather the 'up yours' smile of a man who had fallen on his feet in a big way. There was also a gorgeous secretary called Susan. Actually the whole place was full of beautiful girls attracted by the shop and its wares. It was a great place to be at that moment in time.

Geoffrey drove a Sunbeam Harrington, a rare beast that was a Sunbeam Alpine with a custom built rear end to celebrate the Le Mans cars. As he was having problems (after all it was a Sunbeam), he traded it in for a Jaguar Mark II. It was impressive in black with a red interior but Pupo freaked out at the prospect of sitting on seats the colour of blood. Accordingly it was dispatched to the trimmers to be recovered in black leather.

The next week I went over on Monday, Wednesday and Friday evenings and put in another long Saturday. But maximum effort barely dented the workload. Physically there was no space to bring in more staff and it was impossible to find another room. Tony could have employed a night shift but the security implications did not bear thinking about.

I had a week's holiday outstanding so I booked this in and put in a six day, sixty hour marathon sharing Tony's very small office. It made an impact but more muscle was needed, and we asked Max if he had the time and the inclination to pitch in. He did.

So my dance card was full. Monday to Friday 9 to 5, Wilson Wright; Tuesday and Thursday evenings at the studio; Saturday plus any other time in the week Casa Pupo. We were given a key to the back door and I can recall 7am starts. One Saturday 'Sales' day it was an 11.30pm finish.

There was no time for girls although I did date a couple of the sales staff and no time for studies. I was making good money but at what cost?

My landlady had given birth and the mood had changed. My room overlooked the back garden and the rear of the houses beyond and I noticed that a brothel had opened up directly opposite. My friend Rod came round to take a look and our noise put my host's noses out of joint. Although an explanation and apology was offered up it was obvious that my marching orders were not far away

Back to the search and I found an ideal billet in Belsize Park. Called a garden flat, in reality it was a semi basement that in the days of yore had been the kitchen area for the big house. It consisted of one large room with a bathroom and a tiny kitchen with full central heating. For the first time I was not sharing a bathroom as it was totally self- contained. The rent was just two pound a month more than I was paying for my tiny unit in Tooting so it was a no brainer.

At the weekend I approached my landlords who were still foul of mood and before I could give them the news they told me that with the arrival of the baby they needed my room. Would I please sling my hook which saved me the job of giving notice. The following Sunday I moved in at 47 Belsize Park Gardens NW3; what a joy to get home, shut the door and not have to worry about the bath time rota.

Life was also changing for my good friend Max. Many years earlier he had been engaged to Margaret but she'd had a change of mind or received a better offer, gone off and married someone else. She gave birth to a son at which point, as I understand it, the husband decamped leaving her bereft. So back she went to Max who asked my advice. Usually I would have had plenty to give but on the subject of affairs of the heart I was out of my depth. I chickened out, telling him that only he could make that decision.

Max had been fostered as a child and lived with three elderly sisters on a public housing estate in Bethnal Green. Now in his early thirties, he was still there. With Margaret back on board all that had to change so he bought an apartment in Thames Ditton and swopped his Sprite for a new Ford Capri. I met Margaret several times, thought she was a lovely woman and a good influence on Max. The lad was a well-mannered boy and it was a pleasure to spend time with him.

My Sprite had been giving grief and it was also time for a change. Seeing an advert for a TVR, I phoned the owner Martin Brewer and asked if he was interested in a swop plus cash for my Austin-Healey. He was agreeable and brought the TVR around to Belsize Park for inspection on Monday 1 February 1965.

It was a Mark IIa 1962 fitted with the MGA 1600cc engine and finished in maroon. He told me it was a factory built lightweight and a test drive confirmed it was years ahead of my Sprite. Two hundred and sixty pounds was agreed, handed over and the deal was done.

A few days before acquiring the TVR, I'd been at the Racing Car Show and a small corner on the Bill Last stand was devoted to the resurrected TVR Car Club. I joined as member number 17 was introduced to Peter Simpson, the Coventry TVR dealer who was to be the club Chairman and the spitting image of Frankie Howerd. A friend at first but turned out to be a real snake in the grass. On the Friday I dropped the TVR over to Boothby and Gordon for a service and to introduce myself. A whole new world was about to open for me.

Squadron Leader James Robert Maitland Boothby was the epitome of a retired RAF officer of the era. He was large of frame, large of voice and very large indeed when it came to personality. Naturally, he sported a huge handlebar moustache, smoked a pipe and drank real ale.

Born in Tavistock in 1917, he joined the RAF in June 1936 and flew Hawker Hurricanes with 85 Squadron in 1939 with rank of Flight Lieutenant. In early 1940 he was involved in a car crash, then saw action in France and awarded the DFC on 31 May 1940. He is recorded as having a possible five kills to his name.

At some point the Luftwaffe bit back and his Hurricane came

down in flames. Badly burned, he was taken to East Grinstead Hospital and treated by Archibald McIndoe, a plastic surgeon from New Zealand. McIndoe was renowned for developing groundbreaking techniques in the treatment and rehabilitation of badly burned aircrew. James told me of lying in bed unable to get his mind to work when a doctor approached him.

'James, I see you smoke a pipe. Well when you light up I want you to remember that you must only strike the match on one side of the matchbox. This is really important.'

So when he fired up next, his brain told him that the doctor had told him something important that he must do. It was that very small thing that triggered his mind to start working again. In 1941 he was promoted to Squadron Leader. After the war he took up car manufacturing with JDM whose cigar tube shape earned it the nickname the Flying Banana. Only eight of these Ford V8 based two-seaters were finished before the enterprise failed.

He had married Sylvia Morris in 1953 and they lived in Hassocks in West Sussex. Brought up in an English family in Argentina, her spoken English was truly beautiful to hear. Sometimes a group of us would descend on her home at some late hour and she was always ready to cook up spaghetti bolognese for unruly visitors.

At the end of the day, Boothby would often lead the way from Reece Mews to The Hereford Arms on Gloucester Road and hold forth on all things motoring. It was a scene immortalised in a 1964 book called *Three cheers for nothing* by Peter Kinsley. He ran the day-to-day workings of The TVR Centre and the factory provided him with a red Mark III Grantura that he used for motor racing as well as his daily commute.

It was only many years later that I discovered the factory had removed The TVR Centre from Boothby & Gordon in October 1964 due to a lack of car sales. The title passed to Paddy Gaston, a TVR racer and dealer in Kingston. In his wisdom, Boothby decided to keep this information to himself, leaving both staff and customers in the dark. In fairness, the factory made no effort to repossess the demonstrator, maybe because the factory was in its usual chaos or they decided that taking the wheels away from a war hero would be really bad karma.

Robbie Gordon was more of a man of mystery and certainly took a back seat in the operation in fact, a long way back. I was told that he was the son of a wealthy Canadian banker and if he did make a crust somewhere it was not disclosed. In his late twenties, he was always well turned out when he arrived at the mews from time to time and always in a different car. I remember a genuine Cobra mainly because I was a passenger in it for a fast and furious ride through the Sussex countryside with Robbie at the wheel. He also had a Fraser Nash Mille Miglia 1953 that was breathtaking.

One Saturday he showed up and on the promise of a lunch pressganged all present into a search for thirty plus Minis that he had purchased and parked at various spots around Kensington. He felt his love for the car had got out of hand and a clear out was needed. Despite the association I never saw him in a TVR.

Warren Fisher was a very decent young man who worked there as a general factotum. Warren and I hit it off immediately and we became good friends. He was a big help in keeping my car on the road and out of the shop. He lived in Brighton with his father who was totally blind and he worried that he would follow suit. I know the thought depressed him and in later years he hit the bottle in a big way and was only 53 when he died.

The mechanic was a South African called Sean Power. He'd served in the South African army for a time before going off to fight the Mau Mau in Kenya as a mercenary. He was a magician when it came to throwing screwdrivers. His friend Rocky Morrison-Lowey had a similar background and sometimes helped out. A bear of a man he was a Hebridean and, unsurprisingly, both men were nightclub bouncers.

Buying the TVR had done wonders for my social life. Now resprayed by friend Rod in dark blue, I visited Reece Mews as much as work commitments allowed. A group of club race drivers frequently gathered there: Gerry Marshall, John and Peter Wingfield and their fantastic mechanic Percy Levett, Chris Lawrence, Martin Lilley and Mary Wheeler. She hadn't taken up motorsport until she was 49 after the death of her husband and her TVR was almost identical to mine.

Boothby introduced me to The Steering Wheel Club, a great hangout off Curzon Street. The bar was run by Frank and the dining room looked after by his brother with a private room upstairs available for meetings. It was from outside this place that Roy 'the

Weasel' James stole Mike Hawthorne's Jaguar mark 2, his car of choice. Roy was a top notch racing driver but lacking sponsorship he supported his interest by being a top notch getaway driver much in demand for armed robberies. He came unstuck in 1963 when he took part in The Great Train Robbery and I believe it was his fingerprint left at the farm that lead the Old Bill to solving the case.

Now I was in a typical Catch-22 situation. The rapid expansion in my circle of friends and activities needed plenty of spondulicks to support but it really was impossible to put in any more hours working without cutting back on the social whirl.

Casa Pupo was expanding at a frantic pace with new shops being opened both in the UK and abroad but without any additional management being brought in to govern it all. Tony pressed Max and I for more hours and both of us committed to a full Sunday once a month to simply keep pace with the paperwork. I doubt that any meaningful accounting figures were produced on a monthly basis and the directors were reliant on sales reports as their measure of success which carried obvious dangers.

A new girl arrived on the scene early in the year. I met Sally at a party over the holiday period and we went out a few times. She had been engaged but her fiancée collapsed and died at Heathrow Airport from a brain aneurism. I have no reason to disbelieve the story, other than the fact that she was somewhat off the wall. After a few weeks she disappeared from the scene without a word but I remembered that her parents lived on Jersey. I tracked down the phone number and dialled to be answered by a Colonel Blimp voice. My polite enquiry was met by a pompous, abusive and loud response and an order to 'piss off and don't call again'. Before I could protest that his language and attitude were totally uncalled for, he'd slammed the phone down. I never heard from Sally again and think I missed a bullet with that one.

I'd met Janet through her brother Peter and known her for quite some time and she was a really down to earth girl in contrast to Sally. She lived in a ground floor flat off of the Portobello Road and we started to spend time together, nothing too serious, just enjoying each other's company.

Michael moved his studio from Kensington High Street to a large unit in Elvaston Mews. The parking was a million times easier but our working space was very restricted as we were forced to share the reception area. A few doors away there was a horse riding stables that provided mounts for those wishing to ride in Hyde Park. I was there one afternoon when Chipperfield's Circus arrived with a real live fully grown tiger that was to be a backdrop in a fashion shoot. Although the horses couldn't see the animal, they could clearly sense its presence. They were kicking hell out of their stalls as the grooms struggled to calm the panic-stricken beasts. The male model was also far from happy and although assured that the tiger had been fed very well and very recently, demanded and received an additional fee for his troubles.

Under peer pressure, I started to enter hill-climbs in the TVR, the first being at Firle near Brighton. There was a thrill to it all, charging flat out up a hill with a sharp left turn at the top but that was dampened by thoughts of the cost and inconvenience of damaging my only means of transport. I didn't come first and I didn't come last, which set up the pattern of my short career as an amateur clubman.

My day job continued much as before. The audits came around each year at the same times and the trick was to get the guys you wanted and avoid the lightweights. One Nigerian called Charlie Otabo was generally okay but he had this fixation with London bus routes. His social conversation revolved around which bus ran where, so unless a transport guru was required, he was to be avoided.

Around that time, I was in the reception when Mr Gould returned from wherever looking exasperated. I asked him if he was all right.

'Some clients are just impossible.'

'Who's that?'

'Ralph Hilton. He's just told me that he's bought another transport company without even consulting us, so there's no chance for us to do due diligence. Seems he just plucked a figure out of the air.'

I bit my tongue and left him to retreat to his office. Maybe he asked the Richardson brothers to go round and make an offer that couldn't be refused. Having seen a little of the business, my gut feeling was that Mr Hilton's approach would create serious problems for the firm. And my gut would be proved right.

In September 1965 the TVR factory closed and an administrator appointed. This was the third time in seven years, during which several companies, boards of directors, investors, entrepreneurs and some total chancers had tried to get the finances of the small quality car manufacturing under control. Seemingly a dock strike in the USA that trapped a batch of exported cars was the last straw.

An important project under development at that time was the Trident. Designed by Trevor Fiore (was Frost) and developed in Italy by Fissore, two prototypes were at the Blackpool works and two were in Italy. Great confusion reigned over actual ownership with a queue of people owed money. Many claimed that under English Law, ownership is not transferred until payment has been received.

The East Anglian dealer Bill Last arranged a meeting with Peter Simpson and Nadine Hoyle. As well as being the company secretary at the time of the closure, she was a personal friend of Simpson and the Italians, who thought the whole thing was 'official'. No detailed explanation as to what happened has been made but Last came out in possession of the Trident project and went on to manufacture over a hundred vehicles. Trust Simpson to be involved in that nefarious activity.

Martin Lilley saved the day for TVR by buying the business from the administrator with his father's support but was shocked to find that Trident had disappeared. He's been quoted as saying: 'we thought we'd bought the Trident but a certain bunch of people who shall be nameless, took a lot of stuff away with them'.

If your appetite for the whole convoluted history of the TVR has been wetted, then I recommend a series of books on the subject by Peter Filby (Autocraft Books) and *TVR: Ever the Extrovert* by Russell Hayes. But I've digressed.

One aspect common to many people's lives is that at some stage, we have all made a really minor decision that has led to a major change of direction. So it was for me on Friday 10 September 1965. Having finished an audit in West London I decided to call in at Reece Mews on my way back to the office. There were always interesting people about and it was a chance to catch up on what motor sports activities were coming up. I had parked the TVR and was chatting to Warren when I suddenly realized that nobody else was talking and every conversation had dried up. All eyes were on something or someone behind me. Turning, I found myself looking at a beautiful girl dressed in a plain white top and jeans but without shoes. I knew that it was a current fashion but maybe it wasn't such a great idea on the oily cobblestones of the mews. A young guy was close behind.

I was caught, hook, line and sinker. The escort was another South African and a friend of Sean and Rocky but being much younger, didn't share their military background. A party on Saturday night was mentioned and I knew that I wouldn't miss it. Knowing my little friend back at base would be looking for me, I asked Warren to find out what he could and drove off.

The party was in a basement flat in Kensington and I took Janet along but managed to exchange a few words with the new object of my desires, Rosemary. The evening was spoiled when several men complained that their wallets were missing from their jackets that they'd hung in the hallway. I suggested that they look in the cistern in the toilet as from past experience it seemed to be the favourite place for dumping empty wallets and purses. I was right, which caused a few suspicious looks to come my way. The worst gent affected was a Colombian guy who worked in security at his embassy who had lost his licence to carry a firearm when on duty. We had to take him to the police to report it and then to his embassy where we left him. What a night but at least I had managed to put a stake in the ground.

A couple of days later Janet left for a two week holiday in Spain with friends.

The next two weeks were a blur. It transpired that Sean and Rocky weren't great admirers of the boyfriend. They were happy to join in any conspiracy to help me to usurp him and proved to be a fount of knowledge and information.

Rosemary was nineteen, shared a flat in Cranley Gardens with Cherry and was a secretary. Rumour was that she came from a once wealthy family that had lost a lot but were still in better straits than most.

I think the breakthrough came when after a couple of hours at the pub one evening Boothby suggested that we all drove down to his home near Brighton to share a spaghetti bowl. I had the TVR and my rival was on Shank's Pony. It took but a moment to ease her into the passenger seat not only for a run down to Hassocks and back but to what was to be the very best of times and the very worst.

When Janet returned home I was waiting for her on her doorstep and simply told her that I believed that I had found the love of my life. It left her in the lurch, which was a lousy thing to do and I doubt that I did it very well. But I have always believed that people should not be messed about and if there is something that needs doing, then grasp the nettle and get it done. Don't mess folk about, tell the truth and deal with whatever falls as best you can.

To put a little flesh on the bones, Rosemary Smethurst came from just outside Grimsby and her family had been big in the fishing industry although her father Michael was now an egg farmer. She had three younger siblings, Jackie, John and Bill; her mother had died and she had a stepmother called Jane. Soon after we got together I asked if one weekend we could drive up to meet her family. She explained that Jane had banned her from the house. I wondered why.

The difference in our backgrounds could not have been more pronounced. My formative years had been a raggedy-arsed struggle against the odds whereas Rosemary had enjoyed an idyllic upbringing in the English countryside.

After primary school she had attended Cleethorpes Girls Grammar where she'd obtained a shedload of A and O levels, topped off with a stint at St Godric's Secretarial College in London. Her home in a Lincolnshire village was picture postcard with a solid family background and plenty of exchange student jaunts. The loss of her mother at the age of nine must have been horrendous and the arrival of the stepmother traumatic but overall it was a far cry from the grinding poverty that had been my lot.

As we couldn't visit the old homestead, father Michael came to London. I liked him on sight and my judgement was spot on as he was the kindest and most decent bloke you could ever meet. Too nice I dare to say.

He took us for dinner and brought a Swedish woman along who, I discovered much later, was a psychiatrist. I dread to dwell on what her interpretation of my mental state might have been. I remember being highly nervous and drinking and talking too much. Still, I wasn't warned off so must have passed muster.

Over the next few months I spent a lot of time at the Cranley Gardens apartment. Although I realized that this wasn't fair on Cherry who was forking out half the rent and having to put up with a near permanent visitor. My place was simply not good enough to stay for any amount of time as in addition to being dark it was suffering from a cockroach invasion from the adjoining boiler room.

The landlord refused to acknowledge the situation even after I delivered dead samples to him. I called in the local Council exterminator who told me he couldn't eradicate them but he could drive them out and into the next house. I asked him to crack on.

It was Michael Dunne who offered a solution. His uncle Francis was an author who lived in Italy but happened to own a mews house in Marylebone that he let partially furnished. And at the time it was unoccupied.

We went over to 12 Devonshire Mews West and found it perfect for our needs: two bedrooms, bathroom, reception and fitted out kitchen. The garages were securely locked and, I assumed, contained Francis' property. Some of the chairs looked and smelled as if someone had died sitting in them but nothing insoluble. The problem was that for this wonderful central little gem the rent was horrendous, eighty quid a month. We couldn't afford it, no way, no how.

As an alternative the whole house was offered to us for eighteen thousand pounds but even if we had lived on fresh air it was impossible. It's a great pity as according to information on the internet today, it's priced in excess of seven million.

Knowing that it would be difficult we still took the plunge, with the safety net that at the worst I could flog the TVR and keep the roof over our heads. I pushed for a pay increase at the day job and raised the hourly rate elsewhere to help the finances but it was still tough. The only thing that really mattered was that we were together and didn't have to share our space. Marylebone is a terrific place to live even if you don't have much money.

Two new clients were passed on to me. The first was Cyril Fraden, a famous South African artist who had recently moved to London. An absolute charmer, he was a pleasure to work with and his records straightforward and complete. Please send me more like him, that's all I ask.

Maybe it was too much to ask as the second newbie was just the opposite. Mr & Mrs Hudson had started up a chauffeur driven car hire firm and their first year's records arrived in two huge laundry bags. Helped by one of the lads, we tipped them out onto the floor.

After taking the betting slips and sweet wrappers out, we were left with a mountain of receipts for petrol, servicing and among the detritus, half a dozen hotel accounts. I made as much sense as I could but was left with no alternative other than talk it over with them to fill in the many gaps. I thought that a perfectly natural question was whether the hotel stuff was accommodation for the drivers whilst working or were they pleasure. Mrs Hudson's reaction was totally unexpected.

'We've never stayed in a hotel together.'

The penny dropped. Moron that he was, Mr Hudson had left the evidence of his bed-hopping in amongst the business stuff for us to stumble on instead of disposing of it where his wife wouldn't find it. I mumbled that my assistant must have made a mistake, cleared up my papers and cleared off sharpish.

Back at base Boreham was waiting, as expected.

'Mr Hudson has complained to me that you have tried to break up his marriage.'

'If anyone breaks up his marriage it will be Mr Hudson. He included six hotel bills with his business paperwork and I considered it a perfectly reasonable question to ask if they were related to the chauffer work or were private. Who in their right mind keeps evidence of extra-marital adventures, which I now assume they were, around to be found. Look, I'll finish the job off and drop it in to you plus the hotel accounts separately for you to see. You can take it from there but I'm making no apology for doing my job.'

It was around this time we nearly lost Max. He had felt very unwell and went to his doctor, only to be told be had indigestion. On leaving the surgery he collapsed in the street and an ambulance was called. Once in A&E he was diagnosed with a burst stomach ulcer and could have died. He spent a week in hospital and then some time in convalescence.

On first hearing the news I rushed over to the hospital in Whitechapel and went every evening together with most of the firm's staff. In order to cover my commitment to the studio, I had gone over there very early in the morning, arriving at the firm around nine rather than my usual eight o'clock start. Boreham caught me as I headed for my room and I was not only worried about my friend but weary and irritable.

'How's Max?'

'Why don't you go over there and see for yourself.'

'It's not on my way home.'

'It's not on my way home either. You should know that all the secretarial staff and all the lads have been in to see him and taken presents. Conspicuous by their absence are the bosses, you and Mr Gould. I think that says it all. Max could have died you know. He's been seriously ill and lucky to survive.'

I didn't wait for a response and just walked away to my office down the corridor. I fully expected a balling out for my impertinence but it never came. Nor did any visitation by the top dogs to the hospital, not even a card. Maybe Max could consider himself fortunate in not getting his marching order cards like poor Mrs Trew.

We carried out some decorations at the flat, bought covers for the seating and threw a small party. Rosemary was still banned from the old homestead so John and Jackie came down to visit us

Soon after we moved in I set up a meeting to bring together the London members of the TVR Club at the Devonshire Arms. Some 25 people turned up with around 15 cars and our President Peter Simpson came down from Coventry with his new wife Hilary who was some sixteen years his junior. They invited us to their home, Motslow Cottage in the tiny village of Motslow, near Stoneleigh. I really thought that we had made a couple of friends. As said, in Peter Simpson's case my judgement was way off. Later he showed himself to be a total bastard and not to be trusted, especially where women were concerned.

It was truly a beautiful spot, the house having been converted from a row of cottages and reached by crossing a small stream. They were very hospitable and over the next few months we met regularly at each other's homes and at motor sport events.

When the season started, I took up the hill climbing again. All went well until I went down to Firle halfway through the year and on the first practice run the TVR's clutch burned out. For some reason Rosemary wasn't with me praise be and as a local garage had sent a tow truck, I asked them to take the car back to their garage and drop me at Brighton station. What really galled me was that my merry Band of Brothers all just buggered off without a word of concern or offer of help. When I finally reached home I had resolved that that was an end to it all and put my racing helmet on the shelf and there it stayed.

Rosemary and I agreed to get married. I didn't do the getting down on one knee bit and as there was no spare cash, there was no engagement ring. But I think that we believed it was the natural progression we both wanted. As Michael's permission was needed, we drove up to Lincolnshire one weekend to ask for it. Jane had absented herself and gone on a golfing trip with female friends. I still had no idea why she and Rosemary had fallen out but she certainly could bare a grudge. I had written a letter of reconciliation to her that had gone unacknowledged and judged that she wanted to milk any last drop of unpleasantness for all it was worth. How correct I was to be proved only too soon.

The family home, Great Coates House in the village of the same name was breathtaking. A huge manor house set in its own grounds with a long gravel drive, it was truly magnificent. In one corner were two large sheds that housed the chickens that produced the eggs. I found out later that the family pile was on a short lease and not owned, confirming that the moneyed days were behind them.

John and Jackie were there, as was the youngest sibling Bill who was about fifteen. He was a real likable lad and much of my time was spent building him a proper Subbuteo table and playing the game for hours on end. I also volunteered to help collect eggs and generally showed willing. I took Michael aside and asked him the big question and he was okay about it. Not thrilled maybe but nodded me past the post.

We picked 3 September 1966, the anniversary of the declaration of war with Germany in 1939. Ominous or what? We decided on a small wedding totally due to cost considerations. We had next to nothing and I was sure that Michael wasn't going through a purple patch. Marylebone Registry Office was chosen, a reception arranged and some thirty people invited. I could not have been happier as this was a commitment I really wanted to enter into with all my heart.

At Wilson Wright there were changes in personnel. Mr Smith's office remained empty, waiting for a new partner who never arrived. My office next door was a three desk affair but for some months I had been the only occupant. I was now joined by an Indian geezer named Gagan Patel who was always very smartly dressed and to my mind every inch a nark. We had a couple of Indian lads working there and we got on very well but I could see this bloke running down to Boreham with any tittle-tattle he happened upon. So any personal stuff would be dealt with in his absence and I warned my intimates to be careful when around him.

Also more Mediterranean boys arrived. It was beyond me why these youngsters were taken on as none showed any real interest in learning anything. They were simply following their parent's directives to go into accountancy. It was as though they were just filling in the time but like Mehet in the past, in the eyes of the management they could do no wrong.

Amon Papadopoulos was older than the usual recruit and his hand-made clothing indicated great wealth. His family owned a chain of fish and chip shops and his wedding present from his parents was a house in Finchley; his in-laws gifted the furniture, appliances and two new cars. Rumour had it that he was destined to take over the finances of the chippy empire and he was with Wilson Wright to learn how in double short time. Whether he was paid or not, I didn't know but he stayed out of my orbit until a fateful day in August 1966.

I had been scheduled to set off for the wilderness of Colindale on 8 August to carry out the audit of New Art. The weekly visit guys had fallen behind with the annual summaries and I expected this would take some six days to get to finish even with Ian Keller helping me.

At the same time I was responsible for the audit at a catering supplies firm in Vauxhall. I had asked Eital to take a junior and undertake the routine work and told him that I would get over there straight after New Art, probably on Tuesday to finalise everything.

On Friday 5th, Boreham summoned me to his office. He had arranged that we would start the annual audit of Greville Tinners on the Monday as well. I protested that I had two jobs starting on that day and could this not be put off for a couple of weeks. No it could not. I was to take Amon and two lads and introduce them to the client.

'It will be good experience for them.'

'Listen,' I protested, 'I don't know these guys or their standard of work and experience. Why can't I pick a team that I know I can rely on.'

'No more argument, meet them there, set them up and then join Ian at New Art.'

Three jobs on my plate all over London while the favoured sons sit around the office picking their teeth, scratching their arses and watching the clock go round.

On Monday morning the two juniors arrived on time more or less but Amon strolled in just before ten looking like he had come directly from Savile Row. It was obvious that he deeply resented being removed from his comfortable slot back at base and forced to travel to this run-down dump. I introduced them to the bookkeeper, explained that they were to go through the audit programme and that they should find everything straightforward as the books were balanced.

'Once that's all done, then organise the summations to enable a trial balance to be produced.'

Sounds technical but it was absolute bread and butter to accountancy at that time.

'If you're not sure, simply look at what was done in the previous year and copy the formula.'

Not a word was said in response.

'If anything does arise that you can't deal with, call the office and they'll find me.'

Still no response, so I left to hurry north to join Ian.

For the next few days we worked like dogs amid the roar of the button factory and managed to finish on the following Monday as planned. I asked Ian to take the finished job in to Boreham on the Tuesday morning while I headed south to join Eital who I found was closing as I'd expected. Everything was parcelled up by lunchtime on Wednesday so we ate at the local greasy spoon, Eital headed back to the office and I went west to find what awaited me at Greville Tinners, arriving around 2pm.

The three stooges were exactly as I had left them. I asked for the audit programme and was shocked to find that it was totally blank. I looked at Amon who handed me a large set of papers without a word. My hopes rose as it seemed they had finished the work without my assistance. I took the offering and opened it only to find that they had simply copied the previous year's audit paperwork. They had taken my word copy as gospel.

We were eight days into the audit with nothing whatsoever to show. Straightaway I knew it would be a disaster if the client found out what had happened although the bookkeeper must have known something was wrong. My team had just sat at the table day after day without going into the accounts office even once and without looking at a book we can't carry out an audit. The firm's reputation was at stake here.

Thinking on my feet I told the three of them to return to the office and the minute they were gone I put in a call to Ian Keller.

'Ian, don't say a single word, just listen. I'm at Greville Tinners and am in deep shite. Can you drop everything and join me here at nine tomorrow morning? I need help. Just say yes or no.'

Spontaneously, we shook verbal hands.

'Yes.'

'Good man, I'm counting on you.'

Ian was the best we had. Street wise, he was quick on his feet and when the chips were down I knew he wouldn't flap. We had two days to pull this off and although the client might well suspect that something strange was going on, he wouldn't know exactly what.

Good as gold, Ian arrived early. I told him what had happened and where we were. He was astonished and like me, could not believe that knowing they couldn't cope they didn't make a call for someone to be sent to guide them.

'We can't show the slightest sign of panic or rush about, so we move around quietly in a professional manner. We've got two days to do two weeks work and can't let the firm down at any price.'

I had made a start in what was left of Wednesday afternoon. We couldn't cut any corners as we were responsible for undertaking an audit but from previous experience I knew these folk were as straight as a die. There appeared to be little interchange between the staff, no chitchat, no personal telephone calls; all social activity stopped at the door. Ian and I would have to do everything at double speed and to keep ourselves going we would live on a diet of chocolate and fizzy drinks from the shop opposite. By Friday morning we could see the light at the end of the tunnel. But this job would have a sting in the tail and it just kept on giving.

At lunchtime a few office staff drifted into the retired staff canteen where we worked, to sit at one of the twenty tables and eat their brought-in lunches. They didn't bother us and we didn't bother them. At the table nearest us sat one of the directors, I think Mr Barrett, although in line with the library-like ambience of the place, he had never spoken a word to me, let alone introduced himself. This was about to change.

When he'd finished eating, he stood, looked over at us and I caught his eye.

'You're a bloody selfish bastard,' he shouted.

Nonplussed, I replied, 'Sorry, I don't understand. What have I done?'

'You're a bloody selfish bastard,' he repeated.

'I don't understand, what has happened?'

'You know full well. You are sitting at the girls' table, that's where they like to sit every day.'

'I'm sorry if we're sitting at the wrong table but we had no way of knowing that this was the girls' table unless we were told. We simply took a table near the window. If someone had just mentioned it we would of course sat somewhere else.'

It was obvious that he wasn't interested in what I said and as he turned on his heel he shouted one more time.

'You're a selfish bastard.'

Ian and I looked at each other in despair.

'Ain't this job hard enough without getting abused?'

Still, nil bastardum carborundum. We pressed on. By the end of the afternoon we had covered all the ground but it would need a day over the weekend to get the finished accounts out. But no matter as it seemed the client would never realise what had taken place and our problems would stay in-house. I dropped Ian off at a station, drove home and crashed.

I awoke on Saturday with the mother of all migraines; the first ever and I hope, the last. My guess was the result of a combination of stress with an overload of chocolate and cokes. Spending the day in a darkened room did the trick and I spent Sunday pulling the accounts together for submission on Monday morning.

I arrived before 8am as usual checked the work. I waited until Boreham was served his tea at around 9.30 and walked into the lion's den. Now I'd never expected a red carpet or a brass band but I was certainly unprepared for the reception that awaited me.

'Morning. Greville Tinners,' I said, placing the accounts on his desk. 'And not without some drama.'

'So I have heard. Tell me about the table and chairs.'

'Don't tell me that idiot phoned you about that? It was nothing, a storm in a teacup. What I want to talk about is twenty four days totally wasted.'

'I am not interested in any of that and you are forbidden to talk to anyone about it. Tell me what happened with the table and chairs.'

'Forbidden, you say, to talk to anyone. What about my lawyer?'

'You haven't got a lawyer.'

'That's my next move. You insisted on lumbering me with three chumps who sat for eight days without producing a single scrap of usable work. Ian and I knocked our tripes out saving this firm's reputation ...'

Boreham cut me short.

'I'm not interested in any of that; tell me about the table and chairs.'

'Why didn't Amon call me, or even you, if he was out of his depth.'

He ignored the question.

'You mustn't talk about Amon. His family is very influential.'

'Influential? They own a chain of fish and chip shops! Their influence stops at the gates of Billingsgate Fish Market.'

'You are forbidden to talk about him, speak to him or to discuss any of this.'

The penny dropped.

'I know what's going on. You think if you mollycoddle him now, that when he's CFO you'll get the audit. Don't delude yourself. Greek businesses employ Greek accountants. Your chance of getting the job is between no chance and fat chance.'

'Tell me what happened with the table and chairs.'

'Okay, okay. We were working in what used to be a staff canteen in the distant past. A staff canteen that still has about twenty sets of tables and chairs to choose from. We simply sat at one next to the window without a thought. Why would we have one? One table is much the same as another. Then on Friday, the director shouts abuse at us for sitting at the girls' favourite table. I apologised and tried to explain that we had no way of knowing that this table was anybody's special table. And if we had been told, we would have sat somewhere else. Frankly coming on top of everything else …'

Cut off once again

'Tell me again with more detail.'

'You want a different version? Okay. Ian and I were having so much fun and we thought that it would be really mischievous and jolly to sit at the girls' table. Naturally, we're both mind-readers as well as being accountants.'

'Tell me what happened'

'I've told you, and I suggest you go to Ian and thank him for his efforts.'

'It's none of your business what I do.'

'Let me tell you this, if you make any attempt to cut short my Articles you will regret it. That's a gold plated promise. How you justify your extreme actions to my Institute because I sat in the wrong chair will be really interesting.'

I had always been capable of turning a disaster into a success and a plan was forming in my head as the exchange roared back and forth.

By now Boreham had risen from his chair and moved to the window. He was a man so full of snot that he could have choked himself but for all his bluster he was just a Battersea boy.

'Don't you ever think of looking out for your staff? Why are you always so ready to throw us under the bus where the client is concerned? Don't you see the bloody absurdity of all this? All the tables and chairs are identical and unless there was a reserved sign there was no way of us knowing that one set was out of bounds. I pull in over thirty two thousand in fees all on twenty quid a week, Max is next with eighteen and Phillip with fourteen and the rest can muster a few more grand between them. And here I am, after seven years of service, being threatened with the sack for sitting in the wrong chair.'

'How do you know those figures?'

'Because it's what I do for a living. I don't work in the dark. Knowledge is power, as my friend Charlie Richardson might tell you.'

Silence. So I laid out my stall.

'I tell you what. I would rather wear a dead man's shoes than work for you one more day than I have to. The moment my Articles finish, I will walk out of this place never to look back. That suit you?'

He was totally surprised but before he could answer, I turned and headed for the door. As I grasped the handle, I called over my shoulder.

'Now you can phone Barrett and tell him you have fired me for sitting in the wrong chair, two weeks before my wedding.'

As I walked out I could see that the reception door was open a smidgen and figures behind the frosted glass. We had an audience and I couldn't resist playing it.

Halfway into the corridor, I popped my head back into the office.

'And after lunch, why not pop over there and kiss his arse.'

I shut the door and scuttled towards my office, hearing the phone already ringing. I continued past, down the back staircase and into the fresh air of Holborn.

Why didn't I take the whole mess directly to Mr Gould who was both owner and the boss? After all, Boreham was just the manager. It's the East London background which never leaves you. You don't grass, or tell tales. You deal with your problems directly, face to face and don't go crying for help. It's not a code of honour or badge of morality, it is just how it is and it stays with you all your life. And

Boreham knew that.

That evening I told Rosemary what had occurred and of the plan that I'd formulated in my head earlier that day. She was incredulous hearing at what had happened but agreed with my reasoning: that the most important thing in my life, in our life, was for me to complete my examinations, without which I would never get to the top level of the profession. My Articles would finish on Friday 10 February 1967, some five months away.

Emil Wolfe ran a six week course prior to each examination which was designed to prepare every student for what was directly ahead but it was not a substitute for the completion of the correspondence course. Since the Intermediate exam I had not done a stroke of work towards the two tests needed to become a Chartered Accountant, so it was going to be a massive gamble but I was sure it could be done. Instead of getting a proper job I would continue with Michael Dunne Studio and Casa Pupo and fill in with temporary work as a contractor with Harrison Willis the employment and supply agency.

Sacrifices would have to be made for the greater good. The TVR would have to be sold but the really hard part was that we would have to find a cheaper place to live. Rosemary was unhappy about the last bit but could see the logic of it all. As far as I was concerned, 1967 would be the year that would be make or break.

Ian came to see me the next morning. He was rather puzzled that nobody had spoken to him after he'd pulled hot coals from the fire. Like me, he'd expected a little glad-handing and a 'well done' here and there and couldn't believe the clamour of yesterday's shouting match. Before he could speak I told him that I would come and see him later about an audit coming up and ushered him out. I didn't want to have any conversation in the presence of Gagan.

I took him for lunch at the Noshery in Greville Street to thank him for his efforts of the previous week and express my sadness that they had not been recognised elsewhere. I suggested that we speak no more on the matter and told him in confidence of my plans.

At the end of that day Boreham attempted to reassert his stamp of authority. As I was leaving the office with other staff, he appeared at his office door.

'Peter, be here at 8.30 tomorrow. The catering client is coming in at 9.00 and I want to go over the file with you.'

I carried on walking towards the stairs without breaking stride.

This was a power play set up in front of witnesses but it had holes. Firstly, after all these years he didn't even know I was in the office at 8.00 every morning. And secondly, he had never needed to go over a file with me. What was presented was always topped with a discussion sheet that outlined all matters needing the client's attention.

The next morning I arrived as usual but instead of grabbing a sandwich and heading in, I sat down in the café for a full English with several cups of tea. I timed my arrival at the office for exactly 9.00 and passed Boreham's office with a bunch of guys and girls.

'I told you to be here by 8.30.'

Again without breaking my stride I replied, 'My hours are nine to five'.

He didn't respond. He knew that he had more to lose than me in a public row. I had resigned and truly had nothing to lose but my blood burned with the unfairness of it all. I'd enjoyed working at Wilson Wright and had never thought of moving on but now my hand had been forced, I would make a positive out of it.

Our wedding day arrived and we duly attended Marylebone Registry Office to tie the knot. Michael had arranged a handsome reception and brought Rosemary's siblings Jackie, John and Bill down from Lincolnshire. Some thirty odd friends turned up and for me, it was a wonderful day. Incidentally, Mandy Rice-Davies, who was central to the Profumo Affair, married Rafi Shauli at that same spot the previous week and the photographers were the grubs of Fleet Street. Our cameramen were the crew from the studio and Michael Dunne amazed us with the gift of a two-week, all expenses paid honeymoon in Amalfi, Italy.

Notable by her absence was stepmother Jane. I still had no idea what her beef was with Rosemary but it was going to be allowed to fester forever if she had anything to do with it. So, here I was, newly married and about to become unemployed; love on the dole maybe.

Never having been overseas before, the trip was an eye opener for me. Rosemary took it in her stride having been an exchange student to both France and Germany whilst at school and was pretty fluent in both languages. The TVR was sold for five hundred quid and a Mini estate (a Woodie) acquired and what a great little workhorse that proved to be.

To our amazement, Jane had decided to bury the hatchet, at least for now and we were invited to Great Coates for Christmas. Some twenty years younger than Michael, she made it clear that in her world it was her way or the highway. I did respect the fact that she had taken on another woman's four children but apart from that I thought she was a really unpleasant piece of work. And only too easy to fall out with.

I didn't discuss the situation with my fellow workers, not because it was verboten but because it was so fatuous it wasn't worth spending time on. Everyone knew anyway and I was given a show of silent support when Max and five of the London lads resigned one by one.

As we moved into 1967 a bunch of replacements bailed up, including a couple destined to become future partners. I have no idea what Mr Gould was told but he never asked to speak to me so I can only guess it was a load of cobblers. On my last day I tested out Gagan with a bad joke and, low and behold, five minutes later I get the call. Boreham is telling me that I must apologise to Gagan as my joke had upset him, all within hours of my departure. Wot a laugh it all was.

At 5pm I was gone. No goodbyes, no handshakes, no nothing. I had invited most of the staff to a party at my house which finished up at 5am on Saturday morning, so I guess we can call that a success.

Looking back, the whole business reminds me of a quote by Richie Norton, author of *The Power of Starting Something Stupid.*

'You can be the most productive and the most effective, but politics show up as ego, jealousy and sabotage from bosses who can't perform.'

Postscript: Greville Tinners went into liquidation at the end of 1981.

6 JOURNEYMAN

'Without ambition one starts nothing. Without work one finishes nothing. The prize will not be sent to you. You have to win it.'

Ralph Waldo Emerson

On Monday 13 February 1967, I headed out to my first contract job at CBS Records in Theobalds Road. I was directed up to the first floor where the accounts department was situated. A dozen staffers were working away and I was told that my contact was in one of the three glass fronted rooms at the far end, each of which contained two qualified accountants. I later discovered that the CFO had an office on the ground floor because he was disabled and there was no lift. I often wondered if he knew what went on above his head.

I finally found the right guy, shook hands and asked how I could help.

'We need you to assist with the end of year figures.'

I was a little surprised as there seemed plenty of hands on board but it wasn't my business.

'You can start with the bank reconciliation.'

'Fine, when was it last done?'

'Last year.'

'When last year? November?'

'No, last year end.'

'It's not been done for twelve months?'

'Does that bother you?'

'Not at all, where do I work?'

'There's a spare table over there, here's the cash book; the bank statements are in that box.'

Indeed they were, all still in the original envelopes. This was a serious major corporation, yet no one had looked at the bank situation for a year. Hell's bells, how did anyone know how the business was tracking?

I found my table, sorted the statements into order and started in; it was a huge job and every month took at least a day. When I did finish, I was told to summarise and analyse, which took me into week three.

It was fair to say the atmosphere was toxic. The six musketeers spent their time moving between the three offices and no actual productive work seemed to be undertaken. There was zero interchange between them and the clerks around me and it was obvious that everybody resented my presence. Nobody asked me what my name was or offered their name.

After six solid weeks without lunch breaks, I had broken the back of the annual preparations and moved on. The place was soulless but it had been very good money.

During this period we had moved to an apartment in Golders Green which was a fraction of the rent of the mews place. It was a self-contained one bedroom unit and its main drawback was that the kitchen was tiny. It was planned to be an interim stop while I hopefully completed my examinations and it was close to the station. So overall, I was happy with the place. However I found out much later that Rosemary hated it and probably felt she was moving down in the world.

The refresher course was held in the City and for Final One there were some twenty students. A few had completed the correspondence course and were there to make certain of success. But the majority was less well prepared and for a few people like me, this was their only hope. It could not have been more professional and I really concentrated as hard as I could. And then topped and tailed each day and weekends with solid study. It was hard yakka.

May arrived and the tests were to be held at Alexandra Palace. I just prayed that the Mini didn't let me down. We got off to a shocking start when after a few minutes into the first paper the girl at the next desk passed out and fell off her chair, just missing me. I felt sorry for her but also sorry for me as it was a hell of a distraction. At the end of it all I felt that I had done as well as I could have expected and signed on with Emil Wolfe for Final Two in November. The result came through quickly: I had passed.

Back to freelancing and I worked throughout the summer all over London. There was no shortage of work and at good rates but all unmemorable.

I took Rosemary to Paris for her twenty-first birthday which was the best I could do at the time.

Autumn saw me returning to Mr Wolfe's classes and again with about twenty people. Two stood out: we had the UK's tallest man as a student who stood at well over two metres and a real show-off woman who drove us all up the wall including the teachers. It was all more of the same except for statistics. That was totally new for me and hard to get my head around.

In November it was back to Alexandra Palace. I felt that I had done enough on everything apart from statistics and was so concerned that I drove down to see Mr Wolfe and show him the paper. He agreed that it was very difficult but suggested that a score over twenty would get me through. I need not have worried; the gamble had paid off and I'd passed.

When I received the paperwork to apply to become a member of The Institute of Chartered Accountants, I was horrified to find that it had to be signed off by both Mr Gould and my old sparring partner Mr Hodgson. I sent off a couple of obsequious missives and to my great relief they both returned the necessary reference without comment.

As soon as I'd finished the exams, I phoned my agent and was told to get over to GKN in Ealing as they needed all the troops he could find. He explained that they manufactured scaffolding equipment that they sold and hired out through ninety-two branches. What had gone wrong was a new accounting (too early for computers) system that had been designed to keep track of every nut and bolt. But when the button was pushed to print out the end of year position, all the stock figures had come out negative. As far as I can work out you can have some stock or no stock but you cannot physically have minus stock.

When I turned up I found an office with a dozen regular staff and six freelancers. I was given a desk with an adding machine, a pile of work sheets and told to check the additions. I dived in. The first hundred sheets were perfectly accurate, as were the second hundred and so on. When finished I exchanged these for a fresh batch and it seemed that this work could go on ad infinitum. Over the next few days more guys appeared, decorators' tables were set up in the corridors and we were asked if we could work weekends. Casa Pupo still took my Saturdays but a Sunday shift would help my finances no end.

Christmas came and once again we were invited to Great Coates. Michael was relieved that my exams were out of the way and that his daughter had not married a complete dead beat. Jane was her usual unhappy self, never smiling, quick and dirty with her criticisms. It was clear that she did not like me or my type but it was wholly mutual.

Back in Ealing the madness went on and there was talk of setting up a demountable in the car park to enable more bodies to be brought in. None of us did anything else but collect a pile of sheets, check the casts, return them and collect a fresh batch. On Friday you got a signature on your time sheet, posted it and a big fat cheque would land on the doormat in a couple of days.

Now my accounting mind suggests that if you have a million pages to check and not a single mistake is found in the first ten or twenty thousand, then the problem, whatever it is, lies elsewhere. For the first time in my life, and the last, I was working without the faintest idea of what I was doing or why. Money was being poured down the toilet. I never saw or heard anyone senior, just clerks hauling masses of paperwork from somewhere and after processing hauling them away again. After two months I was going crazy; I called my agent and told him he had to get me out of there.

The Mini had been playing up and had broken down on Christmas Eve during our trip north. Miraculously we found a small garage that was still open who could fix it and get us on our way.

After all my hard work I felt that I deserved a proper car. After discussions with my friend Percy Levitt, I bought a 1966 Alfa Romeo GTV 1.6 for £500 plus the Mini from a dealer in Grosvenor Crescent Mews. Even though it was not very old the driver's door around the handle had rusted through and part of the deal was that a brand new door would be supplied. It turned out to be the best driver's car I ever owned.

In mid-January I was able to escape the Ealing farce and on 17 January 1968 signed in as a contractor with Cartwright Scruton Trup, a local firm of accountants in Totteridge. It was a very happy place to work and in the main, I was used to heading up the larger audits such as Station Garages Group, a clothing manufacturer and local businesses.

There was a flash of high drama at the studio when it transpired that Arlene was madly in love with Ali, a photographer's assistant. Apparently they had abandoned their respective spouses and families and fled. Rosemary worked there for a while but that ended literally in tears.

As far as I was concerned, at the time everything seemed to be fine at 10 Templars Avenue. The manic working and studying for seven days a week had ended, there was enough money rolling in to run a really nice car and live well. We often attended Alfa Club functions and ate out regularly. My plan was to secure a proper job, then start our house search before the year end, not realising how unhappy Rosemary was with our current home. Now she was working for an advertising agency in the West End.

When summer arrived I just couldn't find a way to get time off, so suggested that she took the Alfa and travelled up to her family home for a couple of weeks to visit family and friends. She hit a pair of pheasants on her way north but without any damage except to the birds. I was glad to see that she and Jane were at least on speaking terms but I knew instinctively that Jane would be a source of trouble at some time. If I was asked for one word to describe her, it would be vindictive.

Asked to carry out the annual audit of a client in the Stockwell Road, South London, I chose a couple of juniors and headed off. Walking up to the first floor we were met by Alan the bookkeeper who was the son of the owner. After the initial handshakes we were directed to a table. Alan informed us that he was a very successful gambler, producing from his pocket a wad of notes thick enough to choke a donkey.

Alarm bells were ringing and his constant disappearances to the bookmaker next door did nothing to allay my fears. When we left for lunch we discussed the situation and agreed there were all the signs of fingers in the till.

Bell & Co was a major building firm and well established. The books were in good shape, and after a few days of thorough checking, we uncovered nothing of any concern. But when that Achilles' heel of many a business, the petty cash was completed, it was over six grand short. This was at a time when that sort of money would buy you a very nice house.

How did Alan think he could get away with it? We may have been cabbage looking but we weren't green. My guess was that he was laying down some big bets to make up for previous losses but experience dictates that it never works. It simply makes the hole you are digging deeper and deeper. However this was all above my pay grade so I made a call from outside to John Cartwright asking if we could meet the next morning, on Saturday. He told the three of us to visit his home at 10am.

The matter was laid out with confirmation that all three of us had checked our results and agreed on the shortfall. We had completed the accounts that had shown a very good profit even after the missing dosh. He told us to leave it with him and he would arrange a meeting with the owner. We heard nothing more, so Alan probably got off with a bollocking from his father and the losses written off to experience.

As summer approached big changes were happening in the firm. The senior manager Mike Hurst, a couple of other guys and I were offered partnerships. I turned it down having decided that it was time to find a permanent position with solid prospects and told them that my last day would be 30 August.

I'm not sure of the order of things but Scruton and Trup left to move to Spain and become involved in the property industry there. Cartwright left to take up the position of CFO at Sandell Perkins the massive builders merchants in Pimlico. Mike Hurst became senior partner and the whole shebang moved to Barnet.

Through my agent's introduction I had a job to go to but I had postponed the start date in order to get a holiday. Saffery & Sons were a firm of accountants based near St Paul's and I was very impressed at the interview with Mr Jones who was one of the partners. The whole setup looked very smart and I was offered a position of Senior Audit Manager with an excellent salary to boot. Naturally I accepted and we had agreed on a starting date of Monday 23 September.

Max had experienced a difficult year. Under pressure from his girlfriend he had sold his apartment and bought a house in Surbiton close to the station and the practice he had set up after leaving Wilson Wright. Recently she had gone off with another geezer and left him adrift. Rosemary suggested that we drive to Italy and ask Max if he'd like to join us for the three-week break. He accepted.

On Sunday 1 September we set out, driving down to Lydd Airport and flying to Le Touquet. We motored across France, through Paris and on to the Swiss border by evening. The next day we stopped south of Milan and on day three set off for our first destination, Orbetello.

The reason for aiming for this remote spot was financial. Michael Dunne had been shooting near Rome and had left some excess cash for us with his uncle Francis who lived in Orbetello. Yes, this was the same uncle who'd been our landlord when we lived in Marylebone. He went to the Taverna at noon every day and so would be easy to find.

We were actually heading for the island of Monte Argentario where I expected to find a fishing village in which to stay. More appropriately, it should be called a peninsula as it's joined to the mainland by three causeways. Orbetello is on the middle strip of land and looked like a perfect location for a spaghetti western: dogs lying about in the dust, dirty ragged kids staring at us and the occasional morose villager giving us the evil eye. We found our meeting place at 11.45 and ordered a carafe of Frascati and dead on the stroke the door opened and a sullen elderly Englishman entered.

We introduced ourselves but he went straight to a bar stool without accepting our proffered handshakes. A drink appeared in front of him without a word being spoken. I kicked off what was to be a short exchange.

'Michael Dunne told me that he has left some cash for us with you.'

'Yes, he did,' he mumbled.

'Well, can I have it please.'

'Spent it.'

'You can't have. It's not yours to spend and we're depending on that cash.'

During this brief exchange the glass of red had been drained and replaced. It didn't take rocket science to see where our money had gone. We all realised that we had been screwed over but there was nothing to be done. This little weasel was related to someone we held in high esteem otherwise I think that he would have been joining the dogs lying in the dusty road outside. Without looking up from his glass, a crooked grin appeared on his face.

'After all, this is Italy.'

We drove away to the island where a second shock was waiting for us. Porto Santo Stefano was not the sleepy fishing village we had expected. Rather, it was like a miniature version of Monte Carlo with wall-to-wall beautiful people and fabulous cars; too rich for our blood, especially after our recent experience. We retraced our steps to the mainland and drove south until we reached Anzio. A lovely beach caught our eye where we spotted a trattoria and pension opposite next to a hotel. As we had lunch there, Rosemary asked if they had any rooms available. They were actually full but by moving the two children into the parent's bedroom, they could give us their room.

When I went out to the car that we'd parked in the hotel car park, I found that it had been broken into; they had stolen the radio, spare wheel, tools and box of parts. For practical purposes it would have been easier if the robbers had taken the whole car.

I reported this to mine host and we set off for the police station, stopping at the post office to acquire a stamped paper essential in the making of a statutory declaration. We couldn't understand much of the proceedings except for the phrase that was still ringing in our ears.

'This is Italy,' always accompanied by a shrug of the shoulders.

The place was rustic to say the least and cold showers were the order of the day. If you turned the hot switch, sparks flew and electrocution was a real possibility. The meals provided took on a predicable pattern but the beach compensated for any hardships. We fared better than the guests at the hotel where the food was barely bloody edible.

After two weeks we paid our bill and headed north. I think the family felt guilty at our prospect of a long drive home without a spare wheel, tools or parts and they lent us a chunk of cash that we repaid at the earliest possible moment. When we reached Basel we dropped Max at the airport as he needed to get back a couple of days earlier than us. As soon as we entered France the clouds opened and we drove to Le Touquet through an unrelenting thunderstorm. As we closed in I could tell that the clutch was about to give up and putting the car onto the plane finished it off.

When we landed in England, we found the whole of Kent was flooded and we were stuck with a broken car. In addition, a couple that had been on the same flight were also stuck, as Lydd airport had no taxi or bus service and they were begging us for help. I decided to make a big throw of the dice. I pushed the Alfa to the top of a slight decline and putting the stranded folk into the back seat, let the brake off and spun the starter motor with the car in second gear. It was brutal but it worked and we headed for London knowing that if we stopped we would never get under way again. To add to our predicament, as our headlights were set for left handed driving, oncoming traffic put their lights onto full beam in protest.

We reached Bexley Station where the car and I had both had enough. The couple went off to catch a train and I phoned Colin for help. He didn't let me down and I recovered the vehicle on Sunday. Then I was ready for action on my first day at Saffery Sons & Co.

I met Mr Jones again in his office and he called by phone for a man 'who would settle me in and show me the layout'. After a timid knock, a reincarnated Uriah Heep entered the room, bowing so low to Mr Jones that I thought he might well fall over. I followed him out and along a few corridors until we reached a locked door. With a flourish he brought out a jailer's set of keys, selected one and we went into a stock cupboard. He selected three coloured ballpoint pens, an ink pad and an audit stamp, presenting them together with his ledger to sign. He explained that when the pens ran out, I was to present those to him for replacements to be issued. Seeds of doubt entered my head.

At this point, I must have lost my presence of mind and actually enquired about mileage rates. The look of total shock was followed by the inane question uttered in disbelief.

'YOU have a car?'

After a moment's silence, he continued, pedantry replacing shock.

'You can only travel to a client in a car with the written authority of a partner and you are required to take with you any other staff.'

'You're having a laugh?'

He wasn't. We plodded down more corridors until we paused to view the juniors' room. It was a long narrow space with shelving along three walls. High chairs not dissimilar to bar stools were provided so that the lads could perch to reach the worktops. The seeds of doubt had grown to gonad size.

Continuing down further passages, we finally reached 'your office' and when the door was opened I could not believe my eyes. It was a big room, about 30 by 30 feet. One wall with a large window was fronted with six desks, a blank wall with another five and a further four parked against the wall with the door. One side of the room had no desks but a further five were in the centre. A grey ghost sat at each of nineteen desks. The empty one in the darkest corner was, as I was to quickly discover, my planned destination and the chair was broken.

I stepped outside and told Uriah that there must be a mistake as I was a Senior Manager but was assured that this awful place was where I was supposed to produce my best work. The seeds of doubt had exploded.

There was a great deal of shushing coming from the room and I was to learn that the golden rule was that there was no talking, not even a good-morning or good-night. I needed time to gather my thoughts. I sat in my unsteady chair and looked at the job that had been left for me to tackle.

The only saving grace of this firm was that there was a Billy Walker's Baked Potato nearby where a hot spud with a great choice of toppings could be bought for very little money. It was fast-food sixties style and pretty good too. At lunchtime I acquired a notepad to keep a detailed record of my experiences that I instinctively knew would be called upon.

By Friday my mind was made up and I had a plan. After lunch I bailed up on Mr Jones.

'What do you want?'

'I'm afraid we have both made a mistake here and I would rather we dealt with it sooner than later. The working conditions here are Dickensian to say the least and utterly unacceptable. And I am not prepared to work in a room with nineteen dead people. Here is my resignation.'

'I thought you were a serious candidate.'

'I am a serious candidate but I am not prepared to have anyone accuse me of having let them down. So here is my proposition, we cancel my employment here and I will work for you for three months as a freelance contractor through my agent. The hourly cost will be lower than my salary rate, you will get the jobs done and have time to find a replacement. If you find someone earlier then that's fine and I'll leave.'

He looked back to his desk and then sent me away with a dismissive wave of his hand.

'I'll take that to be a yes then.'

Those were my parting words and I left without a bow. That was for the more servile among the staff. That weekend I set down the arrangement to paper, sending a copy to my agent, as I needed to be belt and braces for sure with Mr Jones. For the next few weeks I was mainly used to manage external audits as I suspected that my disrespectful attitude may have disrupted the peace and calm of the place. That suited me and I think the young lads found me a breath of fresh air.

On Friday 13 December, I put a letter on the partner's desk to remind him that Friday 20 December was the end of it all. I'd carefully maintained my logbook in fine details. Everything had been meticulously recorded, even toilet breaks. Clients I'd worked on, who had said what to whom, all reconciled with time records and hours claimed.

I'd played the game according to Mr Hoyle. It would be interesting to see what game the other side played. When the fateful day came, I walked into the office at 4pm for the last time. Before he could speak I offered him the paperwork.'

'Last job, finish today …'

'I can't see you now, go away and wait until you are called.'

'Better be quick, 'cos at five, I'm Boff and I'm off.'

Dismissed by the hand yet again, I waited until five, rose from the broken chair and shouted to the room.

'Bye everybody, it's been a blast.'

And danced out into the street, free at last.

On Monday I was with my agent, chatting about plans for 1969 when the phone rings. Low and behold it's Mr Jones and he's not going to pay because I had walked out without notice and my work wasn't up to standard … The agent cut him off.

'Mr Roy has presented me with a comprehensive log of his time with you. Not only did he not charge considerable travelling time but he never even bothered with the out-of-pocket expenses and has kept records of all conversations; I believe that he behaved honourably in difficult circumstances.'

Mr Jones hung up.

Two days later the agent called me to let me know that the account had been settled in full. I have always expected a high standard from not only my profession but from all professions and have often been disappointed.

It was around this time that Hilary and Peter Simpson had a son, Scott Tallon. As we had only seen them a couple of times in 1968, we promised to get together early the following year.

Once again the year was finished with a visit to Rosemary's family. It was good to spend time with Michael and the kids but as ever Jane was a real ball breaker and no pleasure to be with. When they made her, I hope they threw away the mould afterwards.

Picking up with freelance work in the New Year, I was shortlisted for the job of CFO at Conway Typography in Molyneux Street. The first interview was at 5pm that was a little late by my measure. I thought the meeting with Stanley Conway went well and I was subsequently introduced to two other directors, Des Edmunds and Trevor Rogers, who insisted we went to the local pub. I didn't realise that this was part of the test.

I didn't want to get into a session mainly because my car was outside and I had to drive home. I had a half and then made sure I shouted a round. We chatted generally for about an hour and I headed off.

Later, I was told that my competitors to a man had got pissed and whinged loudly about their current boss and fellow workers, which did them no favours. I of course had no employer and from memory, rabbited on about cars, football and passed with flying colours.

Before a firm offer was made, I was asked to meet with the firm's auditor, based in Slough. I fixed this up for an afternoon and was surprised to discover that the practice was a one-man band. The actual one man was a middle-aged Jewish gent who was as unpleasant a bloke that you would not wish to meet, if that makes sense. From the get go he made it crystal clear that I was an irritant taking up his valuable time, so I let my CV do the talking for me, whilst he droned on about his own importance. That tactic seemed to have worked and an offer of employment came through to start on 3 February 1969.

7 Conway's Group Limited

'Achievement of your happiness is the only moral purpose of your life and that happiness - not pain or mindless self-indulgence - is the proof of your moral integrity, because it is the proof of your loyalty to the achievement of your values.'

Ayn Rand, novelist & philosopher

Built at the turn of the century, the place had a front on Molyneux Street but ran backwards right through to Cato Street, becoming a concrete pile for the rear half. The three accounts offices were at the front of the top floor above the Managing Director's rooms.

Being the first CFO of the company, I had been allocated a small room with a desk and two chairs. The adjoining space was occupied by a large woman called Hazel who was to be my assistant. When we were introduced, I was surprised to note that she was sporting a fine black eye. The last and largest area formed the general office and was packed to the gills with ten clerks making a total staff of twelve.

I had only been in my new office for a half hour when the receptionist called me to say that a Mr O'Toole from the Inland Revenue was here to see me. That sounded bad but I went down to collect him and we sat on opposite sides of my new desk.

'You were not here on my previous visit?'

'No, I started today, about half an hour ago. I guess that you know more about this firm than I do.'

'Possibly. I'm here to take action to recover PAYE and NI contributions. You are six months in arrears and I am about to call in the Bailiff to take possession of the machinery and equipment.

'You'll appreciate that I know absolutely nothing about the company finances. Currently therefore there is not a thing I can offer you.'

'Look, when I sat down on the tube this morning I noticed that I was wearing odd socks which means it's someone's lucky day. I'll give you four weeks to get a handle on the finances and when I come back I hope you have a firm proposal for me to get your payments back on track.'

'Thank you for understanding and consideration. Rest assured that I will do my very best.'

'I wish you luck.'

Amazing that this company's future depended on a superstitious Irishman. The number one task was to ascertain as fast as possible where we actually were financially. I piled into getting the bank situation up to date only to realise that the business was living hand to mouth. I would not see the directors until I had a full picture available and more importantly, a plan.

My assistant's boyfriend arrived to collect her at the end of the day but where she was large, he was small and German. He had a black eye as well, together with numerous other cuts and bruises. I could only surmise that they had been in a car accident. Much later I was told that their injuries were a consequence of their lifestyle.

A member of staff came to see me on day two when I was toiling away. She could not have picked a worse time.

'I have an arrangement that if the weather forecast is for a sunny day I can take work home and do it in my garden. I just wanted to let you know that's what I'm doing tomorrow.'

'Are you having a laugh? I don't know or care who you think that arrangement is with it's not with me, so forget it. We're not running a holiday resort. If you don't come in tomorrow, as far as I'm concerned you've left.'

She was not a happy bunny but if you let the staff walk all over you, they will. The troops were very overcrowded anyway and I had plans to make conditions better by sacking a few. This lady had popped to the top of my list.

By Wednesday a general picture had started to emerge: the profits were there but cash flow was desperate and it wasn't hard to find the cause. Apart from saying hello to the team I hadn't had any reason to go into the general office but I had noticed stacks of paper all over the place. They reminded me of the Old Man of Hoy, a sea stack in the Orkneys. It was time to enquire so I asked Hazel.'

'Oh, they're just typed invoices ready to be sent out.'

'If they're ready, why are they still here? How far back are do they go?'

'They're January's and they have to be sorted. Some customers like a fourth copy, others copies of orders attached.'

'I understand all that but why hasn't it been done? A whole month of invoices sitting on the floor is no good to anybody.'

'It's a boring job and nobody wants to do it.'

'Wants to do it? Tell someone to do it!'

'It doesn't work that way.'

'It seems to me that it doesn't work at all.'

I decided to leave it with her and see what happened, if anything. By Friday afternoon nothing had changed, so on Sunday I pulled a few friends in, got the job done and the lot was down in the dispatch department.

When she came in on Monday, Hazel was annoyed. She told me that I didn't know what I was doing and the clients would be angry at not getting suppliers' invoices correctly presented. Looking at her punchbag of a face I had a hard time stopping myself from giving her the old heave-ho on the spot.

'At least the clients have the invoices. It's the tenth of the month and if you had your way last month's sales would still be sitting on the floor. What I would like you to do is organise it so the job is done every day and that day's work goes out the same day. No argument.'

Rather than allow a protracted discussion, I retreated into my room. I now had two candidates neck and neck at the top of my wastage list. An appointment was made for me to visit the bank manager of Lloyds Bank Park Lane on Wednesday to introduce myself. I duly arrived but was met with a distinctly cool reception.

'I've agreed to see you but I can't imagine what you want.'

'Nothing. I'm here out of courtesy to explain who I am and simply touch base.'

He interrupted my opening speech.

'You don't need to say any more, all I want from you is to take your firm's bank account somewhere else. I don't want you banking here. The account has a long record of unauthorised overdrafts, dishonoured cheques and false promises and I want it gone.'

There were a few more minutes of nastiness before I was shown the door. I'm sure he felt better getting his angst off his chest but politeness costs nothing.

By an astonishing coincidence, three weeks later I read a report in the morning newspaper that Lloyds Bank Park Lane had been robbed. Allegedly two employees had decided to run away together and had taken as much cash as they could carry to fund their journey. Speculation had it at around thirty grand. I was pretty certain that the obnoxious manager's career path had been badly dented, to say the least. Maybe I'd been a wizard in a previous life.

With a total workforce of around a hundred and an accounts team of twelve, we were obviously overstaffed. Ninety-five per cent of our work was producing a large quantity of small value invoices to a wide client base that were mainly advertising agencies. If one staffer took on the purchase and payment side while I managed cash control and payroll then a maximum of six would suffice. I called a general meeting and addressed the throng.

'I have been given a job to do and it's going to get done. I'm a very direct person and if something needs saying or doing then it will be said or done. I am no good at office politics and don't do the plotting and scheming, nor messing about and wasting time. If you are doing a good job I will tell you and if you are crap ... I'm under the directors' microscope and in turn, I'll be watching you lot. Whatever regime existed in the past is gone. It's not a yardstick for the running of this office in the future.'

I guess you could call the speech a success as I was handed two resignations the following morning. I told them I wouldn't hold them up and that they could head out of the front door straight away. Their paperwork would be in the post. Two down, four more to go and Hazel was next in line.

Some mornings it was all she could do to haul her bruised and battered body up the stairs. But it was clear that she gave no quarter when her man showed up to collect her at the end of the day. I was truly sick of this three-ringed circus and didn't feel it was good for moral. She was meant to be the office manager but none of the others could have had any respect for the woman. I know I didn't. I sat her down, raised my concerns and she told me it wasn't any of my business. There was no point in pursuing the argument so I simply made her an offer: pay to the month end and an extra month free of tax to go, and go now. She went.

In the 60s there was a slogan stemming from the American counterculture 'Make love Not War' and was used mainly in reference to the Vietnam War. This couple could have claimed that 'Make Simultaneous Love and War' was their motto. I really felt for their neighbours. Three more and I should be done.

By the end of week two I had the complete financial picture and it wasn't rocket science. The business was without doubt profitable but the sales achieved were not being turned into cash fast enough. Invoicing went out as and when, and when the clients did pay, they settled what they had on their books as no statements were sent out. If we could get on top of the situation and actually work the phones chasing up payments, we should get enough back income in to deal with the tax guys.

The elephant in the room was how much we would lose in non-recoverable debt. Once an invoice gets long in the tooth there is a natural reluctance on the part of the customer to pay. That's especially true if it goes back to a previous year that has been finalised and closed off. I suspected a solid ten to twenty per cent of book debt was dead in the water.

I arranged a meeting with Stan Conway, Des and Trevor plus the two other directors John Hicks and David Cable. The latter pair had been brought up from the shop floor but it would have been better if they'd stayed down there. I can't remember a single useful contribution that either made to any meeting.

Stan kicked off by voicing his concern that three accounts staff had already left. I told him that more would be leaving. With that out of the way, I explained in layman's terms what I'd unearthed and outlined my solution.

'When Mr O'Toole returns, we'll offer to pay the current month's debt plus one month of arrears. It'll be tough and a lot will depend on all helping to get clients to sign off the old stuff.'

'Do you need extra people?' asked Stan.

'No, I needed fewer people. Look I'm not an empire builder as are many of my compatriots. I liked to work with a small quality team.'

Most of my inheritance folk above were lightweight youngsters settled in to a cushy life and I could only see prospects for a couple of survivors.

A young bloke called Alan Bunce was promoted to manager and we settled in for the long, hard haul. A stud wall was taken down to turn two rooms into one large office. I took the old manager's room and brought a credit controller to work with me. As I'd expected, none of the directors or sales staff helped with chasing up old accounts. It was a tough business and there were write-offs but it couldn't be helped. We coped with the Inland Revenue payment plan right up to month six when we failed in our efforts to pull in enough cash to meet all our liabilities. When I told Stan that the directors would have to sit on their pay cheques for a few days, he threw all his toys out of the pram then ran around like a headless chicken. We got through.

When I'd signed up for this show I hadn't realised that the business was heavily unionized. The National Graphical Association (NGA) was run by and for Neanderthals. The directors were terrified of their own workforce, constantly complaining that the lads were 'worried, upset and concerned'. The level of pay for the typesetters was astronomical especially for those on mid or nightshift and their attitude to management and other non-union workers, disgraceful.

They and only they were workers, every one with a seven-year apprenticeship behind them. Out there were the customers and we were in between them and the customers, the fucking parasites poncing off the sweat of their labour. The Chapel, (as they were called) reported to The House, the Union's headquarters and if we wanted to recruit a typesetter it was The House who sent us a body.

Although the lads lived in open contempt of all non-union folk they were constantly on the hunt for women to bed among the accounting and secretarial staff. One married guy named Richards had picked up with Stan's personal assistant Mrs D'Arcy. Her husband and his brothers were spotted heading for our front door with reports of more following. Unsurprisingly the lovers took off over the roofs of adjoining houses with the aid of John McCarthy, one of the managers. It was amazing how their revilement could be pushed to one side when it came to getting their leg over.

Stan was not impressed and Mrs D'Arcy was shown the door. Her replacement was Ann Jacobs, a wonderful woman and we became lifetime friends up until her sad, sad loss to cancer in 2017. In that place you needed a reliable confidante; politics were high on the menu and the union, constantly on the lookout for trouble.

My vote was to take them head on but the threat of complete anarchy meant that in reality they ran the place and called the shots. Keeping any semblance of order required generous amounts of largesse poured into their pockets.

*****

For Easter 1969, Rosemary and I were invited by Paul Orssich to stay at his home in Menorca. We flew down to Barcelona on the Friday morning intending to catch the short flight to Menorca in the afternoon. But when we landed, the airport was shutting down ahead of the onset of a tropical storm and all flights were cancelled. There was no further information available, no vouchers for refreshments and all the food outlets were closing anyway. Our night was spent in the airport and since we couldn't access our bags, dawn on Saturday saw us wearing the same kit that we'd had on in London only dirtier.

With the rain showing no sign of letting up and a total absence of information from airport staff, mutiny broke out at 2pm as a surge of angry passengers attacked the service counter. Their refusal to return our luggage was ignored by the mob that climbed over the counter. People searched for their bags and once retrieved, headed out to the taxi rank to go off into the city to find food and lodgings.

We joined them, found a guy who could recommend a hotel and left. The taxi got bogged down a couple of times but we put our shoulders to the wheel and eventually arrived. A hot bath, hot food and a bottle of wine just can't be beaten. On Sunday we simply wandered around the town, returning to the airport on Monday morning where the storm had eased.

We were told that as our return flight would result in a trip of less than six days we would have to pay a surcharge. Naturally we refused on the grounds that our original arrangements were less than six days. By this time my charm, patience and quiet English reserve were all used up and I was able to convince them that they were not getting another red cent under any circumstances.

We found ourselves on the first plane home with just six others. One of them was so pleased to be out of Spain that he got totally pissed, smoked through the entire flight, refusing to extinguish even upon landing. We arrived in Heathrow to a beautiful, hot sunny Easter Monday.

Given Conway's' cash problems there was no chance of escaping for a holiday, so Rosemary took the Alfa and headed home. I thought we were on the same page working towards getting our own property and building a career but looking back I think it may have been happening too slowly for her. With her background of having cash readily available to move forward with any plans, my brick by brick approach just didn't deliver quickly enough.

*****

Stan told me that his accountant wanted us to send over the books, so he could carry out an audit. I responded by saying that it was impossible to let the papers out of the building and that we were too big an operation to be a paper bag job.

'Can't the accountant come to us?'

'No.'

'In that case we need a bigger firm.'

'Who could you recommend from the people you worked for?'

'My last lot, Cartwrights are really good guys. I'm happy to work with them or just get a local mob. There are a couple in this street.'

'What about the firm you spent seven years with?'

'Not so happy. We finished up on bad terms. Surprise me.'

Stan Conway did indeed surprise me and chose Wilson Wright. Why? I think it was the religious thing. As Greek business men always have a Greek accountant, I believe Stan Conway felt more comfortable with a Harold Gould than a Mike Hurst.

I guess it is only human nature for people's first choice to be someone from your own clan, tribe, nationality or religion. German Field Marshall Erwin Rommel (popularly called the Desert Fox) made no secret of the fact that he preferred to fight alongside fellow Swabians as he felt that they had a special invisible bond. Anyway, sorry to say Wilson Wright were back in my life again.

When the day of the audit came, our receptionist called to tell me that Mr Boreham had arrived. I simply could not believe the bloody brass neck of this man, after all the history between us showing his face. I was determined to put a stop to this straight away. I grabbed my manager and headed off.

As we approached my nemesis strode up, hand outstretched.

'Hello Peter.'

I shoved a pile of working papers into the offered hand.

'My name is Mr Roy and this is my manager, Mr Bunce. You will deal with him and through him to me. We are putting you in the boardroom and there are eight chairs but one chair is sacrosanct. You're banned from sitting in it but we won't tell you which one. Please will you show them the way Mr Bunce.'

Boreham looked crestfallen.

'I hoped we'd got past this.'

'I'm sure you did.'

I phoned Mr Gould from my office.

'Mr Gould it is not my nature to be disagreeable but the sole solitary reason for my leaving your firm is sitting in my boardroom and I will not tolerate it. I am the client here and I want that man gone from my building now. Please send somebody else, anybody else. Thank you.'

'I'm sorry to hear this. I hadn't heard of any problems between you …'

'I am sure you didn't hear a word of truth about what went on but I am not interested in going into the matter. Please get him away from here asap.'

He didn't say yes and he didn't say no but he did know I could make the audit hell, if I put my mind to it. Ten minutes later I got the news of Boreham's departure and went straight over to greet the junior audit staff properly and make them welcome. One asked about the chair.

'The chair business? Was that a private joke?'

'Private but no joke. I lost my job at Wilson Wright because I sat in the wrong chair. A long time ago, blood under the bridge.'

Peace restored and all went well. Staff came and went until I had a team of six that I could rely on and trust.

The news came through that the NGA was about to call a national strike which would bring the media industry to a halt. Stan called me to his office.

'You know that a total shut down is on the cards. But I'm surprised that you haven't made any financial plans to cope with the situation.'

'Oh but I have. By my calculations we can hold out for eighteen months without a problem. I'm sure that they can't and we can bring these bastards to their knees.'

The blood drained from his face.

'For God's sake don't talk like that! The brothers are already upset, worried and concerned.'

'Well, let them tell The House that they don't support it.'

'They can't do that. Anyway it doesn't matter as I have come to an agreement with The Chapel that they will avoid the picket line at the front door, slip in at the back door and carry on working as normal. Look at this way, as the only typesetting house still operating we'll capture the market and our competitors will be out of business. You should be grateful to the lads, they're risking their union cards for Conway's.'

'I am very impressed with their generosity of spirit but I'm equally sure that I haven't heard the full story. What are they getting in return.'

'Well, it's been agreed that they will continue to received their full pay, plus average overtime while the strike continues.'

He paused and an ominous feeling of dread crept over me.

'In addition they'll be paid normal wages plus actual overtime in cash without deductions.'

'And you've agreed this without consulting anyone? Entered into a conspiracy to defraud the tax office and saddled the company with a cost burden it cannot possibly carry? Well I can tell you that I and my staff will have no part of it.'

'I am very pleased with the agreement and you can get over your concerns by simply grossing up the cash payments to deal with the tax people.'

'Simply gross up! Have you any idea what that will cost?'

'Well, it's a hell of a lot better than shutting up shop for the duration.'

What was the point of having a board of directors when the CEO could take a decision of this magnitude without a discussion beforehand to consider the implications. The brothers knew more of what was going on than the so-called bosses.

In the event the strike was averted and that was the end of it but did teach me a salutary lesson: in reality being a director at Conway's meant nothing, it was still a one-man band.

*****

Heading towards the end of 1969 I took a telephone call at home that brought devastating news. It was Peter Simpson telling me that Hilary had died as a result of a fall from a horse. This was truly terrible especially considering that their son was only a year old.

We had only seen them once during the year and I regarded them as good friends. There were relatives and close long time mates who would form the nucleus of support at this time. My expectation was that we would travel up to Coventry for the funeral and the wake. I ended the conversation and told Rosemary the sad tidings. Her reaction took us into the Twilight Zone.

'I must go to him now,' she said.

Within ten minutes she was packed and out of the door. I ran her down to Euston and asked her to phone me when she could. It was beyond my understanding what she thought she could possibly offer that the nearest and dearest could not provide. That evening no call came, nor the next day and no invitation to the funeral. Nothing but the big silence.

Two weeks later she returned, almost to the minute. Without a word. The lost fortnight was never spoken of and what exactly had happened was left to my imagination. Looking back, I think it was the beginning of the end. It just seemed unnatural not to talk about what had transpired over the two weeks. Even stranger that no attempt had been made to let me know about the funeral arrangements in order that I might attend.

The whole event has caused me a great deal of anguish and provoked many thoughts. My only conclusion is that Rosemary simply couldn't be bothered to make up a story to fill the gap. I wasn't even worth a lie.

What we had here was a failure to communicate. I realised that I needed to deal with the problem and for some crazy reason formed the belief that if we could get our first house purchase achieved all would be well. We had a reasonable lump of savings and a couple of strong lines of credit, so in 1970 a one hundred per cent effort would go into house hunting.

The end of year break took us up to Great Coates where Jane was being her obnoxious self and picking on the kids for no apparent reasons. Having had a real gutful I took her to one side, told her that she should lighten up and stop being abusive to those who couldn't put up a fight. She spat blood as I expected and mentally lined me up as an enemy on whom to take revenge at the earliest opportunity. We were snowed in for a couple of days but the roads opened in time for our return to London.

The Alfa was sold and a Vauxhall Victor acquired for twenty-five quid. It turned out to be a reliable old heap but lacking badly in the braking department.

*****

By this time my value had been recognised at Conway's and my pay had moved up a couple of notches. I left Michael Dunne Studio and handed the work over to Max. I told Tony that I couldn't commit to any more Saturdays at Casa Pupo as I needed to spend more time on my marriage. He really needed to bring in some accounting automation to deal with the sales volumes. But with the programme of expansion pressing ahead at full speed he was having to fight hard just to stay in control. Much later I heard that a major creditor, possibly the Lipton Family, had taken over ownership in the early 1970s and that the business closed in the 1980s. I may not have been in control of my life but I thought I was and had a plan.

Rosemary had left Connell May & Stevenson and joined Van Den Burges who manufactured margarine and was part of Unilever. This had caused a mild sensation as the family firm Smethurst Frozen Foods had been sold to the Unilever Group many years before but the name was still extant in the catering division. The Head Office was situated opposite Blackfriars Bridge North.

She informed me that she had signed up for evening classes twice a week to study sociology, which simply put is the study of the human condition. It seemed like a strange choice but it would be an interest and there is no such thing as too many qualifications.

Back at the coalface Stan had decided to sack Trevor Rogers who had been with him pretty much from the start. I was never privy as to the why but closely involved with the how. Trevor sensed that something was afoot and confronted me, demanding to be told what was going on but I could only tell him that I didn't know. I liked Trevor and he had invited us to Biggin Hill airfield where he took me up in his two-seater plane which I think was a Piper. Anyway for whatever reason Stan wanted him gone, they had a meeting and that was that.

Trevor left his Triumph 1500 (which I used for a few weeks) and moved down to Cornwall to run a ship chandlery. He also left his ten per cent of the company's shares. Stan explained that he would like Des, David, John and I to pick up two and a half per cent each. The firm's auditors had valued each holding at four thousand pounds, meaning Trevor would receive sixteen grand towards his maritime endeavour. In hindsight I shouldn't have got involved but I was young and naive and thought being a shareholder actually meant something. It didn't.

The firm's banking had moved from Lloyds to my bank in Holborn and they were happy to fix up loans to allow the arrangements to proceed.

One morning I arrived to find that a large dog had taken a dump on our doorstep. As there was the obvious risk of it being trodden all over reception, I asked Alan who was trolling up the street behind me to tip a sand bucket over it while I ran around the area to find a road sweeper. It was a small irritant and insignificant in my mind but two weeks later Mr Bunce handed in his notice. He had felt insulted to be asked to deal with a dog's Richard the Third. Precious boy. Living in Barking he did the obvious thing and joined Fords on their assembly line. A year later he killed himself.

Our house search kicked off in earnest and we settled on an area north of London around Abbots Langley and Aldenham with easy access to the M1 motorway and rail links into London. We quickly found a terrific house and offered the asking price that of course was accepted. We paid our deposit, started the legal stuff and paid a surveyor to run the rule over the place. A good job, well done we thought. Until we got a call from the estate agent, to say that a higher offer had been made and accepted. We'd been gazumped but would we like to make an even greater offer? Now I always believed a contract, even a verbal one, was a commitment but not in the world of property where rabid dogs ate rabid dogs. I refused and we lost not only the house but our costs that had been incurred thus far. This type of selfish and nasty behaviour set the pattern for the months to come.

When I got home on Friday 3 April, Rosemary informed me that she had volunteered to help with the firm's stocktaking over the weekend and that a hotel had been laid on to save travelling time over the two days.

Unilever House was the head office not a distribution depot and no stock was kept there. It could have been the paperwork aspect but I knew it was a total fiction without any doubt. To have questioned her would only have produced a tirade over my disgusting lack of trust. So I decided to let it ride and see where this journey would go. My offer of a lift into town was rejected and she left on Saturday morning to God knows where only to return late on Sunday afternoon without any comment. An expression I picked up from an Aussie on my travels seems very apt: 'dogs are pissing on your bluey'. I knew my world was about to implode and I didn't have to wait very long. Three weeks in fact when on Friday 24 April I received a phone call.

'Hi Peter, its Carol, I work with Rosemary.'

'What's happened? Is she all right?'

'She's fine, don't worry. I would like to talk to you personally and in confidence. Can we meet?'

Think mind, where? All the pubs around Blackfriars would be full of the Fleet Street crowd. I wouldn't ask any female to run the gauntlet of the lunchtime session.

'How about the Cheshire Cheese, Carol? It's totally tourist but you will be safe from the grubs in there. If I head off now I can meet you at 12 noon.'

After telling the troops that I would be on the missing list for a couple of hours, I hailed a taxi and headed off. My mind was screaming: what is this all about? Help with a tax return or in looking for a job? Both highly unlikely. Maybe she was planning something for Rosemary's birthday but that was a bit early and a very farfetched. Clear the mind boy, all would soon be revealed.

Walking into the near empty pub, Carol was already there with a colleague. I enjoyed two wet fish handshakes and a mumbled introduction to Mary, I think. I offered drinks but they both already had spritzers on the bar in front of them. I ordered a Smith's Glenlivet and offered lunch which was politely refused. It was an awkward moment but I felt I should kick the can down the road.

'Well, here I am and how can I assist you?'

Carol looked at Mary for help but as none was forthcoming she grasped the nettle.

'We need your influence in dealing with your wife.'

She paused and then got into her stride.

'Look Peter, there are only about twenty females in Unilever House and all are married or with steady boyfriends. But we have to share the space with hundreds of men. A long time ago we girls made a collective decision not to encourage any office flirtations and to make this policy quite clear to the guys, otherwise we would find ourselves pestered from dawn to dusk.' She paused again, took a deep breath and continued. 'Your wife has totally ignored the policy.'

'You mean she's been flirting with blokes?'

They exchanged glances and giggled.

'It's gone a long way past flirting.'

If a pin had dropped I would have heard it loud and clear. At this point I realised that the drink I'd raised to my lips at the start was still untouched. I placed it back on the bar, struggling to keep my composure. All the suspicions that I'd refused to consider now welled up to the surface. Carol ploughed on.

'Have you heard of a Mr Barker?'

'Yeah, Rosemary has mentioned him a couple of times. He's the company's rep for the West Country ...'

Carol cut me short.

'He's the worst pest, a creepy little man who tries it on with all the girls every time he's in the building.'

Mary interrupted, 'He's horrible, like a child molester.'

'A few weeks ago Rosemary told you that she was going to help with stocktaking. Well that was untrue. Obviously we don't keep goods at Head Office. She spent the night with Barker at a hotel. Doing it. Now he's told everybody, the gloves are off and we're regarded as easy pickings. We're sick of it.'

Mary chimed in with words of reassurance.

'Don't worry Peter, you're not going to lose her. Barker's married and it wasn't love or romance or passion or anything like that, just sex, like dogs in the street.'

So this is what we had come to, my beautiful wife viewed by her colleagues as having the same level of morality as a dog rooting in the street. I wished I could unscrew the top of my head and take out all the filthy pictures that Rosemary had put there. So much for knowledge is power. I had the knowledge, maybe too much, but I was powerless. If I tackled her head on, my guess was that she would deny everything and use the situation as an excuse to leave. I just couldn't bring myself to imagine a future without her. I was even sad at her lack of discrimination, having sex with a sleazebag.

Mary piped up again, 'You can always check her diary.'

'I can't possibly do that. It would be a terrible breach of trust.'

They laughed and Carol said, 'You've got double standards here Peter. Your wife is screwing around and you won't even take a peek into her diary?'

We had run out of things to say and small talk was inappropriate. I believed what they'd said, apart from their alleged motive for grassing on Rosemary. I didn't quite swallow the solidarity sisterhood reason and thought it was more basic than that. They simply didn't like her and dobbing her cheating to her husband would cause maximum grief.

I offered to refill the glasses and repeated the lunch invitation but they declined and told me that they had to get back. I thanked them both and with a couple of limp handshakes they were gone. I stood at the bar for a few moments to try and gather my thoughts and then headed towards the door. The barman called me back, pointing at my untouched whiskey. I retraced the few steps, thanked him and downed the drink. My mouth was so dry I couldn't even taste it. Instead of a taxi back, I walked. Where did I go from here?

A couple of weeks later, after the evening meal, I dropped a one-liner into the mix.

'You haven't mentioned your friend Mr Barker from Bristol lately.'

The short answer gave me all the confirmation I needed.

'He always gets want he wants.'

That was it. If the whole thing had been more spontaneous – a drunken Christmas party or a stationery cupboard knee trembler – it would have been easier to bear. But a cold-blooded planned tryst without any emotion, a physical workout nothing more, that was something else.

I can honestly say that throughout my marriage, I never once lied to my wife or cheated on her. That's not a boast, it's bleeding normal for married couples. What is the point of going through the ceremony and bearing the financial cost if the undertakings you make mean nothing? I didn't know it at the time but the disaster put me off marriage for the rest of my life. What's its purpose I'd asked and no one could ever give me a sensible answer. Strange as it may seem, I never learnt Mr Barker's first name. I wonder if Rosemary even knew, after all she was never one to sweat the details.

Meanwhile I had a business to run. My new assistant Marion had previously worked for Matchless/AJS motorcycles and was a first-class bookkeeper. Unfortunately she had a very unhappy personal life and more often than not, hit the sauce at weekends resulting in piss-poor performance on Monday mornings.

Another new appointment was that of Dick Amphlett to the position of Leader of the Chapel. A seriously bolshie guy who together with his Spanish mate Carlos, took over the leadership and we were destined to lock horns at every opportunity.

My first real encounter with Dick and Carlos was on the matter of averaging holiday pay for any of the lads who had made a shift change. Their view was that if the move was from mid or night shift (massive pay levels) to a day shift (big pay levels), then the calculation of the holiday pay should take into account that part of the previous year they were on a higher pay grade than now and the rate for holiday should be averaged over the year.

But if they had moved the other way, then the holiday pay should be based on today's pay rate and the fact that for part or most of the previous year they were on a lower rate was to be ignored. There was no logic at all to their rationale but try telling that to the apparatchiki. They insisted that we take this to Stan Conway who was both horrified and terrified that I would face up to these bastards. He wanted the matter settled tout suite. I started to explain the problem but was cut short.

'Look Peter, can't you see that the lads are upset, worried and concerned and they want certainty on the holiday pay front.'

Amphlett interjected, 'We're prepared to take this up to The House if necessary'.

The magic words caused outright panic and Stan moved to reassure the lads.

'Peter, all holiday pay must be paid at current levels except where they have been on a higher shift in the previous twelve months. Then it must be averaged and that's the end of it.'

'Hold on, what about if they have been on a lower shift.'

'That's irrelevant and to be ignored.'

He went on to reassure the friends of Moscow that he was their pal (and ally), and they wheeled out of the office flashing their smug grins in my direction. When they were gone, Stan reprimanded me for upsetting the lads and told me that he wanted no more confrontations. I responded with a fair question.

'Don't they work for us? And isn't us who pays their wages?'

'You know full well that simplistic approach does not apply here. Your job is to keep the peace.'

'My job is to avoid throwing money away.'

The power of the NGA over the management was amply demonstrated by an exchange I witnessed between Amphlett and his floor manager Paul Benedict. Paul was a deranged man who had been known to rugby tackle women in the street just for fun. His idea of amusement in a restaurant was to throw food at other customers, help himself from their plates or even dive onto a loaded food cart and propel himself the length of the eatery. Luckily for him he was a huge man and most blokes would be reluctant to take him on.

Amphlett was on the mid-shift from 2pm to 10pm, at a pay level twice that of mine and I was the CFO. I would see him most days driving past in his Morgan around 2pm but entering the building around 4pm. To my certain knowledge the two hours were usually spent in the Blue Cockatoo Club, a few streets away.

Dick Amphlett had a way of speaking that was normally exclusive to politicians. In an argument a point is made, then when the second point is laid out the first is repeated and so on ad nauseam. It's intended to wear the opponent down and provides a tedious disquisition. Here I will set out his justifications for his actions in precis to spare the reader a long diatribe.

I had been in reception dealing with a visitor when Dick arrived at 4pm. He went to his workstation and sat without speaking to Benedict.

'Come on Dick, you're two hours late and just march in without saying a word.'

This had the makings of an interesting conversation, so I loitered. Dick's reaction was predictable and he went off on one.

The firm made him work unsocial hours so he never had time with his wife or kids nor could he watch TV like normal men did. Because public transport was not feasible, he had to drive in but the firm insisted on being in the West End where parking was impossible. He was forced to drive around and around until he could find a parking space, with all the petrol costs and wear and tear on his car that that entailed.

It was a long speech, and Paul was no match for him. At the end it was agreed that if Dick tooted his car horn and waved at our receptionist as he drove past at 2pm he would, in effect be clocked in. His actual physical arrival time was not recorded.

The Morgan motorcar has always been an attractive proposition. But although I've owned many vehicles, I never had a Moggie because Dick Amphlett had one.

*****

As we moved into the summer, the house search continued. I still had this mad notion that our own property would provide us with a new start and that the horrors of the past would somehow fall into insignificance. I really must have been crazy.

We were gazumped twice more. On the third occasion our offer was accepted and we thought we were there until the surveyor reported that the owner was a do-it-yourself enthusiast and not a very good one. A lot of money would be needed to put right the botched up jobs he had carried out. Maybe it was not to be on the cards.

Certainly it was a real effort to stay upbeat and carry on normally. Especially with carrying the knowledge of what had gone on and for all I knew, was still going on now under my own nose. Having had plenty of practice, I now knew when she was telling a downright lie. Rather than looking me in the eyes, she'd look at an invisible person standing at my right shoulder. Once I worked that out it saved guesswork.

Another nail in the coffin of our marriage was the holiday in Bulgaria. Unsurprisingly, by September I was exhausted and depressed so booked a last minute cheap two week all-inclusive trip to the Sunny Beach Resort on the Black Sea.

We boarded the Gatwick Express and sat opposite a couple in their thirties who were sharing a bottle of red wine wrapped in a paper bag. Within minutes they revealed that their destination was the same as ours, which struck me as a bad omen. It was. By the time we reached the airport the bottle was empty.

I am sure the plane was ex-military and when we landed it was pitch dark. We were then coached to the resort and told our bags would be taken to the hotel rooms. Rosemary was given the pack of meal vouchers that would enable us to eat in any of the many restaurants.

Sunny Beach Resort was built in the 50s, primarily as a paradise for workers from the Soviet Bloc. But it was also designed to attract people from west of the Iron Curtain in order to bring in much desired foreign currency. For its time and place it was a rare opportunity for ordinary people from the two ideologies to meet, although it was obvious that we were all under surveillance. Every morning during our stay the air force sent jet fighters to hammer down the beach at low level to impress. Some one thousand army personnel that included motorbikes with sidecar combos equipped with fifty calibre machine guns arrested a few gypsy hawkers. A bit over the top by any standard.

On our first evening we were on the beach in the moonlight

heading for our hotel. There was no rush as they would be six deep at the reception counter, so we slipped off our shoes and socks and paddled in the warm water. All very romantic.

After a while we were joined by a Bulgarian kid, about thirteen I would guess. He didn't speak English but smiled, laughed and seemed harmless. After ten minutes we headed off the beach but it wasn't until we reached the hotel that Rosemary realised that she had lost the meal vouchers. We retraced our steps but found nothing. I suspected that the lad had somehow managed to steal them. I couldn't work out how it had been achieved but he was the only other person around.

Now we were in real trouble. Because the holiday had been all-inclusive, I had only brought a little cash for emergencies. The only person we could tap for a bailout was Michael and I told Rosemary that she would have to call her father to get eating money sent to the hotel as soon as possible. We had no credit cards in those days. I put up a notice on the board asking that any spare vouchers be gifted to two hapless travellers. By the end of week one we were running out of money when Michael's donation arrived. God bless him.

The two drunks haunted us constantly. Their room was opposite ours and there was no escape. We would go down to the beach each morning and they would insist on joining us, always bringing two bottles of red wine. Those would last until about noon by which time they would be comatose, waking around 4pm to discover they had missed the afternoon excursions which they had booked and paid for. Their evenings were more liquid than solid, so they would crash until fighting the mother of hangovers when they struggled down the following morning. They could have stayed at home and done that. In addition they suffered from terrible sunburn due to the hours lying drunk on the beach. We got to know a family of East Germans who were a decent bunch and a big plus, were sober.

Now able to afford a couple of excursions we set off for Adventure Island on a pirate ship (powered by an outboard motor) and led by Captain Blackbeard. He turned out to be an ex- university professor fluent in some seven languages who had fallen foul of the country's politburo and been reassigned.

The island was not so much an island but a strip of beach further north up the coast. Any illusion of adventure or beauty was dispelled by the massive construction site next door. A grubby BBQ was serving up burnt lumps of mystery meat and there was the usual rough red wine for drinking.

After an hour or so Rosemary fell ill and I approached the captain with the need to get her back to the hotel. He started in with the island crap but I cut him short and explained that I hadn't come up on the down train; I could see Sunny Beach a couple of miles to the south. If he couldn't whip up a taxi, I was certain that for a drink one of the tipper drivers on the site next door could run us there. And that's exactly what happened.

I offered to organise a doctor but Rosemary refused and took to her bed for twenty-four hours which brought her back to life. The return journey was uneventful until we reached Gatwick when a couple in front of us dropped the huge punchbowl set they had bought as a souvenir and it smashed into a million pieces.

I have always believed in the old theatre maxim that if the show you are in isn't working, by giving your maximum performance your efforts alone might turn it round. Sorry to say, I was finding that my maximum efforts were having no positive effect whatsoever.

Try as I might, I just couldn't get her adultery out of my head and I now doubted that time would be a healer. I had wanted above all else for the marriage to work but I couldn't ever see a time when I could come to terms with Rosemary's breaches of trust. I know it was the swinging sixties but I hadn't bargained for an open arrangement. The solution arrived on Wednesday 28 October.

The morning started like any other but as I headed to the door Rosemary told me she was unwell and would not be going in to work. This was a certain lie as it was directed not to me but to the leprechaun sitting on my right shoulder and as was her practice, untruths always came at the last minute. I offered to phone in for her but she said she would do it herself.

Before I reached the car I guessed that this was the day for moving out, either that or a gentleman caller. What should I do about it? Frankly I was so worn down by the lies and the cheating I decided to just do nothing. It broke my heart but she had disappointed me so much that I couldn't be bothered.

At ten I had a coffee break and asked myself whether should I drive home and see what was happening but dismissed the idea. I would find out soon enough.

When I got home at six, as I'd foreseen Rosemary had gone and cleaned the place out in doing so. I would not have known I'd lived there if it were not for my clothes lying heaped on the floor and a burned out pan on the stove. I went to pour a glass of whiskey but the bottle was not there nor any glasses. And our building society book was gone.

There was a Dear John letter that told me she was going into hiding and that I would never find her. What nonsense was this? What drama had she dreamed up for us all to act out? Always the star and the rest of us bit players in her theatre of life. Suddenly my good friend Max arrived.

'What are you doing here?'

'Rosemary invited me to dinner.'

'She's gone Max so there ain't no dinner or any plates to eat it off. She's cleaned me out.' He had to settle for a Chinese take-away. She had done a thorough job. Not a scrap of food had been left, all linen and towels liberated, books, photos, everything as if by right. Getting into the office next morning I gathered my staff and told them the news.

'I'm telling you this because there'll be plenty of rumours flying about and I want you to hear the story from the horse's mouth. I got home yesterday to find my wife and all my property gone and at the moment, I don't know where. So if the gossipmongers start up, you already know the full story so far and anything additional is fiction. That's it.'

That evening I called on my neighbours who I hardly knew. To my amazement not only had they noticed an American car parked outside but they had recorded the make, model and number plate. It was one I knew only too well. The car belonged to Peter John Simpson of Motslow Cottage, Motslow near Coventry.

Then I put in a couple of calls to friends to bring them up to speed but I instantly realised from their reactions that they were ahead of me. The penny dropped.

In order to justify her 'run and hide', Rosemary had told some terrible tales to our friends, transferring her dirty doings and adulterous behaviour from her court to mine. Apart from a handful of stitched on mates none of whom she had bothered with, I was to find she had done the rounds and really poisoned my well. People who I'd regarded as close friends simply disappeared from sight and sound forever.

On Friday my old friend Dave Stubbs called and I gave him a heads up on the situation. He was furious to learn that I had been left like a shag on a rock by Rosemary and even more so that Simpson had inserted himself into my domestic business.

'I'll pick you up tomorrow morning and we can drive up and confront him. See what he's got to say for himself.'

I agreed and good as gold he arrived in his Lotus Elan. We had known each other since the cycling days and he worked as a draughtsman. I guessed he had a lot of overtime as he always had an interesting car. I remember a NSU Ro80, a Mustang, a Lotus Cortina and even a 1932 Morgan V-Twin.

At around 11.30 we pulled into Motslow village and stopped next to the telephone box that overlooked Simpson's cottage, the bridge over the stream and the meadow where his car was parked. I went into the phone box and called the house. Peter answered.

'Hello Peter Simpson. It's me.'

There was a sharp intake of breath.

'I'm in your area with my friend Dave and if you are not too busy I thought I'd call in on you. Just to catch up. Be there in half an hour.'

My voice was as firm as I could make it and he must have known that to refuse would raise my suspicions.

'Well, okay, half an hour you say?'

'See you.'

I looked at my watch and was not disappointed. A mere fifteen seconds passed before three figures ran from the building – Simpson, a woman I didn't recognise and my 'never find me' wife.

Crossing the bridge, they piled into the Yank tank, roared out of the field and onto the only road. By this time we had walked to the road and they sped past and I think they were so intent on their mission that they didn't spot us. All this stupid melodrama was wearing thin.

An hour later Simpson and his friend returned. I would have bet a year's wages that Rosemary was now sitting at the man's car sales yard. We weren't dealing with a team of espionage experts here, more like the Three Stooges. We had parked up by the bridge and the couple looked as sick as a pair of parrots at their reception committee.

'Aren't you going to ask us in? We have things to talk about.'

Given their demeanour, it was a dead man walking over to the cottage. We were ushered into the main room where we took two armchairs but to my surprise, our hosts ignored the other chairs and sat on the floor. There was no eye contact.

'What's all this sitting on the floor stuff? What's wrong with the chairs?' I asked.

No response. They looked as if Reggie and Ronnie Kray had come to pick up a debt. I decided to have some fun with this bastard Simpson and reached inside my jacket for my cigarettes. They clearly assumed that a gun or knife was about to appear. The girl scuttled around Simpson to sit directly behind him and I watched the blood drain from their faces.

'What the hell is wrong with you two? You look like you have seen a ghost.'

Lighting up, I started to chat about utter trivia: the weather, motor racing, car sales, the price of houses, all the time flicking ash all over his carpet. I knew this minor discourtesy was but a shadow of the rudeness he had shown to me. I saw the confusion on their faces as they just couldn't work out what was happening. Did I really not know what was going on?

No drinks were offered. They didn't want to prolong the meeting. Finally I edged forward on my seat as if to leave.

'By the way, I have a couple of questions for you, they are simple yes or no questions, no multiple choice stuff and the interesting thing is that I already know the answers. So firstly Pete have you been screwing my wife? And secondly were you in my apartment last Wednesday, without my knowledge or permission, stealing my property. Yes or No?'

By this stage I was more out of the seat than on and our faces inches apart. There was no doubt that the geezer was petrified. David sat slightly behind me to the side, had not spoken and I hadn't introduced him. So Simpson had no idea who he was or why he was here but having listened to my dear wife would have suspected the worst.

'Come on! Yes or no? Cat got your tongue?'

Simpson eyes were drilling holes in the floor.

'I can't answer you.'

'Can't answer me? What, you can't remember? I would have thought they would have been notable events outside the daily routine. I'm sure they would have stuck in your memory. So let's try again, think hard. Yes or no?'

'I can't give you an answer.'

'Well, well. Here we have the big racing driver and car dealer who can't take responsibility for his actions. Happy to screw a friend's wife, then march into his flat and help himself to his friend's property. But hasn't got the balls to own up to what he has done. You really are a gutless bastard. I suggest that you sleep with one eye open in future.'

I signalled to David and we headed out leaving the pair on the floor. At a guess, Simpson figured that if he stood up there was a good chance he would be back on the floor double quick.

'Any idea where he's hidden Rosemary?' David asked as we walked back to the Lotus.

'She is at Simpson's garage for sure.'

'Want to go over there?'

'No, I've had enough of this foolishness. Let's head home. Did you see those two? What bloody nonsense did Rosemary tell them?'

We drove back in silence.

On Sunday morning I hit the local supermarket to stock up with the essentials needed for the kitchen and day-to-day living. Larger items, such as vacuum cleaner, would have to be bought later.

I now had a full picture of events in my mind. For her own reasons, Rosemary had decided that our marriage wasn't what she wanted. She'd planned and executed her exit meticulously. I wasn't aware of her thoughts and decisions but she was confident that I was oblivious to her extramarital affairs. By nobbling our friends and family with sad tales of (imaginary) marital strife and my (imaginary) affairs, she was out, smelling of roses.

I took a conscious decision.

As far as I was concerned the marriage had been a happy one and on course until her two week mystery stay with Simpson. After that it seems the wheels fell off. I didn't want the good times swamped by all the dirt being thrown about and swore to myself that I would not encourage the unpleasantness. Therefore the 'friends' who chose to believe the tales that they'd been told could go hang in the breeze and that be an end to it.

The family was a whole different ball game. Jane would be in her element as misery was her oxygen. I imagined that she would be bursting all over with 'I told you so'. For one of the privileged upper middle class to get involved with an East End oik was just asking for trouble. To be disposed of as quickly as possible with no consideration whatsoever to said oik. All her life Rosemary was accustomed to getting what she wanted. Conversely getting rid of something she didn't want, she should be able to do with minimum inconvenience to herself.

What did worry me was Michael and the siblings but what could I do? They would believe Rosemary to some extent I'm sure but they knew her better than anybody and had plenty experience of her melodramatics. Once the dust had settled, the best I thing could do would be to visit, apologise and step out of their lives.

The knowledge that Rosemary had been dropping her knickers all over the town would stay with me. But that was something I wouldn't discuss with anyone, not even my legal guys. David knew some of it but he was solid and I knew he would be buttoned up.

In fifty years I have never discussed the situation, apart from a brief 'no names' mention in an earlier book. Why expose it now? Well why not? Many of the people involved have kicked the bucket and many more are on the edge. I simply feel that somewhere there should be a record of what took place and here it is.

What I have been thankful for all these years is that Michael was never exposed to the truth. He was a really nice man and Rosemary was the apple of his eye. To have learned that she was a woman with no moral compass would have broken his heart and I would have borne anything rather than let that happen.

I had always been capable in coping with setbacks, taking a positive attitude and turning a bad situation around. All the emotions were raw, the anger, frustration, betrayal, loss and a great sadness but I knew that I had to get past all that and get on with life. I was a great believer in karma although my thought was to take some direct action against my old buddy Simpson.

A new officer manager joined us on Monday. Brian Yates was a young New Zealander and had some knowledge of mechanised accounting systems. Now I had seven members of the accounts department including myself, which was my target number. It was still a massive effort getting the sales invoices typed up so I visited an office equipment exhibition with Marion and Brian. Impressed with what Mitsubishi had to offer, we arranged for their representative Tony Bromage to undertake a survey and make a presentation.

When this was done Des recommended that Arthur Anderson run a rule over the proposition. I have to say their reputation at the time for being the best was well justified and the staff we met were all first rate. However in their opinion one machine would not be enough so we told Tony that we couldn't proceed. It was nobody's fault, just one of those things. The Japanese bosses came back with the offer of a second machine free of charge. How could we refuse?

When they arrived we agreed that the weight may be a problem for the wooden floors, so we swopped rooms with the art department and moved to the concrete building at the back. The system produced the invoices very much the same as by typewriter but provided a punch paper tape record that was fed into the machine at month end to facilitate the printing of statements.

Marion was now regularly putting in a four-day week. Almost every Monday I would get a call from her mother to tell me her daughter was sick and wouldn't be coming in. We all knew the reason was an excess of firewater and I was aware of the effect on the other staff. After a couple of warnings, I gave her the old heave-ho. It was a shame as her work was of a really high standard but I like to run a disciplined office. We also lost a machine operator who had taken up with an NGA guy called Greenway. His wife turned up and made a manic scene in the reception area resulting in my staffer being fired while Greenway wasn't.

Now we had the finances under control, the company could operate without constant cash problems. Bills were paid on time as was the tax man and we could meet the immense payroll every month.

Stan introduced a canteen and we found a formidable woman to run it. Ivy was the best judge of character I have ever met, before or since and should have been employed in human resources.

A cigarette machine and an instant meal vending machine were installed. Both were broken into on the first night and cleaned out; replaced the next day and again instantly robbed. I refused to repeat the experiment and I had Dick Amphlett in my office shouting about the withdrawal of a facility without consultation with the Union. The fact that it was his NGA members doing the damage and stealing was lost on him. Once again the lads were upset, worried and concerned but even Stan Conway wouldn't override me on this one. I had put the bill from the vending company on his desk for authorization.

As we rolled into 1971, I bought an apartment off-plan in Harrow for six thousand pounds. It was partly built with an estimated finish and occupation time in June. I left the Golders Green flat and stayed with my brother part of the time and with friends, or bed and breakfast the rest. After all, I was now travelling light.

By April I felt enough blood had gone under the bridge and telephoned Michael for permission to make a short visit. He was okay with it, not thrilled, but okay. I drove up on a Saturday to find just Michael and the two boys as Jane had absented herself as usual. There aren't enough bad words in the English language to describe that woman.

We chatted generally for maybe half hour and then he walked me to the car. I thanked him for being such a decent bloke and told him how sorry I was that things had come to pass the way they had. I made no comment on the why as I was sure he had his own thoughts and he was nobody's fool. I told him that this was the last he would see of me, shook his hand thanked him again and drove off. I had done what I had promised myself and believed that my decision had been the right one.

In June my lawyer contacted me that my new apartment was ready to finalise and I fixed a meeting for the next morning. Just as I was leaving the office to attend, the phone rang; it was the builder.

'Where are you on the apartment?'

'Just heading for the lawyer to complete. Should all be finished in the hour.'

'Well the price has gone up by a thousand.'

'What are you talking about? We have a signed contract.'

'Then sue me. If you pull out you lose all the costs.'

'That's bloody blackmail.'

I told him in no uncertain terms that I wouldn't pay another penny and he informed me that I'd lost the property. He had buyers queuing up.

So six months on and I was back to square one. The property business seemed to attract chancers and carpetbaggers like moths to a flame. Thus I carried on with the nomadic life.

I had sold the Vauxhall to David, one of the folk who had unfriended me for twenty-five pounds which he never actually paid, so I think that says a lot. Somehow I had been allocated the dispatch department to look after and had updated the motorcycle fleet to ten police standard Triumphs backed up by two Mini Mokes. A Volkswagen Beetle was also in service and I used it as my personal transport.

After some nine months I was bored beyond measure at my position of being a married man who had no idea where his wife was. Just how stupid was all this and how stupid was I putting up with it?

On a Monday morning I had had enough, called my lawyers Landau & Landau at 9am and asked them to put a private detective on the case. By 9.45am I received the information I needed: I had an address and telephone number in Nottingham together with the news she was working at Boots Agrochemicals' head office all for ten quid.

Four weeks later I was staying with my brother when late in the evening the phone rang and Jeffery answered.

'It's for you,' he said holding out the phone, 'it's your wife.'

This was a surprise.

'Hello Rosemary, what can I do for you?'

'I hear that you have found me. Jane says I'm in danger and must move away.'

How in hell did she know? I had only mentioned it to close friends. Did I have a spy in the camp?

'Your stepmother is a poisonous and unhinged woman, and please quote me. I have had the information for over four weeks. I'm sitting here in Kenley, you're in Nottingham and nothing has happened. Let me tell you I'm pretty angry with all this hide and seek crap, totally unnecessary and childish.'

We chatted for a long time but what about I have no recollection. I told her I had a wedding to attend in Mansfield later in the year and maybe we could have dinner then. She agreed. My staffer's wedding was scheduled for Saturday 9 October, so I phoned Rosemary to suggest she meet me in the bar at the Albany Hotel in Nottingham at 6.30pm that day. We could have dinner there.

I drove up to Mansfield on the Saturday morning and stayed at the reception until mid- afternoon. Then I drove over to Nottingham and took a spot in the bar around 6.15pm. I felt that I needed my wits about me and ordered a glass of tonic water. When she walked into the bar, I was shocked and my first thoughts were how she'd managed to get past security dressed like a whore. She wore a skintight white top, a white faux micro skirt and leatherette over-the-knee white boots. Every eye was on her and all conversations had stopped. Initially I assumed that the trashy slut look was intended to annoy me and she'd succeeded. But then I thought that maybe this was her new image. I felt more like a prospective client than a husband.

We adjourned to the restaurant, ordered food, a bottle of Shiraz and finished off with a couple of glasses of Drambuie. Once again, I have no recollection of the conversation but it was after eleven when I asked the receptionist to order a taxi to take her home. Would you believe that he refused on the grounds that she could walk home? Looking the way she did, she would not have been very safe. I insisted, put her in the cab, gave her the fare and waved goodbye. That was the end of that, no question.

On Monday I called my lawyer and instructed him to start divorce proceedings.

'On what grounds?'

'Take your pick and please ask Fenton Bresslaw if he can take it on. I've heard he is the best and I want this done without any slipups.'

'Money no object?'

'Correct. And soon as possible please. I want shot of, let her be someone else's burden.'

The following Saturday I went over to Chequered Flag Motors in Chiswick and drove out with my first Aston Martin. It was a 1966 DB6 registered KCD250F in 1968, cost two thousand pounds and was in the best possible colour – gunmetal grey. The downside was that it was an automatic and without power steering which in London was a pain.

I had a high paying job and a fine motor, so I'd sorted two of the four pillars of normal living. What was missing was a home and a woman but I decided to put both those objectives on ice until my head recovered from recent events. The gypsy life would continue.

*****

Fun and games with the NGA never let up. Much of my time was spent helping employees with their personal finances like mortgages, insurances, tax returns, divorces and so on. I was aware that if a late shift worker needed advice, he would have to make a special effort to visit me and that didn't seem fair.

We employed people around the clock so all should have the reasonable access to the management as a right. My co-directors didn't agree but I persevered and announced that one evening a month I would be in my office until 10pm. Accordingly I stayed my first evening session and nobody visited. But I was not discouraged as I believed that what I was offering was the decent thing to do.

The next day a delegation was in Stan's office complaining that I was spying on the evening and night shifts and (no surprise) the lads were upset, worried and concerned. Stan banned any further late working on my part, no argument, end of story.

The actual typesetting had come a long way from hot metal and was now produced on phototypesetters. Des who was in charge of innovation, had introduced Diatronics, the first keyboard controlled phototypesetter with of course, the full participation of the NGA. Nobody could have imagined back then that in a few years it would all be rendered obsolete by personal computers and desktop publishing.

Conway's was the largest firm of its kind in the UK, if not Europe and its range of fonts unsurpassed. In my view, this was the golden age of advertising with London leading the world in creativity with budgets equal to the movie world. I believe that some six million pounds was spent on an advert for tyres by building a bridge across the Bosphorus just to drive a car over it. We worked for most of the major agencies in London and it was a comfortable environment unless the finance people interfered.

I was called to a meeting of suppliers at J Walter Thompson in Berkeley Square, where we were addressed by the wonderfully named CFO, Mr Treasure. A new system was being introduced where every order had to be a written one, in four parts: the top copy for the supplier, the pink one to be returned to JWT with the invoice, the blue one for JWT accounts and the green one to be retained by the ordering department. Without all of which no payment would be forthcoming.

I got to my feet and told him that this simply wouldn't work. This pissed him off no end, as he was probably bursting with pride about his new baby.

'I represent Conway's the typesetting house. Your typographers often demand a two hour turnaround or less or at best overnight, and there isn't time to mess around with paperwork. They have to get their ideas out for the clients and I'm not asking my sales people to insist on orders and antagonize your creative people.'

He was even more pissed off, telling me and all the others present that his scheme was the way it was and if we wanted to stay on the firm's books, we would have to play along.

I was still standing.

'It won't work – you'll see.'

It never happened. Who knows whether they had actually listened or their staff just ignored it but the avalanche of multi-coloured paper never arrived.

The dark side of the industry, as in many others, was corruption.

I had no problem with the routine entertaining of customers and

I'd heard of cash money being slipped into the pockets of senior typographers in the pub on Friday night with a whispered 'have a good weekend'. But that was small potatoes compared with a rival typesetter who had bought a West End apartment, stocked it with food, drink and women and then offered its use to clients free and gratis. This was exposed some years on and the two instigators received substantial jail terms.

One of our sales guys Peter Bennett told me that we had been summoned to a major advertising agency in the City of London to meet with their CFO to discuss our future relationship. On arrival we were ushered into a massive office and greeted by a middle-aged man whose desk was clear apart from one car brochure. We took the seats offered.

'I have decided that this firm has too many suppliers on its books and this needs to be rationalized. Therefore I am setting up a record of approved suppliers and in future no orders will be allowed to be placed outside of that list.'

I had suspected something of this nature and had already prepared a monthly discount scheme that we could live with to present at the meeting; it wasn't needed.

A podgy hand pushed the brochure across the desk – it was for a Lancia Fulvia 1600HF. We both looked down, then back up to make eye contact with a truly bent accountant.

'That is to be parked outside with a note of where to take it for service and petrol on your account. That will secure your inclusion as a trusted supplier.'

I was aghast.

'Sorry no can do, no way, no how, not in a million years.'

'Well, I'm sorry. I'm certain that one of your competitors will see this as a real opportunity. Good day gentlemen.'

'Your creative staff will not accept this. They will insist on the freedom to use who they want and as we are the best, they will continue with us no matter what you say.'

'Shut the door on your way out.'

When we hit the bricks Peter was shell-shocked.

'That was unbelievable, to have the front to demand a car for himself! Do you really think we will keep the work?'

'I'm sure of it. Anyway, let's report back to Stan. If we do suffer I'm prepared to go to his Board.'

Stan agreed with our thoughts and actions. If word got around that we were giving away Lancia motorcars, there would be a long queue at the door.

Interestingly, nothing more was heard regarding the matter. Maybe the CFO had tried his luck with other suppliers and been rebuffed or maybe even he had listened to my words of wisdom. I suspect he had given it more thought and realised that he was putting his high paying job on the line. If his ultimate bosses in New York had learned what he was up to he would have been out on his ear. Creative guys can, and do, get away with gross liberties but not the pen pushers.

Conway's threw parties, big no holds barred parties. The core problem was that the head typographer of one of the top five London advertising agencies was a skinhead who dressed straight out of Clockwork Orange and he'd bring along a dozen mates of a similar bent. We couldn't avoid inviting him as in our small world he would soon know he had been blackballed and the consequences would be dire. So we hired security and lots of it.

One year the do was in a club on the first floor and when the yobbos arrived, they caused mayhem. The leader poured a full pint of beer over the head of Erwin Wasey's Chairman's lovely wife and battle commenced. A howling, roaring mass of muscle descended the staircase and with heroic effort, the dirty dozen were forced into the street and the doors locked.

The next morning Stan received a hand delivered thank you note: best party ever, thank you, looking forward to next year.

I stopped going to these gigs early on in my term of employment. Definitely not the NGA boys most favourite co-worker, with free booze washed down their necks, I could well imagine some unpleasantness heading my way, with prejudice. So I was on the missing list for the Thames River evening river cruise where tempers flared and two combatants ended up being rescued from the water by the police.

The firm also attended the annual National Advertising

Benevolent Society (NABS) bash where limitless drinks were dispensed by a couple of topless girls who, towards the end of the evening, became bottomless at the drop of two fifty pound notes.

Early in 1972 Conway's started up an audio-visual department to add another string to their bow. Judy was recruited to manage the department and I was impressed. Having just climbed out of the bear pit, I was in no rush to start up a relationship, especially with anyone working in the same firm. But I spent more time than was necessary in the a/v operation, helping with transport and clients. Eventually we got together and rented a small apartment in Battersea.

The sales team had a new leader brought in, one Stanley Paine. As there was no natural candidate in house, a professional salesman was recruited to beef up our marketing. Within a few days of joining us it was obvious that he had a serious drinking problem. The night shift had found him passed out on the back stairs at 10pm one evening. None of us wanted to admit we had made a big fat mistake so we turned a blind eye for the moment.

When we discussed the budgets for 1972/73 with him, he asked for a special fund of one thousand pounds to be spent as he saw fit on staff morale; this was unusual but was granted.

Our financial year kicked off on 3 April and Mr Paine gathered his troops that very evening to set off on a bonding exercise. The next morning he requested the whole of the special fund without a single receipt proffered. I refused but Conway signed off on it so I let it go. No one outside the sales people could find out what the hell happened and even under the influence, everyone involved kept buttoned up. The only fragments I gleaned was that the evening kicked off at Trader Vic's restaurant and possibly ended up in a hotel room with a couple of ladies of the night.

We took a stand on a trade fair in Chicago and those unlucky enough to travel out there with Paine came back with terrible tales of the man being pissed 24/7 and utterly out of his mind. Plus Stan Conway returned with a mega dental problem, so it could be said that the US adventure was not a success. Sorry to say, Mr Paine's boozing was out of control and we fired him. The last time I saw him was on Victoria Station around 11pm, three sheets to the wind and trailing his raincoat behind him while trying to find a train to get him homeward bound.

The south London pad had always been intended to be a short-term stay. Property prices were rising fast and I simply had to get on board. The proposition of a house in the suburbs was no longer of any interest but in an estate agent's window, I spotted a flat, within twenty minutes walking distance of our work in Maida Vale.

Carlton Mansions in Randolph Avenue comprised two Edwardian Blocks separated by an entrance to Paddington Recreation Grounds and tennis courts. Consisting of 94 apartments, number 43 was a first floor walk-up and on viewing, it was very clear that a total refurbishment was essential. The former occupants were a couple of female schoolteachers who had done a job of work moving out, right down to taking all the electrical fittings and even the lagging off the pipes.

I made an offer at the asking price that was accepted. Don Nichols my insurance man, arranged a mortgage with Norwich Union and my lawyers got to work. The surveyor reported some minor bomb damage from the war but all that could be fixed without any great cost.

With heavy heart the Aston Martin was sold. I needed every penny to get the transaction done so needs must. I got back my two grand exactly.

After three weeks the estate agent phoned me to ask how it was going.

'All good,' I assured him. 'The mortgage is signed up and the lawyers are working towards completion. Should be about ten days I guess.'

'Peter, I have to tell you that you're in a race. There's another buyer and the first to complete gets the apartment.'

I was furious. Bloody agents, here we go again. From his voice I was sure he was lying and I decided to call his bluff.

'No, there's no race, I'm out. Let the other geezer have the place, I'm not interested in these games you play. Please send my deposit over to my solicitors today and I will tell them to cancel everything.'

'No, no, hang on, what about your costs?'

'Lost, I guess. Look, I'm busier than a one-armed paperhanger so gotta go. Bye.'

I hung up, told our receptionist that this fella would be calling and that I was unavailable no matter what. Three days later I took the call.

'Peter, are you still interested in Carlton Mansions?'

'Maybe, but I've cancelled everything. Has the other guy dropped out?'

Silence while he decided whether to tell the truth or field another lie. I hadn't cancelled anything, so I pressed on.

'If I have your word that there'll be no more playacting, I'll press on with the purchase.'

'You have my word. I was just trying to speed things up.'

'Your plan worked a treat. I'll get things moving again.'

The word of an estate agent? Don't think you could take that to the bank.

We moved in and it was as rough as guts. I had a credit line with Selfridges so we were able to sort out some basic furniture and linen and an electrician made the wiring safe to use. It was a good feeling to have our own place in a nice area although we were soon to discover that the park was unusable due to its role as a dog's toilet. The groundsmen were as dedicated to tea and cigarettes as their brothers in West Ham and were never to be seen outside their hut. Shame as otherwise it would have been a safe and pleasant place to jog or just enjoy the open space. The block did have a garden running the length of the buildings that was underused and well cared for.

The first major snag came in the shape of our elderly downstairs neighbours. The smallest sound of saw on wood or hammer on nail and the bloke would be screaming blue murder for us to stop. This resulted in materials having to be measured up in situ, then taken to the basement workshop at Conway's to be cut to size, predrilled and returned home to be fitted. It was a painstaking business and extended the time needed to complete any job by a factor of two. Much of the work we did ourselves and brought in tradies as needed to undertake the difficult stuff.

We bought another Mini 'Woodie' which was stolen and reported to the Old Bill. A month later we received a call from the police pound saying that they had the car towed in from Manchester Square two weeks earlier. Why hadn't we collected it? They were well upset that we refused to pay the fine for the forty parking tickets stuck to the windscreen. Find the driver who dumped it, I suggested.

It was around that time when I saw a car crash actually happen in Marylebone. Driven at speed, the car clipped the kerb and flipped over onto its roof. I ran to help and passed two traffic wardens writing up tickets. I called for them to give a hand and their reply was what you expect from pond life like them.

'Not our job mate.'

It was a great slice of luck that no one was hurt, just shocked.

Next to the loading bay in Cato Street, a derelict building had been pulled down and was to be replaced by two town houses. We worked well with builders until a high wind brought down a wall on top of one of the motorcycles. They refused to accept any responsibility or give us details of their insurers, so relations deteriorated. That proved to be a precursor to problems when the nearest building became occupied.

I cannot understand for the life of me how the new owner did not realise that he would be living next to a commercial operation. One that was open twenty-four hours a day Monday to Friday, with motor cycles coming and going constantly. Maybe he only came to view at weekends.

But from the day he moved in complaints came by the bucket load. He would call in the police on a nightly basis as staff came and went, slamming doors, starting cars, talking, shouting, whistling, you name it. I had made arrangements for a skip to be delivered on a Friday afternoon to enable an overdue clear out of old machinery and left over building materials. Phil the maintenance man with me to help was going to do it on Saturday. We had tried to do this on a weekday but the lads simply pulled out everything we threw in, took the stuff back to their workplace to be taken home at some later date. Which totally defeated the purpose.

When I arrived the skip was already full to overflowing with a smashed up piano. When our neighbour exited his home it was obvious that it was his doing. Accordingly we took the pieces out and piled them up against his house. When he returned he called the police and the council and in thirty minutes a group had formed to hear his allegations which we didn't deny. But under questioning he admitted that it was his piano and yes he had under cover of darkness disposed of it in our skip, without our knowledge or authorization.

The balance of the official opinion was that he was a dirty scoundrel and that he must find a way to dispose of his rubbish at his own cost. He was not a happy bunny and continued to be a thorn in our side. However the police were sick of being pointlessly called out and thereafter gave him short shrift.

When we kicked over into 1973, I was given a date by my lawyers for the divorce hearing. The morning I headed out of the apartment to go to the High Court in Aldwych I picked a postcard up from the doormat. It had been sent from Monte Carlo and, bearing Rosemary's signature, it read: 'In Monaco on a yacht in the harbour – this is the life. Good luck with the divorce.'

I thought it was a really mean thing to send me and luck that I didn't need. If you need a fast way to burn money, hire a legal team. They had made first class preparation and had extracted a 'my fault' statement to file. I was on the stand for just two or three minutes. Afterwards I offered a round of drinks but they all declined, so I went back to work. Three months later the final clearance came through and I was a free man. A sad end to what I had thought was a great romance. And a ball-breaking experience, never to be repeated.

A friend offered me a 1963 Sunbeam Alpine Mark II and it was a disaster. It burned as much oil as it did petrol and changed gear of its own accord. It was a short-term experiment and I was very relieved to be able to sell it for what I had paid.

The dispatch department had swopped the Mini Mokes for two Renault 4s and their dash-mounted gear lever took some getting used to but they were terrific workhorses and performed very reliably.

The company was doing well, so at last we were able to take holidays to the Canary Islands and have weekends away.

There is no doubt that trade unions were fundamental in bringing decent conditions and fair pay to the working classes and ending the exploitation by the industrialists at the close of the 19th century and the beginning of the 20th. But by the 1960s in the UK, I think that many were being led by militants bent on anarchy. The automobile industry had been irreparably damaged, coal mining was heading for self-destruction and the print trade workers rushing towards a cliff of their own making to jump off.

Conway called a meeting on a Wednesday at 2pm to discuss the next year's NGA pay increases. This would involve the Father of the Chapel, his deputy, their treasurer and the five directors. It occurred to me that perhaps I should warn my leader that a special informal arrangement had been made between Amphlett and his manager that his mid-shift started not at 2pm but at 4pm to compensate for the hardships we put him through. Clearly, I was the only director to the wise. My mischievous streak took over and I let it ride. After all, even Dirty Dick would make an effort to report in on time for such an important meeting, wouldn't he?

Came the hour and seven assembled. Two hours passed in silence and on the stroke of four the door opened and the waft of the brewer's dray floated in followed by Mr Amphlett. He was dressed to cause offence wearing a filthy vest with hair pushing out at both front and back, dirty torn jeans and Dr Martens 16-eye boots, all topped off with greasy hair and a weekend stubble. It was a wind-up, no question. He took his place without a word and hoisted his boots onto the boardroom table.

'Thank you for coming, Dick,' said Conway.

I couldn't stand anymore.

'What the hell are you talking about "Thank you for coming Dick"! He's two hours late, offers no apology and he can get his feet of the boardroom table.'

That fired Amphlett up a treat. He swept his feet from the table, jumped up and launched into a replay of the speech that I'd previously eavesdropped on with much use of his favourite description of the management. Him being half-cut added to the pathos of it all. Conway's first reaction was to kick me in the shin and then he was also on his feet trying, unsuccessfully, to calm Amphlett.

Wot a way to run a business!

I was judged to be the villain of the piece but you couldn't have a finance meeting without the CFO. An hour's adjournment was called during which interval calmer heads prevailed; it was time for amelioration.

The lads prevented Dick from returning to the drinking club and in truth I think they were tired of his antics especially when it came to their wages. Stan had rushed to the canteen to stop Ivy from closing for the day and arranged for her to get fresh bread and some expensive fillings to set up two trays of sandwiches, partnered by pots of fresh coffee. My colleagues insisted that I did nothing more to antagonize Dick.

'Don't you four ever resent being constantly referred to as fucking parasites and having to swallow it? It's more than disrespectful and yet we're expected to grin and bear it!'

'It's just trade talk, it means nothing,' Conway offered.

'Rubbish, it's what they believe.'

However I had to agree that we had to deal with what we had. We reconvened at 5pm but I refused to join the feast, something about breaking bread with the enemy.

The talks went as expected. They demanded a three year deal at an outrageous percentage based on upping the ante. We spoke in single numbers based on common sense, inflation and what the business could handle. The Chapel agreed to seek advice from The House on what was being achieved in our industry generally and it all wrapped up in fifteen minutes.

The special arrangement was never mentioned and continued unchallenged allowing Dick to enjoy ten hours a week free time.

Another union was impinging on our business. Over the years there had been a series of strikes within the coal industry and it is generally agreed that the miners were responsible for bringing down the government of Edward Heath.

Another pit strike came into force on 1 January 1974 and a three day working week was imposed. This would prove to be a disaster for Conway's as much of our work had very short lead times. Equally we could be sure that any co-operation from the NGA would come at a fine price. So we hired the mother of all generators and had it installed in the loading bay. Wired into the electricity system, at a throw of a switch the huge diesel motor would fire up and power would transfer from the grid to in-house. The benefit to the business was obvious: while our competitors juggled to meet orders, we traded on without any interruptions. Apart from our neighbour, who of course called out police and council officials about the noise. They would not, or could not help him and by then his solicitor was on the case. The strike had finished on 7 March and the generator returned to base.

I was overpaid by some 35% in the marketplace, we all were, and I wondered how long this could be sustained. Although I enjoyed the income I resented the fact that I was effectively trapped as if I moved on my standard of living would take a big hit. The actual work was fine and my staff made a good team. But apart from Des, I had little respect for my fellow directors and pure contempt for 'the lads' on the shop floor. Throwing money at problems and difficulty was the only solution the directors ever offered and that attitude needed no skill set whatsoever.

The company pension scheme was a prime example of this management style. We had set up a contributory plan for directors some years earlier but Stan Conway wanted to expand this to all staff on the completion of two years' service. This would be non-contributory and the company would pay into the fund an amount equal to 6% of the worker's pay which I thought was very generous.

Naturally the first person to be informed was the Leader of the Chapel together with his deputy. As the latter was on the night shift, I called for a meeting with them at 10pm. No other director volunteered to help.

I asked our broker, Don Nicholls to attend and we arranged to meet at the local Thai restaurant at 8pm together with a representative from the insurance company who were setting up the plan. We were all very careful not to drink too much, not only because we were all driving but needed all our full faculties at the meeting.

We all bailed up in the canteen, Dick displaying his usual sartorial elegance and I explained the plan. The reception was not what I expected.

Dick lounged back in his chair with his cock-of-the-north attitude.

'Is Ivy included in this?'

That was one question I could not have expected.

'No, Ivy is a self-employed contractor and the canteen is her business.'

A silence fell and then Dick launched into one.

'It's not fucking good enough.'

I felt my two guests tense up.

He continued with his well-worn monologue regarding the fucking parasites standing between 'his lads' and the customers, living off their skills hard learned on a seven-year apprenticeship and if there is money around to pay for a pension scheme then that money should come to NGA members only in the form of extra pay.

'I did an apprenticeship as well,' I pointed out.

'Not a real one like us. All you did was walk around with fucking papers under yer arm.'

At this point it could be said that I had reached the end of my rope.

'Your behaviour in front of guests is a disgrace. I can't speak for the directors but as far as I'm concerned the pension scheme is dead in the water.'

My two companions realised that it was time to go as nothing was to be achieved by continuing. They rose to their feet and headed out of the door. I apologised for wasting their evening and they sympathized with what I had to deal with on a daily basis.

The next morning Stan Conway called me to his office.

'You obviously made a real mess of last night's meeting over the pension scheme.'

'Really? I thought it went rather well.'

'What's your version?'

'Dick was against it. He felt that if there were profits then the directors should have them for doing such a good job.'

'What rubbish is that? I've been called to the House to explain why profits earned by the lads are being withheld from them.'

'Look as far as I am concerned, the pension scheme won't happen.'

'I've have sorted out your mess and the pension scheme will go forward exactly as planned.'

'And?'

'And the NGA members will all receive a 6% pay increase backdated to 1st October last year.'

'Good grief. Have you any idea what that will cost?'

'No I don't but it has solved the problem you created.'

'And this pay rise is for everybody, accounts, dispatch, art department etc?'

'No, just NGA members.'

'And you decided all this without talking to the other directors?'

'I had to act quickly and decisively to stop the House getting involved.'

And that was that. The owners of the business lived in fear of the workers. The tail didn't just wag the dog, it beat its head against the wall.

This was not exclusive to Conway's. Much of the print industry was hidebound with arcane language and practices, blissfully unaware of the changes soon to come; changes which would decimate the workforce and therefore the power and control of the various unions.

I came across an excellent example of the rotten state of affairs whilst on holiday in the Canaries. One morning the hotel breakfast buffet was very crowded and I found myself sharing a table with a young guy and we struck up a conversation, as you do. After introductions, he told me that he was a machine operator at The Times newspaper on Gray's Inn Road.

'I'm doing up a house in Preston and commute.'

'Commute from Preston to Central London every day? How long does that take?'

'It's not too bad, I have a very fast Audi. But I haven't been in for a year.'

'How come?'

'I fell off a ladder at home and hurt myself pretty bad. So I got the girlfriend to drive me down to town and to cut a long story short, I claimed that an accident had taken place with the printing machinery.

I just send a doctor's note in every month and my wages keep coming. We've got the place pretty sown up. It had been agreed with the bosses that my machine needed seventeen men to operate it but in reality one man was enough. So there's plenty of time for rest and relaxation. I miss the overtime money though.'

'Don't you worry that they will check up on you?'

'They wouldn't bother. It would just cause trouble for them.'

*****

One morning reception called me to tell me that a Mr Smethurst was downstairs. Which one I thought?

Since my fleeting visit to the family home, my only contact had been with Jackie and her boyfriend Nick, taking them to dinner just the once. Otherwise I had deliberately not made any approaches to any of the clan; we were all moving on with our lives and the only thing we had in common was my now ex-wife. Enough said.

It could be Michael, John or Bill but I was pleased to discover that it was the last of the three. As it was close to lunchtime, we headed for the pub. It transpired that Bill hadn't been certain exactly where my place of work was, so had been pounding the pavements all morning before he found a street he recognized.

We ordered some drinks and pub grub, then found a corner table.

'So what are you doing these days?'

'I'm an accountant.'

'Really? Why?'

'Because you are.'

For me this was a defining moment. After all the horror show that Rosemary had laid at my door with all the lies, the cheating and the hurt to so many people, this endorsement that I wasn't an entirely bad person came like a rainbow into my life.

From that moment we stayed in touch. After he moved to Toronto we experienced large gaps between meetings but even so I regard Bill as an important person in my life.

*****

I had fully expected the beginning of the end for me at Conway's would stem from my constant battles with the NGA, but when it did actually happen the roots sprung from a totally surprising area.

It all started with the art department run by Keith Woods who was a decent enough manager, his PA and staffed by about ten artists. But the art department was a thorn in Stan's side because it produced a loss every month. Strangely, this didn't bother me as it generated a mass of work for the typesetting side. All Keith needed to do was demand a major customer discount, thus turning loss into profit but he didn't. One day he quit and we advertised for a replacement at £7,500pa which was only a little less than I was paid. So we thought we were entitled to the very best.

We did attract a solid response and chose a final five from the applications submitted to interview. Stan, Des and I conducted these and two guys stood out, so we called them back for a second viewing.

After all this performance we agreed on a Michael Andrew Pratchett. He stood out as being very personable, well spoken and had a CV to envy that cited Shell, Dunlop, ICI and other blue-chip outfits as previous employers. It was a no-brainer and Stan agreed to offer him the position. A directors meeting was called and Stan informed us that he had made the call and Michael would be joining us on two conditions.

'He wants £8,500 plus a car.'

I was the first to speak up.

'Tell him to get stuffed! He applied at a salary of £7,500 and that's it. No way José.'

A heated discussion followed and it was agreed, but not by me that he would be offered the extra money but not the car. The majority vote won.

I had my objection put on record and my guess was that he was a conman.

He started and on day one informed Conway that he needed one day off a week to have dialysis to cope with his failing kidneys. What a joke, a four day week and paid top dollar.

When Stan told me I erupted.

'Told you, a swindler. Demand medical paperwork or better still, send him packing.'

Again, I was outvoted and the man was to be given a chance to perform. Just don't go looking for him on Wednesdays when he was supposedly in hospital. He knew from the outset that I was on to him and I made no secret that I thought he was a spiv. Maybe it takes one to know one.

After three weeks Stan took him to meet an important customer, BOAC as it was known then, and they went to lunch with a couple of senior guys. Halfway through the main course Michael fell asleep and rested his head on the table. Stan tried to explain it might be the effects of the dialysis but whatever it was it wasn't a good look

The staff didn't take to him and he seemed to be on the missing list more often than not. The showdown came around three months into the programme. We had a meeting to go over the budgets for the studio which had been distributed a few days earlier. Michael had a question.

'These cash flow projections? I don't understand why there is a big fluctuation every three months, is this a mistake?'

I knew it, a fraudster and he had just cooked himself.'

'That's the rent, payable every quarter.'

'Nonsense. What kind of accountant are you? Rent is paid monthly, like everything else.'

Parcelled up like a kipper.

I watched Stan's face as the blood drained.

The meeting wrapped up and the room emptied, leaving just Stan and I.

'Okay, you were right, he doesn't have a clue.'

He was fired, sued us and with the kidney failure business, we were hammered by his lawyer. If the case had gone to court, we would have looked to be the worst ruthless bosses in the world. To get the problem gone cost Conway's £20,000.

For some months this was the elephant in the room. There was no doubt that Stan was to blame for the fiasco by pushing hard for Pratchett even after he put the bite on, which for me was a big fat warning sign of a charlatan. Des, Dave and John were simply not really interested in the machinations within the art department and happily took a back seat.

I did some research on my own, which of course should have been carried out before the job offer. Telephoning the employers on Pratchett's CV, I received an interesting selection of responses. Often I was brushed off with the confidentiality excuse and once I was just hung up on but a global cereal producer had their lawyer return my call and he was very cagey. I decided that I would have to come clean if I was going to learn anything, so I laid out my stall and went through the super interviewer, the extra demands, the dialysis, the swift downfall and the humungous cost.

When I finished I could hear an intake of breath and he spoke.

'This is confidential. My clients don't want it known that they can be taken in but they were, just like your company. They normally carry out detailed checks but this man seemed so outstanding that they didn't want to lose him and went through an almost exact replica of your experience. I think this is how he makes a living.'

'A lucrative method, if you have the gall.'

'Oh, he had the gall all right.'

I thanked him for his openness and hung up.

Stan was both furious and embarrassed. He announced that he would head up the art department and knock it into shape. He later informed me that he had changed the staff payment scheme after discussions and with their agreement; from wages plus overtime to a flat salary basis with the understanding that they would stay late if necessary, to finish that day's workload.

A few weeks later Stan told me he had recruited some freelancers to help with busy periods and give variety in the creative field. They would be paid in cash weekly on Fridays, giving an extra chore to my department.

Stan wasn't putting through a charge for his time or that of his PA which effectively gave the department a subsidy from the rest of the group. Even so, I couldn't see how all these extra labour costs would bring the division to profit. Let's watch and wait.

The department continued with mixed results, most months achieving near break even and it was such a small part of the whole it attracted little of my attention.

One Friday evening in late September 1975, I received a phone call from Brian Cox. From the background noise I deduced he was in a pub and was more excited than pissed.

'I need to see you tomorrow. I've stumbled onto something serious and I can't talk on the phone.'

'Can we meet at the office around ten?'

'Yes, can't talk, see you then.'

Puzzled was the word. Saturday morning we both arrived early and sat down with cups of coffee and doughnuts.

'OK. What's up Doc?'

'When I left yesterday evening, I knew that I couldn't catch my train so slipped into the pub for a quick one. The art department were in there, well almost all of them, and they were on a bender. They invited me to join but I explained that I was only in for one and bought myself a pint. I noticed that they all had wads of brand new notes and funnily enough the cash I had got from the bank for the freelancers was all brand new. I don't believe in coincidences, so I called my wife, told her I'd be late and pretended to join the session. It was one of the girls that blew it when she let it slip that they got their overtime pay cash in hand, no tax.'

We settled down to comb through the contractors' invoices and it soon became obvious that the majority were completely false. Streets that didn't exist, untraceable names, a tissue of lies.

What hurt the most was the lack of respect for me and my department. If a tax audit had turned up they would not have believed that I wasn't in on it. No accountant could be that stupid and this would have damaged my reputation irreversibly.

What had happened was that the arts people had reneged on their agreement with Conway and refused to work overtime for free. They weren't NGA but had worked cheek-by-jowl with the union guys and knew the power of collective labour.

If I had been in charge I would have reversed the salary arrangements and they could take it or leave it. But as ever, Stan solved the quandary by throwing money at it, as usual without a word to his fellow directors.

After festering over the rest of the weekend, on Monday morning my mind was clear and I called a board meeting for ten o'clock. Four bewildered faces stared at me when I entered the room and rather than taking a seat, I stood at the end of the table and read a one page letter to the directors

It summarised what Brian and I had discovered: that we were looking at a conspiracy to defraud the Inland Revenue, false invoicing, fraud, false accounting and obtaining money by deception for starters, all perpetrated on my watch. I would insist that the Company remedy the situation, after which I would distance myself by my resignation effective that day. I was contracted to work out six months notice and I would honour that.

While Des, Dave and John looked totally dumbfounded, Conway sat with a smile throughout. No shame or even embarrassment. I had no doubt that my decision was solid. Later in the week I was informed that meetings had been set up with both our lawyers and accountants to discuss how to proceed.

The solicitor was very decent and commended me on my taking the high road. He lectured Stan on the seriousness of what he had done and that involving staff, including junior staff, in a plan to commit a crime was foolhardy in the extreme. A secret is no longer a secret when a second person knows it. We then took a taxi over to Wilson Wright, where a completely different reception awaited us.

We were ushered into the inner sanctum where Messrs Gould and Boreham stood waiting. They rushed forward to greet Stan Conway with double-handed handshakes and much squeezing of his elbows and shoulders. Then virtually carried him to the visitor's chair. I was the invisible man, no handshake was offered, not even eye contact. Mr Gould placed a hand on Conway's arm and leaned forward.

'Mr Conway, I cannot tell you how sorry I am that this has happened. Let me reassure you that WE will put everything right.'

The obsequiousness was causing my stomach to react and not in a good way. I decided to stir the pot.

'Well that's good news for me, that you're going to carry out the work. I'll call the office and get a desk made ready for you.'

'That's not what I meant, you will carry out the calculations and we will supervise.'

'You really think that I need your supervision?'

You had to be there to witness this unedifying spectacle. I would rather say goodbye to a customer than demean myself like these two were. Even though their client had committed a series of crimes, they would not utter a word of admonishment and did not care an iota that these actions had led directly to the loss of MY job. It is said that there is honour among thieves but there certainly wasn't much honour among accountants.

Boreham had already thrown me under a bus over the seating arrangements at Greville Tinners, so I didn't expect anything from him. In the past I had always had the greatest respect for Mr Gould. He had given me a chance long ago which I had repaid by seven years of hard work and commitment. To see what was being enacted in front of me was crushing.

Mr Gould spoke in Conway's ear, 'Peter has always been too emotional'.

'You're right. I get very emotional when someone commits fraud and theft right under my nose.'

'Mr Conway has done nothing wrong. He owns the company.'

'Two points, he doesn't own the company because there are other shareholders. Secondly, conspiracy to defraud the Inland Revenue is a crime whoever you are. And if there had been a Revenue audit I would have been the one shoved straight up the barrel.'

When I had seen the meet and greet, I decided to remain by the door and not move into the room. My left hand reached behind me for the knob, which I turned, and started to back out. 'Where are you going? We are not finished yet,' said Mr Gould.

'I have to leave. I need to go outside and throw up.'

I backed out, shut the door and walked away. The sight of Conway's beaming smile as he was being washed clean by his friends when he should have been hung out to dry stayed with me for a long time. I walked back to Molyneux Street which was a fair hike.

Stan had beaten me back and had regaled his co-directors with the hot news that in the senior auditor's own words he had done nothing wrong. All that was needed was some technical accounting work and that was it. I imagine that all this business was of little interest to them as long as their stipend kept rolling into their bank accounts. An accountant leaving would be replaced with another pen pusher and in their minds did not add up to a row of beans. Life goes on.

Clearly the company had been hamstrung for future development and expansion as any major plans would involve due diligence. It wouldn't take a genius to find the fingerprints of dirty dealing and that would automatically kibosh a deal before it got off the ground.

Wilson Wright's attitude did not totally surprise me except that they had very recently been on the front line: a client's directors had falsified their company's accounts, the culprits had ended up in the dock and the case became the subject of a Department of Trade report. Wilson Wright were the auditors to Roadships Limited (formerly known as Ralph Hilton Transport Services limited).

I had always taken time out to chat with the auditors when they made their annual visit to Conway's and the talk of the town from 1970 to 1975 was always Ralph Hilton. He had continued to upset Mr Gould by buying up business after business without consulting the professionals, preferring to rely on his own business acumen to get the deals done. The company had gone public in 1970 and the first year's accounts were up to speed. However in 1972 it came to light that the previous year had been achieved by the aid of £68k of false sales invoices which the auditors had failed to detect and another £150k of 'errors'. This led to the rise and fall and rise again of Mr Hilton. With the help of the most excellent archives of Commercial Motor to fill in the gaps, this is the chapter and verse of a wild ride.

By 1970 Hilton had taken over some 40 transport companies throughout England and Scotland, controlled over 1000 lorries and had in excess of 1500 employees. A ten-acre site in Charlton was acquired for a central base and was opened by Richard March MP. The two ocean-going speedboats owned by the company were also kept on site, known by some as Gestapo Headquarters.

November 1970 saw the business floated on the stock exchange backed by Industrial and Commercial Finance (ICFC) and Thomson Mclintock. The joint auditors were to be Wilson Wright (who had held the role since 1959) and Peat Marwick Mitchell. The accounts for the year to July 1971 showed a turnover of £4.3 million and a profit of £626k. So far so good.

In June 1972, an independent audit was called to report to the Board. At any one time some 28 accountants were toiling away and although the findings were never made public, in July the stock exchange quote was suspended.

The July 1972 accounts were produced with heavy qualification. The loss for the year was £1.159 million. In addition the previous year's profit had been overstated by £218k by fake invoices and other devices, and even the 1969/70 profits overstated by £42k. The net liability stood at £2.3 million.

I have not tracked down the results for July 1973 but the first 28 weeks, unaudited, showed a loss of £435k that I guess would extrapolate to around £800k for the year. In April 1973 Ralph Hilton resigned. In September of that year the Department of Trade ordered a report. Year 1973/74 continued with more of the same with a loss of £948, reducing to £536 after tax.

Directors came and went as the struggle to get the business under control continued but in May 1975 the ICFC pulled the pin and appointed a Receiver and a name change was made to Roadships Limited. In June 1975 the court actions instigated by the Department of Trade came to a finale at the Old Bailey.

Accountant Rob Withers had turned Queen's Evidence. When this was announced to the court, I was told by someone who was there that Hilton leaned over and whispered into his ear; Withers collapsed on the floor. Maybe it's an urban legend but I can believe it.

Financial controller John Skinner received a suspended prison sentence. Ralph Hilton was fined £2,500 plus £2,500 costs.

Justice needs to be seen to be done but personally I don't think it was done in this instance. I know that all the people who sold their companies in exchange for Hilton shares will agree with me.

At some time in 1976, Mr Hilton acquired from the Receiver of Roadships Limited the William Beadle Subsidiaries and also J & H Transport, the latter alone having 240 vehicles. He was back on the road again.

The Department of Trade report came out in September 1976. Roadships Limited (formerly known as Ralph Hilton Transport Services Limited), investigation under section 165(b) of the Companies Act 1948; report by Benet Alan Hytner & Alexander

Noble Irvine for the Department of Trade - 401 pages.

As expected, it was critical of many of the parties involved. It stated that the company 'was not fit to be floated as a public company' and that neither Ralph Hilton nor John Skinner were fit to be directors.

It was highlighted that at the time of SIH negotiations, Hilton declared that his salary was £6,000pa, whereas in fact he was drawing (in one form or another) £16,000pa, plus £2,600pa in false expense vouchers.

(That last bit rang a bell somewhere in the back of my head.)

'Wilson Wright & Co, auditors, bore part of the blame for the state of the accounts department of the company.'

There is one part of the report I would dispute. It stated 'that rumours of gangland associations were discounted'. I know who I saw in the yard at Vauxhall all those years ago: Charlie Richardson, Eddie Richardson and Frank Fraser. At the time they were the toughest of the tough and it's no secret that they were very capable debt collectors.

I know the individual who was scapegoated for the audit failure but will not share it here. The reason for setting out this saga in detail is that my visit to Wilson Wright with Stan was in late September 1975 and although the DoT report was not yet completed, those involved would have known what to expect when it was published.

In the light of that, it is even more bewildering that Conway's false invoicing caused such little concern and their assertion that it could all be put right at a stroke of a pen.

Ralph Hilton died in 1981 aged 58.

The matter surfaced again in 2002 when Parliament investigated the relationships between auditors/accountants and their clients and the facts behind audit failures. In many cases, the inability of many firms to face up to their clients' bad behaviour stems from not wanting to bite the hand that feeds you, as simple as that.

I now faced a difficult six months. It was too early to launch myself on the job market as I was not going to be available until April 1976 and I was in a bad spot having to deal with Conway on a daily basis, who asked me several times to change my mind. It would have been an easy path to say yes and collect a pay increase but my self-respect would not allow me to do so.

It is fair to say that the black dog arrived. I was very angry. This was my job, which I had created and had paid a high price along the way, putting up with abuse from 'the lads' and dealing with a freewheeling CEO who spent money like a drunken sailor in port. I had brought the business into a secure financial position and some geezer off the street would arrive and enjoy all the benefits of my sweat and toil. Not fair.

In January I contacted employment agencies, reporting my salary as £8k whereas with bonuses and pension contributions it was nearer £12k. I attended a few interviews and finally received an offer that strangely, I didn't want; the meeting consisted of half an hour of the CEO talking and I don't think I spoke a dozen words. Every fibre of my body, my gut instinct, my intuition, all told me 'don't do it' but it was the only game in town so I accepted.

My replacement James McDonnell came to see me and he was a presentable fellow. I showed him round and made introductions as appropriate. I advised him that sourcing replacements for the accounting machines was top of the to do list. The existing equipment had been almost flogged to death and by my reckoning had the maximum of a year left. Brian and I had written a detailed user's manual to help him with the task.

Judy decided to move out and I didn't blame her as I must have been hell to live with. She had found a flat in Covent Garden that was ideal for her. I was sorry but it had been my fault, so no excuses.

On item still to be settled was my shareholding and I fully expected to be stitched-up. I was not to be disappointed. Stan asked for a meeting to discuss the matter and I was prepared.

'The auditors tell me that your shares in the company are worth nothing and have suggested that you be given £1,000 to transfer them.'

'Really? Are these the same auditors that valued these same shares at £4,000 some six years ago?'

'They say that when you acquired them, they were part of a bigger parcel and that's what they were valued at then.'

'You know Stan, I couldn't give a monkey's toss for the opinion of anyone at Wilson Wright. I have known them for fifteen years and their philosophy of life and mine are light years apart. Six years ago this company was only a short pass from going down the toilet and now it's a success story. As you know full well sales in 1968 were around £200k whereas in 1976 were well over a million with profits in line and now there's a rock solid balance sheet. I have made my own calculation which I have discounted by 50% to take into account the small amount of shares, which will just about cover the interest I paid on the bank loan, and you can take it or leave it, as frankly I don't give a shite what you do any more.'

I dropped my offer in an envelope on his desk and departed. That afternoon his cheque arrived in an envelope on my desk for the full amount. Working on for six months had been a mistake and had drained me. I was more than ready to turn mother's picture to the wall and walk away.

I had learned a lot over the years but I could never adopt the approach of appeasing the client at all costs. Generally I found that people appreciated straight talking and straight dealing. Ego stroking was never my forte.

I took my department out for a slap up Chinese meal and thanked them all. Stan and Des took me to Claridges for lunch and a very nice presentation. So what happened to this colourful cast of characters?

James McDonnell did nothing about the machines and after a year of breakdowns they both gave up the ghost, so it was back to paper and pen for the accounts. A little beforehand he was heard to boast to a visitor about his input into the department.

'When I arrived there were only seven people in accounts and now I have built it up to seventeen.'

Ironic. So many people that a building had to be found to house them all on Edgware Road near Church Street market, a mile from head office. In my view it might as well have been a million miles as I believe it is fatal to have accounts distanced from the action. Soon after the move James left to be CFO at Ogilvy & Mather, the heavyweight advertising agency. By coincidence, their outgoing CFO David Wheller joined Conway's. James died in 1988 aged 48.

Two years after I had moved on I received a phone call to tell me that my nemesis Dick Amphlett had dropped dead from a heart attack on a Spanish beach whilst on holiday. He really was a miserable bastard who lived in this out of date world of workers doing battle with the capitalists in a dance to the death. I had never seen him smile or heard him say a pleasant word and Lord knows how he found a wife. I raised a glass or two not to him, but to his departure. He was 39.

The NGA, whose members totalled some 130,000 in 1982, gained some fame with a picket line blockade of the Messenger Newspaper in Warrington. Together with other print unions, they met a man willing and able to take them head on. Rupert Murdoch had purchased Times Newspapers together with their 8,500 unionised workers. During 1985/6 he had secretly built Fortress Wapping staffed by 650 electricians with the latest technical equipment and massive security.

One day in early 1986 he moved all the newspaper production from Fleet Street to Wapping and effectively fired 6000 workers. At that time I lived some two hundred yards from the old works and could watch the passing marchers calling out.

'We want our jobs back. When do we want them? NOW!!!!!!'

No chance, the jobs no longer existed and whose fault was that?

The shrinking NGA merged with Graphic Paper & Media Union in 1991 and that lot joined Transport & General Workers Union in 2007.

Conway's continued on and in the 80s created some dozen subsidiaries out in the London suburbs. When times became hard, a plan was hatched to sell them to their respective management people for a total of £750k. But the wheels fell off because some bright spark had included in the contracts a guarantee that 100% of the debtors list would be recovered. The reality was that they fell far short of the mark with a shortfall of 90% and the grand total collected in was £75k.

Companies were created for Stan's son and son-in-law to run, doing what I am not sure but we can be sure that the salaries were high and handsome.

One afternoon in June 1990, Stan Conway called a meeting of all staff in the basement of 26 Molyneux Street and announced that there would be no more wages as the NatWest bank had put the entire business into receivership that day. I bet that the lads were upset, worried and concerned. Violence arose, heavy threats made and the directors made a hasty retreat.

Stan went full circle – he had started the business from his garage and that's where he returned. He later moved his home to Harrow and set up a print shop there. Des bought the best gear from the auction and started a phoenix in Victoria.

The lads wandered off to their spiritual home, The House and the dole office.

Peter J Simpson has proved a little elusive. A guy of that name married Ms Marian Groocock in 1976 and a PJ Simpson died in Rugby in June 1994 but beyond that nothing has come to hand. I'm sure a determined chase would bring forth a detailed history but to what end?

So what became of Rosemary I hear you ask? In truth I had met very few of her relatives and friends and knew little of the family history, apart from the fact that Smethurst Frozen Foods had been sold to Unilever to become the catering side of Bird's Eye. I kept in touch with Bill but we avoided the subject of his big sister, then he upped stumps and migrated to Canada. I have always believed in the maxim 'never go back' but around 2005 I googled her name and up she popped on Friends Reunited.

> What I'm doing now
>
> I used to live at Great Coates House, Great Coates with my sister Jacky and two brothers, John and Bill. We all went to St Martin's, then Jacky and I to Clee Girls and John and Bill to Clee Boys.
>
> Worked at Boots Agrochemicals in Head Office in the good old days with JCB and the gang! Love to hear from anyone who remembers me.
>
> My husband, Ivan and I have lived in San Diego, California, since 1978. We have no children but have two enormous black dogs and six cats. Our hobbies are stock car racing and growing orchids.

She mentions her schooldays and Nottingham but omits her exciting years in London. Now a girl who is tired of London is tired of living. Not having a surname I put in 'Ivan & Rosemary San Diego' and to my amazement found a mountain of information at my fingertips. Firstly she had achieved every pre-pubescent girl's dream by marrying Ivan Harrison, the lead singer in the rock and roll band Ivan Jay and the Jaycats based in Nottingham. In 1962 the name changed to simply The Jaybirds and then part-morphed back to become Ivan Jay and the Jaymen. They never had the break-through to launch into the big time. After their marriage in 1977, they followed Rosemary's father to San Diego in 1978 and set up a business producing a fertilizer for orchids named Aussie Gold. Ivan also set up a workshop repairing furniture.

I had caught up with 20 years in 20 minutes. For me that was that. A passing thought but sometime in 2007, I think I heard that Ivan had cancer and died on 9 February 2009. Rosemary had borrowed from the bank which foreclosed on the house, knocked it out for $203,500 and it was sold a while later for some $300k, presumably after redecoration and updating.

Michael died in 1997 but I can't imagine Jane going to the party. I picked up an appeal on the internet posted by an Eric Visconti who was asking for help for Rosemary, who was apparently in dire straits following the loss of her husband, home and business.

His calculation was that she would only have $600 per month for rent, which wouldn't go far in California. He said that it would be the best thing in the world if someone could donate a low rent small property or mobile in a trailer park. Good luck, my son.

I know for certain that I would not have been on Michael's list of potential suitors for his daughter and that he would have preferred someone from his strata in life. Probably he would have liked a local lad from a quality family with an established business to support them and not a penniless oik from the East End of London. But on the other side of the coin, my profession would have at least produced a reliable and comfortable way of life.

Michael was always courteous and generous to me and I liked him very much. There was no doubt that his family was wealthy but somehow he seemed distanced from the movers and shakers, without the support network I would have expected. Maybe I got it wrong but that was the vibe I got. They lived as very wealthy folk would, in a listed Georgian Manor House with stables, a cottage with extensive beautiful gardens but it was all on a short-term lease. He had his army of some 7,000 hens working their tails off producing as many eggs as they could but could the birds meet the bills? I doubted it.

Still, it was none of my business then and it's none of my business now.

I came across Peter Mullin's blog on the internet setting out his research into the east window of St Michael's Church at Little Coates. This is in memory of Joseph Smethurst who died in 1908, the year Michael was born.

It was installed in 1910 by Joseph's widow, Maria Isabella and their daughter. Maria gave her home address as 20 Cornwall Terrace, Regents Park, London that today is recognised as one of the finest private houses in London. I understand that if it were on the market, it would command a price in excess of £100 million with minimum annual running costs of half a million quid. So early in the 20th century there really was a few bob in the Smethursts of Grimsby family.

The blog also answered one thing that had had me puzzled. Back in Victorian times people did not move about like they do now, so how did a family with a Lancashire surname like Smethurst wash up in Grimsby?

The Smethurst Grimsby saga started with the arrival of a hawker of that name originally from Oldham. His son William was the father of Joseph (1844-1908) referred to earlier and the younger brother of Henry Carl Smethurst (1819-1892). A leading figure in the town, he became Mayor and a statue of him was erected in the People's Park that had been set out on land donated by Henry, so I was told.

When the railway reached the town in 1848, it gave a major boost to the fishing industry, greatly expanding its market reach. The trawler owners were known as the 'fishocracy' – Smethurst, Mudd, Sleight, Aylwards, Black and Lambert. Other wealthy families included Wintringham and Chapman, both timber merchants and Spinks who traded in fine art and jewellery. The recycling of given names and the intermarriage amongst these worthies together with the tendency towards large numbers of children, makes tracing the lines through Victorian times a near impossibility. Henry married Phoebe Winteringham and Maria's father owned fishing smacks.

Michael's mother was a Mudd woman and in 1938 Colonel William Wintringham Smethurst OBE, chairman of the Grimsby Fish Merchants' Association, gave away his daughter, Honor Wintringham Smethurst in marriage to Paul Spink. This was the pattern among the Grimsby area's elevated families during the 1800s and 1900s. Maybe it still is today.

In contrast the lives of the fishermen were hard and dangerous, made worse by the practice of being paid in direct relation to the size of their catch. A poor result at sea would mean little or no money to feed the family. In 1901 industrial action was taken which resulted in the Great Lock Out by the trawler owners that lasted 14 weeks and caused huge suffering. Towards the end a riot broke out: 400 extra police and 125 soldiers were drafted into the town to suppress the disturbance. Three troopships lay at anchor in the port.

A ruthless man by all accounts, Henry Smethurst tried to bring in Swedish crews without success while the Mayor Harrison Mudd tried to arbitrate but that also ended in failure. Finally the owners made a few concessions and the workers caved in.

If life was grim for the fishermen, it was a lot worse for the apprentices who were mainly recruited from orphanages and workhouses. Any attempt to break their contract and they would be brought up in front of a Justice of the Peace for sentencing. The practice lasted until 1929.

In the early 1900s the Smethurst family employed 80% of Grimsby's workforce, directly or indirectly. They started Smethurst Frozen Food factory, employing hundreds of people and doubtlessly making a shedload of money.

During WWI all the fleets were requisitioned and used for mine laying and sweeping. Many were lost, either by colliding with mines or sunk by U-boats but one assumes that the owners were compensated.

In any event Smethurst sold two trawling businesses, White Star and Excalibur, in 1924 to Sir Alec Black making a net profit of £32,000 (roughly two million today). In the thirties they even owned Grimsby's Zoo.

In 1946 the frozen food factory was sold outright to the Lever Brothers (Birds Eye) for £292,803, according to published accounts. This is equal to some thirteen million quid today. I could not track down who in the clan benefited from this windfall.

Maybe if Rosemary had stayed in this comfort zone her life would have been easier and smoother. Still, not my business as she abandoned this particular ship long ago.

From owning a magnificent mansion in London early in the twentieth century to be asking for a gift of a mobile in a trailer park in San Diego early in the twenty first century is a big stretch. There's an old north England proverb that runs: 'there's nobbut three generations atween a clog and clog'. Might be apt.

8 Empire Catering

'We took risks. We knew we took them. Things turned out against us. Therefore we have no cause for complaint.'

Captain Scott of the Antarctic - last words of his journal

The head office was just off Oxford Street, a block from Selfridges. The company owned some ten high-end restaurants and was a franchisee for Wimpy.

On Monday 5 April 1976 I arrived, with some trepidation, to take up the role of CFO and went straight into a board meeting headed up by the CEO Alan Da Costa. I had nothing to contribute whatsoever. Just before we broke up a young man joined us and was introduced by Mr Da Costa as his son who had recently returned from New York. Apparently he was on his way to the Oxford Street Wimpy to start at the bottom as a kitchen hand.

When I returned to my office I was surprised to find that the number two director had moved his office down the corridor. A signwriter was removing his name from the door and replacing it with the said sons moniker and description Director. A little after noon the young man reappeared and took up his place in his new office. So it could be said in truth that he had worked his way from the bottom to the top. A bit smoke and mirrors for my liking.

After lunch my first month's pay arrived in advance. This was as unexpected as was the company credit card. On the second day my gold Parker pen set was stolen from my desk. Was this an omen?

By Friday the 9th I knew my initial feelings had not been wrong. On Sunday I delivered my resignation to Mr Da Costa's desk, simply informing him that I was positive that we both had made a mistake. The way forward was to recognise this and bring to an end my appointment. On the Monday I sent my keys over to the office, a cheque to repay in full my salary, (which was only fair since I had made no contribution during my five days) and my unused credit card. Why was I so keen to throw myself into the mighty ranks of the unemployed?

In the past I had always taken a lead in whatever I was involved in as it was my nature. In this case I judged that this was not expected and that I would be in a passive role looking after the number crunching and not much more.

The decision to cut out was never a subject for second thoughts; it would never have worked for me.

9 Napper Stinton Woolley

'Advertising is based on one thing: happiness. You know what happiness is? Happiness is the smell of a new car. It's freedom from fear. It's a billboard on the side of the road that screams with reassurance that whatever you are doing is okay. You are okay.'

Don Draper played by Jon Hamm in the TV series 'Mad Men'

Free time meant that I could get a medical problem sorted out; my nose had been broken twice and it not only looked a mess, my breathing was restricted. Dr Toszeghi arranged for me to check into a hospital in Essex and get it fixed. All went well. The only downside was that the neighbouring ward was for burn victims. It was hard to sleep with the many screams that came out of that sad place. My stay lasted four days and Max picked me up in his Ford Capri to take me home. I looked odd for a couple of weeks with a massive plaster in the middle of my face but by early May I put myself out in the market place looking for work.

A recruitment firm called to tell me that the advertising agency Napper Stinton Woolley were looking for a Financial Director and arranged an initial meeting their auditor. My heart sank when I realised that they were also auditor to my previous employer. As soon as I took a seat, I put my cards on the table.

'Before we start I have to be straight and tell you that in April I walked out of one of your clients after just one week. And that's not on my CV.'

'Really? Which company was that, and why?'

'Empire Catering. I simply felt that I would never fit in and rather than prolong the agony, I left.'

'Okay, that's fine. Thanks for letting me know.'

The rest of the interview went well and an appointment was made to meet the Chairman, Peter Ryan.

On Friday 11 June 1976, I made my way to the NSW offices on the top floor of the London Brick building at York Gate, Regent's Park. Later I was to discover that until recently they had occupied the top two floors but had relinquished the lower to London Brick, apart from a small area at the rear where a kitchen was located together with the dispatch department.

Peter Ryan was very welcoming and I took to him immediately; a large man, he appeared open and straightforward which was refreshing. The three gents on the masthead had formed the agency after they were released from the military at the end of World War II but they were long gone. Peter himself had served with the Fleet Air Arm and had flown a Fairey Swordfish at the sinking of the Bismark. I was offered the job on the spot, to start the next Wednesday 16 June.

I spent the first morning with my predecessor Ian Pinkerton, who was leaving to take a year's sabbatical to, and I quote 'sit on the top of a mountain and get my head straight'. He took me for an early lunch and ordered a bottle of red wine. I had one glass and drank about half. After an hour I left him to finish the bottle by himself and thankfully he didn't return in the afternoon.

The agency had a total staff of 50 and to my horror but not surprise, 11 of these were in accounts, plus me of course. That translated to 25% of the total, which was utterly crazy. In addition, Ian had allowed flexi time that was openly abused. The small accounts office once again resembled a furniture store. An old biddy called Margo had made a mini room for herself by siting her desk in a corner fronted by three metal filing cabinets topped with massive pot plants, next to a cupboard. When she opened the cupboard door, it formed a door to her private space. Assessing the crowd I could see two girls worth their weight: Linda an Australian who was to be the best of the bunch by far and Alice the accounts machine operator. Calling the other nine lightweights was being kind.

To my amazement, we had a voucher clerk which might work in a big agency but not here where he would struggle to find half an hour's work per day. He was a nice enough bloke but after a couple of weeks he was gone. Then I called a meeting to tell them that I would honour the flexi arrangements but demanded a 35 hour week whichever way you sliced the cake. The next morning I was happy to receive resignations from Iris and Beryl the worst two layabouts. The only thing I can remember about them was that they were big Brian Ferry fans. The message was getting through that a very different type of accountant had arrived. I heard rumours that Ian, who was a married man, was in a relationship with not one but two of the accounts girls. That can't have helped keeping discipline and respect in the place.

It was around this time that I received a call from Brian Cox one evening at home. He sounded crazy, not drunk but mad as a cut snake. He was very unhappy with James McDonnell and needed my help. More to get him off the phone than anything else, I suggested we meet at a fish restaurant in Baker Street the next day at 6.30pm for an early dinner.

When we sat down, it was more of the same. McDonnell had introduced a reporting system and took no active part in the management of the department, leaving everything to Brian to sort out including the credit control. He was so unhappy with his lot and was there any way I could take him over to NSW?

'That would be really difficult. I've only been there for a few weeks and chopping out dead wood out as fast as I could. There's no plan for recruitment in the near future. And to be honest, given Conway's pay policy your salary there as office manager is greater than mine at NSW as CFO, so there's no way I could match your pay level.'

'Please Peter. I really am desperate. Help!'

'I'll try to work something out but I can't promise anything.'

As he was a good worker who got along with everyone and could be relied on, I put a plan together: we would reorganise with me, a manager and four staff, thus halving the numbers but not the cost. It was a hell of a job to sell it to Peter Ryan as he had so little experience of my abilities. But he took the chance and guaranteed support for my decisions.

I had been in regular contact with Brian, assuring him of my best efforts and was excited to be able to call him with the news.

'The chairman has backed my scheme and I can offer you the job at £6,500. In addition, I can drop you into a Saturday morning slot with a firm of cladders not far from your home that pays £1,000 plus a car you can use full time. So there'll be no change financially with the plus that you get transport in exchange for a half day.'

The part-time post was through an accountant friend of mine, David Cohen.

There was a strange pause that I found odd.

'I'll think about it.'

'What the hell do you mean you'll think about it? I have only been in this job a few weeks, and I've put myself out on a limb with the directors to get you this opening. What's going on?'

'I'll think about it and call you back.'

The line went dead. Two days went by before the return call came.

'Sorry, I can't do it. My wife won't let me take the chance.'

'Thanks. I could do without this! You've made me look a complete fool in front of the board.'

The line went dead. What was it all about?

Later I heard that Brian had gone to James McDonnell with the story that I had made unsolicited contact with him. He said that I'd offered him the same money to join me at NSW, plus a motorcar and paid running costs. Of course James panicked and being so dependent on Brian, offered him a massive pay hike. Which is exactly what Brian had been aiming for all along.

I had sown the seed so well with Peter Ryan that he came to see me to ask when our new accounts manager was starting. Being honest I simply told him that his wife wouldn't allow him to change jobs.

'Sounds like we are better off without him,' was Peter's response.

I was disgusted. Several months later, word on the grapevine had it that Brian wanted to resume our friendship. My message back was unprintable.

At our short get together, Ian had been insistent that I attend the monthly meetings of accountants in advertising held at the Advertising Association, as these were not only important but informative. I was dubious to say the least but with nothing to lose, I went along to one.

Obviously, this was where filmakers got their inspiration for zombie films. Wall to wall miserable looking geezers in similar grey ill-fitting suits and the only subject of their conversations was boasting about their latest company car. It was horrendous and I couldn't escape fast enough. What Ian saw in this God-awful assembly I will never know. Not a smile let alone a laugh, these were just dreary pen-pushers, every one with an undeserved sense of entitlement and importance. Never again.

More and more it occurred to me that I really wasn't interested in the company of other men in the evening. Much like Bertrand Morane, the hero of 'L'Homme Qui Aimait Les Femmes' (The Man Who Loved Women) who would not tolerate the presence of males after 6pm. In my youth I would spend time in the pub with mates or going to a football match with them. But I had moved away from that way of life and found that I was happiest with women around. Or no one.

Margo was an enigma. Every morning, sometime after eleven, she would appear with a mug of tea in her hand but I never saw her arrive. I frequently spent time in London Brick's reception area on the ground floor chatting with Kate the terrific receptionist but never saw Margo pass by. It took a while but I eventually twigged that she was slipping in the back door and walking up the stairs to collect her tea. Then she'd take herself up to the main floor and as if by magic, there she was.

Her job was to charge out production costs which, I would estimate, required one or two invoices a day. She treated this as if it were a secret freemason's art that required powers known only to a sacred few. The fact was of course that each client required a different approach with regard to presentation: some liked copy supplier's invoices, others insisted on an authorization order. Back then it was 15% for us on everything (equal to marking up by 17.65%), except where a fixed price contract was in place and everything charged at cost. It wasn't rocket science.

Another staffer resigned so I took the opportunity to dismantle Margo's 'office' and rearranged the furniture to accommodate the reduced numbers. The next morning, as predicted, she came to see me to complain. I cut her short.

'I'm in charge here and you will sit where I put you. If you really can't deal with it, please leave. Now go back to work.'

I hated it when people were so stupid that I was forced to remind them who was the boss. She put so much time and effort in swinging the lead. If this time and effort had been directed at the job in hand, we wouldn't have had problems between us. By my estimate she was nearing sixty and without being ageist or sexist, in my book she should have been bloody grateful to have a well-paid and comfortable job and giving it her best possible attention.

The following weekend I brought in a pal who was good with locks who got her desk open pretty quickly. I was horrified to discover work to be invoiced out over a year old. Common sense will tell anyone that the likelihood of recovering any of it was slim. I sacked her.

She wrote to Peter Ryan and he took it up with me. I simply told him what I'd found and that was that. And I got the billing up to date.

The ancient stuff was for a furniture manufacturer and the charges related to an exhibition. They refused to accept the invoicing on the grounds that their books had been closed for that year, audited and NSW kissed goodbye to some eighty grand. I discussed the legal aspects with Peter and we were of like minds, that we had been at fault and there had been plenty of chances to have picked it up. Seemingly Ian, the auditors and even the account handler lived in fear of Margo as if she were the wicked witch of the east. At the end of six weeks, I had a department that worked well.

I reconsidered the plan I'd cobbled together to accommodate my old assistant and adopted it, just not with Brian Cox! Linda and Alice had stayed with me as had two others from the original line-up. Now I recruited a young man to run the office. He was a Scot named Stuart Townsend who had a military background and would provide a counterbalance to some of the frivolity of the ad world. I had my sensible six in place of the dirty dozen.

The layout of the floor consisted of an open space running the full length. On the right hand side sat the secretaries, personal assistants and the accounts machinist. Alongside both walls were offices for directors, account executives/handlers, creative and media department with two larger units for meetings and the production department

The TV series 'Mad Men' set in a New York advertising agency in the 60s and 70s caught the flavour of that time and NSW was a miniature version. We had some very major clients and household names but as with every agency in the world, winning a new customer or losing an established one, could have a dramatic effect either for the good or the bad.

Peter Ryan was exactly as my first impression had indicated and I would have been happy to work with him anywhere.

I had very little contact with the managing director Jon Van der Byl but then nor did anyone else. I was told he was the brother of the Rhodesian Foreign Minister PK Van der Byl but I totally disbelieved that. He spent most days in his office with the door shut and there were some colourful suggestions as to what he was doing in there.

Jim Bridgeman and Bert Pyne ran creative, David Noble was media and I think Mike Boland, J Hooper and Philip Dale were account executives. Sorry if I have slotted you in the wrong place, it was all a long time ago.

I have left the worst to last: Chris Munds, Deputy Chairman and head of creative. In my judgement, he was a man to avoid at all costs and I did just that. In addition to the day job he had appeared on TV in 'Braden's Week' and starred in TV commercials for the client Trebor Mints. How can I put it? He preferred to get his own way and woe betide you if you got in his face, caused him any inconvenience or annoyed him.

Outside my office was Peggie, Peter Ryan's secretary and we hit it off straight away. She was a bubbly, vivacious woman about my age who I found later was engaged to one of London's grand old men of advertising, Michael Manton. Next to her was Lucy, another terrific young woman who, other than looking after Van der Byl, was in charge of in house dining.

Credit control was contracted out, a system I had not come across before, to CPA owned by Chris Pearson, no surprise there. We had a regular visits from his staffer Derek Webb and they were paid on a complicated formula based on improvement in performance from the day of inception. To me it all worked out roughly what we would pay an in-house controller, so no reason to make a change. On the last working day of the month I would go with Derek to visit our biggest client Sterling Winthrop in Surbiton. We'd go to meet with their accountant, have lunch at the Italian restaurant by the station, collect a cheque and head for NSW's bank in Mayfair to lodge it. That worked well and was a break from the routine.

The agency's fleet of cars were all Citroen CXs. As Ian had returned his, I used that for a few weeks before selling it back to the dealer. I could have had a car but preferred a higher salary and I was still using Judy's Mini as she had no parking at her new flat in Neal Street.

I hate to see anybody humiliated, especially women, and Munds soon showed his colours. It was no secret that he was having an affair with his assistant (name suppressed) and a couple of mornings a week they would walk into work hand-in-hand. Than he would phone his wife to tell her that he had been out with clients all night and he needed a fresh set of clothes. An hour later she would arrive with a garment bag, walking into the agency and passing his paramour on the way to his office. To not know what was going on she must have either been trusting beyond measure or maybe just accepted his behaviour and let it ride. I am not the morality police but to drag in her in time after time like this showed a total disregard for her self-worth. All that was needed was a change of clothes kept in the office.

Peter Stevens' conduct was more nonsense straight out of 'Mad Men'. He was an account executive who sat in the next office. Once or twice a week he would go to lunch, have a skinful and return to the office off his head. He would then try to maul Peggie who would flee into my office and hide behind me, causing him to stop at my door, eyeing me to gauge my reaction as best he could in his befuddled state. Realising that the situation could swiftly move out of control he always backed off but it was tedious to say the least.

The agency had been presenting to Dunlop Sports for some months and a luncheon was arranged where it was hoped we could land a new client. Despite best efforts, it did not go well with some hard questions being fielded. When the meeting broke around 6pm everyone had left and finally John was the last man standing.

The next morning, we arrived to find the meeting room in chaos with broken furniture and holes in the ceiling. John was so exasperated that he took it out on the furniture and fittings, only stopping when security arrived, quickly followed by the police. It took a shedload of diplomacy by Peter to calm the situation down and a heap of cash to get the damage fixed and the furniture replaced.

It was only a month later when the dining experience again took a turn for the worst. An established client's marketing people had come into the agency for a planning meeting that concluded with lunch. As always an excellent spread was laid on, accompanied by fine wines. When the brandy was passed it did not circle the table as was the custom but was hijacked by the client's head honcho who, over the course of the afternoon, drained it dry. At 6pm a halt was called and the participants headed home. Our hero popped into the gent's toilet where he attempted to grab the private parts of a production guy taking a leak. He then staggered into Peter's office where he threw up and when he got into Mr Ryan's car to be driven home he was substantially sick again.

Sex in the Agency? Apart from Munds' adventures, two of the production crew announced that they had left their spouses and set up home together. The receptionist and an account handler were an on, off item and I'm sure that there were others but unless the tittle-tattle came to me, I didn't seek it out.

Towards the end of the year a worrying event occurred which gave me serious doubts as to my long-term prospects. Chris Munds decided that he needed a second team of creatives and gave his requirements to a firm of headhunters. Two guys were selected, arrived for work, allocated an office and introduced around.

In due course the invoices for the recruitment costs came in, were signed off and paid. I noted that they were non-refundable. Just two weeks later on a Friday, a fired up Munds came to see me – which was a first. He wanted to know what it would cost to sack the new creatives and handed me the contracts which he had signed without asking any advice from any source. I read through them carefully. Unless they had committed a crime, they were entitled to a year's salary each, plus of course the finder's fee, all amounting to around twenty grand. I walked up to his office (also a first), gave him the news and backed out.

It was lunchtime, so off I went. When I returned an hour later, the place was as empty as the Marie Celeste and I soon realised why. The new guys' office was smashed, the furniture broken, artwork torn to pieces, photographs destroyed and to cap it all one bloke's raincoat had been torn in half. If a message was being sent it couldn't be missed. When Peter returned he asked me who had done it, I told him what had transpired and that my guess was Chris Munds. His anger simply drained away; with a shrug and an 'Oh', he headed for his office.

In September, I received the sad news that my old friend John Wingfield had been killed in an accident whilst club racing at Thruxton. I'd been angry with John for continuing to race after his younger brother Peter was also killed six years previously in a similar crash at Croft. Now his widowed mother had lost both her sons to the sport. Max and I attended the funeral.

On a happier note, I met a person who was to take a big place in my life for almost fifteen years. I'd first met Tina back at Michael Dunne Studio when she came in for a modelling job and we'd chatted amiably to pass the time as she waited in reception for her husband to collect her. By sheer chance I bumped into her in Selfridges one Saturday morning. Over coffee she told me that since our last meeting she'd got divorced, bought an apartment and now her career was headed in a positive direction. We arranged a dinner date for the following week.

It was clear from the outset that she didn't want any kind of domestic arrangement. She was loving her new found independence too much and wouldn't give it up for anything or anyone. That suited me down to the ground as I was becoming accustomed to the bachelor life. From that point on we met on a regular basis, often at weekends and when I had to work she would shop. We went for dinner together, sometimes go to the theatre or to see a film. Both of us respected each other's space and it played out to be an excellent arrangement.

Back to NSW. One evening, I took a very drunken John home with the help of a couple of the production boys. It was doubtful that a taxi would take him and if he stayed in the building there was a chance of a contretemps with the security guards. His wife, a charming Indian lady, greeted us at the door and thanked us for our good deed whilst dragging her husband over the threshold.

As we neared Christmas, I was asked to provide £3,000 for a client, to pay for their Christmas party. The arrangement was that they allowed us a certain amount of license within our production costs and the cash was the quid pro quo. Obviously it needed a director's signature for the books.

When it came to the firm's Christmas party I went AWOL. Having observed what went on between nine and five, Monday to Friday, I dread to think what it was like when they really let their hair down.

1977 started with a bang. Mrs Munds had been called to bring down a fresh set of duds for her spouse and en route she crashed her husband's Lancia. Fortunately she was not hurt.

A South African called Simon was a new account director who had recently been appointed. A few weeks in, he came into my office and closed the door. This was ominous.

'Can I talk with you confidentially?'

'Sure, take a load off.'

'I've been going through the TV production costs on the two varnish commercials we shot and they don't make sense. One has the varnish being applied to a chair and the second to a table.'

'Yes, I saw the storyboards. Where's the problem?'

'It's the backgrounds: firstly a kitchen and the second a gazebo.'

'So?'

'I would have expected that we would have hired locations for them, after all they are only props. But I have supplier's invoices for a whole new kitchen and a brand new gazebo. What has happened to them? Where are they? The client isn't going to pay this totally unnecessary expense.'

To me it was obvious where they were.

'Look Simon, just don't worry about it. Charge it all out as is, add 17.65% and there will be no comeback from the client I guarantee.'

'I can't do that, the whole thing is ridiculous. I'm going direct to Chris Munds.'

'Please don't do that. Listen to me, charge it as is and if you like go over the final draft with me. It will all go through as smooth as silk, no worries.'

He left shaking his head and sat in his room for an hour. I thought he had taken my counsel to heart. I was wrong. He took up his concerns with the creative department and was sacked on the spot.

It was common knowledge where the background props were. It was an extension of the practice of giving away bits and pieces after their usefulness is over. For example NSW had a pharmaceutical company on the books and they would send over boxes of product to be used in commercials or still photography. After the event there was no question of returning them to the client as it was not worth the effort, so all of us had a well-stocked medicine cabinet at home.

What had taken place with the kitchen and gazebo was forward planning, designing the advertisements to leave items that were useful to those in charge when the job was concluded. I know it is not a healthy business practice but life is what it is, not as it should be.

David Cohen phoned me to say that he'd gained a new client but being a one-man band, needed help with the audit. I called Bill Smethurst and we both arranged two weeks holiday, meeting on a Monday morning to travel down to Essex to the premises of Ferry Freighting. For David, this was a big job and it took the two of us working flat out, including the weekend, to get it sown up. David was happy, as was the client and we were well paid.

In most ways NSW was a great agency with an enviable portfolio of clients but there was an underlying instability. The day would come when it would be announced that we were in a merger with a bigger outfit that in reality would be a take-over. You could bet our leaders would be looked after but the other ranks thrown to the dogs and the cost savings would be at their expense. I know Peter would do his best for everybody, but Chris would look after Chris and probably prevail. John reminded me of a quote by David Ogilvy:

'A boss who never wanders about his agency becomes an invisible hermit'.

Rarely seen on the floor, he showed no interest in the day-to-day workings of the firm, he stays a mystery to me. Certainly he was not the archetypal ad man.

It seemed like perfect timing when an invitation came through to attend an interview for the CFO slot at Gordon Proctor, a major ad agency. On my arrival at Buckingham Gate, I was ushered into the office of a director.

After exchanging a few pleasantries and him telling me that the accounts people were working in the attic, we moved to the interview proper. The first question totally wrong-footed me.

'When you arrived at NSW what did you find?'

'I'm sorry, I don't understand the question. What do you mean, what did I find?'

'It's simple. Was the accounts department in good order? Were regular management reports flowing through to the directors and were the staff capable? Was there a good atmosphere?'

It quickly dawned on me that there was only one possible reason for this line of questioning.

'From your enquiry, I deduce that Ian Pinkerton is a candidate and the sole purpose in my being here is to supply you with a free background check. Sorry, I'm going to disappoint you and I am not best pleased at being brought here under false pretences. You've wasted my time.'

I pushed my chair back, turned and went out the way I had come in so fast the guy didn't have time to think of anything to say. Did Mr Pinkerton get the job? No idea; I guess the bloke thought he was as sharp as a knife with his cunning plan. According to the London Gazette they appointed liquidators in 1981.

It never ceased to amaze me how little importance some companies pay to their image with the outside world. Spotting a newspaper ad by Young's Seafood for a financial director with an outstanding remuneration package on offer, I applied for an interview enclosing my CV.

The rejection letter was a 'one size fits all': a thousandth photocopy flush with spelling mistakes that was used whether the application was for the Chairman's spot or a fish filleter. To add insult to injury, the staffer dealing with it must have been in the middle of a hamburger lunch as the missive was covered in spots of grease, finished off with a long tomato ketchup stain north to south.

Late in April I was at home one evening when the telephone rang. It was Barrie Carmel-Smith, one of the influx into Wilson Wright back in 1967. (He dropped the Smith bit in 1982.) After all the grief this mob had given me over the years, I should have hung up but I was intrigued and in truth, I had no quarrel with Barrie whatsoever.

'Hi Peter, how are you?'

'Good, and you?'

I was on my guard.

'Yes, I'm fine. If you don't mind me asking, what are you doing workwise at the moment?'

'I'm the FD at an ad agency near Regent's Park. Look, let's cut to the chase Barrie, you're not phoning me after ten years to be sociable. What's on your mind?'

'You're right, we have a client who needs a financial man and I wondered if you would like to look at it.'

'I'll be frank, you must be really bloody desperate to have the gall to call me after the treatment dished out to me by Boreham and Gould in the past.'

'No, we just thought your set of skills would be an ideal match to what they need.'

'So they're in the shite. Who is it?'

'Theatre Projects.'

I knew the name from the old days but had never worked on the client.

'Okay Barrie, get them to call me and I'll take a look.'

'Thanks Peter.'

A few days later I was in the reception at 10 Long Acre at 5pm for a meeting with Richard Pilbrow, the boss of Theatre Projects (TP). When a guy walked in from the street to be greeted cheerfully by the receptionist, I instinctively knew this was the man. Slightly built, about seven years older than me, he sported strange wispy facial hair. It is a style much favoured by Japanese artists as part of a shared identity with the world. He wore a felt hat that had been fashionable twenty years ago with a badge hanging down from it in the shape of a light bulb.

At the time I had no way of knowing that this geezer was to be the most dishonest, disloyal and disgusting excuse for a human being I would ever meet in my entire life. That joy was yet to come. A few minutes later, I went up to his first floor office, we shook hands and sat at a circular laminate table. The first thing I noticed was a fierce case of halitosis wafting in my direction.

His opening speech was well rehearsed. The business had started in 1957 in the back room of a theatre with sixty pounds loaned to him by his father. Now it was a 'highly successful' group of companies spread over several buildings in Covent Garden.

TP Services was the largest element, involved in the sale and hire of equipment to the entertainment industry. TP Consultants designed places of entertainment or the refurbishments thereof and Light Ltd was working mainly on projects in Nigeria. In addition there were film and theatre production divisions and prop hire. But the big news was saved for last and he demonstrated his party trick that I was to experience ad nauseam during my first year at TP.

He pulled an old envelope from a waste bin and wrote down a dozen names with a value next to each, totting it up to come to a predictable result. Then took a percentage that amounted to six and a half million pounds, plus he emphasized 'overruns'.

'This is the Iran Project. Twelve new concert halls and conference centres to be built. TPC has a fully staffed office in the capital Tehran. It's fantastic and will take TP to a new level.'

'I don't understand why you need me. A monkey can be trained to pick money off the table.'

He then produced a memo that he had sent to all staff informing them that until the Iran tap turned on, cash was tight. When they left a room, they should ensure that lights were turned off.

'We need someone with the financial skills to get us through the next few months which will be difficult. Our CFO, Tony Webb, has left us and although we have another three Chartered Accountants on the payroll, we don't think they have the experience to carry this out.'

'Four qualified accountants? How many people work here?'

'About a hundred.'

'And how many other accounts people?'

'About a dozen.'

'So 16% of the total crew are bookkeeping and accounts? That's crazy.'

'Given your experience, how many would you envisage?'

'Six or seven maybe, tops.'

Pilbrow knew of my career record from the auditors and I was who they had recommended. But I quickly realised that I was not what he wanted, a rough boy from East London with an accent to match. What he wanted was a cultured chap with a middle England background who would fit in and be 'one of them'. I could tell that he felt he was being foisted with someone who was not afraid of telling it how it is and that was not what he wanted to hear. He loved sycophants as they gave him the feel good feeling and he'd already started his collection.

'What salary do you have in mind?'

'I wouldn't sign on for less than eight grand a year. But no car.'

'We couldn't do that! You'd be the highest paid person here. This is the Theatre.'

'Yes, for doing what I suspect is the toughest job in the place. I have the reputation of an axeman and the first order of play is to weed out the deadwood in accounts which is never nice. Eight grand or let's stop right now.'

'I'd like you to meet a couple of other people, so let's leave the final discussion of salary for now. Can my secretary call you to make the arrangements?'

'Sure, any time.'

That was that. I know he choked on the money side of things but I could sense his desperation. We would see.

I knew little of Iran but as it was a major factor in TP's future I thought I had better brush up on the current history. Ruled by the Shah, the oil price rises of 1973 had brought a great deal of foreign currency into the country that in turn had helped fuel massive inflation. In 1974 many large projects had been initiated in order to combat unemployment and recession but they were not helped by endemic corruption. TP's big deal must be part of this move to modernize.

But here was the warning shot. In 1976 protests had started against the Shah and his family and were gaining momentum during the following year. I put in a call to a mate working at The Guardian in the overseas section; it was their general opinion that things were going to get worse, not better.

An invitation came from Pam Hay to have lunch and we met at an Italian restaurant off Saint Martin's Lane. It was all very pleasant and we chatted for about an hour. My guess was that she was making a personality assessment to report back to Pilbrow. I discovered later that she was very good at reporting back. Unswervingly loyal to Pilbrow, she had been with him since the early days, although I never found out exactly what actual work she did. I realised that Pilbrow some times used her as his personal Rottweiler to carry out the dirty jobs he couldn't. I never knew exactly what talents she had but whatever they were, they were brutally wasted at TP.

The next call was to meet John Ball, the head honcho of TP Services. Now this was my kind of a man who had none of Pilbrow's theatrical affectations with all that luvvy stuff. With a background in engineering, he was a man's man, a straight talker and we hit it off right away, working well together to the bitter end. One unnerving item he dropped into my lap was that he was so dissatisfied with the current accounting records that he kept his own books which were more accurate than those produced by the sixteen accounting staff.

What was crystal clear from our discussions was that his part of the business was starved of capital. Like everybody else, he'd pinned his hopes on the Iranian adventure coming good but as this was a TPC matter, he was in the dark as to the actual true situation on the ground. At least I now knew there was one real businessman in the place.

Another call from Pilbrow's secretary Liz Lomas.

'Richard would like you to meet the three accountants.'

'Whatever for?'

'He feels they might be upset by someone being brought in over them and a meeting would reassure them.'

'I don't think I can do much reassuring. After all, if all three are being overlooked then the management can't have much confidence in their abilities.'

I don't know why but I agreed. I had so many chances and reasons to walk away and still to this day don't know why I didn't.

The trio arrived at my apartment and after a drink we walked down to an Italian restaurant. Paul appeared to be the unelected leader of the three and by my measure, a sanctimonious sort of bloke. The other two, Peter and Robert, struck me as total lightweights. I was astonished when they revealed their pay levels which were half of what I would have expected, which they attributed to being in 'the theatre'. What bloody nonsense that was! In my book you get proper pay for the job whether you're making bricks or running the country.

Tony Webb was a decent bloke by their accounts but bullied by many to the point he just couldn't take it anymore. It was obvious that they resented my possible recruitment and had no answers to offer as to why TP needed 16% of its workforce to account for what the other 84% were doing.

I gained little information and knew they were not reassured; quite the opposite I suspect. Another call from Liz Lomas.

'Richard would like you to meet Woulter Poldervaart, FD at Polygram who owns a third of TP shares.'

I protested that we were now in the Twilight Zone. Five interviews for what was a small business. I was not applying to join MI5. I really, really should have hung up. But I didn't.

Podervaart was an accountant at the big end of town and I suspected that the running of a small struggling outfit was really outside his compass. I decided to take him head on in the matter of my predecessor.

'Excuse me saying but I have been told that you ran Tony Webb ragged with demands for reports. If that's correct, I have to tell you that it won't work on me. If you need information the books will be open to you at all times. You can send someone over whenever you need them. My energies will be aimed at culling staff in the accounts department, cutting it by half or more and finding out what is really going on there. I am not being rude but I don't want any misunderstanding between us.

'I'm convinced that TP is in serious trouble and that this total reliance on the Iran business bailing them out is flimflam. From all I have read and heard, a major uprising against the Shah is not very far away and then every penny committed will be lost. I think the ambition should be to get every element running in profit and forget castles in the air.'

He didn't comment on my approach and the interview was over. The following evening, it was her again.

'Look Liz, if this is to arrange to meet another geezer, you can forget it. All this could have being settled by just one meeting with Richard and John. Pam, the three stooges and the Polygram bloke are really not relevant.'

'No Peter, Richard would like to meet and make you an offer.'

'A serious offer, I hope.'

One fact had emerged from these discussions: many of TP's employees were content to be on very low wages in exchange for the kudos of being in the theatre. In theory the business should be making a mint of money but in reality low income births low self esteem and usually piss poor performance. I remember my first job only too well, with a wage packet containing very little being delivered every Friday by an obese man in a chauffeur driven limo and smoking fat cigars to boot. No one working for me would ever be treated like that.

There was a story going around about the guy who worked at the circus and his only task was to clean up after the animals. He constantly complained about shovelling shite but if anyone pointed out that he could just walk away any time he liked, he responded angrily.

'What and leave show biz?'

A meeting of senior staff at NSW had been called, without Peter, John and Chris. I think it was Philip Dale who explained to the group that an idea had been floated to expand the share ownership of the company to the other directors and maybe some staff. This gathering was to test the initial reactions.

I needed to be elsewhere and quickly explained that my previous experience ruled me out. It was nothing to do with the agency but I preferred to remain a working stiff rather than a part owner. Okay, coming from the accountant, it might not have been the best of starts to the discussions but I'd said my piece and was gone.

More and more I was deadly certain that Munds had plans to change the balance of the status quo. Perhaps he thought that if he could weaken Peter and John's shareholding strength by getting equity in his supporters' hands, he could assume control. There was nothing to base my thoughts on apart from gut instinct but that had never let me down in the past. I was sure that my future lay elsewhere.

On the evening of Thursday 12 May I was back in Pilbrow's office. Frankly, I thought I had been pissed about enough and was unwilling to waste any more time. He asked me how it had gone with the various chitchats, although I was very sure that he had received feedback already. After that marathon, I knew John and possibly

Woulter would recognise that I was what was needed. The theatrical types would be against and the three accountants must have realised that they were on borrowed time. So the dance began. A few people entered, were introduced and left. Finally, just the two of us were sitting at the table.

'The salary you requested is agreed and I'd like you to start as soon as possible.'

'Fair enough.'

'Your job title will be Company Secretary and you will be on a six month trial.'

I stared at him for several long seconds.

'Are you having a laugh?'

'No, a short period to see …'

I cut him off.

'Look, I'm 38 not 18 and I don't need a trial period to prove myself. A Company Secretary is a little man running around with bits of paper, with bugger all respect or clout. I am tired of all this nonsense. It's Financial Director from the get-go as far as I am concerned or forget it. You decide.'

He grudgingly agreed but it was obvious that my style was not to his liking. Despite all the bravado, I know that deep down he realised that Iran could be slipping through his fingers and in that terrible case only someone like me could be his salvation. I'm sure that for Richard Pilbrow this was a deal with the devil.

Very early the next morning the telephone rang; it was George Grant, the head of a recruitment agency who had held my CV since I'd left Conway's. He came straight to the point.

'A major advertising agency has seen your history file and wants to talk to you in respect of the post of CFO.'

'I wished you had called me yesterday.'

'Why?'

'I agreed to join Theatre Projects last night.'

'Look, this comes with a fantastic package, five figures and a car. Can't you at least go for an interview. Have you signed anything?'

'No, but I have given my word and that's an end to it.'

Ironic or what? I had always tried to be a man of principle whose word and handshake meant something that anyone could totally trust. But here I would find, in the fullness of time, that I had given my word to a man totally lacking any principles.

'Are you sure you can't just take a look?'

'Sorry, but yes I am sure. Thanks for thinking of me.'

This really was a mad period as every opportunity was popping up to turn my back on TP but I just ignored them. When I reached NSW that day I handed my resignation in to Peter Ryan with three months notice.

In early July I received a call from Bastable Advertising. Their accounts department was in chaos and my name as a troubleshooter had come up. I arranged a visit.

The joint MDs Messrs Manning and Chipperfield explained the situation. Their new CFO could not take up the position for a few weeks and the accounting had slipped behind; the accounts people were either unable to, or unwilling to take steps to correct the situation. Their system was based on good old-fashioned paperwork and I figured that a few hands over a weekend could get it sorted. They were really nice guys and I was to find, appreciated everything I did. Working the phones I recruited Bill, Max and a couple of other good workers and spent a long hard weekend in a basement. By the end of the weekend everything was up to date and balanced. Job done. A few weeks later I was asked to pop in on a Monday morning to help welcome the new CFO and show him round. After meeting the directors we went to his office and I offered to introduce him to his staff. He asked me to give him half an hour.

Bearing in mind that I was still working for, and being paid, by NSW, I didn't have time to waste. When at 9.30 I re-entered the room he told me he was too busy to see me or meet his crew. I noticed the desk was covered in car brochures and scribbled calculations. He had been given a budget for his company car and was trying to spend right up to the top including accessories. This was his order of business. My being there was doing him a favour but I wasn't his servant, so I said goodbye to the staff and shoved off. Bastables sent me a charming thank you letter:

Dear Peter,

Thank you for your letter and copy to Ian.

We would like to take the opportunity of giving you our sincere thanks for all the work you have put in and, more importantly, the very helpful and enthusiastic attitude you have shown in solving our problems.

We hope everything is going to settle down now (about time it did) but please let us keep in touch at all events.

Kind regards.

Yours sincerely,

The postscript was interesting: Hope the new job goes well. If it doesn't, feel free to give us a call.

Peter Ryan gave me a very nice letter. My only hope was that my replacement didn't see the need to bring in more staff for the sole purpose of increasing his sense of importance.

19th July 1977

Dear Peter,

I find to my distress that I have not formally acknowledged your letter of the 13th May, sadly advising us of your impending departure.

I am sorry that your stay has been so short but you have made important contributions in your restructuring of the Accounts Department as well as in other areas and we are sorry to see you go.

As you know, we are struggling to find a replacement in which I hope we shall be successful, but it is nice to know that you are so willing to pop back from Covent Garden should we have any problems in interim period.

Yours sincerely

The set was completed with a note from Sterling Winthrop, who I visited once a month with Derek Webb. For the last couple of months this small pleasure had become a tiresome chore. Our accountant Jack had effectively been demoted by the arrival of Andrew, a young bloke to take charge of his section and this guy wanted in on the free lunch. Unfortunately he wasn't satisfied with the Italian restaurant and would book an expensive eatery a taxi ride away and boy, he was a real gold plated trencherman. Instead of one course with a glass of wine, he would do three courses, a couple of bottles of wine with brandies to finish and we had to follow his lead. It was a struggle to get away even after three hours at the trough and we could never get back to town before the bank shut.

My final day was Friday 12 August and another leaver from media and I were treated to a drinks party.

Some months later I heard through CPA that NSW had changed its name to the Munds Partnership after a coup where Peter was ousted. I really did lose touch with everyone there. Apart from sighting a familiar face around the town from time to time, the chapter was firmly closed.

Chris Munds joined Lintas as Chairman on 18 December 1991 and the name was changed to CM Lintas, referred to as CMLI. A few months later Hugh Salmon was appointed Managing Director on 15 June 1992. According to reports in 'Campaign' and 'Marketing Week', Mr Salmon uncovered an arrangement involving the booking of economy class air tickets for business trips while charging business class fares to the clients. The travel agent paid the difference into an account linked to Munds.

Chris realised what was afoot and, just as I would have expected having worked with the man, sacked Mr Salmon on the totally untrue claim of clients complaining about him.

The ad world is small and although I had never met Hugh Salmon, I knew that he had the highest possible reputation in the industry. Munds' panicked knee jerk reaction was due to the fact that his dishonesty was about to be exposed.

Salmon took his case to the top, the ultimate parent company in New York, Interpublic, without any success. He was left with no option but to go to the law. It took four years which must had taken a terrible toll on Mr Salmon and his family but he won. On 3 April 1997, Lintas Worldwide issued a Public Statement that he had been wrongfully dismissed, badly treated and that he was completely in the right bringing legal action against them.

It was a big fat and very public grovel. Their legal bills must have been humongous with the case estimated at costing in excess of one million pounds.

In 1999 Hugh Salmon set up his own agency and I have read that he may be putting himself up for election to Parliament. Good luck to him whatever he does.

As for Munds, I cannot find any record of any retribution. He seems to have retired from CMLI on 30 June 2005 and died in 2014 having had a wonderful life, 'loved by everyone'. Well, maybe not everyone.

10 THEATRE PROJECTS

'A man is not an orange; you cannot squeeze out all of the juice and throw the rest away.'

Guiseppe Garibaldi

On Monday 15 August 1977 I walked into Long Acre half expecting to find TP out of business having heard nothing since signing on but there it was. My office was on the top floor, shared with Pam Hay who was responsible for TP Associates, the theatre production side of things. Other occupants were TP Film run by Neville Thompson, Light Limited and Pilbrow's office.

The first morning was taken up by the ten cent tour. The main buildings situated between Langley Street and Mercer Street were massive and in the past had been a banana warehouse. Now they were home to TP Services, TP Consultants and an entire floor devoted to a bloated account's department. In one dark corner there were two guys running a specialist prop hire business dealing in police equipment going back to the time of the Bow Street Runners. After a couple of hours pounding the bricks, shaking hands and forgetting names I was ready for lunch.

In the afternoon I gathered up the Three Stooges and explained my approach. Under these circumstances I was surprised to meet all three of them. Four qualified accountants were at least two too many and it was obvious that a big axe was going to fall. Job hunting time was now. But apparently not.

My immediate tasks were to ascertain quickly where TP was financially, get the truth of Iran and then put a plan together for TP's future. In the meantime they could continue to run the accounting until I was ready to take the reins. However I had made up my mind that our department was to be much reduced and told them that if anyone resigned, I'd help them on with their coat and open the door.

I made an appointment to visit Ivor Mylecreest, our bank manager at Lloyds.

The first job was to gather up the accounts for the previous year. There were 26 companies in the group but 20 dormant. It would seem that these were registered to either prevent the name being used by an outside party or simply wishful thinking.

TPL was a holding company and its only income, the fees paid to it by the subsidiaries. TPS and Light Ltd were trading normally and TPC consumed by the Iran situation. TP Films were at that moment inactive and TP Associates had nothing in the pipeline that I could find. Easy savings to be made here?

On the personal front a bad case of hay fever had arrived at the same time as starting at TP. The drugs to control it were debilitating and it lasted some four months. Judy's Mini had been sold and a Vauxhall Victor arrived. It was cheap to buy, cheap to run and had no street cred whatsoever.

John took me to meet Tony Corbett, managing director of Light Limited with an ominous warning beforehand.

'This man is the worst possible product of the public school system.'

Large of frame, Tony could be the charmer but if he didn't get his way, he could quickly change to being very unpleasant.

'Accountants are a waste of time. All I need is a young girl for a couple of hours a week and I want the central charge stopped as I don't use any of the services.'

He went on in that vein for a while and I really wasn't interested so we moved on. As it was to turn out, Light Limited needed vast amounts of both my time and John's, and even Pilbrow's, to deal with the complex problems Mr Corbett brought to us. The business involved lighting design projects and at that period most of its work was in Nigeria.

In addition to Corbett, two young men were employed as well as Marion, the super PA. There was no doubt that this little outfit punched above its weight and they were to be commended for working in West Africa which can't have been easy. After all the doom and gloom it was a wonder to see that they made a profit on a regular basis.

Critical to our near future was the strength of the various debt lists and more surprises were to be found here.

Second on the TPC list was The National Theatre for close to twenty grand. Before I picked up the phone I did a bit of research that quickly revealed that this would never be recovered. It related to the design of the drum revolve which didn't work as it should have and I understand that it's rarely used even today. Peter Hall's excellent book refers to the problem and his dealings with Pilbrow that are not flattering. No one in TPC would even talk about it and when I tackled Richard he just brushed the subject aside. It was truly dead in the water and would have to be written off.

Light Limited deals in Nigeria were usually paid by Letter of Credit but just under ten thousand was owed by Calabar University according to the books. It took me a whole week to sort out the paperwork but, to cut the story short, the money was irrecoverable. The guys weren't working in that locale any more, restricting themselves to Lagos and by my reckoning only a personal visit by someone with incentives to offer would winkle the money out. When you added up the cost of such an enterprise together with the risk factor, it was a non-starter

We had a credit controller who was the brother of a director and I would guess considered himself fireproof. I sat down with him and asked him how he operated.

'I choose two or three debts at the start of the day and go after them hard, often making a personal visit.'

This tied in with my regular sightings of him wandering about Covent Garden with a file under his arm. However in my judgement he was a waste of space and would be totally unreceptive to any suggestions or advice. After Christmas I would sit down en masse with my department and show most of them the door and regardless of who his sibling was he was gone.

I had a meeting with the CPA guys, Chris Pearson and Alan Ifford. Obviously the advertising agency formula wouldn't work but Chris offered to bring in his brother Charlie and we would work on a fee basis. I accepted, hit it off with Charlie and we worked well together.

Clearly it was time for me to dig out the truth of the Iranian project, beyond the used envelope trick of which Pilbrow seemed so proud. TPC had rented an apartment in Tehran which served both as a residence and office for the three staffers based there. The unit had been furnished and equipped, a car purchased and a driver employed.

The Shah was engaged on a course of reforms to bring about a greater measure of political rights and freedoms but he was facing three main streams of opposition: Islamist, Marxist and

Constitutionalist. Within each of these groups there were additional factions but all were joined in spirit by a common enemy: the Royal Family and its governance of the country. Maybe Shah Mohammad Reza Pahlavi could keep a lid on this powder keg of insurrection for a while. But whether that would be long enough to get the building of our projects done and the fabled six and a half million pounds, plus overruns of course paid, I doubted.

The undertaking had been running since early 1977 and each and every month monies were remitted to Tehran to pay salaries and overheads. On top of this the TPC staff here were working on technical drawings to send over by courier.

Two shocks were in store for me. Not a single contract had been signed by the Iranian government, nor a sod turned nor a brick laid. Not a penny piece had been paid by the government of Iran to TPC either locally or remitted to the UK. Much later Pilbrow claimed that he had personally been to the Ministry and collected funds but that is a false memory. I do know that David Staples who was in charge of our office went above and beyond in trying to get our invoicing paid but neither in our UK books, nor in the accounting received from Tehran, was there a single payment of any kind.

I now knew that Pilbrow and I were looking at this from diametrically opposite ends of the spectrum: he believed it was a crock of gold, whereas I knew it was a crock of shite.

In summary, TP Films, Associates and TPC Iran were haemorrhaging cash faster than the rest of the group could make it. My early estimate of the loss for 1976/77 was eighty thousand pounds and that was without providing a bad debt reserve for the Middle Eastern adventure.

The meeting with Ivor Mylecreest at Lloyds Bank in Covent Garden was pure déjà vu. He was a tall man from the old school of bank managers whose reactions to a customer would be as much based on personal judgement as to any figures put in front of him. However we now have a new era of banking where decisions are made based on formulas dreamt up by a bunch of graduates at head office and not by the people on the ground.

I introduced myself and gave him a copy of my CV.

'Why are you here and what are you asking me for?'

'Just to introduce myself. I'm not asking for anything because I think that would be a waste of time for both of us.'

'Look, I'll come to the point. I want all your accounts gone from here. You have been nothing but a pain to us for a very long time. Where are you with the so called Iran project your boss believes will be your saviour?'

'If you'll excuse the pun, I wouldn't bank on it.'

I think he was warming to me, maybe a little.

'What you are up against here, as are all businesses with stocks and work in progress, is that my head office discounts their value on your balance sheet by 90%, down to 10% which is fire sale value. Here on my desk I have your last group accounts and their interpretation. Look, I have to step out for five minutes and I trust you not to look.'

I couldn't believe it. Taking a quick peek, I saw that Ivor was right, TP's figures which were rubbish anyway, were absolutely destroyed when the head office knife was stuck in. I don't know why he was so open but it was a good start to a good relationship.

When he returned, I promised to keep him informed, we shook hands and that was that. I seemed to have passed the bullshit test.

In order to set up a line of credit I contacted my old friend Peter Glenister of United Dominions Trust. We had written a lot of business together whilst I was at Conway's and I knew he would help if he could. We met up at Stone's Chop House, just off Leicester Square. After catching up with the gossip and news, I asked him if he could arrange some finance.

'Sorry Peter, Theatre Projects is blacked. As is your boss Pilbrow.'

'Blacked?'

Yes, all the credit agencies have them zero rated. There's bad history.'

'I won't try to kid you, they are in bad shape but the base is solid and I can cut out a lot of waste. I know I can get them on an even keel within a year. Is there any chance of setting up just a small line so we can get some essentials and make a start to getting a decent record.'

'We have done a lot of business over the years and you've never let me down. I will get something moving on your assurance that I won't be made to look foolish. I'm not asking for a guarantee, that would be unreasonable.'

Nevertheless, if things had gone pear shaped I would have made good out of my own pocket. I believe that if people put their trust in you, then you have to show that that trust is justified. Peter was as good as his word. A couple of small hire purchase agreements followed, one of which was to get Pilbrow some new transport, his ancient Audi 100 being a bloody disgrace for any CEO to drive.

It soon became obvious that over the years, Pilbrow had built up an inner circle, a clique, of people who were experts in various aspects of the theatre industry: David Collison, John Macintosh, Robert Ornbo and Pam Hay, to name but a few. Tony Corbett was either in or out depending on his whim. He lived in a village close to Pilbrow's in Oxfordshire. John Ball and I heard of business decisions taken over the Sunday breakfast table but had never been invited. Richard Walton was TP's insurance broker and an external member of the circle. En passant, his brother was Tony Walton who for a time had been married to Julie Andrews.

What should have been a good thing wasn't. They were all truly untouchable, free to operate as they saw fit and unaccountable to anybody. For example, David who was the top man in theatre sound announced a couple of years later that he couldn't tolerate the commercialism of TP that I had brought about. In future he would work from home, coming in once a month to collect his pay cheque and deal with any chores that needed his attention.

The workforce was the biggest asset and it was clearly evident that staff were totally committed. But the group lacked capital, sources of credit and was being dragged down by the loss makers. Coupled with the lack of solid management, failure was around the corner.

I asked Liz Lomas to call a directors' meeting. When I walked in it was obvious that Pilbrow was up for a fight with the ubiquitous Pam Hay by his side. John Ball and Dick Brett completed our pentangle.

John had been with TP for several years and although he was MD of the Group, the greater part of his energies was devoted to the running of TPS. A couple of years older than Pilbrow, he was his opposite in almost every way. Well known throughout the entertainment industry, he was highly respected and trusted by all he met. His ability to find a sale or hire was uncanny and he was one of the very few men whose handshake was his word and his word was bankable. I was proud to have been his friend right up to his death.

Dick had an engineering background. I found him straightforward to deal with and he had not been infected any of the affectations shown by others.

I tabled my results on one sheet of paper that I had typed. I knew that anything I asked Liz to do would be shown to Richard at the first opportunity. Richard threw all his toys out of the pram.

'A loss of seventy eight thousand? That's totally wrong and totally unacceptable. What have you brought in for Iran?'

'Nothing, of course.'

'That's ridiculous!'

With a flourish, a used envelope appeared and that well-known list of places and numbers appeared before our eyes.

'Six and a half million pounds.'

'And overruns,' I added sarcastically.

'I demand that a proportion of these profits be taken into account, enough to show a reasonable profit.'

'No can do. Not a single contract has been signed nor any work started and, here's the rub, not a red cent paid. Frankly I am tempted to show the whole 'investment' so far as a bad debt and that will double the loss.'

John turned to Dick with an exasperated look.

'Dick, is this true? That you've not even received a down payment?'

'Sorry to say, that is the current situation.'

John turned to Pilbrow and asked why he hadn't been told, but was ignored.

'These figures are not to be shown to anybody,' Pilbrow commanded.

'Look, in all honesty I cannot see what all the fuss is about. The results are a reflection of the year and I have a report being prepared to tackle the problem areas. There is the basis of a good business here and if we treat it as a business rather than a dream factory we can pull it round. It is common knowledge that Iran is heading for revolution within twelve months, so my advice, which you will ignore I'm sure, would be to abandon the whole thing. Remember Saigon.'

'This so called report, where is it?'

'Being typed off premises. If I'd asked for it to be done in-house, you would be reading it page for page, hot off the press, so to speak. I like confidentiality.'

Pilbrow looked at me malevolently and the meeting ended. Two years ago I'd thought that the trade union lads were a bastard to deal with but they were a walk in the park when compared to this idiot who surrounded himself with yes-men and insisted his decisions and determinations were accepted without question. That's why he was in deep trouble and why I was there. It would prove a rough ride.

I always accepted that the man was a brilliant lighting guy, no doubt about that. The problem was that there was so much ego massaging amongst his magic circle that he really believed he was the bee's knees at just about everything including running a business. But he wasn't. Set up in 1957, Theatre Projects had staggered through to 1977 and was now on the brink of bankruptcy. Of course he and his staff had done some wondrous work in that twenty years but there was no money to show for it. As for the Iran project, making such a commitment without payment was seriously bad judgement. But to press on with the project when everything pointed to a brutal end of the Shah and his government in the near future was beyond stubbornness. I worried about the staffers and what risks we were exposing them to.

A few days after our meeting Liz informed me of another get together. What fun! When I entered the small room I was surprised to see ten chairs set up around the circular Formica table as four or five was the usual complement. John and Dick followed me in and the seats filled anti-clockwise with me, John, Dick, John Macintosh, Brian Boreham, Harold Gould, David Collison, Richard Pilbrow and Pam Hay. Additionally between David and Richard sat an elderly man who John informed me was Richard's father. This worthy gentleman was a dead doppelganger for Boris Karloff and was to spend the entire meeting glaring at me like an Easter Island Moai. If he was looking for his sixty quid back he was going to be out of luck. Then it was standing room only: behind David was Robert Ornbo, Bob Stanton (Head of LAMDA) and Bill Stiles.

Just as the meeting was about to begin, Liz ushered in two young men. I had no idea who they were but maybe she had stepped out into the street and waylaid the first two swinging dicks to happen past. They took places next to Bill. The intention was clearly to intimidate me, as crude as that.

But if there was a vote at the end, what legality would it have? Some of those present didn't even work for TP in any shape or form. But if Pilbrow wanted the world to know all about his foolishness then so be it, as frankly I didn't give a damn. I had reached a point where very little was needed for me to walk away from this strange little man. I decided to press him into a corner of his own making. Richard indicated that he would make a start, but I interrupted.

'Excuse me Richard, shouldn't we wait for Mr Poldervaart as he's a major shareholder?'

His face turned red.

'He's not coming.'

'Really?' I asked, feigning surprise.

Of course he wasn't coming – he would know nothing of this ragbag assembly. To my amazement Richard had a used envelope to hand and the party trick was run out yet again. Why couldn't Liz type up a proper schedule to hand out? He explained TPC's presence in Iran at length. He eulogised about what the wonderful buildings would be like when they were finished and that our expectations could be as high as ten million pounds clear profit. Then came the bombshell.

'Our new accountant Peter refuses to bring any profit into the accounts which is of course, ridiculous.'

I wasn't sure what he expected would happen next – would they hiss and boo or even throw things. What actually happened was nothing but looking at their faces most were wondering why they were here and what this situation had to do with them.

I leaned back in my chair.

'It's very hot in here. Could somebody open the window.'

While that was being done, I opened the file in front of me and consulted my papers, simply for effect.

'Okay, Richard has laid out the good news. Now I will tell you all the reality and the truth. Firstly, not a single contract has been even signed. Two, not a single building has been even started and three, most importantly, nothing has been paid to us whatsoever. Not a penny.'

I paused to let the information to sink home, then quickly continued.

'And another truth is vitally important. Iran is heading for a revolution in the next few months and the new regime aren't going to be interested in any of this. They're burning down cinemas with people inside for God's sake! Frankly I think it's disgusting that you're keeping our good people out there and at risk. Their blood could be on your hands!'

I had deliberately used 'you' and 'your' to spread a little collective guilt around the room and I could see the effect. Despite our recent history, I really did expect our auditors to back me up but yet again I was to be sorely disappointed. Mr Gould took the floor.

'I think I have an elegant solution to all this. We could hold over our audit to the last minute and Peter, you could bring in a figure that would make Richard happy. Then when the audit does take place, hopefully the money will have started flowing and we could take a view.'

There we are again, keep the client happy at all costs.

'And the purpose of these accounts would be …?'

Richard grabbed Gould's idea with both hands

'You could take them to the bank and get an overdraft to tide us over.'

'So your joint solution is that I turn a seventy eight thousand loss (that caught my audience's attention) into a profit by slotting in money that doesn't exist, will never exist, then take that to Lloyds Bank and make an overdraft request. Everyone in this room is committing a conspiracy to defraud the bank by even being here, listening to this.'

Gould tried to bring it down a notch.

'It doesn't matter what figures you produce, after all you are not a real accountant.'

'What the hell are you taking about, not a real accountant? You know full well that I am a Chartered Accountant and I guard my solid reputation. Last week an accountant was jailed for doing what you are suggesting and the Judge said, and I quote: 'A company's accounts must be sacred for the market to be able to trust it'. And that's my mantra. In any event TP's chance of an overdraft is between no and fat. All Lloyds Bank wants is for TP to go away. You don't know just how bad things are. TP's credit rating and yours (I pointed to Pilbrow) are nil. You are black listed all over town.'

Richard was reeling by now but he had brought it on himself.

'That can't be right. My car is on hire purchase.'

'Yeah, through UDT on my credit rating and with my personal guarantee,' I shot back.

Most of those in the room were transfixed at the revelations. I decided to pull the plug. Gould tried to correct his misstatement by explaining that what he'd meant was that I wasn't an auditor, just an in-house accountant. I looked him in the eye and fired the last shot.

'I think I too have an elegant solution. Start the audit on Monday, we are ready, then YOU can put in a sum for Iranian profit. You know take a view, arrive at a figure to please Richard and then sign YOUR name to it. I am not interested in getting us through to the next crisis, my job is to sort out TP here in London and get it financially stable. Simple as that. I have work to do and I have nothing more to say, so I'll leave you to sort the world out.'

I rose and left the room with John and Dick following.

As I started to descend the stairs I heard Pilbrow shout: 'I've met the Shahina.'

I thought the alternate title for the Empress of Iran was Shanbanu but I could be wrong.

On the way down John asked Dick to confirm that my revelations on Iran were correct and if so, as the managing director why hadn't he been informed.

'Yes John, Peter is completely correct but I don't know why you were kept in the dark.'

John was neither impressed nor best pleased. It's called mushroom management. As we three hit the pavement I told them that I was going for a much needed drink and threw out an invitation. Dick declined, probably because he didn't want to be seen with the pariah of Theatre Projects. However John agreed and we took an early lunch.

'What the hell was that all about and who were the last two guys?' I asked him.

'They're lighting designers.'

'Why were they there? And the other lot? Only three people spoke and only those three were actually needed. His father, Bob, a bunch of lighting guys, what was the point?'

'It's Pilbrow, his modus operandi. He always makes a huge drama over everything. Where a couple of blokes could sort out what to do in ten minutes, he will bring in a cast and turn the whole thing into a three act opera. Fifteen packed into a tiny space with most of them not even knowing why they were there. I must say you didn't give an inch and dropped a few bombshells on to the table. There will be some juicy conversations all over Covent Garden as we speak. Look back on your recruitment, five interviews when a chat between Richard, you and I would have done the job. Everything's made bigger than it is.'

'Well, as he invited them I assumed they were privy to the details of our finances.'

'Liar, you played him like a fish on the hook.'

When we finished lunch, I strolled back, ready to clear my desk and make an appointment with my lawyers but to my surprise there was no dismissal notice. John had told me that working at TP could be like Florence in the Middle Ages with Niccolo Machiavelli and the Medici family vying for power. I had worked out who represented Lucrezia Borgia.

I will never know why I wasn't fired, as I had parcelled him up like a kipper. But I did know that he wouldn't forgive or forget in a hurry and the more I got to know the man, I learned that he carried grudges and resentments to the death.

For me there was never any question of knocking up dodgy accounts. I was very proud of my qualification and although we don't sign an equivalent to the doctors' Hippocratic Oath, the public is entitled to rely on a high standard of honesty; there are bent accountants, always will be but I wasn't one of them.

My mind was made up. I needed to get rid of the auditors. The predicament that I was in was largely my own fault. When they phoned to offer the introduction to TP, I should have sent them away with a flea in the ear, simple as that. But I didn't. When Pilbrow put me through a long series of interviews for a two-bit job I should have told him to stuff it. But I didn't.

I had been assured that Boreham had nothing to do with TP and I wouldn't have to deal with him, yet here he was a few weeks later backing up his boss. Praise be, he had nothing to contribute to the famous meeting. How could I have expected anything more than grief?

After seven years of good hard productive work, I was in effect sacked by Boreham for sitting in the wrong chair, when I had no possible way of knowing it was reserved. Then I exposed Conway's long running fraud, not only on the Inland Revenue but on his fellow directors. Not only had that directly cost me my well-paid job, but they treated me as an irresponsible nuisance causing such a fuss when their client had done absolutely nothing wrong.

Now for upholding the long established rules of accounting according to GAAP, let alone the rule of law, I am told in front of an audience that I am not a real accountant and therefore by definition, a fake accountant. I decided that enough was enough. I had been abused, insulted, maltreated and the auditors had to go. And wrote a letter to explain why.

It set out how disappointed I was with their obsequiousness to clients and I needed a firm who would back me when a customer is behaving badly (if there is such an animal). In our recent meeting every accounting standard supported my decision on the Iran farce, but they had openly backed Pilbrow to keep him happy and even had the audacity to refer to me as 'not a real accountant'. That was the very last straw. I needed people with me on the task ahead to stand up to be counted when the going gets tough, as it will.

They wrote to Pilbrow claiming that I was taking revenge for events in the past. Frankly, I didn't care and if Pilbrow had interfered I would have walked straight out the door. The new auditors were Melman Pryke, now I believe part of Grant Thornton.

Soon after this I circulated my report; it contained nothing radical, just common sense. Close Films and Associates, no pay rises until we are out of trouble or any new staff unless absolutely essential and sort out the accounting department. No mention of Iran, no point.

A meeting of directors was set to adopt it. There seemed to be a different attitude and for once, there was no mention of the millions from the east. The film production's inactivity was simply resolved by Neville Thompson resigning with immediate effect. In fact, he went on to have a wonderful career until his death in 2002. Pilbrow announced that TPA would go dormant and that Pam Hay would be absorbed into his staff, to do what was never made clear but I was soon to find out what he had in mind.

The only written response was from John Macintosh who suggested that his annual pay increase could be funded by sacking the secretaries and replacing them with young girls who would work for peanuts because this was the theatre. Would you believe that he dictated this to his secretary to type up? Must have done wonders for her feelings of security.

I was fast learning that this place was a bed of intrigue, a symptom of too many people doing too little work. I had just the remedy for that.

Paul approached me for a private word. With very obvious delight he informed me that John had heard that I was rubbishing him around the town to all and sundry and therefore my hope of a good working relationship was at an end. I told him in no uncertain terms that what he had heard was 100% bollocks and that I would sort this out pronto.

Straight away I walked over to John's office where I related what Paul had told me.

'Look John, I have only known you a very short time and I like what I see. Frankly I don't know you well enough to offer any opinion to anyone, so whatever you've heard is pure crap.'

'I know it is.'

'What the hell is going on here? People seem hell bent on making bloody mischief and cause problems for the sake of it.'

'It has always been like that and maybe always will be. When I joined it had a real hippy atmosphere – flower power and all that. I remember walking into Robert Ornbo's office to find his secretary stripped to the waist and sitting on his lap. It was all cheesecloth shirts and sandals. Some folk haven't changed and never will.'

We shook hands and agreed that when anything needed sorting out we would deal with it at the earliest possible time. Later, I discovered that the culprit was a previous accountant.

I received a message that Bob Scott and Steve Batiste who ran Commercial Presentations (CP) from Neal's Yard wanted to see me. All I knew was that they were major customers of TPS, so I took myself over to get some background from John.

'Essentially, they produce product launches and organize corporate events for an impressive list of clients. And they're very successful at it, both creatively and financially.'

'What do you think they want to see me for? To say hello?'

'No, it's more than that. You need some background. A few years ago I was good friends with a dear old chap named Stanley Coleman who owned a photography business in Neal's Yard which produced work for both TP and CP. He wanted to retire, so I negotiated a deal for TP Associates to take over the business and the staff all at no cost.

'From that it was agreed that Commercial Presentations would exchange 25% of its shares for 25% of Theatre Projects Associates, which at the time made sense.

'Pilbrow had never liked Coleman or his setup. He thought it was a grubby little company and didn't fit into the grand TP vision. In 1975 I went on holiday and prior to setting off asked Pilbrow to please do nothing in respect of Coleman's and when I got back I would convene a meeting to discuss the whole situation.

'On my return, I discovered that Pilbrow had sent Pam Hay over with fistfuls of redundancy notices to sack the entire staff and close the business down. Bob and Steve were furious as all their photography work had been carried out by Coleman's and were not consulted or even informed about the action. As a result today's situation is TP has a quarter of a terrific business and that business has a quarter of TPA which is worth nothing.

'I was furious about what he'd done and that I'd been totally ignored and offered my resignation, which he refused. I should have insisted but I was sweet talked into staying and here I am.'

Now that the books were closed off for 1976/77 I could finally take a good look at the accounting department I had inherited. I moved my base over to Langley Street and set up a desk in the corner. I kept my spot at 10 Long Acre for any private activities, such as interviews. To my surprise a day after my move, Pam Hay arrived in the accounts area and acquired a desk as well. Frankly I didn't care where she was but I couldn't see the point. I still didn't know what she did for TP but it certainly wasn't accounting.

Then I went off to see Bob and Steve and introduced myself. Steve was on the boil.

'Two years ago we did a deal where TP Associates would hold 25% of our stock in exchange for 25% of their stock. Today we're a success and TP Associates are total losers.'

'I understand.'

'We want the transaction reversed and as soon as possible.'

'I can see that.'

'If not, we'll run CP down to nothing and form a phoenix. That will be a massive waste of energy and money, but we are not prepared to let it all drift on.'

'Sure, I agree with you. Leave it with me and I'll get it sorted.'

I got up to leave but Bob stopped me.

'Is that it?'

'Sure, give me a couple of days.'

It took me a morning to sort out the paperwork and get everything signed, but job done. We had lost nothing as I am sure they were not bluffing.

But something strange was happening. I started to notice that whenever I left the office, irrespective of the time, Pam was still there. I did a few late nights and there she was beavering away as I made my exit. So one evening I put her to the test.

Opposite our building was a similar unit that was occupied by Pineapple Dance Studio. So after saying goodnight, I shot down the stairs, crossed the road and shot up the stairs of Pineapple, until I reached a point overlooking my desk. And Pam was sitting at it, going through my papers.

Finally she left the building with my files, returning after twenty minutes to replace the paperwork. I had a spy in the camp and decided to milk it to the very last drop.

The next day I churned out a mass of paperwork, including sheets of totally meaningless figures. The staff had gone by just after five and I headed out at half past and ran to take up my watching spot. Armed with a Polaroid camera, I was going to secure unchallengeable evidence of her dirty work. The following day I repeated the entire exercise. I was ready to drop the hammer.

Pam came in at 9.30 to find her desk clear apart from a couple of photographs. She turned on her heel and left the room. When she reached Pilbrow's office she found him also examining some pictures and reading my memorandum. It explained that I did not know what skill sets Pam possessed but that using her as a spy was a despicable abuse of power. If he wanted copies of my work all he had to do was ask. I also added that I had had a gutful of his tomfoolery and if there was any more of his foolishness, I would walk away and let his wonderful Theatre Projects to go into liquidation in the very short term. He never spoke to me on the matter but Miss Hay quietly left the accounts office and returned from whence she'd come.

I felt that I had fallen down the rabbit hole into an unreal world inhabited by some very strange and pretty disgusting people. It would have been so easy to leave them to stew in their own juices but the bottom line was that the rank and file were a decent, hard working bunch. I felt that it had fallen to me to get the company out of this financial pit. The business was there and run properly, the profits would follow. With John to share the load we really could get the show on the road. What Pilbrow would come to realise was that if he fucked with me, he was fucking with the best.

The organisation now had three clear profit centres.

Services, under John Ball, was by far the largest, dealing with the sale and hire of lighting and sound equipment. The biggest money-spinner was getting a rig into a long running West End show. Its origins sprang from the acquisition of Stagesound in 1974 and Rank Strand South in1976. Rank Strand had retained 25% of TPS shares and two or three of their directors would attend a monthly meeting to review the company's progress or lack of it. There was a small retail shop, the beginnings of an a/v unit and a special project department developing mixing desks under Sam Wise. But the whole business was starved of capital.

Consultants under Dick Brett designed places of entertainment and the National Theatre had been a major client. They were engaged in the design and construction of theatres, concert halls, art centres and the like across many parts of the globe. But it was clear that Iran was their Achilles Heel and I could only watch as we got financially deeper into the hole every month. Pilbrow would never face the facts and it would take blood in the streets for him to walk. Dick was quietly reducing the level of work leaving London but we had to support our guys on site and that cost money.

At the time, Light was crewed by four staff. On meeting him, Tony Corbett brought to mind the image of Harry Flashman from Tom Brown's Schooldays. The main business at that time was turnkey lighting projects for clients in Nigeria. I found Tony could be difficult to work with as the slightest affront, real or imagined, would send him off to complain to the Chairman.

When I'd visited Pilbrow's office to drop off my memo, I noticed copies of the share transfer CP/TP on his desk that Pam had obtained for him with his hand written addendum, 'He is giving away our heritage'. There is no doubt in my mind that if the deal had not been done Steve and Bob would have carried out their threat to phoenix CP, rise from the ashes in another guise and we could have lost a TPS client at a stroke.

When I bumped into John, I told him of the James Bond adventure that I had uncovered and he wasn't the least bit surprised.

'You know Peter, if he would just stick to what he is good at, namely lighting, creative, front of house, all that side of things and leave the commercial and financial stuff to you and I we could make a real success of what we have. But outside of his clique he respects and trusts no one. He tries to micro manage everything and meddle. The only way we can influence this is to never have money to spare, always be on the brink of disaster and that might put a brake on him spending on one whim or another.'

'Well, that's where we are now and for the foreseeable future.'

'Watch what happens when we do have any money available. He'll be impossible to control, wait and see.'

A little before Christmas I returned to the office after lunch to find the three caballeros with their coats on and ready to depart with four of the staff.

'Early finish lads?' I asked.

Paul spoke for the group.

'No, we're going to the Opera House to see the rehearsals of Wagner's Ring Cycle, so we won't be back today. It's a perk of working at Theatre Projects,' adding in a petulant tone, 'and if you say we can't. I will resign on the spot.'

He was putting great temptation before me but I let it pass. The empty desks portrayed a vision of the very near future.

It was clear was that we were on the edge of insolvency and trading in such circumstances could result in each director being liable. Of course many of the directors could claim that they had no idea what was going on as they were only officers of the company as far as salary and prestige were concerned. Financially, they were totally in the dark and responsible for nothing other than themselves.

Cometh the New Year, cometh the axeman.

I called a meeting of all accounts personnel on a Friday afternoon in the basement of 10 Long Acre. In they trooped, the unfed, unmotivated and uninspired. I explained that TP had lost a lot of money and continued to do so, meaning that cuts had to be made and promptly sacked ten clerks with immediate effect. I retained Barbara the machine operator who, like Linda at NWS, was worth more than the rest of them put together. I also kept Trudy who was 50/50 to my mind.

I was reluctant to fire any of my qualified guys, although I only needed one of them, because having a sacking on your CV is not good thing; it's not a blood brother society situation, just a professional courtesy. I hoped against hope that they would see what was clearly ahead and find another job or convince me that they were worth their weight. I was heading for sore disappointment.

I had prepared for the following Monday. Paul, Peter and Robert duly arrived and I asked Paul to take control of TPS, giving TPC and Light to the other two with a suggestion that they helped out wherever they could. Max had agreed to give me a weeks worth of help and I had booked a couple of contract workers. With Brenda and Trudy that made eight, plus Charlie and me, total ten. I was fairly sure that I would lose another two quickly, so in the short term I had cut the department in half. Within a week we were up to date on all fronts.

The second week we moved lock stock and barrel to rooms at the back of 10 Long Acre and I handed over the massive warehouse to John so that TPS could fill it with productive money generating activities. My belief is that cash flow is the cornerstone in any business; get that right and everything else follows.

So a routine emerged. I was always in before seven and would go through the debt lists, setting up the day for Charlie to chase the money. If deemed appropriate, we would visit a client together to pick up a cheque and generally make ourselves known. And sometimes collect an order for John to follow up.

I interviewed people to replace the temporaries and recruited a couple of Antipodeans. Trudy didn't last long. She took a day off sick (to look for a job) and we found a pile of unbanked cheques stuffed in a drawer. Now she knew as well as everybody how much of a bind we were in, so when she did show up words were exchanged. She went out, got pissed and when she returned to the office stinking drunk, I threw her out on her ear.

There was no doubt that TP's reputation for slow payment meant that in many cases we worked on a cash with order or cash on delivery basis, which exacerbated our financial situation. That couldn't be improved overnight but I had found that in my experience a creditors' list could be made more controllable by paying off the small debts quickly. As much as 70% of a list could be settled by maybe only 10% or 15% of the total cash owing.

This of course leaves the bigger accounts to be handled but as our solvency improved we would have the resources to tackle them as well, unless foolish expansive ideas damaged the day-to-day operations.

Paul was a hard worker but I found him dour. He asked for a

word. If this was to be more scurrilous gossip I was ready to send him away with a flea in his ear and the result would have been much the same if it was some claptrap about rehearsals of The Nutcracker. We were in a new era where being in the theatre was not all pervasive. In actuality, he wanted to complain about his old muckers Peter and Robert. Paul had a job which kept him busy all day, every day and he was fed up watching the other two swan about with little or nothing to do, and never, ever offering any help to others. He was dead right.

I had put it off for too long. Here were two intelligent, educated, professional men well aware of our financial hole, yet seemingly content to take wages for minimum effort, strolling around the town like a couple of Queens of May. I had truly expected them to come to me and talk about the future, but no. I mentioned it to John but he had no magic solution, so the axeman had another dirty job to hand.

I called Peter to my office who duly arrived and took a seat. We started our chat by me stating the bleeding obvious: try as I might I could not find useful employment for him and, frankly, he had made little effort to make himself indispensable. I had hoped that he would have worked to find himself a niche under the new regime but he hadn't. So he now found himself part of the cost savings, could leave right away and his entitlements would be sent to him next week. We both stood up, I wished him good luck, we shook hands and he left the building. I had no qualms about losing him. I had been patient beyond measure and had given him enough rope to hang himself and he did just that.

Minutes later I heard footsteps heading up to my office. Robert was incandescent with fury and outrage.

'I have just been told by Peter that he has been fired. I consider that an absolutely disgusting and an abhorrent act committed by a vile person.'

I leaned back in my chair.

'I'm glad you're here Robert.'

'Why?'

Because you're also fired.'

'What? How dare you?!'

'You know our financial position as well as anyone and the fact is that neither you nor Peter have any work to do. Nor have you looked for any or pitched in to help the others. Do you seriously expect to be carried along like a pair of old retainers?'

'But the Iran money will arrive any day and that will sort everything out. There's no need to sack people.'

'There ain't no Iran money now and never will be. There are major demonstrations on the street in Qom as we speak and the Shah's army is busy killing civilians. The country is about to explode. Anyway, none of that is relevant here as I have made my decision, you are fired so please go, and go now.'

Robert was still standing, so I rose and offered my hand. He refused it and stormed out. It was only a few moments later that my presence was required in Corbett's office and I was joined on the staircase by John Ball on a similar errand. We were both surprised to find Peter, whom I had so recently given the chop, sitting there grinning happily.

Tony launched into us.

'Peter tells me that he's been let go.'

'Correct. So what?'

'Bloody disgusting. Why wasn't I consulted?'

'Because it's got nothing to do with you. I don't interfere with Light Limited's staff arrangements, so keep out of my department.'

'Well gentlemen, I'm announcing that Peter is to be my personal accountant.'

'To do what exactly?'

'Manage my books.'

'You tell me again and again that you only need a girl for two hours a week. What do you suggest that he does for the other 33?'

'I will find something.'

'No you will not. You want your management charges down, you want TP to survive and you have employed me to do all that. I can achieve all of those things and a lot more. Respect that. We cannot afford to carry passengers and the gravy train has stopped.'

I turned to Peter.

'I am sorry that you have lost your job but there is nothing whatsoever here for you to do. For a business to have four Chartered Accountants and twelve support staff out of a hundred people is ludicrous. Pen pushers represent 16% of the total and still being in a bloody mess is ridiculous. I have tried to do this in a nice way but if you think you can stir things up for me you are sadly mistaken. You have been given every chance and you have blown it by spending your time poncing around as if you are at Butlins. Tony can't help you and why should he when you couldn't help yourself. You're finished and I want you out of here.'

'I have to agree with Peter Roy,' John interjected. 'We have employed him to rescue the TP Group and we will achieve nothing if we fight his every decision.'

Tony said nothing. I stood up and headed out. As I passed Peter, I whispered into his shell-like.

'On your bike mate and now.'

That was the last I saw of Peter and Robert; if they had a leaving drink I wasn't invited. A couple of weeks later Paul announced he was off. So out of the original crowd I had only retained Barbara and she was the only one I didn't want to lose. The rest of 'em could go home to their mothers.

Every month John and I had a meeting with two directors from Rank Strand to discuss TPS' monthly results. Normally it was Phil Rose and George Templeton who would turn up. Phil was a quiet spoken man who had six beautiful daughters but no sons. He complained that even his dog was female. George Templeton was from Glasgow and very direct, telling you how it was in no uncertain terms. Any attempt at bullshitting or gilding the lily and he'd be all over you like a cheap suit.

Our February Monday morning 10am meeting was due the week Paul was leaving and I impressed on him that we must have the January figures on time. He assured me that all was well and they would be ready. When Monday came, Paul told me that he was just making the final adjustments and the accounts would be presented on time.

As the conference room was in use, we had to meet in my office.

When John arrived, he grumbled about having to work with his paperwork on his knees and then Phil and George turned up. At the stroke of ten Paul appeared, handed round the accounts and left.

As soon as I looked at the figures it was obvious why Paul had engineered this situation. The figures were terrible, showing an unbelievable loss. Even a quick glance showed that he had made a massive bad debt provision (everything over three months old), stocks were written down to fire sale values and everything viewed as pessimistically as could be possible. Paul's leaving gift. Phil and George exploded and the tough Scotsman had some choice words for the management of their investment. It was a very short meeting.

After we broke up, I thanked Paul for his efforts. He was holier-than-thou with an attitude that the figures were realistic. I pointed out that decisions that affected people's lives were taken on what we accountants produce but he was unrepentant and I suspect, totally unconcerned about other people's lives.

Fortunately, John was well aware of Paul's bastardly act but Phil and George were not. But Paul's attempt to hurt the hand that had fed him was to lead to one of my finest hours in the very near future. In March I replaced Paul as accountant with Mr Ian Archie Gray ACA. He was not made a director.

At the end of the first six months of 1977/78 our financials had improved but staff termination costs had hurt; the second half should reflect the actions taken. Cash flow had improved dramatically thanks to the amount of serious time and effort that had been dedicated to the task. Scam artists could no longer place an order with good old TP and expect to get away without paying. An Argentinian restaurant ordered a sound system and then cried poverty, so I rounded up a bunch of lads, went around at lunchtime and ripped it all out in front of their horrified customers.

The overarching problem was the lack of capital but there was no way of rectifying that until we could display steady profits across the board; a typical chicken and egg situation.

Iran was hotting up daily. February had seen violence erupt in Tabriz with over a hundred people killed and at the end of March hotels, cinemas, banks and other western symbols were attacked. It goes without saying that not a copper coin had been paid.

Although Corbett had made clear his accounting needs, huge

chunks of my time and of John Ball's were committed to his company. The first export to Nigeria to come across my desk was for the external signage for the NET (Nigerian Telecommunications) building in Lagos. We had a Letter of Credit that backed our orders to suppliers. The Nigerian government had introduced a new scheme to protect themselves from empty containers or cargos of scrap being sent down to them. We had to get every shipment cleared by a Swiss Inspectorate based in Wiltshire, so a mass of paperwork had to be generated and all invoicing matched to suppliers bills to ensure profiteering did not take place. And finally we had to ensure that everything tied in with the Letter of Credit and the Bill of Lading. It was a hell of a job but there was a good margin albeit eroded by the commissions paid out to the middlemen. Add to all this the time it took to drive over to meet the Swiss guys, go through everything and come back. It killed off the two hours per week nonsense.

The next hurdle to jump was with the suppliers. Given our track record, I found that even with a Letter of Credit they were unwilling to release any goods without payment in full. And that was money we simply couldn't find. Many of the supplies came from Rank Strand and of course, they had access to the TPS accounts and knew the precarious state of the TP Group. We had deadlines to meet with the shippers and customers and it was exhausting pulling it all together. The only way out was to give my personal guarantee, which was in itself was ridiculous as I was only a staffer. I kept this arrangement to myself, for obvious reasons. It was a potentially dangerous gamble to take but there was no other way to get the goods released.

The government droned on about 'export or die' and 'help for small businesses' but it all meant nothing. It simply provided easy lines for civil servants to spout. I did the rounds of government agencies, completed endless forms, attended dreary meetings and shook countless sweaty hands, all for nothing. The bank? I asked, they refused, end of story.

It took time to build up the accounts team and mistakes were made. A thirty something woman named Sally was brought in to help with TPS sales and though of nervous disposition, her work was fine.

A party to celebrate TP's twenty-first birthday was announced which would be held on the top floor of our Langley Street premises. So great was the excitement leading up to the party that I invited a few mates to join us in what was promised to be an extravagant spread. The staircase in the old warehouse was open tread and four of us had to escort Sally up, as she was terrified by the lack of risers.

Organised by Pilbrow's handmaidens Pam and Liz, what greeted us was a joke and an embarrassment. All that was laid out were a few bowls of crisps and Twiglets, not even any nuts or sausage rolls, to be washed down by boxes of the cheapest of wines.

Pilbrow started to make his speech, the same old hackneyed fable of starting off in the back room of a theatre. We had heard this so many times that we could all recite it by rote. My rough group ignored him and talked amongst ourselves, prompting Liz to fly over.

'Be quiet,' she hissed, 'Richard is speaking.'

What a laugh. I know I wanted economies but if you can't afford a real party, don't bother. Then the music started up and Sally, who was absolutely wasted, took to dirty dancing with a TPC guy who looked like a flasher. After an hour or so she wandered over in the direction of John Ball, threw up over his shoes and then Dick Brett got a spray. Corbett grabbed her in a fireman's lift and took her down to the street but not before she was sick over the back of his jacket. Barbara offered to make sure Sally got home as they lived in the same suburb. I hailed a cab and handed the driver a fistful of money to get the problem away and off our hands. I later found out that before hitting the wine she had consumed a dozen tranquillizers.

A few weeks later I returned to the office around 4pm after a client meeting, to be regaled with the story of Sally and a Hungarian temp called Maria. Apparently they had returned pissed and abusive after a long lunch, caused a massive disturbance for an hour and then gone home. When they arrived the next morning, it was straight up to my office, sacked, and out of the door.

David was another mistake. The guy could have been Bob Hoskins' double and he started well. He was allocated the central TPS ledger to control and made a good fist of it for a few months. David had an irritating habit of accosting me each and every time I walked through the accounts office, always with an irrelevancy, and then he started to need bits of time off. His wife's hospital appointments were the favourite.

One morning I was working with Charlie on a major debt and was about to leave the building when David arrived in a panic with a strange tale to tell. He had taken the ledger home to work on, (which was peculiar in itself), and had left it on the bus. Later that evening he had received a telephone call demanding a hundred quid reward for its safe return. The story stank. How did the finder get his phone number? Common sense told me that this was a shakedown but I couldn't afford to lose those records, so I agreed. Although he gave me a story about the cloak and dagger operation of recovery, it was a complete fabrication.

So he was finished. A week later he asked if he could leave at 1pm to visit a friend in hospital. I followed him across Charing Cross Road into Newport Court, where he dived into a porn shop. I hadn't had lunch so I took a window table in one of the many Chinese restaurants, ordered some sweet and sour and a beer, and waited. When I finished an hour had passed and he had not reappeared so unless there was a back door exit, which I doubted, he was still in there. The following morning, I told him that his story was false, as were his many others I suspected and he was fired. I think he interpreted our kindness as stupidity. We're not as green as we're cabbage looking.

In his book *A Theatre Project*, Pilbrow is somewhat sparse in spelling out actual year end results, which I plan to rectify. However he does claim and I quote: 'The TP Group by 1977 had a financial turnover of £1,744,000 with a net profit off £164,000'.

This is incorrect and I wrote to both Pilbrow and the publisher enclosing the group's results as lodged with Companies House and signed off by the directors and auditors, along with various other matters. These are in my procession and I have supplied copies to other interested parties, so everything can be verified.

The final figures for the year ended 30th September 1977, expressed in thousands were as follow:

| Sales | 1,734.7 |
| Trading Loss | (68.4) |

The simplified balance sheet at 30.09.1977 was:

| Share Capital | 21.0 |
| Reserves | 53.6 |

Deferred	3.7
Minority interests	23.5
	101.8
Assets	101.8
Current Assets	712.3
Current liabilities	(712.3)
	101.8

It was a total freak that current assets equalled current liabilities and I have to confess that I have never seen this before or since.

So we have an error of some £232k between RP's record of what the profit for 1976/77 was and what was reported. Only a few years later a remarkably similar situation arose.

We were closing in fast on the end of my first year and I knew we were tracking well but there would always be surprises.

As ever, TPS was hampered by lack of capital. John would receive an order but was unable to meet it due to a lack of equipment and the means to buy any. It was painful to hear staff referring customers to our rival Donmar to buy supplies because our shelves were bare.

TPC were working hard on several solid projects but still stuck in the morass that was Iran. Whatever money was made was largely leaving for the Middle East to fill a bottomless pit.

Our audited results for 1977/78, signed by the directors and auditors and filed at Companies House, and expressed in thousands were as follow:

Sales	1,846.2
Profit	110.7

The simplified balance sheet at 30.09.78 was:

Share capital	21.0
Reserves	109.6

Minorities	<u>43.3</u>
	<u>173.9</u>

Assets	121.7
Current assets	762.8
Current liabilities	<u>(710.6)</u>
	<u>173.9</u>

What had to be borne in mind was that I was writing off all the cash sent to Iran together with invoices for the design work as they happened. Without that continuing nonsense the profit would have been increased by £35k to a tad short of £150k. The Chairman's report didn't mention Iran.

As far as I was concerned my methods and I had been vindicated but I know for a fact that many were sorely disappointed that I hadn't fallen on my face. The list would have been long, to include those who had lost their jobs and but others who relied on their special bond with Pilbrow to maintain their stipend. They pined for the good old days of a few guys, a girl and flower power and who knows, maybe they would all return. It's a strange world.

In the summer of 1978, assured by the USA that they had his back, the Shah introduced martial law and banned demonstrations. Unimpressed, the people were out on the streets of Tehran and other major cities as the mood for change gathered pace. There was still no sign of any money whilst the debts continued to rise as did the risk to our beleaguered staff. Ayatollah Khomeini who had lived as an exile in Paris for many years was awaiting the call.

Of course there were a few fringe benefits gained by working at TP but not enough to sacrifice a decent wage. Tickets to shows were often available, especially when a production was poorly attended and bums on seats were needed.

I managed a couple of mediocre seats for the Royal Gala of Evita, arriving well before the start. I had drinks in the bar, placed an order for the interval and the barman indicated my spot for collection. Being at the end of a row I was first to collect our drinks but it was six deep at the bar within seconds. Some of the PolyGram directors wandered in but didn't recognise me. They took one look at the scene and realising it was mission impossible, spotted some drinks set out on a shelf prepaid by some poor punter but not yet claimed.

'Here, these will do,' said one and handed around the drinks.

Morality isn't dead, it's just hiding in shame.

John had been de facto managing director of the group for some years but on 11 July 1978 Pilbrow sent him the following letter.

PRIVATE

John Ball Esq,

10 Long Acre,

London WC 2

Dear John.

I was, both personally and on behalf of Theatre Projects, more than delighted with the very detailed and frank discussion we had last night.

I would like to confirm that at the Board Meeting on this coming Friday I am going to propose that you become Managing Director of Theatre Projects Limited with myself as Chairman. This will mean effectively that the company is run by a triumvirate of myself as Chairman responsible for creative policy, you as Managing Director responsible for commercial affairs and Peter Roy as Financial Director responsible for finance. It is our intention that we will, as aggressively as possible, go out and seek sufficient capital for the presently intended scheme of things.

It is obviously very essential that the three of us work together as a closely knit unit and I would suggest we have meetings like last night's at not less than monthly intervals.

I understand that, following our conversation, you discussed the question of salary with Peter Roy, and I would agree with the suggestion that it should be raised to £12,500 per annum forthwith and with an increase to £15,000 as from the 1st October 1978.

Once again, may I express my personal pleasure in this development and I look forward to the future.

Yours, with thanks,

Richard

However, within 24 hours he had added CEO to his title of Chairman, rendering John's promotion an irrelevance.

John and I were of one mind as regards the management of a business: we did the rounds. That way we knew almost everybody and everybody knew us and that we were approachable. We met every day, often for lunch in the Kings Arms, and were aware of what was going on in our industry on a day-to-day basis.

By the end of 1978 I was in a good place. My apartment had been finished to a high standard and I had a reliable but boring new car. Tina was my regular date and I had a short list of ladies with whom to have lunch or go to the theatre or whatever. Most importantly I had proved myself and although Pilbrow didn't actually like me (or John for that matter), he had to admit that as far as financial ability was concerned, I was the man for TP. My salary had also seen a good increase, which was most welcome.

The situation in Iran was desperate. The Islamic revolution was well and truly on the move. In August 1978, Cinema Rex was burned to the ground, killing the 420 people trapped inside. I sent a memo to Pilbrow expressing my serious concern for our staff's safety and welfare. The Shah and his Empress fled the country in early 1979, leaving the way for Khomeini to return.

In early February Pilbrow finally called a meeting and announced that due to the circumstances existing on the ground in Iran, he was proposing to close the branch immediately. I told him that he didn't need a meeting, just do it, and now. He made the call.

The property and contents were abandoned and the driver managed to get them to the airport through streets packed with people. Our instructions were to get the first plane out, to anywhere. As a last gesture our car was signed over to the driver who deserved nothing less.

I can say with certainty that I would never have left it so long. There is no job in the world worth dying for and it was wrong for us to have taken that risk. And I can say with hand on bible, no payment was ever made. Nothing whatsoever arrived in the UK and the finance reports from the Iran office show the same. I admit that some actual cash may have been paid and used for everyday expenses but I doubt it. Was a lesson learned here? I don't think it was as history repeated itself a few years later.

Later that day John told me that when the Iran business first came up, PolyGram forbade TPC to proceed in any shape or form. Poldervaart was adamant that there were no resources available for such a risky adventure in a very unstable part of the world politically and they would not support it. In fact the top brass in Holland sent Pilbrow a cable emphasizing their position but he choose to ignore all their warnings and set up shop there.

I have never understood the big deal about having a company car. The personal taxation charge takes away a large part of the benefit, especially if you do not use it much for business. But for many, it's a badge of honour, a sign that you've reached the top of the greasy pole and you've arrived. I always preferred extra salary, then choose and run my own vehicle.

At TP we had just three vehicles: Pilbrow's new wagon, John's Peugeot 405 and Corbett's Citroen SM (a DS with a Maserati V6 engine). Corbett asked me to join him in reception. What foolishness was this? Being over six feet tall, he towered over me and switched on the charm.

'Three years ago my car cost eight grand that with inflation would be ten grand today.'

'So?'

'So, that's the exact price of my new car parked outside. Could you deal with the man and sort out the finance.'

'What new car?'

'The Cadillac.'

'Are you having a laugh? There is no money for new cars, and even if there was there has been no directors' meeting to approve the funding. My new car is over the road and paid for by me. Why not try that?'

The charm was gone in a heartbeat and he loomed over me.

'I'm telling you to see the man and sort it out.'

'NO. There is no money for cars at this stage of the game. Tomorrow's weekly wages will be paid out of my pocket, that's how tough it is right now. You got the bloke here, you get rid of him.'

I don't know if Corbett took his complaint up to Pilbrow but I heard nothing more.

Light Limited had moved into manufacturing lamps. The basement at 10 Long Acre was cleared out and a workshop set up under a very pleasant young man called James Wadsworth. I don't know if it was even legal but I think if the health and safety guys turned up they would have been very unimpressed. Another string to our bow.

One of my objectives was to have no empty rooms and apart from the top floor of number 10, that had been achieved. Technical Projects, part of TPS, which produced mixing boards under Sam Wise was so cramped for space it moved to Marshalsea, South London.

But the lack of capital hog-tied us from taking advantage of opportunities for sales and hires in TPS and the new profitability couldn't generate funds fast enough. There was no real prospect of raising loans or overdrafts as Lloyds Bank still wanted us gone and the 1977/78 results were regarded as either a flash in the pan or overoptimistic. It wasn't just John and I struggling; people were frustrated and tired at having to deal with worn out equipment that was well overdue for updating.

Although Rank Strand still held 25% of TPS, the monthly meetings had died out with only Phil Rose continuing to show an interest. So over lunch with John one day, I floated the idea that if Rank Strand bought our 75% and took the whole thing over, they had the financial clout to take the business forward, run it as it should be run and realize its full potential.

John was unimpressed but agreed that treading water was not the future and would achieve nothing. He suggested I run it past George Templeton on my own and gauge his reactions. I hoofed off to Syon Park, expecting a rough ride and that's exactly what I got.

With George there is no chitchat to warm up, it has to be straight down to business, so I jumped in.

'Obviously you know that TPS is struggling through lack of capital. Although we have slowly improved, without funding we are never going to be able to take the business up to it's full potential.

John and I have talked it through and I am here to run an idea past you to see how it bounces. The proposition is that you buy out our 75% which means you own 100% of the business because you have the resources to make it work.'

Seeing George's body language, I could see he was unimpressed and he'd lost all patience with TPS and its management long ago.

'What are you asking for your majority stake in this pile of crap?'

I whispered so quietly that I could barely hear myself: 'Seventy five thousand'.

'You must be bloody joking. I wouldn't give you seventy five pence! It's worthless, nothing you hear, nothing. You couldn't give it away.'

All in his gruff Scottish accent; I was deflated. That was it, back to the drawing board. I reported back to John who was expecting such an outcome. Back at base, I festered. Then it came to me. If our majority interest was worth nothing, then what was the value of their minority interest?

When John and I had visited Rank Strand in the past, we'd often had a drink with them at their local tavern and I'd got on well with one of the accounts guys. He was a real boozer often buying himself an extra pint between rounds from his favourite spot at the end of the bar. After one Homeric evening he let it slip that they had written down their share in TPS to only eight grand. Great insider information.

I phoned George and I could tell he wasn't pleased.

'Sorry to bother you but I had a thought. If TPS is worthless why don't we buy your holding, you'll be rid of us and with 100% we can get some loan financing.'

'Look laddie, I didn't exactly mean that the shares are worth nothing.'

'Hear me out. You have them on the books at £8,000 so if I could find £11,000, you would show a profit on the transaction. What about it?'

'I'll be able to do that. Send the paperwork over.'

What a coup! What a big multi-coloured feather in my cap. £11,000 was a steal.

John was as amazed as I was but felt it all went back to when Paul had set us up with an on the nose set of accounts just before he left our employ. George had pretty much given up on TPS there and then and we had done nothing since to improve his frame of mind. Coming to visit Long Acre to be exposed to bad news month after month must have been demoralising, and he and Phil were never even treated to lunch for their trouble.

But although the transaction had no effect on actual cash flows, it meant that whatever profits TPS managed to make, the Group would enjoy 100% of them in the consolidated accounts and not have to hive off 25% to minority interests. It was a win-win situation, without question.

Richard was unimpressed. He liked to have respectable names attached to TP and I don't think he understood the ramifications. Once again I guess he thought that I was giving away our heritage. It wasn't until 1981 that I was able to clear out the other fag ends of external shareholders, so that TP Ltd shareholders actually owned 100% of everything.

The group's banking had now moved to Standard Chartered Bank. Regular changes in accounts staff had been made but it was settling down and a sense of purpose was more evident among the troops.

My second year, 1978/79 was disappointing; turnover was up but the bottom line was down. Wage levels had been held since I had taken charge but inflation hadn't, so that costs had increased across the board.

Our audited results, signed by the directors and auditors and filed at Companies House, and expressed in thousands were:

Sales	1,923.9
Profit	107.6

The simplified balance sheet at 30.09.79 was:

Share capital	21.0
Reserves	155.8
Minorities	13.4
	190.2

Assets	221.4
Current assets	883.1
Current liabilities	(914.3)
	190.2

The TPS share deal is reflected by the reduction in minority interest from £43.3k to £13.4k.

There was no shortage of unusual tasks coming into my department.

The film director Tony Palmer had plans for a ten episode TV production of the life of Wagner and had discussed these with PolyGram. They had agreed to put up fifty thousand pounds in seed money for outline scriptwriting, location research and preparation of a final total budget. I was informed that TP was to handle the funds; there must have been a political justification but I was never privy to it. My guess was that if Tony needed additional money he knew it would be a waste of time asking TP for more, whereas if he was dealing directly with PolyGram the possibilities of extra costs being picked up were more realistic.

We were not to be paid a fee for our trouble and I had the pleasure of dealing with Mr Palmer on a regular basis. As predicted, the money ran out, I was asked for more that I didn't have nor could I get. It was a very unpleasant business, especially since we were working for free. The production was completed with Richard Burton in the lead role.

The strangest business of all was the matter of the Milton Keynes town clock. Corbett turned up one day with a signed contract for TP to build a town clock for Milton Keynes for £75,000. It is fair to say that nobody in the whole organisation had the faintest idea about clock manufacture but that wasn't my problem. I think Tony found a man through Yellow Pages who lived in Clapham and he in turn was contracted to take on the task.

Some months into the job, Tony's head appeared in my room while the rest of him remained on the staircase.

'Milton Keynes is sending you a Writ for seventy-five thousand, so you had better sort it out.'

With that he was gone, having abdicated all responsibility. I could have chased him and told him to shove it. But obviously this had been discussed over the famous kitchen table where the dynamic duo had decided on this course of action. The next Saturday morning I picked Charlie up and we went to see Steven, the sub-contractor.

'Honestly, I'm doing my best,' he assured us, 'but the problem's a lack of transport as I don't drive. That means going to Victoria Coach Station every day and getting the long distance coach to Milton Keynes and vice versa at the end of the day. And I can't carry anything but the smallest tools and parts. So I've got a daily commute of six hours and all the smallest alterations have to be done in my south London workshop. Which is why the job's behind schedule.'

What was needed was a driver and Charlie put forward his friend David who happened to be unemployed and owned a car. We went to see him at his place in Streatham. It would be a long boring day for whoever took it on, so I offered a straight cash deal of £200 a week plus expenses which David happily accepted. He turned out to be a diamond, picking Steve up at the crack of dawn and not only chauffeuring him but also helping with the work as much as he could. Also at my suggestion he found a local mechanic and rented a short-term spot where Steve could work.

All this put the costs above budget but in the circumstances that just didn't matter. The clock had to be finished. Steve and David got the contract completed, signed off and paid for in six weeks. Did we get any appreciation for our efforts? Of course not! Corbett never mentioned it, not a word.

He had ordered the mother of all sample cases built to carry a couple of our new lamps, and set off to Houston on the trail of a sale. The first morning at the hotel he awoke to find that sometime in the night the room had been robbed and he had been cleaned out. It was a professional job and they'd taken everything: money, passport, suitcase, clothing and the beautiful sample case and samples. He called John, who called me, but there was nothing to be done until the bank opened. And he still complained at the central service charge.

He did invite me to his cottage for a weekend, which was strange in itself. I arrived late afternoon to meet his wife Anne, daughter Sara and two couples who had also been invited. We ate dinner, had drinks and chatted, as you do, but frankly I had no idea why I was there. Tony and I rarely socialized and we had bugger all in common. Around nine Sara went off to bed and around ten-thirty I followed suit.

In the morning I came down around eight-thirty, made breakfast for one and then Sara appeared. We cleared up last night's detritus, washed up and then waited. By eleven I gave up and drove back to London. Nice to be asked, but I'll never know why.

John and I had regular meetings with Poldervaart in PolyGram's swish offices off Oxford Street and a couple of times in Amsterdam. He may have seen us in Convent Garden but I have no recollection of a meeting there. I had great respect because PolyGram was a massive international corporation dealing in hundreds of millions whereas TP was a dollar and dime operation even then. With this difference in scale his advice was sometimes off the mark but it didn't matter as John and I had a clear vision of where we were going and how we were going to get there. He never gave any indication that PolyGram was struggling and after a period of aggressive trading, the end of disco music in 1979 had left them with overproduction at a time of falling demand. In 1980 group losses were over £200 million and in 1983 the workforce was cut almost in half from 13,000 to 7,000. Despite all that, Woulter kept the image of a big finance man and we played the game, whatever it was.

John asked me if I could dispose of a small suite of offices above a shop that was surplus to requirements. 3 Chertsey Chambers consisted of three rooms, a toilet and store cupboard with a lease that still had some five years to run. I had a look and it seemed ideal for Max who was working out of a seventh floor walk-up at Ludgate Circus. He came over to take a look.

As it was too big solely for him, I suggested that we share the space and that I could use the back room as a quiet refuge when necessary. John suggested that for a rent share he would have access for private meetings or interviews. So we asked our lawyers to draw up a sublease with an annual rental of three hundred below cost. Max moved in and I furnished my space with a dining table, chairs and some shelving.

Our solicitors Kingsley Napley were also in Long Acre and we usually dealt with Laurence Sherman who went on to become the banking ombudsman. They were a top-notch firm and over the years did some great work for us.

It was in March 1980 when a regular customer of the shop asked to meet John Ball. Geoff Courchaine and his wife ran Courage Light out of Haarlem; John and I took them for a modest lunch at the Kings Arms. They operated a very small light hire business and wanted to have a working relationship with TPS, so a few weeks later John and I travelled to Holland to take a look at their operation. It was a terrible trip for me as the hotel had the central heating going full blast with those old-fashioned massive radiators and the windows were screwed shut. I woke up in the morning feeling like death and everyone thought I had a hangover.

We reported back to Pilbrow and it was agreed that this could be our gateway into Europe in the fullness of time. No loan or capital would be involved, just a modest line of credit and co-operation on any work too large for them to handle. At this stage it was really small potatoes but in November 1981 Theatre Projects BV was created and the whole thing mushroomed into a huge problem and an equally huge loss for the group.

Light Limited just kept on giving. A secretary/PA had recently resigned and left. Subsequently I received a letter that was addressed to me, marked private and confidential. It was from her father, a brigadier no less, who claimed that during her employ she had been sexually assaulted. He gave no details of by whom, where or when, or even what he expected me to do about it. I took a copy over to Tony Corbett and after glancing through the missive, simply said: 'tell him Brown's Hotel'. And that was that.

So I did. I wrote a very polite letter, telling him what I had been advised to say in reply. The matter ended there. Maybe I was better off knowing nothing.

An order floated across my desk from Eddie Kulukundis. To my shame, I had not heard of him at the time. When I called John, I heard him actually stand up at the mention of the name.

'Eddie is solid gold and we must make sure he gets the best. Actually, send the order over to me and I'll deal with it personally. He is totally bankable. He's also married to Susan Hampshire.'

What a wonderful way to be spoken of and something to aim for, to have your name revered in such tones. My third year, 1979/80, I think proved that Theatre Projects could be run successfully financially without the hand to mouth conditions of the past. For the first time ever, we had instigated a monthly cheque payment scheme for creditors rather than paying a bill when the creditor screamed.

Our audited results, signed by the directors and auditors and filed at Companies House, and expressed in thousands were:

Sales	2,349.6
Profit	126.9

The simplified balance sheet at 30.09.80 was:

Share capital	21.0
Reserves	273.0
Loan capital	317.0
Minority interest	19.3
	630.3
Assets	454.6
Current assets	1,157.9
Current liabilities	(982.2)
	630.3

Christmas 1980 brought the worst incident during my time at TP. Most staff were paid by monthly cheque but a few holdouts in the stores still insisted on weekly cash. We had become very lax with security and it was routine for a couple of the girls to go over to the bank each Friday and collect the relatively small amount of cash. Before the holiday period we had a double week to draw and as the staff exited the bank they were robbed by a couple of guys on a motorcycle. Thank God they were not hurt but it must have been a terrible experience for them both. At the end of the day it was my fault for letting things slide. Around three thousand was lost. I have no doubt that it was an inside job but there's a big difference between knowing and proving. There can be nothing more disgusting than putting your fellow workers at risk.

My department was more settled than it had ever been. Mr Gray had an assistant whose name I have been trying to forget for almost forty years. Barbara had left to run a bed and breakfast place and we had an excellent Kiwi temp in her spot. Ruth and Lesley looked after sales and receivables; Babs and Francis covered purchases and payments.

An early form of computerisation had been introduced. Made by DEC (now part of Hewlett Packard) the actual kit was reasonable but the supplier's staff were a bloody disgrace. One day late with the monthly service charge and they would refuse service bringing our operations to a halt. Many times I was reduced to a screaming match and, if I could have afforded the gesture, I would have slung the whole lot out into the street.

However, TP could move into 1981 with an optimistic outlook, or so we thought.

One morning Chief Appio from Nigeria arrived at the office and it always fell to John and I to take our African friends to lunch, usually at the Greek restaurant in St Martin's Lane. Appio had been a good friend and facilitator to our guys working out there and lunch was the least we could do.

He asked for a favour. He was due a commission from an English company but didn't have a UK bank account. He asked if he could have the monies parked into our account for a few months; it was £107,000 and he wasn't asking for interest. That presented no problem for me as we knew this man very well and were satisfied that he was kosher.

A few days later it showed up in our account. I have never regarded money as sacred but I do believe that other people's money is to be treated as such. This belief was to bring trouble to my door further down the pike. Incidentally, back then a Nigerian naira was worth more than a pound sterling (1 naira = £1.25); today £1 will buy you around 475 naira.

Brother Jeff informed me that our sister Anita was visiting the UK, mainly to visit Ireland and the sites of the Irish Catholic Martyrs; whatever floats yer boat I guess. The last time I had seen her was when I was eight years old and she'd emigrated to Australia. I was excited to meet her after over thirty years. I had decorated the spare room and purchased a new bed and linen in anticipation.

We collected her at Heathrow and took her back to my flat for breakfast. Then drove her to Kenley where she would stay with Jeff for a couple of days before setting out on her pilgrimage. I told her she would be very welcome to stay with me on her return.

A couple of weeks later, she phoned to say that she was at Victoria Station and couldn't continue to Jeff's house because of a rail strike. I told her to stay put and I would collect her in twenty minutes.

'Oh no, don't bother. I've booked a bed and breakfast here in Victoria for a couple of days.'

I couldn't believe it, to prefer a B & B to staying with your brother.'

'So, why have you called me?'

'I thought you would like to know.'

'Okay, I know, good luck.'

And hung up. When I next visited my brother I asked the reason why and Anita had told him that I was like a stranger. Well after half a lifetime I guess I was. That was the last contact between us and the excitement short lived.

Disappointment back at the office as well. I have always encouraged the accounts staff to actually interest themselves in what the business does, what makes it tick and know the people involved, be approachable and be aware. So many accountants build themselves an ivory tower and measure the company solely by the reports that pass across their desk and wouldn't dream of going down to the factory floor and talking to the workers.

Heading out with Charlie to do some extreme debt collection, I was stopped by funereal faces and informed that Services' monthly result was a disaster with a loss of £45,000, no less.

'You don't know how tired of this rubbish I am. Services has produced a profit of around £15,000 a month for a long time, so what catastrophic event has taken place to cause a £60,000 hole to appear?'

Shoulders shrugged.

'Check the figures.'

'Everything has been checked twice.'

'Show me.'

It took less than five seconds to spot the error; I crossed an item out and walked off to do some real work. When I returned two hours later there was no eye contact and not a word was spoken. Just before going home time I enquired. Yes, a year's depreciation instead of a month's had been charged to the accounts.

'All the wages paid out in this room and no one can divide by twelve.'

I started a speech about folk's livelihoods depending on what we produce and if Pilbrow had seen their figures, his Rottweiler would have been sent on a sacking and closure mission. But I stopped as I was wasting my breath. They weren't interested and they didn't really understand; too philosophical, I suppose.

TFA was a company similar to TPS but in rock and roll. When its parent company collapsed and the receivers moved in I suggested to John that we arrange a meeting with Brian Croft the MD. We ended up buying the assets for twenty grand which was another fine bargain by my reckoning. The equipment alone was worth double that at least and Brian continued to run the joint. But my plan to simply continue our steady progress was to be thrown out of the window.

I was invited to meet some visitors and made my way to Pilbrow's office to find John and Dick already there. We were introduced to Duncan Fitzwilliams and Chris Cussons of Venture Link and Sam Stevenson of Foreign and Colonial.

Now I have always respected the right of a company's owner to make decisions regarding the future as long as they are not illegal or immoral but Pilbrow was about to pull a rabbit from the hat.

'I have agreed with these gentlemen to take Theatre Projects to a private placement later this year.'

I could see the picture in Pilbrow's mind. He was alone on a large stage, the spotlights were on him and him alone. Waiting in the wings were the magi, the three wise men from the east and they were bearing homage to him and him alone. All achievements bore his name while we were the village people: Peter the store clerk, salesman John, draughtsman Dick and Sparky Tony. It was a fait accompli.

The £800,000 of new money would enable TP to clear the debt to PolyGram and expand TP in all directions. I should have been happy but I wasn't. I couldn't shake the feeling that this was all too early, after all we had only three years of decent profits under our belt. And that was after two decades of stagnation. For a decision of this magnitude to have been taken without a single word with his key directors confirmed that our opinions weren't worth Jack Shit. The only opinion Pilbrow valued was his own.

There was no doubt that at last we would have a solid working capital base and being backed by the City was no bad thing. But I was watching Pilbrow closely and I could see from the look on his face that these new monies would not be used for boring things like consolidation of current activities and strengthening middle management. This would be his money, allowing him to indulge in flights of fancy that would quickly leave us as thinly spread financially as before, only worse. But my disquiet was to some extent mitigated by the fact that we would have professional directors on the board and investors to whom we would be answerable.

A lot of the new money would be coming from the pension funds of ordinary working people and I admit that it weighed on my mind as it was a big responsibility. Pilbrow's egocentricity was off the scale.

The bankers knew that they were powerful men. Their control of such massive wealth meant that everyone they met showed great deference, after all their decisions could mean life or death to a business. Theatre Projects must have been a million miles from their usual remit of manufacturing, retail and IT but with Pilbrow namedropping for all his worth, I think they could envisage an interesting investment.

Their plan was of course to take equity, draw dividends and nurse the Group to a point where it could justify an IPO and a fine capital gain all round. That was the plan. Richard was in his element and was bursting out all over, with tales of genius all flowing from that infamous sixty quid in a back room of a theatre. John, Dick and I just made up the numbers. I could think of a thousand places that I would rather be but here I was nothing more than a spear carrier.

Towards the end of the meeting, one banker enquired as to net profit expectations for 1980/81, looking at me for an answer. I had projected around £165k after interest that would be a 30% increase on the previous year. It was ambitious but without any craziness it could be done. Before I could open my mouth a shout of two hundred thousand went up. It was, of course, Pilbrow. A figure plucked out of nowhere without any basis in reality and now we were hoisted with £200k to find. If we fell short in the final accounting, confidence levels with our new investors would take an early hit and could scupper the whole deal.

Now began my nightmare but there were two aspects to pulling it off. Firstly all potential punters would get the ten cent tour of the better parts of our business, skirting past the stores in the dark and dingy basements under Mercer Street; then meet and greet the team leaders, followed by the high spot, a mega lunch at Inigo Jones.

Secondly Due Diligence and that was my slice of the cake: the exhaustive examination into the financial history of the whole business to wit a super audit. Mr Gray informed me that his current workload precluded his involvement in this extra burden. So it would fall to me to rise to the challenge.

I was informed that Chris Cussons would be my liaison man and my point of contact to Venture Link. He explained that they would need photocopies of all accounting 'stuff' going back six years, all contracts for ten years plus leases and any sub-leases. For the period under my control, that would be straightforward but the earlier years really could be anywhere. All this in addition to my day job.

Searching through the dark corners of the many buildings, I started to find the old accounting records and the copying could begin. Ruth was a great help often coming in at weekends, pitching in with hours at the copier, then collating, and bundling up the paperwork. Our lawyers were a terrific bunch, dragging the property files out of the archives although naturally charging for their time and effort.

Contracts were another matter. TPC filing was in good shape but you couldn't just pull out a pile of papers, copy them, and dump them back. You had to respect their sense of order, proceed piecemeal and it all took time. Then there were the theatre and film activities which meant dealing with the Rottweiler whose blind loyalty to Pilbrow made her a difficult person to work with. You could be sure that everything you said or did would be reported back. John and I found everything we could on TPS but when it came to Light I just didn't bother.

Corbett would have been uncooperative to put it mildly. I couldn't be troubled with it, so I just left out their contracts and waited for the shout from Venture Link but it never came.

I was already putting in a long day but over this period I was working a seven day week, often twelve hours a day. The abnormal became the normal. Waking many mornings before five and with a head on fire with all the things needing attention, it became routine to arrive at work before six, before even the breakfast cafés were open.

One morning a traffic cop pulled me over in Regent Street.

'In a hurry to get home after a night out?'

'No, I'm going to work.'

'Before six in the morning? What do you do then?'

'I'm an accountant.'

'Well, you must love your work. Just take it a bit slower getting there.'

Did I love my work? Maybe not any more. I couldn't shake the notion that we were a ship of fools sailing towards oblivion.

To prepare for the new investment it was necessary to repay the PolyGram monies and to do so put great strain on our everyday cash flows. That lead to giving up the monthly cheque run, resorting to ducking and diving with the creditors, thus losing a lot of the goodwill we had worked so hard to build up.

It is fair to say I had never really got on with our insurance guy Richard Walton who was a long-term good friend of Pilbrow's. I found his attitude patronizing and I am sure that in his mind, I was yet another bean counter parachuted in and destined to go the way of the many others. He would come in once a year to run through our various policies which at that time totalled around £75k pa, no small sum. He could have simply mailed them in to me but he liked the personal touch, so it seemed. We were battling to find the monthly salary bill when I got a message he was coming in to pick up £3,500 outstanding. As had become common practice, I left my personal cheque with reception for him that apparently caused enormous offence and it was rejected. That surprised me as where I come from money is money. Still there it was, he was furious which wasn't my intention.

More important by far was the question of where the extra profit we needed of £35,000 was coming from, for if we failed we would all look like a bunch of chumps. I met with every director and asked each one to ensure that all their invoicing was bang up to date. But in the end I had to ask John to sell a rig that had been hired to a long running show. He was not a happy man and nor was I as this short-term profit in effect robbed the future of continuing hires.

As we approached the year end I phoned Brian Croft and asked him for an estimated result for TFA and he thought that there would be a profit of around eight grand. A few days later I asked one of my troops to check and they came back with eight grand all right, but as a loss. I had to ask John again and he really was as mad as a cut snake.

At the final accounting we had scraped the bottom of every barrel to publish a net profit of £198,000, two grand short but £33,000 more than we had budgeted for. Pilbrow was unimpressed and screamed that we wanted two hundred thousand as promised but by that stage I didn't give a monkey's toss how he felt.

The lunches had become a regular feature and Inigo Jones must have enjoyed a purple patch. We in the supporting cast weren't expected to contribute anything to the conversation but required to look animated and fascinated by what the big cheeses had to say. I was so dog tired that I stuck to water as I was afraid that if I got into the vino I might well give my very personal views of what was taking place an airing.

In both August and September I had sent Pilbrow a memorandum setting out the real problems that the private placing had brought, that it was time to consolidate and not get into any expansion planning. Time to batten down the hatches, bring all the various activities under full management control with budgets and safeguards built in instead of flying everything by the seat of our pants.

But the signs were ominous. Pilbrow flew to New York, by Concorde no less. I wondered how many years of salary sacrifice to his pension fund the average gas or water worker would have to make to pay for that.

On his return he sent me two instructions. Firstly he had met Patricia MacKay who owned the magazine Theatre Crafts and he had agreed to give her $12k. Please would I send this off tout suite.

Secondly he had appointed Wally Russell to head up our USA consultancy and open two offices. He would need money sent out to finance all this and I was not to harass him for expenses returns.

So much for consolidation. As far as I knew no one had been consulted on any of these decisions and there was no paperwork whatsoever: no feasibility studies, projections, budgets, cash flows, nothing. I walked over to his office and told him that I was not sending money anywhere on the strength of a couple of bits of paper.

'I am not your personal accountant. I am accountant to Theatre Projects and its shareholders and much of the new money is coming from folk's pension funds, ordinary working people. We owe the highest fiduciary duty to care for their investment. I need paperwork and board approval.'

His face distorted with hatred. I walked away. I never sent anything to Theatre Crafts. What was it anyway? An investment, a loan, a gift? After I was sacked, the cash was sent and lost.

The board approved the USA move without a scrap of arithmetic produced. That horrified me and opened the gate for Buffoon Wally to be on the phone demanding dollars on a very regular basis. From my experience it would take maybe two or three years before they could exist without head office funding and by my calculations that would amount to at least a quarter of a million quid. In fact by October 1983, £300k had been sent out.

Calling people I knew at Strand where Wally had worked previously, I got the impression that he was ineffectual at best, useless at worst. But he was Pilbrow's close friend. What was happening brought back John's words of wisdom just after I started with TP.

'Watch what happens when we get any money available. He'll be impossible to control, wait and see.'

I had waited and now I had seen.

October found me at the end of my rope both physically and mentally. I took myself off to Dr Toszeghi who arranged a vitamin injection once a week for six weeks.

It wasn't just the long slog to get to where we were but the foreboding that I would not be able to steer the ship anymore and nor would anyone else. I had relied on the City men to be strong on corporate governance but Richard's foray into the USA and the cash splash had hardly raised an eyebrow. If they thought he had the Midas touch they only had to look at the first twenty years of TP where it struggled from crisis to crisis. Somehow they had been blindsided by all the hype and razzmatazz and were missing the obvious warning signs.

In the early days of the placement discussions, Pilbrow had mentioned that his goal was to have a personal team of six including a young man by his side to write down his every word. I hadn't paid much attention assuming it was just hyperbole but now I wasn't so sure.

Outside of the interminable lunches, I had very little contact with Duncan, Sam or Chris. I did see the latter moving around the place but I can't recall exchanging a word apart from the initial meetings. Maybe I should have been more sociable.

Year four 1980/81 and the audited results, signed by the directors and auditors and filed at Companies house and expressed in thousands were:

Sales	2,491.4
Profit	198.0

The simplified balance sheet at 30.09.81

Share Capital	21.0
Reserves	458.6
Loan Capital	317.1
Minority Interest	0.0
	796.7
Assets	815.8
Current Assets	1,448.4
Current Liabilities	(1,467.5)
	796.7

The Chairman's Report centred on the Private Placement which was to be finalised in November and on all the various participants to the transaction. I was mentioned in dispatches for my efforts which was a small degree of satisfaction. However when the revised version arrived from the printers my name and contribution had disappeared. I asked Mr Gray who dealt with the printers but he avoided eye contact and mumbled something about space limitations. I smelt a big fat rat but as I never bothered about words of praise just let it go, having no way of knowing that this was the prelude of things to come.

The last meal before the completion was another bash at Inigo Jones and the usual suspects assembled in Pilbrow's office. Suddenly he was standing in front of me.

'I hope you don't mind, I've asked Ian Gray to join us.'

'I do bloody mind!'

He walked away and as I headed for the door, Cussons and Gray entered; I left the building and drove home. Later I called John and asked him to tell Pilbrow that unless he phones me with an apology for interfering in my staff decisions I was gone for good.

Pilbrow did call but his apology was half arsed at best. I should have told him to stuff it but I had come so far I wanted to see it through. So business as usual or maybe not. Richard, John and I had seven year contracts pressed upon us and they were signed. Later there was some misunderstanding but be assured they were completed and legally binding documents.

The very worst day was yet to come. Called to our leader's office, Duncan and Sam were at the table with an unknown couple, discussing their investment into the future of TP. I understood that it was Pilbrow's sister and her husband who had inherited £100k and were about to tip it in. My whole being wanted to shout, 'don't do it, run away'. But that wasn't my role and would have had a large negative impact on the whole deal.

Duncan came over to where John and I were talking.

'I don't know why you two don't get a part of this?'

John quick as a flash spoke for both of us.

'We're just a couple of hired hands.'

End of conversation

Although we met every single day, John and I really didn't

discuss the placement but our thoughts were the same. It could be a wonderful opportunity to take TP to a whole new level and make it a real force within our industry but the operative word was could, not would. The ego massaging knew no bounds and the more our new friends told Pilbrow how wonderful he was the more he believed he was bulletproof and this in turn encouraged him to follow his ideas without consultation.

As I observed before the City types pretty much regarded the rest of us as worker ants, disposable at will if the need arose and this in its turn, encouraged Pilbrow not to even pretend to value our contribution.

November saw the handover of the moolah in the City. I attended and was ignored as the custom had become. The cheques were presented to Pilbrow who handed them over to me and like a good little serf, I scuttled off to the bank.

A week later I was in a taxi coming back with Pilbrow from a meeting with Poldervaart and he told me that he wanted me to make friends with Richard Walton. I explained that to me he was just a supplier and I couldn't help it if he got angry because I offered him my personal cheque to clear his account because TP was pot-less. I could sense that now money was raining down, my shelf life was coming to an end.

'Look Richard, if you want me to go, simply sit down with me for ten minutes and we can sort it out. I've put up with enough crap here to last a lifetime.'

When I next met John, I related the story.

'You expect too much. Simple isn't in his vocabulary. If he wants rid of you he will make a Greek tragedy out of it, mark my words.'

A couple of days later, John appeared in my office with a pile of paperwork. Walton had decided that I was persona non grata and for the annual insurance renewals he would have a meeting with John. Everything had been due on 1 October and now we were at the end of November, so it was all a bugger's muddle.

Just before the year end I was hit with influenza. Happy days, I had three top tasks needing attention. Max had introduced me to two guys running a business in the heart of the West End theatre area who wanted to retire and I was close to finishing off a proposal to bring to the TP board. As always, this was being prepared off base for all the obvious reasons.

The Holland connection was a good thing and needed encouragement and monitoring, which had been agreed by everyone concerned. Europe was a huge market and Courage was seen as the ideal way in. My concern was that we needed a presence on the ground. I had found an answer in a Danish woman employed as a part-time accountant by Max who spoke fluent Dutch and was prepared to make a regular visit to check how everything was running.

Over the past few months I had experienced some concerns as to a senior staffer's commitment. When I felt strong enough I would have to make some tough decisions. Given the drastic changes that had impacted our finances, I would need a level of backup which I felt was sorely missing. However, before I could even make a start a bombshell landed in my lap.

On Tuesday 5 January 1982, I arrived in my office a little before 8am to find an envelope sitting on my desk that I guessed must have been dropped off the previous evening. It contained irrefutable evidence of financial malfeasance by a director. At 10am I walked over to talk with John about what action we should take and in his view, it should all be taken directly to Pilbrow.

There is correspondence on file dated 16 August 1979 from David S Simpkins of Kingsley Napley regarding a similar incident with the same person. That was followed by a meeting at the lawyers' offices on 21 August at which I was present. The 'impossibility of locating certain monies and accounting for payments and other unauthorised expenses' were discussed. This directly resulted in the said director resigning. On learning of this outcome Pilbrow refused to accept his resignation and the status quo was restored. Emboldened with this free pass, working relationships were hard to maintain.

At 10.30 we arrived at Pilbrow's office and put the documentary evidence before him. Stuffing the paperwork into an inside pocket he forbade me to discuss the matter with anyone. I protested that this was serious stuff and it couldn't be swept under the carpet, especially as this was not the first time the director had been caught stealing. I also pointed out the irony that John and I had been running around like blue arsed flies scratching up profits to achieve target when the thousands that had been purloined would have filled any shortfall very nicely. He was immovable and I realised that it was the messengers that had brought the bad news that were to get the sharp end of the stick, not the thief. So we had to continue working with this guy, knowing he had his hand in the till.

On Monday 11 January at 10.30am, Pilbrow arrived in my office bearing a gift, namely a copy of his latest book on stage lighting. Inside on the flyleaf he'd written: To Peter, with love, affection and admiration.

All very nice. He then spent a few minutes talking about my health, having heard that I had been ill over the holiday.

'You really must take care of yourself, you're essential to the future of Theatre Projects,' were his parting words.

Praise is rare, mendacity less so.

At 4pm on Friday 15 January I was sacked. Not in person of course. I returned to my office from a client meeting only to find a letter of dismissal awaiting me. I immediately went over to Pilbrow's office to have it out with him, only to find he had run away and left for the country.

The missive contained many fingerprints and merely two pages of utter trivia. There was not a word regarding the sterling work to get the placement done and dusted or turning a basket case into a force within our industry. However, my lack of respect towards some of his special friends was noted. Obviously you could steal from TP with impunity but not display disrespect to the brotherhood of the luvvies. The following Monday I returned his book. I'm sure he could find another Peter to have love and affection for and admire.

Did Pilbrow ever discuss this situation with the Board? Were they not surprised that having insisted on a seven year contract, one was to be torn up a few weeks later? Maybe not. For them, one accountant is much the same as another. They do the same training, sit the same exams and simply report on what the movers and shakers have achieved, the creatives, the clever people, people like them. Did they ever know that the last nail in my coffin was my point blank refusal to send monies to Wally Russell and a woman at a party without proper paperwork to protect their investment?

Only a few weeks earlier I told him we could sort anything out between us in under ten minutes flat. But no, he needs Barnum's

Circus, the whole bloody drama involving staff and outsiders. The he sends his handmaiden creeping about with letters whilst he scarpers off to Oxfordshire double quick. Ain't that all something to be proud of? Now, I really was totally convinced that it would all end in tears and lots of them.

I also handed him a letter that repeated yet again the need for consolidation and improvement of middle management. It spoke of my disapproval of him involving my staff and others in his dirty deeds when I had told him that if there was a problem we could sort it out in ten minutes. I also strongly recommended that TP recruit a strong mature accountant to take my place who I would gladly help recruit and that he should rely more on John Ball for commercial guidance rather than trusting the bunch of sycophants with which he had surrounded himself.

I doubt if he even read it.

The board had authorised him to offer me five grand to shove off peacefully and I reminded him of my seven year contract. But I was on the horns of a dilemma: Pilbrow was the enemy not Theatre Projects and I would not do anything to harm what I had given so much to build.

I took fifteen grand to go which, coupled with 9 months back pay, gave me thirty thousand plus. I appointed a lawyer who did nothing, charged like a raging bull and wanted cash to settle his account.

Nothing happened and after a few days I caught Pilbrow in reception.

'What the hell is going on with my replacement? Time's passing.'

As soon as he started to speak I knew a lie was on the way as I'd been on the receiving end of so many.

'Don't worry. You'll be included in every aspect of the recruitment process.'

Looking back I was so naïve; the recruitment process had started months ago and my replacement was already here. It took me two days to put it all together: my name dropped from the Chairman's report, the attachment of Mr Cussons to my assistant, the inclusion in my letter of termination of information that could only have come from my department. I must have been totally cream-crackered and never realised that I was keeping the seat warm for someone else. I asked Gray to join me for a drink.

As we stepped out onto Long Acre I said, 'So, you have the job.'

It was more a statement rather than a question.

Awash with embarrassment he nodded and I left it at that. We adjourned to the pub where I ordered a couple of drinks.

'Do you think you can handle it?'

He nodded again.

'Well, my prediction is that you will be gone in under two years and the whole bloody thing will be finished in under five, mark my words.'

Nevertheless, I wished him good luck and we drank in silence.

Shortly before my departure I was in Pilbrow's room where the City boys were at the table and in front of a dozen witnesses, Duncan Fitzwilliams asked me to telephone him when this was all over.

'We will have a use for your expertise.'

I did call him, seven times, but was never put through. I whinged to John who called me back.

'Call him now, he'll take the call.'

I did and got put through.

'Yes Peter, what can I do for you?'

'You asked me to call you after I left as you said that you might have work for me.'

'I have no recollection of that whatsoever, you must be mistaken.'

And hung up on me.

I am a massive believer in karma and that belief would soon prove to be justified. Pilbrow issued a memorandum to all staff to inform them that my leaving was 'by mutual agreement to enable Peter to pursue his other interests'.

What other interests I ask? Did he really think that the troops were all deaf, dumb, blind and stupid. They all knew what was happening in the business and telling downright lies only added to their lack of credibility in management.

On 18 January I was so concerned with the developing pattern of taking financial decisions without any planning or discussion that I wrote to Pilbrow yet again, telling him that the investment from the City meant we had to be more disciplined not less.

'Again, for the record, I am watching Theatre Projects repeating the mistakes of the past. I feel that all your efforts should be put to getting what you have under control and into profit. Do not rush on into new ventures before you even have the management to control what you have now. There is a real need at this time to consolidate.'

This wouldn't work for Pilbrow. He wanted new toys to play with, shiny new gizmos to throw money at and new friends to impress. Consolidation? He would die of ennui.

I was convinced that my predictions would be realised, not because I had been thrown out but because in my opinion, Pilbrow did not have the ability to manage a business the size that TP was rapidly growing to be. The only person with any real experience of a corporation was John Ball and I could see him being sidelined in the very near future. Something would go wrong, it would be shovelled into his lap and he would be made a scapegoat. Neither he nor I fitted into Pilbrow's oleiferous fan club, nor wanted to.

I have said this a million times: if Pilbrow had looked after the creative side and been the face of TP but given John and I the authority to manage commercial and financial matters, the outcome would have been a very different. But no, he liked to micro-manage and play games with people's lives and see where that all ended up.

He has claimed that the finances were built on shifting sands. They were not. Everyone was well aware that cleaning up the balance sheet to facilitate the private placement put an enormous strain on everyday cash flows. We were working hard to get back trade confidence. Bearing in mind that the PP on its own cost some £75k to achieve and $20,000 was disappearing off to the USA at very regular intervals, I think we were making a fine fist of it. I took many notes of how we were on the day I departed and for the record, our exposure to Holland was £14k and in Nigeria less than £8k. Both of these two areas of activity seemed to have got completely out of anyone's control in a very short space of time.

In May 1982, Pilbrow made an interesting statement: 'It is my intention that we should move away from consultancy ... I hope that by1983/4 TP will be a very large business indeed'.

Friday 29 January was my last day and it was interesting that Pilbrow stayed at home, maybe wanting to avoid an emotional farewell. I took John, Anne and my staff out for a Chinese meal, handed in my keys and that was that.

Although I wasn't there for the full year, I have always regarded 1981/82 as my fifth and final year. When I walked away everything was in place for a £300k annual profit, even allowing for a dead loss in USA. It would have taken a deliberate act of sabotage to have missed that target.

The year's audited results signed off on 22 November 1982 by the directors and auditors, filed at Companies House and expressed in thousands were:

Sales	3,782.6
Profit	309.8 (before tax)

The simplified balance sheet at 30.09.1982 was:

Shares	41.0
Reserves	1,290.9
Loan capital	366.3
	1,698.2
Assets	1,778.0
Current assets	1,814.5
Current liabilities	(1,894.3)
	1,698.2

Amongst all the hubris of the Chairman's Report is a gem of a paragraph.

'The year has seen a major reorganization of the accounts department under your new financial director and a consequent improvement of controls. A substantial increase in turnover has been met with faster and more accurate reporting, which of course greatly aids planning.'

Sad to see that the CFO is now relegated to just number crunching in Pilbrow's view. Ian Gray took over my role on 1 February but not as a director; that came on 2 August 1982 after a six-month trial period.

Although I continued to work in TP territory, I rarely saw anybody apart from the shop and store guys, so I had little knowledge of how TP were tracking. Certainly it appears in good health at 30 September 1982 when on top of the solid figures produced, an agreement had been reached for the City to deliver another tranche of £800k investment in January 1983.

The high point of this whole adventure must have been the shindig thrown by the Big Cheeses of TP for their benefactors in a private room at the Garrick Club. (I hope there were no ladies present as I don't think they were allowed in at that time. Have things changed?)

A Mr Porter referred to 'an impressive record over 25 years' but I think he had only seen the last five. Pilbrow offered 'to give growth in earnings per share in the long term'. Really? Did he even know what that meant? John Ball reassured the gathering that 'together with my finance director Ian Gray, we keep a tight control on our operations'. Then Pilbrow spoke of 'our ambitions to make TP the premier company in its field in the world'.

I believe that this could be called an expensive dinner as it was going to cost £800k of somebody's money.

Back in the Venture Link office, Mr Cussons opined that 'we seem to be very over-subscribed on the TP issue'. Mrs Rust commented, 'Good, if they grow as well as they predict and as we believe, they will need more money in the future and our institutions will be there in support'.

Oh dear Mrs Rust, no they will not.

The arrival of the investment cash coincided with the departure of Tony Corbett. The Nigerian trading situation had become more and more difficult, so he had visited Singapore during 1982 with a view to opening an office there for Light Limited if the business prospects looked promising. In the event he decided to open up shop on his own account.

Without its leader, Light was reduced to being little more than a manufacturer of lamps. There was also the matter of some £100k stuck in Nigeria and the problem of its recovery.

In August 1983 Richard Pilbrow asked a management consultant to undertake a review of the business and she reported back at the beginning of October with mega bad news. With a great deal of angst, she gave the opinion that the financial systems and leadership were dangerously weak. However, on 27 October a board meeting was informed that the provisional profit for 1982/83 showed a profit of £280k. Pilbrow did promise faster and more accurate accounting and got a result within a month of the year end which you just couldn't improve on.

Oh what about the accuracy bit I hear you ask? The final accounts for 1982/83 for the Theatre Projects Group showed a loss of £420.8, a margin of error amounting to £700k! OMG. Pilbrow called out for help and it arrived in November in the huge shape of Wally Russell who was made CEO of everything. I don't know what he did that the management consultant hadn't already done but I heard that he was good with children and dogs.

How the £700k of losses were exactly made up and not known about when the provisional figures were offered has been hard to track down but the Holland venture looms large. Over the course of the year, good people were sent over but were presented with a very confused situation. It appears that an expected loss for the year of under £20k mushroomed to a deficit of around £292k when missing stock was factored into the equation.

An equipment hire to a show called Juke Box went belly up and turned from a good debt to bad with a loss of some £60k. Nigeria losses proved to be £156k, despite the efforts of Dick Brett and others to mitigate the situation.

The Chairman's Report expressed Mr Pilbrow's desire to 'resume the profit growth achieved from 1978 to 1982'. It wasn't going to happen as the architect of that stellar period was in the dole queue at the Unemployment Office where you had put him.

He also reassured the investors of 'improved management systems and financial controls' and under (another) new financial director 'the necessary improvements and reporting'. I think that the financial systems must have been reorganised to death.

On of the first jobs that TPC (USA) took on was for a building in Thousand Islands. It seems that no contract was actually signed and that no money had changed hands when John met the sister of a member of the Council at a wedding in New York. She was horrified when John told her that TPC were working hard but the project wasn't actually real but a political sop that was run out at election time. Somewhere between £200k to £250k had to be written off. Doesn't anyone learn from past mistakes? I don't know if the hit was in 1982/3 or 1983/4.

For the record the audited results for 1982/83, signed off on 24 May 1984 by the directors and auditors and filed at Companies House, and expressed in thousands, were:

Sales Loss	4,500.3
Loss	(420.8)

The simplified balance sheet at 30.09.1983:

Shares	1,376.0
Share Premium	185.8
Reserves	104.6
Creditor long term	391.3
	2,057.7
Assets	2,345.4
Current Assets	2,098.1
Current liabilities	(2,385.8)
	2,057.7

The year of 1984 kicked off with the resignation of Ian Gray on 13 January bringing the first of my prophecies to come to pass. Then the blackest dirty deed that could ever be imagined took place at a board meeting on 23 January when John Ball was dismissed. He was the best man that TP had by far but as I had guessed, he took the rap for the Dutch fiasco. To add insult to injury, John was escorted off the premises by Dick Brett and not even allowed to collect his personal possessions. On his way out of the door he told Dick that he would be next and John was almost right.

The following morning John drove over to the stores to give his crew the news that was received with a mixture of shock and rage.

Ten minutes after his arrival Wally turned up and with extraordinary stupidity, he ordered John to leave immediately totally failing to read the angry mood among the men.

Wally only escaped being violently attacked by some of the men by John stepping in while others opened windows and threw equipment out into the river below. John then forcibly got Wally out onto the street and watched him drive off before leaving himself.

He made a claim for compensation, bringing into play the fabled seven year contract and after a protracted battle, settled for £11,000 with legal costs mopping up most of that.

John and I met not long afterwards when he passed me a copy of a file of correspondence he had received from people in the industry. They informed him that Pilbrow was making slanderous statements regarding the reasons behind his departure from TP, together with letters from his lawyers, Kenneth Brown. I don't know if he actually took action, but it is shameful that a man who had worked so hard and done his level best in difficult circumstances over an extended period of time should be treated so disgracefully.

I also heard that Pilbrow went to see the TPS top customers and got pretty short shrift. He walked into the office of a man who I knew and held in the highest regard, opening by assuring him that John's leaving was by mutual decision and got an immediate response.

'If you think you can walk in here telling me lies you are mistaken. Now get out!'

It is not an exaggeration to say that John was loved and respected in our industry. Walking through Covent Garden with him was like walking the royal mile, always greeted by so many people. If you went into one of the many clubs in the area, drinks would be arriving faster than we could get them down. He was a hell of a guy and it was a privilege to be his friend.

Wally had taken it upon himself to prove a case against John Ball and I for our supposed misdeeds in the past, especially concerning the Holland disaster. He ignored the facts that TP been thoroughly audited, had gone through at least one tough Due Diligence and maybe even a second for the recent tranche. He employed accountants and lawyers to conduct a forensic examination of the records going back a few years.

Of course they found absolutely nothing because there was nothing to find and all at a cost of around £95k without telling the other directors. He must have wanted it to be a surprise, a coup no less and all at a time when TP was in desperate financial straits.

The next CFO to arrive was Tony Field, previously with the Arts Council. He joined as a director and it would seem that the six months trial period had been dispensed with. In turn, he brought in David Pelham to help him with the day-to-day accounting. New auditors also arrived. Unimpressed with the new recruit, Wally returned to the USA.

After a few days into the job, Tony phoned me, asked if we could meet and I invited him over. I liked him on sight and would have helped him in any way I could. He explained who he was and the work he had been appointed to do.

'I have been told that you're the only accountant who has understood how Theatre Projects works and has ever made it profitable. And I wondered if you have any advice for me.'

I was puzzled as to who would have told him that. Richard Pilbrow perhaps?

'I wouldn't presume to give you advice but on a personal level I'll say this to you, never trust him. He's the most dishonest, disloyal and despicable excuse for a human being that I have ever met.'

I couldn't bear to speak Pilbrow's name aloud. I then regaled him with my TP story and my sorry end. I told him that I hadn't followed their progress since my demise but I understood that they were struggling and I really did wish him well. He looked shell-shocked, thanked me and left.

Afterwards, I was sorry that I had been so blunt as he'd done nothing to deserve such a verbal assault. But the mention of that name caused an automatic reaction in my head that is still with me today, forty years later.

On 21 February 1984 Tony Corbett wrote to John Ball.

Dear John,

The news has only just percolated through to this part of the world and I am very sorry to hear it. Richard seems to lack any gratitude either for the help or the long dedicated service individuals have given him. It's very unfortunate and in the end I think he will be left with no one of any substance around him; he's got very few dependables left at this stage. Mainly due to the way he has personally handled things, people have slowly drifted off and done their own thing. Anyway, I am upset to hear of your misfortune and hope that you find something to go into as soon as possible, even if it is the opposition, at least it would give you the opportunity to hurl the rocks back good and hard!! I am afraid it's what he deserves the way he treats people.

We must catch up when I am next back in the UK, which is April 19th for three weeks. Let's have some lunch or even better dinner together and a good few drinks under the belt. Please let me know how to get in touch with you. You can always contact me through my London office.

Life out here is pretty busy, as you may well imagine, and we have already established ourselves as the number one lighting design company in the region. We don't get them all but certainly not many slip through our nets. We are also in the process of setting up a small design unit based in London and that all looks very promising. You probably have heard that David Hersey and myself have linked up and there is every possibility of Andre joining us, but it's not for sure yet, so I would appreciate it if you keep it under your hat.

Anyway let's have a good chat when I get back, unless of course you happen to be coming out this way at all, there is always a bed in the house, or at least most of the time!!

*****

When John and I ran the joint, problems arose with staff from time to time. Our methodology was to sit down and sort out whatever needed to be dealt with face to face. With the new management's style, those days were behind them.

A Frenchman came into the shop and placed an order with a thousand pounds cash deposit. The staffer realised that if he passed the cash to the accounts people and the customer changed his mind he would never be able to get the money back, so he hid it. Sorry to say, he forgot where, so without hesitation the very first item on the agenda was to call the police. Arrest and conviction followed, only for the cash to be then found and the conviction overturned. What a wake up and a disaster for the young man concerned. He was a really decent bloke, and honest to the core.

Soon after this I left my office one evening to find two strange blokes hanging about, who turned out to be private eyes employed by TP. Another shop guy was suspected of breaking in through the roof and nicking stuff. What a waste of time and money. The man in question had suffered terrible injuries in motorcycle accidents and his legs were held together with metal plates; he couldn't climb a ladder let alone a roof and why should he since he had a key to the front door. I featured in the report as a scruffy bloke aged about fifty leaving Chertsey Chambers. Maybe the scruffy bit is okay but they were ten years out with my age.

The worst incident I heard of was when Chief Appio returned to recover his money and was refused on the grounds that the cash was laundered. The poor man had to take it all to Court where he won, of course. If I had known what was afoot, I would have willingly gone as a witness.

As 1984 progressed it was no secret in the town that TP was in trouble. They had moved TPS down to Nine Elms in 1983 at a terrible cost and buildings were sitting empty in Covent Garden but still costing rent.

For the record, to paraphrase Emperor Hirohito: the war has developed not necessarily to Theatre Projects' advantage.

Cape Dalgleish had resigned as auditors and Thomson McLintock appointed in October 1984 and their first accounts were a shocker.

The results for 1983/84, signed off on 5th March 1986 by the directors and auditors, and filed at Companies House, expressed in thousands were:

Sales	4,987.0
Loss	(848.8)

The simplified balance sheet at 30.09.84

Shares	1,376.0
Share Premium	185.8
Reserves	(759.2)
	802.6

Fixed assets	2,677.7
Current assets	2,223.8
Current liabilities	(3,872.7)
Liabilities after 1 year	(226.2)
	<u>802.6</u>

Why it took 17 months to get these signed, I know not; maybe it was the shame of it all. I had predicted that in five years, TP would be gone. Looking at this lot, I think they had done it in half the time. They had looked insolvent the previous year, but with creditors 174% of debtors prima facie, they should have called it a day.

It amazes me that Tony Field kept his directorship as, more than anyone, he would have been aware of the risks of continuing to trade on while the business clearly couldn't pay its bills on a normal basis. But there he was juggling with all the balls in the air, pulling off payment plans with all and sundry.

Believe it or not, the worst was yet to come.

With the boot of the bank on its neck, a plan had been formulated with the catchy title of The Way Forward that aimed to raise £450k. A board meeting had been called for 9 October 1984 and the usual suspects assembled. Duncan arrived with a colleague, resigned, said a few words and walked out. It seemed that this put a damper on proceedings.

The Way Backward was chosen instead, with the intention of flogging off TPS, lock stock and barrel. If, as Pilbrow had written, that 1983/84 had ended as a year of difficulty and disappointment, 1984/85 had started very much in the same vein.

Samuelson Organization stepped up to the plate, paying £1,750k for the bulk of the business at the end of 1984. They didn't take on the Nine Elms property and TP were stuck with the costs relating to that. Other parts in which they showed no interested included a/v, photographic, lighting design, conferences and were simply closed down.

You might remember back in 1977 when I sorted out the Commercial Presentations/TPA shareholding mess that Richard had scrawled across my paperwork 'he is giving away our heritage'. On

January 27 1985 Richard Pilbrow sacked his friend Dick Brett. January seemed to be the month for firing and resigning.

I heard that Sam Wise's outfit Technical Projects had been separately funded and had moved to the Isle of Wight but they'd only taken the equipment that they wanted, the reminder left behind to be written off by TP. Additionally the Light Limited lamp business had been subject to a management buyout. I bumped into James Wadsworth near London Bridge and he was doing well.

Somewhere along the way Technical Projects, which was also supported by Venture Link, died by association. After they realised that the investment in Theatre Projects was lost, they were keen to distance themselves from the whole business and pulled the plug. That left Sam Wise high and dry, not only out of pocket but out of a job.

By this stage all that existed of the business that had received the private placement was TPC and TPA, namely consultancy and production and 25% of TPS that was under the control of another company altogether. However the bulk of the structure that had housed the lost operations still existed with rent, rates and other property costs to be found.

It just could not be done. There was no way on earth that any profits from what was left could cover the costs for the Nine Elms and Mercer Street buildings. TP had not only gone full cycle but almost disappeared.

The results for 1984/85, signed off on 21 April 1986 by the directors and auditors, and filed at Companies House, expressed in thousands were:

Sales	2,501.1
Loss	(1,217.2)

The simplified balance sheet at 30.09.85:

Shares	1,476.0
Share Premium	185.8
Reserves	<u>1,942.4</u>
	(<u>280.6</u>)

Fixed assets	552.1
Current assets	1,235.3
Current liabilities	(1,568.8)
Liabilities after 1 year	(499.2)
	(280.6)

The Chairman's Report mentioned the refinancing of TP by selling 75% of TPS early in the year and of the plans to return to profitability.

I thought that was mission impossible but, believe it or not this situation continued for another two years and nine months. The 25% of TPS shareholding was sold to Samuelson in 1985/86.

The last hurrah:

1,000s	1985/6	1986/7	1987/8
			9 months
			Guesswork
Sales	1,081.1	1,434.5	?
Loss	(293.6)	(225.3)	(200)

The simplified balance sheets are:

Share capital	1,476.0	1,476.0	1,476.0
Share premium	185.8	185.8	185.8
Profit & Loss a/c	(2,236.0)	(2,461.3)	(2,661.3)
	(574.2)	(799.5)	(999.5)
Fixed assets	104.1	48.6	50.0
Current assets	701.3	531.8	500.0
Current liabilities	(1,227.9)	(1,310.7)	(1,500.0)
Creditor after 1 year	(151.7)	(69.2)	(49.5)
	(574.2)	(799.5)	(999.5)

I have wondered why no one was ever brought to book for this malfeasance.

In September 1986, Pilbrow claimed that: 'although we were technically insolvent, the position of the creditors was not deteriorating'. I don't think that there is such a state of being 'technically insolvent' in the same way that a woman one can't be half pregnant. The business is either insolvent or solvent and looking at the accounts, back in 1983/84 the numbers were tight. Certainly according to published accounts, the net creditors rose every year from 1984/5 to 1986/7.

When I heard that a big fat show-off biography was on the way, I wrote to him on 20 December 2010 advising that if I was mentioned then he must be highly circumspect, as any libel would elicit a very positive response. The fact was and still is that I would love to get him into a courtroom and let the world hear the truth.

My name and contributions were omitted from the book. However, buried in acknowledgements he refers to the 'ugly events that occurred during the late 70s and early 80s and that his legal eagles had forbidden him mentioning them'. Of course that period coincided with my period of employment and was the only time that TP actually made any money. So if that is 'ugly', let it be.

To summarise the financial results for the life of Theatre Projects Group 1957 to 1988, there are three distinct periods:

1957-1977 Pilbrow control – accumulated surplus after 20 years	£50k
1977-1982 Peter Roy CFO	£853k
1982-1988 Post private placing & £1.6 million investment	£(3,026k) loss

(The loss figure is partly estimated and before crystallization on liquidation.)

So was it a coincidence that during the five 'ugly' years when I was in control of the finances (as much as I could be), were the only years that TPG made a decent profit? I don't think so.

I know that the inner circle hated the brand of commercialism that John and I brought to the business and my attempts to shine a spotlight on the lack by some of any useful productive input. But in this big bleeding ugly world if you don't make a profit you ain't gonna make it.

I had been warned at an early stage that Pilbrow took all slights, slurs and disrespect personally and they were never forgotten. He had borne massive resentment against me from the day of the mass meeting he'd organised early in my tenure. It was designed to bully me into including a value for the Iran adventure in the 1976/77 accounts, in order to sweeten the bank manager into allowing us an overdraft.

When I realised that that was the plan, (which wasn't difficult) I 'assumed' that having invited the flash mob, he would be happy if the facts were exposed for all to digest. I laid everything out clearly, warts and all. Deep down, he must have known that the Iran project was a total dead duck but he persisted in his belief that it would be a triumph. In any event, I don't do bent accounts to please anybody. He wasn't accustomed to anyone speaking back, let alone making him look like a chump. So he decided to bide his time, waiting for the most apposite moment when he could wreak his revenge and the private placement provided that moment.

He didn't lose his company, he threw it away. On 15 January 1982 to be precise. In his book Pilbrow states that the 80s had been a 'personal disaster' for him with the 'loss of my company and virtually all my personal savings'. Now I don't want to be pedantic or a nitpicker but he wasn't exactly sleeping on a park bench. I believe he still had his apartment in Wigmore Street, his house in Scotland and of course his beautiful place in the States. He also had a job with TPC's phoenix.

To succeed in business you need to be a businessman or businesswoman. At the end of 1981 he had two of these on the payroll, namely John Ball and myself. Since 1977 we had brought a solid profit home every year without any injection of capital or even help from our bankers. When the City money arrived in November 1981, I was ambushed and subsequently sacked in January 1982. John followed two years later in disgraceful circumstances.

For me, Pilbrow was an unapologetic one-eyed Jack and I was one of many who had seen the other, darker side of his face.

A myriad of excuses for the failure of Theatre Projects Group has been offered up: recession, adverse trading conditions, over expansion, inflation, lack of financial backing when needed (all the time), competition, climate change, adverse weather conditions, a shift in the earth's crust. And the worst of all was that 'the finances were built on shifting sands'.

At the end of 1982, a few months after my departure, five years of solid profit had been achieved and the City had made two major investments into the business. Everything financially was in place to take the organisation forward, with confidence rock solid among customers, suppliers, investors, financiers and staff. All the minority shareholders had exited and TPG owned 100% of all its many enterprises.

The failure of the business was entirely due to Pilbrow's dysfunctional management, ably abetted by his bunch of cronies. And you can take that to the bank!

The recklessness of travelling to the US (by Concorde no less) and recruiting staff for a whole new venture without a word to senior management or new investors demonstrated how little respect he held for any of us. Not even an old envelope with a few figures scribbled on the back to demonstrate a financial plan. Then to take on new leases without finding new tenants for vacated buildings in Mercer Street beggars belief. Paying new rent whilst still carrying the old rents is a burden few businesses could bear.

The most common reason for business failure is a lack of funding but not in this case. The inability to control expenses, the total lack of effective and strategic leadership and the employment of myrmidons in key positions was behind it all.

Sometimes I did wonder if he actually enjoyed the laager mentality, circling the wagons with his trusted foot soldiers to form a barricade behind which to fight the enemy. It most certainly was more exciting than the ennui of day-to-day running a business with all the proper paperwork, procedures and routines that are required.

Maybe, back in the old days, the New Row days, things worked. It was a small band of light and sound designers and other theatre types all very much doing their own projects, not having to get involved in the murky world of finance. But TP in 1982 was far removed from those halcyon days and needed a management discipline beyond the capability of Pilbrow and his ilk. The fact that it took so long for the City people to realize that they had tied their clients' pension savings to the wagon of a blagueur was a mystery to me. Like a fairground barker, Pilbrow set out his stall and as a man, they all rushed to throw money at him, a man who would lie as easily as others breathe.

Come on man, tell it like it was: the Theatre Projects Group crashed and burned. And it was you who stuffed it up big time; you own it!

Where would the path of TPG taken them if I had stayed at the helm? It's something that I have dwelled on for many years. Would have I retired in twenty years having built up a giant within the entertainment industry? Would I have an apartment in Jermyn Street, a house on the south coast with a couple of mighty fine autos to carry me back and forth?

In truth the answer is no. Richard still resented that I'd opposed him on the non-existent Iran project and refused to play the role he had chosen to simply kick the financial can down the road until the riches arrived. Then he could find someone more Stratford-Upon-Avon than Stratford East London.

In effect, the City monies provided him with a Persian carpet. Our working lives would become more fraught as I fought to keep his spending in check whilst he plotted and schemed to be 'rid of this man'.

My voice and John's were lost. Our first tranche of new investment was being eroded at a fast pace and I could foresee us going back for more within twelve months, which is actually what happened. When they took the bowl out for a third run they found the tap firmly shut. A few months further down the pike, Pilbrow would have pushed my buttons and I would have blown up. I have never been very good at polishing egos which seemed to be a necessary requirement for working at TPG.

One of the rare pieces of good news to come out of the debacle was that New Consultants was successful and after some 35 years is well established and profitable. I guess that there's nobody left who I would remember or would remember me but I am sure that lessons were learned from the disaster.

Certainly they would not have repeated the commitment to work on a project beyond the initial outlines, without signed contracts and the beginnings of a cash stream. Iran and Thousand Islands could never be forgotten, could they?

In the forty years since I departed TP, other disgruntled ex-employees have contacted me and all have been highly critical of Pilbrow. Not to mention them giving some very salty descriptions of the person and his lack of moral fibre. This peaked around the time of John Ball's death.

One question they all ask is: 'what the hell happened?' and I can only answer that I don't know because I wasn't there.

I have used this opportunity to try and put together where the finances went after the private placement. Some of the following is extracted from TP paperwork or using from educated guesswork. All numbers are an approximation, not anybody's Gospel.

INVESTMENTS	11/81	1/83
Gross	800k	800k
Less costs, loans and overdraft repaid	580k	75k
Net funds available	220k	725k
What happened to it all?		
Two Mercedes		24k
Dividend paid		131k
Holland – missing stock & guarantee liability		400k
Investment in Technical Projects		185k
USA New offices, staff and costs		300k
Thousand Island w/off – no contract/no money		250k
Canada bad debts		70k
TPS Juke Box - production failed		60k
Move to Nine Elms		50k
Acquire Court Acoustics		21k
Light Ltd Debt in Nigeria		160k
Niara a/c		60k
Administration/Management audit		20k
Forensic audit (Wally Russell effort to discredit John Ball & Peter Roy)		95k

Trips to Singapore, Malayasia and Hong Kong (6):	
aborted plan to open office in Far East	30k
Gift to woman at party in New York	6k
Theatre productions	?
TOTAL	£1,862k

In November 1982 a memo circulated with a plan to recruit 12 new staffers with a recommended additional salary bill of £163k pa and attendant costs. And let's not forget the lawyers: with all this heavy-duty activity, notes for fees payable must have been arriving by the barrow load. Then another thought: back in the day interest rates were running at 9-10% on term deposit.

Light Limited. How did the major debts build up? We never supplied anything without a Letter of Credit, never, ever. And the Naira cash account of £60k? That was around £8k when I departed, held in Lagos by Mr Elms. Another shock was a landlord's claim for dilapidations of £100k on 10 Long Acre when those premises were given up.

So while it is accepted that these figures do contain a slice of pure guesswork, the totals roughly show that whereas one million was received, two million was spent or simply lost! How does that work?

As previously stated, this is in no way an audit but the majority of information is taken from paperwork donated by some of those who were there, their shoulders to the wheel at the time so to speak.

What a long, long way it had all come from that Homeric last supper at the Garrick Club. Fine people, fine food, fine wine and most importantly, fine speeches; the golden promises made by TP luminaries of tight financial controls and planning, reciprocated by golden promises of more funding as and when required. Oh, what heady days they were.

Did anyone, anyone, give a single brief thought to the calloused handed men and women of the soil, whose superannuation savings were being committed to this fool's paradise? I very much doubt it.

Give everybody another drink. Cheers, down the hatch everybody. And a fond farewell. Goodbye to £1.6 million that's gone forever.

On 11 July 1988, Tim A Clunie of S G Banister & Co was appointed Administrator to what little was left of Theatre Projects.

He reported to the creditors on 4 August that in order to maximise the assets, he was looking into the possible sale of the business. In reality that was just Theatre Projects Consultants and he received one proposed offer to acquire following an independent valuation. This must have been from Pilbrow and the senior management and I heard that £80k was on the table. The same party had also offered to acquire the American and Canadian businesses for a token five pounds as although it was claimed that they were profitable, they were both in deficit financially.

Information is a bit sketchy, but I tracked down a company formed as Law 29 Limited on 2 July 1988 whose name was changed to Theatre Projects Consultants Limited. It is this vehicle that achieved the management hive down of the old TPC.

Crystallization of the various leases were estimated at £3.5 million, so the final shortfall must have been not far short of six million quid. With the active help of Companies House, I approached the accountants for the actual figures but without success.

The Administrator was discharged on 20 March 1991 and a winding-up order made on 28 January 1991. One Mr John P Richards was appointed liquidator on 15 April 1991 and was finally released from his duties on 10 November 1997.

For some bizarre reason, on 16 October 1990 Theatre Projects Limited changed its name to Magnolia No 5. Why?!

On 25 August 1988, very soon after the wheels had fallen off, Pilbrow and family left the UK for 'a house in Connecticut in the USA' leaving those less fortunate to sort out the mess. Many accused him of running away and frankly, what else could you call it? Like an Italian ship's captain might say, the best place to supervise any rescue is on the shore.

The final disgrace was the quote he was credited with by Pro Sound News: 'We see this move as the final stage in rationalising Theatre Projects activities'. What a weasel word – rationalising. His cash savings as well as those of his father, sister, family, pension fund members and many other investors, together with creditors, banks, Inland Revenue (tax and NI) and HM Customs and Excise (VAT): everything lost forever in the name of ego.

Rationalising? Please!

11 HANGING THE SHINGLE OUT

'Honesty is for the most part less profitable than dishonesty'

Plato

On Saturday 30 January 1982 I awoke after the first decent night's sleep in months and felt that a heavy load had been lifted from my shoulders. For the first weekend in almost a year I didn't have to go to work; that was someone else's responsibility.

I was going down to Brighton for the day with a girlfriend but before I could set off I had a visitor. An old friend called Ted had somehow heard that I had joined the mighty ranks of the unemployed and asked if I would take on his tax stuff, worth some £2k a year. It was a good omen and naturally I agreed. I walked him down to his car to find an Aston Martin V8 series 3 which was a serious wake-up call. What the hell was a petrolhead like me doing running about in a Ford Cortina? I should be ashamed.

Brighton was great, it always is: lunch at English's, a curry supper and a night at the Imperial. Slow morning, breakfast in the hotel and a day of leisure. I could get used to this, I thought.

When Monday morning came, I was so thankful that I had an office to go to rather than be stuck in the apartment waiting for the phone to ring. It wasn't even 10am when I noticed a letter slipped under the door. It was from Pam Hay my old master's acolyte and typed on what appeared to be a child's toy typewriter. It informed me that I was a trespasser and that Max and I must be off the premises by 5pm.

Isn't it sad and indicative of the state of the man's mind? He arrives on Monday morning with a hundred tasks needing attention and harassing me is at the top of his list. Obviously he hasn't bothered to check on the status quo and just assumed we were squatters. TP had no use for the rooms as the top floor of Long Acre was empty if space was required. No, it was all the product of a very strange, sick mind and Pam Hay was carrying out orders as she always did.

I sent over a reply that we were not leaving as we had a lease and were up to date with our rent. The next morning another envelope had been slipped under the door containing a notice putting up the rent. Again I sent over a reply referring to the Landlord and Tenants Act. When another missive arrived on Wednesday requesting a copy of the lease, I referred her to Kingsley Napley.

Why couldn't she simply ask for a meeting? I wasn't a Gorgon so she wouldn't have turned to stone by talking to me face to face. It was all part of that spying, snooping, creeping about way of conducting herself; slipping notes under doors and running off fitted right in to that.

I had planned to phone John and tease him about buying me a good lunch and handing over the file on the business I had been cultivating to bring into the TP fold. It took two men with a solid knowledge of the West End theatre to run it together with a secretary/bookkeeper. The guys wanted to retire and their offer was 10% of the net profit each as a pension, with no down-payment or capital sum whatsoever, so even if it was screwed up TP could walk away as free as a bird. It was a win-win without doubt and put TP right in the real theatre heartland which was always an ambition. The numbers showed a trading profit of about £225k, less staff and accommodation at say £75k, giving a net around £150k. After the two pensions of £30, that left some £120k on the table every year and rising. What's not to like? And the cherry on the top: payment from the box office each week that meant no build-up of debt.

I would have been happy to introduce John and arrange the meetings to do the deed for the future of Theatre Projects. But this dirty dog stuff of trying to throw us out on the street for no reason other than vindictiveness had stopped me dead, and the deal likewise. I phoned the guys and told them I wouldn't be able to help them and that was the end of it. It couldn't have saved TP on its own but to have a solid £10k every Friday wouldn't have done any harm.

That first Monday was spent getting my CV up to date and phoning round employment agencies to let them know I was on the market.

A nice surprise came with a call from Bob Stanton who'd been given the word by you know who.

'Hello Peter, it's Bob. I've just got the news that you're off to do your own thing.'

'Hi Bob, thanks for calling. It wasn't voluntary, I was sacked. One day I'm essential to the future and then four days later I'm not.'

'I'm sorry Peter, that's not what I was told.'

'Look Bob, let's not get into it. I'm happy with what I was able to do at TP and it's up to the others now. I really appreciate your call and if there's anything I can do for you just whistle.'

'Thank you Peter, all the very best. It's been a pleasure.'

He really was a lovely man. It was a busy day. My next call was also unexpected, Chris Pearson.

'Charlie told me what happened. It's bloody disgrace.'

'Well, let's see how they track without me, it may be enlightening.'

'Would you be interested in helping a start-up media shop, maybe four or five hours a week, in Henrietta Street?'

'Sure, get them to call me.'

He was as good as his word and Jeff Upward arranged to come over with his partner Michael Short on the Friday. That would give me time to get the smell of furniture polish in the air as Max didn't have a cleaner. We had a great meeting and agreed five hours a week for £100pw to start. So with the fee from Ted, I was already at £7,200pa, equal to 36% of my old salary after one working week.

Pam was still busting my chops over the lease. I think she believed that she had stumbled on the heist of the year and that I'd used my power as CFO to let my mate have the suite of offices at under cost. She was ready to call in Slipper of the Yard. As far as both Max and I were concerned our arrangement for John, or any other TP person come to that, to use the space to have a confidential meeting or conduct an interview still stood, but I had no intention of going into any of that with Ms Hay. She would, without doubt, report to her beloved leader that John was part of a conspiracy with Peter and Max to rob TP of £300pa. Because that's all it was and there was no way I would provide her with bullets to fire.

There were only a couple of years left on the lease, so I suggested that we ask the lawyers to have the head lease transferred to Max and I. A renewal was unlikely as we knew the landlord had plans to redevelop the whole area as Covent Garden was booming, so there was no long-term benefit to be considered.

I did bump into David Collison in Mercer Street. There was no doubt that we didn't see eye to eye on many subjects but he was a likable bloke and we had no problem on a social level. He told me that he was having terrible pain in his back and it looked like an operation was inevitable. He also gave me a friendly warning.

'Be careful Peter, Richard is out for revenge.'

'Revenge? What the hell for? I rescued TP from collapse in '77 and in four years took it to the door of the Stock Exchange. He should be talking about reward not revenge.'

'You were very disrespectful to him and his friends and he will never forget that.'

'Please tell him for the sake of his health to move on, he's got a big job ahead.'

We shook hands and went our separate ways. I don't know if my advice was passed on but it did not bode well for TP if its chief honcho was fixated on petty intrigues and past slights while ignoring the dirty deals swirling around him. Still, if he really needed enemies to fight to complete his life then so be it.

It all reminded me of the story of Don Quixote; didn't he lose his marbles fighting imaginary foes?

Agents were coming back to me with job prospects, although to be honest I was really enjoying the sense of freedom my new situation had brought.

Although my working life was in London, I had rarely visited the City. I inhabited the West End and Holborn and I was a fish out of water in the Square Mile. Nevertheless, when a well paid opportunity arose I was happy to take a look. The interview was with a very pleasant man who coincidentally was wearing an identical tie to mine but it wasn't a sign. The work was for a charitable trust looking after its investments but I had zero experience in that field, so no cigar.

The second contact was mad, there is no other word for it. I was asked to meet the prospective client in a hotel bar at 11am on a Saturday morning and found Mr and Mrs Tobias at a corner table. They explained that they were in the clothing industry with factories in Essex. After a short conversation we arranged to meet at his accountant's office in Soho the following week and from there, went to lunch at a Jewish restaurant. The accountant was typical surly sort, scoring zero in charm, or table manners come to think of it.

Another get together in a bar and I expressed concern that I had seen no figures, nor his business premises and didn't even know the name of the company. He still did not disclose any of this vital information and I left the meeting none the wiser. Mr Tobias called yet again, this time wanting to meet in the forecourt of Golders Green Station.

'Are we going to your offices from there.'

'Oh no, I thought we could have lunch and talk.'

'Forget it. I've met you three times and still have no real idea of what's happening. I just don't have either the time or interest in pissing about which you seem to enjoy. Please don't call again.'

And hung up. I seem to attract strange people. Or are all people strange?

The third, and as it happens last, effort at job finding was at an automobile windscreen replacement company near Watford. I didn't like the idea of a commute, but at least this would be in the opposite direction to the rush hour into London.

I met with a couple of directors and was shown around and taken to lunch where recent accounts were handed over. It was an impressive business, profitable, well run and the lunch was pretty good too. However there was a fly in the ointment. Isn't there always?

There was another company that they owned, which from memory was in auto brakes and suspension. That was run by a nephew and he was determined to take his activities away from the centre and be totally independent. We drove over there to meet him.

The man in question was the worst possible specimen you could imagine and ready for a fight. He would rather have punched me than shake my hand. Then the penny dropped: if chosen, I would be used as some kind of moderator between two warring sides.

Driving back to town I realised that I just didn't want to work for anybody ever again. I had picked up more clients, I had got my life back and was enjoying it. No more boardroom battles, office politics, long hours, dealing with absolute stinkers and, most importantly, not having your future lying in other people's hands, especially the unhinged ones.

I phoned the windscreen man and withdrew my application which upset him because he was about to invite me to join. Sorry mate, not your fault. I've had an epiphany. Soon after this I caught my last sighting of Pilbrow.

One early evening Max and I were walking past the entrance to the car park in Upper St Martin's Lane when he and his special friend Duncan came round the corner. Amazingly they appeared to be pleased to see us.

'Oh, there's Peter and Max,' Richard exclaimed.

I cannot stand hypocrisy and people who piss down your back and tell you it's raining. These two had thrown me out of my hard earned job without a qualm, were as happy as pigs in mud to be rid of me. And here they are all smiles and seemingly expecting a toothsome hello as we passed by.

They had as much chance as a three-legged cat burying its turd on a frozen pond. Max walked on without breaking his stride, looking straight ahead and I followed suit with the addition of the soldier's farewell: left hand middle finger raised in the truly international gesture understood by all.

No one could know back then but a heavy price was going to be paid for the superordinate patronizing attitude I'd seen displayed: it's called kismet.

Poldervaart called out of the blue and asked if I could visit him at noon the following day. I agreed. Perhaps it was for a thank you lunch for my work at TP. Especially getting the monies that they'd invested back to them which they must have written off years ago. PolyGram had no interest in TP for over six months now and the directorships had been given up at the time of the repayments.

I took a taxi over to Oxford Street and was ushered in to his palatial office, shook hands and I sat down. I fully expected that he would ask how I was and what I was doing to make a crust but I was to be sorely disappointed.

'Your seven year contract. Was it signed?'

'You've brought me over here to ask me that? You could have asked me on the phone.'

He smiled.

'I thought you would at least have a few words of appreciation to offer rather than ask me a question about something that has nothing to do with you. You're pretty generous with other people's time.'

He was still smiling. No free lunch here mate. I stood up, turned and walked out. He was just like his fellow directors supping other folk's paid for drinks at the theatre. Those people believe they are entitled to everything and the little people can make do with the crumbs.

Viva la revolución!

I reckoned that I was overdue for a piece of good luck and it came from an unexpected source – The Surbiton Liberal Club.

Let me explain. Max often visited the club for a drink on his way home and one evening he was approached by another member called Jack Heap (you can't make this stuff up), who made several disparaging comments about accountants. Jack owned an engineering works in Wandsworth and he'd let a couple of rooms out to an accountant who was behind with the rent and owed money all over the town.

Max told me the story and it seemed that there might be an opportunity to pick a practice up cheap. So we arranged to meet Peter Davies. In his early sixties, his situation was worse than we thought. The Inland Revenue were taking him to court for non-payment of PAYE and NI and were going for bankruptcy, so time was of the essence. He employed one guy full time and a part time secretary but had no idea what his annual fee roll was.

I drove over to what was no doubt Clockwork Orange territory. Leaving a car unattended was a serious risk so here again, speed was of the essence. Climbing an oily iron staircase to the offices the first sensation was the noise of the machines next door and then the smell hit me. Mr Davies' assistant had the worst body odour known to man; hurry up called upon to get out into the beautiful air of York Road.

A rapid burn through the files gave me an estimate of maybe twenty grand a year with most cases running behind. That would give a sporting chance to get three year's work out in the next two years, mitigating the purchase price. It was not rocket science to calculate there was not sufficient income to pay the assistant, the secretary, the overheads and leave anything for the principal. In addition to the Revenue men and Jack Heap, Mr Davies owed VAT and a couple of weeks salaries: in total, also about twenty grand.

My proposal was that I would pay all the debts and take over the practice, giving Davies a stipend of £100pw plus 10% of fees received. It was a gamble but I was confident that this could be the nucleus of a whole new beginning for me.

He readily agreed and his number one job was to make his helper redundant. His secretary on the other hand was very competent and came to work for Max and I. My next job was to pay Mr Heap his back rent as he was spoiling my friend's quiet drink at the club. The books and papers came over to my office and a lawyer drew up the contract.

In the meantime the court hearing arrived. Taking the contract with him, Mr Davies explained that everything would be paid within fourteen days. The Inland Revenue officer found that unacceptable and told the Court that they were not interested in the money but wanted Peter Davies bankrupted as a matter of principle. Unbelievable. Another problem to solve.

When my calculations of the debts were complete, I tried in vain to agree an amount with either the tax office or the VAT guys but received not an iota of help. Letters were lost and telephone calls given the run around, so I had my workings typed up to use as the final debts to be paid. Luckily I found that a tax allowance had been missed in the past and used that to reduce the outstanding debts.

We called the Bankruptcy Office and appointment was made for Peter Davies and me. When we bailed up, we were met by a seemingly, self-satisfied geezer. I presented him with all my work as well as proof that enough cash was available to meet all liabilities. He glanced over everything fairly quickly and then looked up from the paperwork.

'If you can provide me with a banker's cheque by 3pm, bankruptcy proceedings would be ended forthwith. However, there is also the issue of my fee.'

'Fee?' I piped up. 'What fee? With respect you haven't done anything.'

'There's a fee for my supervision and oversight. It's the law.'

'How much is it?'

I'd not had more than a few seconds to digest this bombshell but it couldn't be more than £500 or so, could it? The guy couldn't have spent more than ten minutes total.

'£4,675.'

'Good God! How much?'

'£4,675.'

'That's ludicrous! How is that calculated?'

'It's a complex formula that I can't explain, but if a banker's draft is not here by 3 pm, the arrangement fails and bankruptcy proceeds.'

I would have respected this geezer more if he had a mask and a gun. What a racket, it was legalized theft no more no less. So Catch 22 – you scrape up the money to pay the debts and then have to find another dollop on top for nothing, absolutely nothing. My savings on the tax bill were wiped out and more but I was committed and had to finish what I had started. Without taking my time into account, the final spend came to £21k; work to be done, and fast.

I never understood how Peter Davies came to be working out of two rooms at the back of a factory. He mentioned that he had been ill but to be where he was and skint really was the end of the line. Working from home would have been a better fit but maybe that would have caused marital strife. He was a grumpy bugger and that's for sure. Maybe he was born that way.

Certainly he never expressed a word of thanks for getting him out of the hole he'd dug for himself and always referred to the customers as 'his' clients. It suited me that he carried out the legwork necessary to service the practice while I churned out the physical stuff; except in the cases of three major businesses where I got directly involved.

What I was able to pay him wasn't much but I think it was a long time since he saw £100pw on a regular basis. He would soon be able to draw a state pension and get free travel that would make his life easier than it had been for many years.

Unexpectedly there was a backlog of work; the catch up together with modest fee increases resulted in putting out some £75k of bills over the first two years. I had taken the risk knowingly and if it had failed would have had no cause to complain. But it didn't fail.

While all this was going on, I was looking for an Aston Martin V8 and working the phones trying to find a manual rather than the usual automatic. The factory called me to say that a customer had purchased a new car and I could have the trade-in at cost.

I drove up to Newport Pagnell and bought it on the spot, subject to mechanical checks. A couple of days later I was back with one of Max's clients called John Summers. A brilliant engineer but a very difficult man; a genius with his hands but short of temper and you trod on eggshells when in his presence. He was happy with the car and we agreed on £10,000 with a little work to be completed before collection and my Cortina was sold to a builder.

After a break of too many years, I was back in the driving seat of a real car, a 1978 series 4 V8 Aston Martin in Madagascar Brown with a manual gearbox designed for a truck. What impressed me was how polite everybody was to me at the factory, culminating in the reception area prior to departing when I was chatting with the Sales Director. The receptionist called to him that Sheikh Yamani was on the line.

Now this bloke was Saudi Arabia's Minister for Petroleum and Mineral Resources and top man at OPEC. But the director, cool as a cucumber asked the receptionist to put him on hold.

'Would you please ask him to give me a minute as I'm with a customer.'

I couldn't believe it, to ask Sheikh Yamani to wait while he talked with little old me. Real old school.

Our new secretary was very efficient but a terrible timekeeper. Moneywise this didn't matter as she was paid on an hourly basis but it would have been beneficial if she could have been in place by 9.30am just in case we were all out and she could field any telephone calls. But day after day she would turn up looking like death warmed up around 10.30 or even 11.00 and I never found out the reason. Peter reckoned she was having a relationship with a projectionist at the National Film Theatre but knowing him that could be just tittle-tattle.

Max was impressed by my new car and started to look for a similar vehicle. Very soon he found a 1979 example in light blue and headed north to Manchester with John to go over it and as all was well, returned to town as the proud owner.

Another character to enter our lives was Richard Graham who Peter brought in to meet us. He was an accountant/bookkeeper who was looking for work. Tall, thin and unkempt, he didn't impress but if the need arose there might be an opportunity. In fact he was given many opportunities over the next fifteen years but never seemed to be over bothered in making much of a success of what came his way. I should say he was very capable but without ambition.

Ever since leaving NSW I had kept in touch with Peter Ryan's secretary Peggie Roberts, now Peggie Manton and we met up for lunch from time to time. She was great company and I thought her a great friend. She and her husband Michael lived in a beautiful house in Tufnell Park with a large garden running down to tennis courts.

Michael had been a partner in the famous ad agency Kingsley Manton Palmer but was now heading up Manton Woodyear & Ketley. There should have been a fourth name on the door, Daz Valladares but maybe the other three felt it didn't have the right ring to it.

I met Daz a couple of times and although he is the same age as me he's still heading up an advertising business. Gossip reached me that there had been a boardroom coup and Michael Manton had been voted out by his partners. The more I got to know him the more I believed the rumour.

Anyway, I had lunch with Peggie and told her I was looking for business, not a job but contracting work. She suggested Gold Greenlees Trott who had recently moved to Bedford Street off The Strand. They were an ad agency of the moment producing fantastic creative work reminiscent of CDP in the 60s and 70s. They were looking for a senior finance man so I called them, explained who and what I was and was asked to an interview.

Walking in on Monday it was obvious that they had just moved in as there were unopened boxes everywhere. The creative director Dave Trott was going to be talking to me which amazed me. Normally creative heads only deal with what directly concerns them and finance stuff is outside their remit.

Dave Trott had a desk in the middle of the chaos with two chairs and I was invited to sit. He looked at me, then at my CV that I'd sent over ahead of the meet. He asked me to excuse him whilst he made a call, dialled, put his feet on the desk and talked to his mate on the other end about his adventures on the previous Saturday. After watching soccer he'd gone up to the West End, had a few drinks and a meal, then a few more drinks, pulled a bird and gone back to his place. They chatted on in this vein for a few minutes and after arranging a get together later in the week, hung up.

He turned to me again, looked, picked up my CV and scanned it. Once again the 'excuse me' was followed by a phone call to another mate, the boots were back on the desk and an identical conversation to the earlier one followed, with the addition of a good laugh over the name of the bird which he had known but had now forgotten. Who said the age of romance was dead?

The call ended, once again my CV was given a scan and after a glance in my direction the pantomime was repeated. Another mate, another laugh. It occurred to me that all this may be some kind of crazy test to see how much rudeness I would put up with and I was about to fail with flying colours.

Leaning forward I picked up my CV, stood up, turned and headed for the door.

'Just a minute. I'm almost finished, come back.'

I gave him a backward wave and was gone.

Dave had a reputation of being difficult at times and was fired by his partners in 1990, going on to form a new agency Bainsfair, Sharkey, Trott & Walsh. Unfortunately in 1993 his old firm GGT bought out that agency in 1993 and he was fired once again.

The biggest client I had acquired was an asphalt business that specialised in flat roof repairs and relaying on commercial buildings. A family affair, it was run by a husband and wife, Bill and Christine with their son Bill junior. Bill dealt with the black stuff, Chris kept a fine set of accounts and the job was a pleasure.

As far as I could tell, they were as straight as a die so it came as a surprise to be 'invited' to a meeting with the Inland Revenue. These were usually no cause for concern and together with Peter Davies we attended the tax inspector at Battersea expecting a reasonable conversation. The reality turned out to be quite the opposite.

As soon as we were seated he started to scream at the four of us that he had information that they were carrying out work off the books and putting personal expenses through the company. He said he was going to press for maximum fines and prison sentences. The young assistant sitting behind him looked at us and rolled his eyes which tipped me off that this insane behaviour was his standard approach.

I stood up and informed him that the interview was at an end and that I would be sending a report to the Chairman of the Inland Revenue. The others followed my lead. The Inspector demanded the books be sent to him and I agreed on the strict understanding that they would be collected at the end of two weeks as to hold to them longer would have a seriously adverse effect on the client's business.

Back on the pavement, my clients were visibly shaken. I did my best to reassure them that all was under control but they didn't believe me. I asked them to get all their paperwork for the past two years to me by the weekend. When it arrived I went over everything and could trace no horrors, so put in a call to two brothers from a South London family who specialised in dealing with tough assignments.

They arrived on Monday morning, loaded the boxes and took them over to the tax office, together with a letter confirming that they would be back on the Monday in a fortnight. As I suspected, when they arrived at 10am on the day, the boxes were exactly as they had left them. They explained that they had instructions not to leave without them and the reception staff were most uncomfortable at having two very tough looking geezers hanging around.

It worked. At noon they were allowed to remove everything and bring the boxes over to my office. The inspector had inspected nothing and in addition, was acutely aware that we meant business. It was all at my personal cost but that was how both Max and I operated when it came to back duty cases where the client was subject to a fishing expedition.

The inspector requested another meeting and we refused; everything by correspondence please, no meetings or telephone calls and all on the record.

Basically there are two ways to tackle these situations. If the client has been on the high diddle-diddle then you're on the back foot from the word go. You don't know what evidence the IR has and if the client lies, cheats and tries to get away with as much as he can, you are moving into dangerous waters. That's what happened with the famous jockey Lester Piggott who had forgotten to declare some of his prize money. He made a full disclosure, came to a very large settlement and then paid it with a cheque from a bank account he had not included in his full disclosure. It went downhill from there. The taxman is always keen on a speedy conclusion, so if you confess and grovel a bit you can often get a reasonable result for the client that he doesn't deserve.

But if you have every reason to trust the customer then put up a fight; much of the work will be pro bono but I cannot suggest a settlement when one isn't justified. An efficient snow job is required entailing long letters with tons of schedules, replying to their missives superfast, even hand delivering to always keep the pressure on and being ready and willing to complain to Chairman of the Board at the drop of a hat. It is difficult for any inspector to close a case without a penny piece. Even a few quid can be chalked up as a win, rather than having to admit that their time and effort has been wasted.

We didn't know at the time but it was their home that was at the root of the problem. They lived on a new estate in Essex where all the properties were very similar. There was a double sized vacant lot next to their place on which the developer had intended to build his own house. However he changed his mind and offered it to Bill and Chris who bought it, building a huge mansion complete with a heated Olympic sized pool and landscaped gardens. In addition, there were numerous large lorries towing tar boilers going back and forth and hoary handed boys from the black stuff milling around. Unsurprisingly it gave rise to some of the neighbours feeling envious and resentful, a toxic mix.

The inspector banged on about who they used to move house and demanded the name of the removal firm. He couldn't grasp the concept of passing stuff over the fence. The basis for it all was that he thought they were general builders and had hidden the cost of the build in the company's books. But Christine had all the legal paperwork to hand so we could snuff out that flame.

After some four months the inspector called. In an effort to bring some resolution, he told me that a neighbour had complained and informed on the business. He alleged that the business dealt in cash work and paid its troops with folding money without deductions. The first part was pure nonsense as they only dealt with commercial buildings and payments on the doorstep were weekly wages to the legitimate work force. There were no casual cash workers.

I phoned Chris with the news and she immediately put two and two together. A few weeks before the interview, she'd been watering her garden, had failed to notice her neighbour's children on the other side of the hedge and gave them a sprinkle. It was an accident, an everyday very minor incident. However the neighbours were already in a state of agitation: over the trucks, the men, the mansion and the pool. I nearly forgot, and the two new Mercedes. They were quick to instigate a feud, claiming that Christine had soaked the kids on purpose.

Before I could consider our next move, I got another call from the Revenue: the inspector dealing with the case had suffered a nervous breakdown and when his replacement reviewed the case, he closed it down.

*****

The introduction to Upward and Short Media had been a very good one. Jeffery Upward was the archetypical advertising man and had cut his teeth at NSW before I washed up there. Personable and outgoing, he was definitely the driving force behind the agency and it was a brave move to start with just one client. His partner Michael Short was a much more complicated person. He'd finished his education at an expensive school in Switzerland, was fluent in some eight languages with a working knowledge of a further seven or eight and a very talented pianist. But his street smarts were non-existent and his main ambition was to find a wife who he believed would rid him of all his problems. I tried to convince him that in my experience finding a wife was the prelude to a whole raft of new problems that you never knew existed. Nevertheless, every female he came across he regarded as a potential Mrs Short and his clumsy approaches led to many unhappy moments.

Apart from one exception, the staff were a very happy bunch of young women which included Jeff's wife who controlled the client billing. I just didn't take to the odd one out let's leave it at that.

The nature of the business meant that there were regular social happenings and the dynamic duo could really hit the bottle in a big way. One favourite was to clear the restaurant table, climb aboard and dance like crazy people. That would invariably result in the restaurant's staff having a majorly adverse reaction and the night would come to an abrupt end.

Michael was always affable but his appearance was so poor he could be mistaken for a homeless person. At the end of the day he would without fail, retire to The Swan pub in New Row, drink himself senseless and have a minicab called to take him home to Woodford where he lived with his parents. This arrangement meant that he could spend all his pay on himself and fund his unhealthy lifestyle.

The business was invited to make a presentation to a public company to handle all their media, both domestic and international. A couple of the girls persuaded Michael to go with them to Moss Bros where he purchased a new off the peg suit, shirt, tie and a pair of brogues to wear for the occasion but insisted on wearing the rig for the day. Big mistake. He did look rather strange, like a monkey on horseback. Nobody knows what happened that night apart from the fact that he set off for the pub as usual but the rest is speculation.

The boys had arranged to meet at the prospective client at 10am the next morning. Jeff was horrified when Mike appeared, dressed exactly as he had left the evening before except he looked as if he'd slept in the street. His new suit had acquired smears of blue paint and his shirt was spattered with blood. It was obvious that he hadn't washed or shaved or even combed his hair and smelled like a brewer's dray. Before Jeff could usher him away they were shown into the client's boardroom and Jeff had to pass Mike off as an eccentric genius media man which was not inaccurate.

On another occasion Michael was walking to the station to catch the train to work when he passed a convalescent home, decided it looked wonderful and checked himself in without telling anyone. How the management could admit someone off the street without a referral beats me but they did. Information as to where he was only surfaced when Upward and Short Media received an invoice for a massive amount for his first day. Just a couple of days would wipe out a month's salary. His parents were informed and dragged him away. This just couldn't last.

Jeffery was as keen a theatregoer as me although he was more drama than musicals and for many years I was his backup invited guest. It was a bit strange to spend an evening with a bloke but he was great company and always bought the best seats. Many years later we went to see Richard Harris in 'Henry IV' by Luigi

Pirandello which was about a man who had lost his mind and thought he was the King of Burgundy and Holy Roman Emperor. When we stood up to leave, I was amazed to find a huge block of young Japanese sitting behind us looking totally bewildered. My guess was that they'd assumed that this was Shakespeare's 'Henry IV' and had found Pirandello's play incomprehensible.

As we moved into the second half of 1982 my income had already passed my salary level at TP and without the daily madness that had gone with the job. I realized I should have gone self-employed years ago and let the employment agents know that I was out of the market, hopefully for good. I did get head hunted for CFO for a chain of department stores in South Africa with a breathtaking financial package. However a chat with the Embassy revealed that I would be liable for two years military service as my father had been born in South Africa so I declined. They would have held the position for me but fighting for a country to which I held no allegiance just seemed too much Beau Geste for me as well as being over forty.

My mind was made up that I would take no crap from any client and that tenet was soon put to the test. I was walking along Garrick Street when my shortest client shouted from the other side of the street giving a diabolical commentary on the invoice that I had recently sent him. By the time I had crossed over and reached him I had decided that our relationship, such as it was, had ended.

'What's your problem shouting at me in the street?'

'Your invoice is a bit strong.'

'Tell you what, throw it away. My costs for the work I've done are cancelled. It's all free of charge.'

'That's very nice of you, thank you.'

'Don't thank me just find yourself another accountant. I'm not working for anyone who shouts at me in the bloody street. And I'm not kidding. Go away and stay away.'

Later he phoned and asked me to reconsider but I simply sent him the paperwork he would need for his new and cheaper guy.

As we moved towards the end of 1982, Max told me that a client of his called Clive Knapp had looked at a property in Holborn that was for sale. He had felt it was too decrepit for his purposes but it had potential.

My flat was ideal but the block had its problems. The managing agents had spent the contingency reserves on fire proofing the doors and were planning a major restoration that would have cost us owners a fortune. However the most irritating part of living there was the difficulty in parking. As no off-street parking was available, both sides of the street were constantly lined by cars and many people returning late in the evening would simply double park. I found myself unable to get out in the early mornings quite frequently. There was no harm at taking a look as houses that were still homes in central London were becoming rare beasts. Most had been converted to business premises or apartments.

The property was on the corner of Northington Street and King's Mews. In its original state in 1792 it comprised five small mews units that housed the horses and carriages belonging to the large houses in John Street. Clearly it was in a sad state but the general area was terrific for me apart from the huge block of 1930s public housing where Camden Council put its worst of the worst on the other side of Grey's Inn Road. Here lived the criminal classes. The asking price was £65k.

I called in an agent to assess my place, did the sums, talked to the bank and went to take another look. Only to find that the agent had a new improved asking price of £120k.

On inspection I was surprised to find enough space on the ground floor to park nine cars. It was full of junk but an obvious opportunity. The first floor was pretty beat up and the presence of two dead mice added a touch of pathos. At first I thought the place was unoccupied but in one room I came across a little old Spanish lady who spoke no English but was described as the caretaker by the agent EA Shaw of Covent Garden. She didn't come with the property.

I offered £108k and it was accepted. The Maida Vale property sold in a couple of weeks so maybe I should have asked for more. I raised a loan from the bank and moved into Northington Street but it was a bit like camping indoors.

A crew came in and cleaned up as far as that was possible and a skip arranged. It was impossible to drop the container off as the street was too narrow so I gave the driver some cash to leave the whole rig for ten minutes and we piled the rubbish in as fast as we could. The problem was that there was a garage workshop, W Godleman & Son, on the opposite side of the road. Bill the owner was to put it mildly a difficult man and his physical altercations with customers were legendary. Certainly he was not a welcoming figure and much of the junk in the garages was his junk. The first evening at the house noises from downstairs proved to be a couple parking their car. Apparently Bill had 'given them permission' which was bleeding generous on his part as he had no right to do so.

I formed an entity to manage parking in the garages and took flyers around John Street. Within two days I had let them all for daytime parking only to a firm of accountants which was not surprising. Not only was parking on the street expensive but a pain to manage because of the prowling packs of wardens.

CPA had their contract cancelled by TP within a few days of my departure so friend Charlie was out of work. We came to an arrangement that he would manage the project of house restoration.

Tradesmen needed to be found. I decided that due to the age of the house it would be a sensible scheme to line the interior walls with concrete and then add a plaster skim to finish. A man was found who would work evenings and weekends and turned out to be a star, working room by room through the house. One evening he introduced his new partner and as soon as I laid eyes on him I found my mind thinking of Honest John the Fox in Pinocchio. The impression was spot on. On Saturday the pair arrived at 9am with an apprentice in tow and set to work. At 11.45 the three presented themselves suited and booted and announced that I owed them three days money because Saturday was double time in their book.

I rejected this as our original arrangement was based on an hourly rate, period. I had plenty experience of unions with all the penalty rates and loadings and none of that was going to wash with me. I hadn't come up on the down train. I paid them what I calculated and sent them on their way. We found another guy who was happy to take my cash and a couple of sparkies came on board. Progress.

On the corner of Gray's Inn Road was a launderette run by two elderly women. Its claim to fame was for its appearance in the first episode of Minder. The girls had been in situ for many years and informed me that in the 60s the house had belonged to Diana Dors who used it as a party place. On many evenings the mews was crammed with fancy cars delivering the glitterati of the show biz world. The main room had a duck egg blue ceiling with gold stars that gave credence to the tale and by coincidence Charlie's father remembered working on the property at that time when he was in the building trade.

I had met Michael Manton through Peggy and had even been to dinner with them at their home. I gave him the respect he was due as one of the very top men in the advertising business in London. Did I like him? Not much. I found him to be a cold fish looking most of the time as if he was suffering from a bad case of farmer Giles (piles) and there was no doubt that he was accustomed to getting his way in all things. I assume he had a lighter side but I never saw it. Back then I thought they were my friends but I now realise that I was mistaken and was simply being used.

Peggy called me to say that Michael wanted to see me and a meeting was arranged at the Direct Marketing Sales Bureau (DMSB) in Covent Garden. The DMSB was an unusual setup: although its shareholders were all individual members of the direct mail world, it was little more than a division of the Royal Mail. They had invented and supported it with a solid six figure annual stipend and in addition supplied a stream of work researching aspects of the business. It did carry out contracts for other clients but these were incidental. It was run by Michael Manton as Chairman and Michael Schlagman as CEO; the latter also kept the books but as he was moving on Manton needed to fill the gaps of both CEO and CFO which is where I came in. Frankly I didn't have the time but contacted Richard Graham who did. I took the responsibility for finances and Richard became the part time bookkeeper. With the backing of Royal Mail this just couldn't fail. It would take a complete idiot to screw this up, wouldn't it?

The CEO appointment was filled by Frank McGinty. One of his first decisions was to make a donation to sponsor The Seven Dials Trust which aimed to restore and maintain that area of Covent Garden. What this had to do with direct marketing was lost on me but there was cash for pretty much anything.

There were about a dozen staffers but the smartest by far in my opinion was woman in her twenties called Jo Howard-Brown. She may have been a tad young at the time for the top slot and of course was a girl that the decision makers would have resisted to a man!

It proved to be an easy billet for both Richard and I. He would put in a couple of visits a week to tackle the routine stuff and I would drop by for two or three hours usually on a Monday. Because the

Post Office represented 95% of the sales, credit management was a doddle and the cash flow was a magic carpet. Regular parties were held and we were always included. It was to last eight years.

No prospective clients ever came through our door carrying the famous three Ps – profit, prestige and potential although many had the three Ds – desperation, danger and dead broke.

Max had been approached by two couples who planned to enter the hospitality industry and wanted to meet at Max's house in Surbiton rather than come into town. I was last to arrive at about seven and being Max there were no refreshments on offer so after introductions it was straight down to business. One guy was to do much of the talking and he kicked off.

'We've looked at a hotel in Redhill which has been closed for a couple of years. We're planning to buy and restore it and then run it as an up market business. We all have past experience in the trade.'

So far so good. We then got down to the nuts and bolts of finance, time scale, areas of responsibility and all seemed doable. The main man stated that they saw this as a five-year plan and I chipped in.

'So at the end of five years the plan is to sell up and take a tidy capital profit?'

'Oh no, we'll burn it down and claim the insurance.'

He was serious and said it in a totally matter of fact way as if this was normal everyday planning. My blood drained and I immediately rose to my feet.

'I was never here.'

In one movement I was out of the room, out of the house and heading home. The next morning Max told me that he had asked them to leave and find another source of advice. It's not that we were holier than-than-thou but we just didn't tolerate folk wanting to involve us in their criminal activities and in effect shove our heads up the barrel.

Centerpoint Design was one of Max's major clients and by the nature of things over the years, many of their freelancers had signed up with him to look after their finances. So it was no surprise when an ex-staffer phoned to ask for a meeting.

Shirley had been the firm's bookkeeper and was now working for a print outfit called Satellite Group, owned by Derek Absalom and Dennis Bickle. Both were in their fifties but these guys were absolute chalk and cheese. Derek carried all the trappings of a rich man with a big house in Purley, a boat moored on the Thames and a Rolls-Royce to boot. But it was all on borrowed money and as we were soon to discover, borrowed time. In contrast, Dennis was an ordinary man and I say that as a compliment. He was a printer and simply wanted to make a decent wage to keep his family secure. He was not interested in the baubles of wealth.

When Max heard that Absalom was involved he refused to have any part of it. He had met the man through Centerpoint, didn't like him and under no circumstances would take him on as a client. Shirley was in real trouble so, ever the soft touch, I offered to meet Derek and Dennis. The business was that of a jobbing printer but Derek had ambitions for a printing empire and wanted to expand but was mightily hindered by an £80k overdraft, the servicing of which was crippling the cash flow.

There were two bases of production: Crawley that was run by Derek and in North London run by Dennis. Absalom took me to see some premises in King's Cross that he planned to be the central hub of the business with the Satellite operations spoking out from there and it was a shocker. A lease had been signed but there were no funds to equip or staff the unit. It was just a drain on already stretched resources and its physical position could not have been worse in an area that was a magnet for people on the margins of society.

It did not take me long to ascertain that the situation was hopeless. They were running at a loss with no prospect of turning it around and had been for some time. My old friend Lloyds bank had its boot on their necks and it was purely matter of time. Neither of the partners had any cash resources so there was not even a chance of salvaging something from the wreckage. It had been a long time since I had seen anything as bad as this.

I went with them to the bank where two miserable gits sat in judgement, reminded the lads that their guarantee was joint and separate and the legal team would be coming for them. The case went to the Official Receiver who called me to produce a final statement of affairs. I explained that the guys had no cash to pay for my time to date let alone additional work and she promised me payment from the debts she would be collecting. I worked over Christmas and submitted a nominal charge that she reneged on. Civil servants, don't you love 'em?

Dennis approached the bank and offered to re-mortgage his house for £40k to settle his half, they agreed and he had managed to get a job that at his age was a miracle. He contacted me some eight years later and said that Lloyds had changed their minds and were coming after him for Absalom's half. From my experience dirty dogs are everywhere but are particularly prevalent in Lloyds Bank.

An unusual aspect of Satellite was that they only utilised one supplier for their materials, Howson-Algraphy. When the plug was pulled the debt was in excess of £130k so it was no surprise when Dennis phoned me in the New Year with some bad news.

'I have been summoned to their head office in Leeds to explain the situation. Derek won't go and I know it's a lot to ask but can you give me some support?'

Normally, I think I would have politely refused but I knew that if I attended I had an ace card to play. In any event my role in all of this was brutally short but not very sweet.

We went up to Leeds together and took a taxi to the factory complex. I asked the taxi to wait as I had a hunch that we wouldn't be long and would benefit from a fast getaway. The receptionist took us to a door that opened up onto a very large room with the biggest table I have ever seen. King Arthur would have needed another dozen or so knights to fill it up.

It was a circular affair with fifteen dour looking geezers seated around one quadrant while the opposite quadrant sported two chairs for us. The guy at the centre who was obviously the chief honcho gestured us to sit. He then kicked off proceedings by introducing himself as the Chief Financial Officer of the Vickers Group of which Howson-Algraphy was a part.

If this was designed to impress then it certainly did. Vickers was massive, incorporating shipbuilding, engineering, weapons and military equipment, defence systems and even at one point Rolls Royce with in the region of fifty subsidiaries. If this guy was CFO of the Vickers Group then we were up against a tough opponent and words needed to be selected carefully.

He introduced his fourteen-man team as lawyers, accountants and credit people and left it at that.

Looking at Dennis he said: 'I assume you are Dennis Bickle.'

Dennis confirmed.

He switched his eyes to me.

'And I assume that you are the firm's accountant.'

I quickly put him straight, explaining that I was a practising Chartered Accountant and a short while ago had been approached for advice on the company's finances.

Looking back at Dennis, he addressed him in a quiet voice that was very effective. In a nutshell they were not going to stand for a loss of this magnitude and they knew that the business must have traded whilst insolvent which would make the directors liable to the full. They were determined to come after Bickle and Absalom for the debt through the highest court in the land.

As he finished I glanced at the filthy fourteen, their smug, self satisfied faces happy to watch their big boss kick the southern arses sitting in front of them. This was a good day to be working for Vickers.

It was my turn. Let's change the mood.

'Excuse me Sir but may I speak for just two minutes. I may be able to shine some light on the background of all this.'

'Frankly I don't consider that any light needs to be shone as the matter is cut and dried. But if you have something useful to contribute go ahead.'

'The gentleman on your left has a sheaf of papers in front of him. I assume that they are the record of the account. Would you please take these up.'

Chief honcho did as I asked but I could see his patience was at its limit. Hell, this bloke walked the big halls of industry and dealt with top industrialists and ministers on a daily basis, not grubby jobbing printers.

'Please look back to October two years ago. You see a payment of three grand which brought the balance down to just over a thousand?'

'Yes, yes, I see that.'

'Would you please follow the account from that date to the end.' I paused. 'You will see that the three thousand over two years ago was the last payment ever made and on the other side you will also see invoices for weekly and sometimes twice weekly deliveries. Surely it wasn't beyond the wit of man to arrange for the driver to pick up a cheque for something at the time of delivery. I am not trying to shift the responsibility.'

I stopped talking. I had a lot more to say about credit controllers sleeping at the wheel and so on but it wasn't necessary. The main man was keeping a poker face but was well aware that a large and smelly can of worms had been tipped into his lap. Was what he had just heard an example of the performance of the accounting people here and what losses were building up without any control? Smug and self-satisfaction had left the room and a couple of blokes at the far end of the line had a halo of unemployment hanging over them.

In any event, if they had taken Bickle and Absalom to court I think a Judge would have given them short shrift and say that they were large contributors to the losses due to a total lack of basic credit control.

The Man sat back in his chair.

'Gentlemen. I expect you can see that I have some internal matters that need my urgent attention. I want to thank you for coming and wish you a safe journey back to London. Thank you.'

I rose and started hauling Dennis out of his chair.

'What happened?' he asked.

'Time to go mate, and now.'

As we headed for the door, to my horror Bickle turned and called out: 'We were always loyal to you'.

I hustled him through reception and into the waiting taxi.

'What happened in there?'

'It doesn't matter, you won't hear any more. It's finished.'

For us, yes, but not for the geezers we left in that room.

We will never know the ramifications of what happened after our visit. Nobody, big or small, likes being made to look a chump and left hanging in the breeze. Someone in that room must have known the history but had kept silent hoping that the truth would never come out. Vickers sold Howson-Algraphy to Du Pont in 1989.

Dennis treated me to lunch on the train and that was the sum total of my 'earnings' from the Satellite Group. That meeting is etched in my mind. I never was a card player but I knew that I had an unbeatable hand before I sat down; it's a good feeling.

A year after my departure from TP, I was in a far better place. I lived in chaos but it was a means to an end. One day the house would be finished and worth a great deal more than I'd paid for it. My practice was growing underpinned by the fees from Upward and Short and DMSB and new clients were finding their way to my door. My social life was getting better by the day and I had a nice car to tool around in.

On the down side the flat roof in my office leaked and the landlord wouldn't move on it. With a couple of associates I had bought a wharf in Rochester and had taken a share in a greyhound. Other projects floated past and as my relationship with the bank was never better, I could take a serious look at everything.

One morning Jeffery told me that I was to be replaced with a full time bookkeeper who was starting Monday, no warning or discussion. I guessed that they could get someone full time for little more than they paid me. Michael was raving on about her huge breasts and no doubt his imagination was rushing ahead of reality. I went in to say hello, show her the ropes and offer my help.

'I won't be needing any help, thank you. I am fully qualified.'

So that me put in my place. For the record, her boobs were a normal size but she was petite; it was simply a question of scale. A month later I got the call. The new bookkeeper had failed to come in, the books were in a mess and could I help.

'In a mess' was the understatement of the year. The first job was to get the cheques out to the National Publishers Association (NPA) and I set to work. Being at the month end these payments should have been on their journey to comply with our recognition agreement but we were a long, long way from that. I put everything else on hold and worked late into the evening to bring about some semblance of order. By this stage the firm had moved from its basement offices to a very smart first floor unit in St Martin's Lane and that evening I was grateful that we had a pizza place right next door.

The next morning I checked in at 6am and a pile of cheques were ready for signature by ten. The important ones went out by courier and another couple of heavy days got the situation under control and up to date.

Jeffery received a call from the Daily Telegraph and told that we were to attend a meeting the next day. This was ominous. We were received by the company secretary and the chief financial officer, two most unprepossessing geezers. They sat in their tired shiny suits with self-satisfied grins and refused to shake our extended hands. Once seated, the secretary told us what we already knew – that we were late with part of the payment for the month's account.

Jeffery explained what had occurred but he was wasting his energy. These two bastards were having the time of their lives, letting Jeff finish his explanation and apology. I think we both knew what was coming.

'We have already reported you to the NPA with the request that you be stripped of your recognition. We had no choice, it's the rules.'

'Of course you had a choice, don't hide behind the rules. We won't get anywhere with these two Jeff, let's go.'

I could see that Jeffrey wanted to renew his pleas but also realised that any words would fall on stony ground. We rose and walked out without a backwards glance.'

To be blunt, we were screwed.

Christine Upward told me much later that she had seen the 'fully qualified' referring to a book in her desk drawer called Bookkeeping for Dummies or something similar. The moral of the tale is don't hire someone just because she has big boobs.

Only a week after these events The Evening Standard ran a piece claiming that the Telegraph's accounts department was in a mess and that they couldn't produce management accounts on a regular basis. Sounds like the cobbler and his shoes.

It wasn't the disaster that it might have been as Jeffery was well liked and respected around the industry. For most of the NPA members it was a case of turning a blind eye after a few calls, a little refreshment and some pressing of the flesh. A couple insisted on payment with order but allowing discount. But one publication did play hardball, demanding payment in full with no discount. We circumnavigated by getting another media shop to place the ads with a split commission. No prizes for guessing who was the difficult one.

We took on a bookkeeper in the shape of a Welsh woman named Rachel and she was the real deal. The new arrangement was that I would come in for an hour a day and look after the monthly accounts while she would be full time keeping the records and this worked out just fine. It goes without saying that our media cheque run got top priority and after six months we applied for reinstatement.

Summoned up to Fleet Street, we were ushered into a room with four long tables forming a square. The leader of the committee was a good friend of Jeffery and he was on our side but the acoustics of the space were terrible. It was truly difficult to understand what was being said and I struggled to answer questions I could barely hear but was able to lay out our stall with the improvements made to our systems. We passed the test. In the pub afterwards I told Jeff that there was no money that would get me to go through that experience again.

A month or two after this Jeff informed me that they had chosen an auditor and the audit was to start the next day at ten. Why they never consulted me in these matters is a mystery but they never did and were to pay a heavy price further down the pike.

At 10am the following day an orthodox Jewish gent arrived with an Indian in tow and I naturally walked over to introduce myself with hand outstretched which he ignored.

'Are you a director of the company?'

'No, I'm a freelance accountant.'

'I only talk to directors.'

'Well, I wish you luck with that.'

'What do you mean?'

'You'll see.'

What he didn't know was that the boys had gone out for a stiffener and were to my certain knowledge in the pub around the corner, probably on their second Oranjeboom and well on the way to a third. Whether they would go straight to lunch having forgotten the visit of Finchley's finest or stagger back in a very jovial mood was anyone's guess. I greeted Mr Patel who at least shook my hand and we sat at the board table.

'What does the company do?'

I was appalled – to arrive at a new client's office without having done the most basic research was unprofessional to the core.

'It buys and sells media.'

'What's media?'

My reaction was automatic.

'You're an idiot!'

I walked over to Rachel.

'Can you please deal with this, I just don't have the patience.'

Good girl, she handled it well and the audit, for what it was worth, went off without a hitch. The man who only spoke with the honchos outshone himself at Christmas by inviting our two directors out to lunch. He took them to Claridge's and pushed the boat out big time. They were especially impressed by the fine wines and the big cash tip that he threw down on the table. The next morning I opened the post to discover his invoice for the lunch, the tip, the taxis and the time from leaving his office to the return.

The expression 'there's no such thing as a free lunch' must have been his family's motto. Over at DMSB a new client had asked for help with a mailing to advertise their product – a garden umbrella. Not any old garden umbrella but the mother and father of all garden umbrellas that retailed at one grand each, yes one thousand pounds! This at a time when a Fiat Panda was under three grand and a Mazda 323 started at four thousand.

I never found out who handled the mailing lists but it was a dog's breakfast. In a large part the mailing was sent to residents of public housing at Toxteth in Liverpool and St Pauls in Bristol. In 1980/81 both were engulfed by riots and among the worst areas of deprivation in the country. Most people didn't even have a balcony let alone a garden. In addition the roll of addressees contained the names of many people who had died or were close to doing so. The net results were zero sales and a very hostile response. Not the finest hour.

Over the years I had tried many of the European resorts for

holidays such as Spain, Portugal, Italy and Greece. But I'd often returned to Tenerife; with its perfect climate and gentle pace of life, the island was ideal. However, in 1977 two events took place which changed all that forever.

The airport, Tenerife North, was the site of the world's worst air accident. Unsighted in the dense mist that shrouded the island a KLM flight collided with a Pan Am one resulting in a massive loss of life. The authorities decided to build Tenerife South on the totally unspoiled Silent Coast paving the way for massive development.

This headline event coincided with a visit by Mr John Palmer famous for his part in the Brink's-Mat robbery. He realised the potential of timeshare where a property is sold in slices of weekly occupation thus achieving a much higher sale price than if it were sold as a single unit to one buyer.

In due course the island changed and in my opinion, for the worse. Mr Palmer operated his timeshare empire with extreme prejudice and many holidaymakers were pushed into buying into it whether they were willing or otherwise. The sales touts were highly visible on the streets offering cash incentives to attend information meetings and people found it was hard to escape without signing up.

Lanzarote was a beautiful alternative but a very small island. I tried Madeira, loved it and started to make many return visits. Later in life the island would provide an epically hard journey for me that would last some years.

Of course, now being self-employed any holiday was a luxury as while you were away you were spending but not earning. But everybody needs a break.

By the way, Mr Palmer came to a violent end, shot five times with a .32 calibre pistol by Spanish gangsters it's believed. The police reported that he had died from natural causes. Maybe there is irony there. Maybe in Mr Palmer's circles to be shot five times was a natural event.

Because of our backgrounds the client base for Max and I was the advertising world while Peter Davies was strong in the building trade.

An exception to this was Sylvan Estate Management. The original Sylvan Estate in Crystal Palace was a Housing Association but residents realised that turning it into owner-occupiers would bring windfall profits across the board and any dissenters were swept aside. The legal work had been undertaken by Michael Rowe who had an office in Holborn.

A management committee had been set up. At its head was Jeremy who rated himself a tick above the hoi polloi; his apartment hosted the portraits of all of the Kings and Queens of England and other royal regalia. Being a staunch republican, I offered no comment.

The secretary was Norman who was a printer and naturally a member of the NGA. He lived 24/7 in the same track suit and trainers and was obnoxious in the extreme.

I spotted a recognizable face on the estate on my first day: Charlie Kray who I knew from my East London days. I had never met his younger brothers, the twins Reggie and Ronnie that, on reflection, was to the good. He was sharing his life with Diana Buffini and had changed his name to hers as although the Kray moniker carried great clout it could I guess be a hindrance in everyday life.

I knew the Richardsons from my time in Peckham and New Cross and had come across Frank Fraser from time to time. Another lad I had made the acquaintance of was John Bindon, who was a tough guy who happened to have an Equity card and made a good living acting. He was always cast as a heavy and said to be a natural.

One evening John was at the bar in the Coach and Horses in Soho. As with all of these guys, it paid to be careful and John was known to pick a fight just to demonstrate how hard he was. On this occasion he was in a happy frame of mind and had spotted the busty barmaid approaching, wiping down the bar, lifting any obstacles such as glasses or ashtrays, replacing them as she moved on.

John didn't hesitate. Hoisting his large frame up, he unzipped and placed his three-piece suite on the bar and watched the woman approach. She didn't even blink. She picked up his manhood, gave the counter a wipe and placed it back down when she finished. It brought a large round of applause.

Anyway, back to the Sylvan audit. The vast majority paid the service charge by direct debit, just a handful settling by cheque or cash but I was soon to discover that Jeremy, for all his airs had not paid a red cent. I took this up with him and he explained that he expected the other residents would vote him a stipend for his efforts and that would cancel the debt. But there was no evidence that anyone, other than himself, had any notion to vote him anything. Michael came down, read him the riot act and he had to clear the arrears before I could sign off the accounts.

An invitation to the Mantons for dinner was not perhaps the thrill it should have been. Firstly there were the dogs. In a normal house with normal people and normal dogs, the latter will greet you at the door and after a pat on the head and a word of greeting they would wander off. At Chez Manton the two animals in residence were Vizslas, a large Hungarian breed and their hello was to shove their big noses in the visitor's crutch. Maybe they had been specially trained to do this but I wouldn't under any circumstances tolerate eighty kilos of mutts sniffing out my private parts. I shoved them away which Michael and Peggie thought was hilarious. Secondly, while I was there Michael didn't say much and I got the impression that I wasn't worth his effort. He would just sit there staring at you with eyeballs resembling two piss-holes in the snow.

At one such event they informed me that they were planning to take more holidays on their yacht. This was to be moved to Turkey via the French canals and then they would regularly fly out to enjoy messing about in boats in a warm and cheap environment. Where did I come in? Would I visit the house from time to time to check the post and bank any cheques? The dogs of course would not be there. I willingly agreed thus lumbering myself with a thankless and unpaid chore several times a year. I couldn't think for the life of me why they didn't ask one of their children.

A few months after this kicked off, the Mantons were away and I received a midnight call from Peggie's son saying he had crashed Michael's Mercedes. There was nothing I could do about it and frankly I was unimpressed that my name had been given out as the go-to when problems arose. In my book if you're old enough to drive you are old enough to sort out your own crap.

The end of our lease was closing fast. In reality we knew that the landlord would not renew. The flat roof had leaked for a good two years and no letter or telephone call of complaint produced any response, so on rainy days we had to deal with clients whilst the water ingress was caught in an array of buckets.

Our landlords had opened a public display of the proposed

redevelopment of the whole of the Mercer Street/Langley Street block into a monolithic office/retail/apartment complex and our small unit was swallowed up. The writing was on the wall. So the search for new offices was under way.

Max found a spot just off Fleet Street but the larger part was a basement and the lighting was rubbish. Peter took us to view a three floor office space with no plumbing, so no toilet or wash up facilities and 1,200 square feet to boot. We only needed 400 – no wonder he went bust.

Finally Max's client Bob Price who ran a design studio in Holborn needed to cut costs. We took over the first floor at Tudor House, Princeton Street, leaving Bob with the upper two floors. We had a large front office and a small meeting room at the back which was ideal but the toilet and tea making areas were on the top floor. As the move was left to me to organise, I asked Charlie to round up a few guys for the Saturday and we got it done. No one was happy on the Monday morning but stuff the lot of them. No effort equals no reward.

Work at the house continued, sometimes at a glacial pace. Our carpenter Emil had decided to move his family in a camper van to the south of France to enjoy a slower paced and cheaper way of life notwithstanding they couldn't speak or understand a single word of French; bon chance avec ça.

His replacement Pat produced an amazing standard of work and his high hourly rate was worth every penny. He built all new windows, a beautiful staircase and went on to replace all of the doors. Finally because I couldn't source a suitable kitchen, Pat hand built one in situ.

Towards the end of 1985, tragedy hit. Peggie rang me at 9am to tell me that Manton's daughter Jenny had been found dead. When she couldn't be contacted, they called the police who had made a forced entry to find her dead in an armchair. Not knowing the cause the rozzers realised this could be anywhere between natural causes and homicide. Accordingly they investigated thoroughly that resulted in the apartment being seriously upturned and, not surprisingly, the Mantons were struggling to cope.

Telling her that help was on its way, I grabbed a wad of cash big enough to choke a horse from my emergency fund. I asked Charlie,

Pat and an electrician named Derek to take a taxi to north London and help in any way they could. The next day they told me that they had really pitched in and dealt with the smashed front door, the general mess and the disposal of furniture. The wad was gone.

Apparently her death was due to a drug overdose. I never received a word of thanks nor any offer to repay, which at the time didn't bother me. But with a dollop of hindsight I did wonder why I was called in the first place. To be honest I had met Jenny a couple of years back but very briefly and only to say hello. And why call an accountant? Now I realise that they had my measure, were certain that I would rise to any occasion and could be easily exploited.

Nevertheless it was a bloody shame. Jenny was a very talented writer who had worked for Brian Davis at Creative Review until 1984. I don't know what she was working on at the time of her death.

The memorial service was at St Brides Church off Fleet Street and the place was packed. The vicar had obviously never met her but babbled on about a girl bringing home birds with broken wings which was too much puff for even the hard-nosed advertising types that made up the gathering. I think she was only 27 or thereabouts.

Over at Upward & Short Media, Michael's search for a female was reaching new heights of craziness. He was so desperate that I wondered why he didn't simply resort to a knocking shop. After all the cash he spent getting nowhere, that would at least get him somewhere.

At a party thrown for clients and suppliers, Michael roamed the room stroking with grubby hand any exposed female flesh that came within reach. Some of his adventures were becoming urban legend, such as the evening where he had spent much time and money chatting up a couple of Scandinavian girls.

Insisting that he escort them back to their hotel he called a taxi and the threesome sped off into the night. Sitting between two young blonde beauties, Michael lost track of time and space, added to which he hadn't noticed the address given to the driver. When the taxi finally pulled up, the ladies shot out of each side, slammed the doors and melted into the night, leaving Michael alone and bewildered.

'Where to now guv?' asked the driver.

'Where are we?' asked Michael.

'Brighton,' replied the driver.

'Woodford, please.'

The driver obliged. In the early hours of the morning mum and dad had to be awakened to settle the humongous taxi fare. How much longer could it be tolerated?

Michael's home life didn't help. His mother ruled the roost with an iron fist and in order to give his elderly father a break, Michael employed him as the voucher clerk which was a completely non-existent position.

Mr Short was delighted and turned up each morning with all the daily newspapers, took up a large chunk of space and produced nothing. This went on for a few weeks until Jeffrey, weighed down with staff complaints, fired him.

Soon after Jeff asked if we could have a meeting on Saturday morning at the office and when I saw Michael coming down St Martin's Lane, I guessed that this was to be the final showdown and I was right. When he arrived, Jeff laid into Michael and sacked him. It puzzled me at the time as Michael was a 50% shareholder in the company and could have put up a fight but he didn't and was gone.

Shortly afterwards Mrs Short died. Once the family home had been sold, father and son moved to Northern France, rented a small cottage and adopted the life of the lotus-eater. A sad business to be sure. A brilliant man but conflicted beyond measure.

Tony Brown moved from Young & Rubicam to replace Michael and in due course the name changed to Upward Brown Media. No tasking the imagination there. Rachel resigned to return to Wales to run a wine bar in a university town, so I had to rack up my hours to fill the gap.

Then the lease ran out and the ad agency which held the head lease wouldn't renew. Jeff found us a top floor in Charlotte Street. At least he thought he had but there had been a misunderstanding with the agency who occupied the building. They had gained a clear impression that we had merged with them and were to be absorbed. It beggars belief how it happened but the bottom line was that we were on the move again.

Because pressure was being applied, we found ourselves in a full service temporary office nearby where conditions were unworkable.

Desks were crammed together so tightly it resembled a storeroom and I was surprised that the staffers put up with it all. To add to the madness, Jeffery and Tony had recruited Rachel's replacement. What had greatly impressed them at the interview was that during a transport strike he had walked seven miles to work and back again. That didn't score any brownie points with me but I wasn't asked.

Two weeks after he started, after I had been presented with a thank you party and gift, and having been told that this worthy didn't need my supervision, I got the call. George had gone, never to be seen again. Could I help?

This time I pulled Richard in and we worked over the weekend to get everything up to date. What we soon discovered was that our hero had drawn £200 in petty cash every day and pocketed a total of two thousand quid. Not bad for a plonker. Jeff called him and he denied it but the evidence was irrefutable.

We got everything straight, the guys found another accountant, moved to excellent offices in King William Street and almost lived happily ever after.

That was the end of my business association with the media shop although I remained friends with Jeffery and Christine. I was content that I had assisted them in their formative years and help bring them to a point where they were well established and successful.

All was going so well that in 2001 they were approached by WPP with a buy-out proposition and there were millions on the table. I met Jeffery and he was so excited at all the people and good causes he would be able to help, such was his nature. But a problem arose at WPP who asked if the deal could be put on ice for twelve months, but not cancelled.

Unfortunately Jeffery and Tony had smelled money. In addition to the auditor they had a financial adviser who took on the task of finding them an alternative buyer and introduced two guys who seemed to have neither a trade nor a track record. They were asset strippers.

Upward Brown Media's only asset was cash: they had no property, pension fund or physical assets other than a few worthless sticks of furniture.

Christine and I pleaded with the guys to wait for WPP and to kick these two geezers into touch. But we were ignored and the gangsters moved in. They arranged for Jeffery and Tony to receive a large cash payment which provided temporary emollience but of course it was their own money.

For a year they ran the finances until they reached the point where they could empty the bank account, change the locks and disappear, leaving the business in ruins and creditors hung out to dry. It was a crime. The financial adviser was just a flimflam man who took no responsibility for the debacle and offered neither help nor recompense.

I talked to Jeffery about taking action against the culprits by unorthodox methods but he walked away. He was a good man, too good. If I'd been turned over like that I would have been after them with every fibre of my body to the grave. Both Jeff and Tony went to work for Total Media in 2004.

Back to my own business. All was motoring well but its success depended on Peter Davies being happy to do the running around and he was past retirement age. Who knew how long this status quo could continue, the great unknown. I did the working and he did the walking, and much of the travel to see small clients was in the evening. That was a task that I would never have undertaken. So I decided to try and find a buyer.

Like all things it is easier to buy than to sell. As practices go we were small potatoes and unlikely to attract the major players. I think the strangest approach was a Hasidic Jew who apart from Good Afternoon and Goodbye said not a word during our ten minute meeting.

Then finally Alan Brison arrived. As he was actually older than me, I did think his interest a little odd but he'd worked overseas for much of his life and had nurtured the idea of a small practice in London for many years so here he was. He carried out due diligence, met with Peter Davies and Max Thorne and we agreed a price and monies to be paid half now and half in a year's time. The lawyers did the rest.

I did offer Alan all the time and help he might need but he wanted to find his own way and that was fine. I did drop into the office once or twice a week to show support but all appeared to be sailing along without me. He brought in a new secretary and she made it clear that she resented my presence. I have to say that she didn't set out to impress. She habitually discarded her shoes on arrival and spent the day with her big sweaty feet exposed to the world. It wasn't a good look for a professional office but then it wasn't my concern.

My business was to be run from my home and that was nearing completion. The roof had been replaced with a flat area accessed by a spiral staircase to provide an outside space. The garages had been improved with new concrete floors and electric operated doors and there was no shortage of demand for reasonably priced parking.

I'd acquired a mobile phone so no secretary was needed and any typing was done by me or dropped off at a first-rate secretarial agency. I really was on my own and it suited me just fine. If I went on holiday I could organise Max or Richard to cover for me as I would do for them.

Tina was still my regular lady for weekends and I had a number of female friends for dinner, theatre or any other social events in the evening. It was an ideal bachelor life and would be perfect when I could say a final fond farewell to my restoration guys.

While all this was going on, I seem to have attracted a stalker although I didn't know it at the time. I have always liked to think I had street smarts, the school of hard knocks and all that stuff but like a sleepwalker, I stumbled into a world of aggravation when Alice, my machine operator from Napper Stinton Woolley phoned. I hadn't seen her since the Theatre Project days when she helped out as a casual when we were short of staff.

She told me that her second marriage had failed and she needed my advice. Well, she had helped me in days of yore, so it was only fair ... I arranged and paid for her to stay at the Royal Scot Hotel as I didn't want to have her staying in my home. Her tale ran that she had a son from her first attempt at wedlock called Jim who would then have been about 15; the second try produced a son Ned (7) and daughter Mary (6). She had reached an agreement with her husband that the house would be sold, that he would buy a flat and that she and the three children would acquire a small house. He would take the furniture.

For the life of me I couldn't see what advice she needed from me as everything seemed sorted and two lawyers were drawing up the paperwork. Support for the kids had been agreed, she had a couple of domestic cleaning jobs and on Saturdays worked at a department store, so there was an income of sorts to keep everything afloat.

A few days later I drove down to Kent to view the situation for myself and then phoned around to drum up some furniture. When the moves actually took place I rented a van and went around town picking up the offerings and took the lot down. I saw my role in all this as supporting an old friend, treat her and the kids to a meal from time to time or buy some kid's clothes. I didn't realise that Alice had a very different agenda.

One Sunday I went down to take Alice and the two younger kids for a drive and lunch. When I'd parked, we noticed five pound notes flying around and gathered up about two hundred quid. There was not a soul in sight so the source remains a mystery. Later Alice quietly said that she'd like us to get together which was an electric shock wakeup call. Time to run screaming from the room! There was more chance of a one-legged man winning an arse-kicking contest.

I'd tried marriage before and found it to be the most ball-breaking experience of my life. Consequently, I had absolutely no intention of shacking up with anybody, never, ever again. Friends I could handle but that's it.

Anyway, I'd found out ages ago I really couldn't understand children. Initially I tried treating them as small adults but when that failed I thought that maybe one should train them like dogs but that didn't work either. What I really couldn't understand was their selfish ways and habits. Was it just the kids I met or are all kids innately selfish? For example, seeing Ned take off his coat when hot and just pass it to his mother to carry drove me up the wall. I wasn't like that but that was at a different time in a different world. I worried about children wrapped up in cotton wool, throwing tantrums until they got their way. There was no way that this lot was coming to my door and I was just a visitor.

Feeling that my life had enough craziness in it, I decided to make a tactical withdrawal and cool the situation down. We spoke on the phone from time to time and Alice would talk with Charlie who she'd known from the TP days.

I had a dental implant fitted and it got infected, so it was necessary to go to the Harley Street Clinic to get it removed. I chose a Friday morning to get it done and by 11am I was back on the street heading home. On arrival I was horrified to find Alice there chatting with Charlie. She'd brought a flask of soup for my lunch. What the hell was going on? I quickly worked out that the two of them must have had a chat and that Charlie had let slip that I needed a minor operation. Naturally, Florence Nightingale had rushed to be by my side.

Tina was coming for the weekend and the last thing I needed was Alice in residence. To quote Roger Vadim, I knew the difference between a diamond and a bottle top and here I had the bottle top. At 4pm I eased her out of the front door only to see her approaching the house again at 5pm. When I reached the door Tina was there as well.

Rather than a heated discussion on the street, I let them both in only to find Alice had found a whiskey bottle and was doing her hardest to empty it down her throat. I got both of them out into the street, into a taxi and off to the main line station where Tina and I frog marched Alice to her train and watched as it departed. Tina was a great girl and laughed it all off; we had known each other for a very long time.

Contact with Alice fizzled out. She found a new man and did call to ask for the £3,000 back that she'd left in my safekeeping. Her new man was sure I would steal the money. I returned it immediately and her new man stole it. Another guy arrived and left and after few years she found what she wanted, another husband.

I can't imagine what the children thought of it all this – different blokes wandering in and out of the house at all hours. But kids are resilient and, as strange as it may seem, they may have come to the conclusion that this was normal.

When Jim left school there was no work to be secured locally and as he had a creative streak I had talked to Max about possibly finding him a slot with one of his clients, a retouching house in the advertising industry. Gone were the days of tiny brushes and pots of paint, now they used highly expensive equipment to remedy problems on both still photographs and film. They stood tall, offered a training position with a proper wage and paid for Jim's season ticket. It was an amazing opportunity to learn a trade in a highly paid field. Later on I heard he had simply stopped going to work without a word of explanation. He produced two kids with two different girls, taking not one iota of responsibility for either of them. Some people are just born to be bums.

The last major job on the house was to update the garaging. We put up a complete false ceiling over a weekend by bringing in a small crew and having all the materials pre-cut to size. New lighting went up as we moved from wall to wall. Concreting the walls and floor proved to be more of a drama. Charlie tracked down a Rastafarian who quoted a solid price for the complete job but we would have to expel our parking clients for a few days and give them a suitable refund. What we didn't know was that our man and his assistant chain-smoked marijuana and the property stank of the stuff for weeks.

The guy owned a basement flat off Portobello Road and was so crazy that he had excavated under the main road, supporting it with various pipes. Then he went and installed a hot pool that he fitted out in a Roman style. As you lay in the tub, the sound of heavy traffic rumbled over your head. That might have spoiled the romantic ambience.

The guys worked at a great pace and although the final job was acceptable, it was a couple of weeks from hell. The deal was half up front and the balance at the finish but I returned home every night to find the guy in ambush demanding cash. You can't reason with a bloke on weed every waking hour but I quickly learned that giving him just a few quid would get rid of him. During that period odd stuff went missing like a leather jacket, a watch, tools and the assistant was free with my telephone. But the job got done and I was relieved to be shot of them.

Meanwhile, some unsettling events were taking place at DMSB. It could never fail with the Royal Mail annual commitment being around half a million pound per year but some management decisions just didn't make sense. Richard and I stayed right out of office politics and simply rendered a service, so we were often late in hearing any news.

The Bureau was booked to make an appearance at a direct marketing expo in Switzerland and had built a small display to erect there. Personally I would have hired a rigging outfit to transport, erect, maintain, break down and return and the staffers fly over. I couldn't believe it when I heard that a Renault people carrier had been hired, all the seating apart from the front row removed, the materials piled in and staffers were putting it together on site and then reversing the whole process. Why? It couldn't have been to save money, we had the resources to do everything to a gold standard.

Then came the book. Jo had led an effort to produce a guide to direct marketing and the final result was published in a two-volume set. It was decided that Frank would attend a marketing fair in the US with the intention to sell as many copies as possible and off he went. When he returned he dumped a Tesco carrier bag on my desk.

'There are the orders for the book. Can you get them invoiced out.'

I tipped the bag's contents onto the desk to find a mixture of business cards and order sheets. My first thought was that it all looked unprepossessing but in fairness, the working conditions could not have been ideal. I punched out a schedule for invoicing and off they went in the post. At the end of the month I sent out reminders but after several weeks without a single payment, it didn't take a genius to work out that something was very wrong. Allowing for the time difference, I telephoned every number that I had but none of them worked. Every fibre of my body told me that I was on a fool's errand.

Before sharing my concerns I took myself over to City Library where they held telephone and trade directories for the US and many other countries. I spent a whole day there searching for the names and addresses of the businesses and individuals that I had been given. I found nothing, not a single lead. What the hell was going on?

Of course there was no financial loss here as no books had been sent out, nor would be without payment. In any event, the total sum was of no significance in the Bureau's income. The cost of the trip to the States had been absorbed in routine expenses. But it was a total mystery to me how fifty pieces of paper turned out to be meaningless, each and every one. Was it some mad hoax? And with what motive?

As McGinty was away, I caught up with Manton the next time he was around and explained my problem in one sentence. As per normal, I got the cold deadeye stare and the distinct feeling that neither I nor my news were welcome.

'Write it off and forget it.'

'I can't just cancel fifty sales ...'

He cut me off.

'Take them off the books and say no more about it.'

'Shall I talk to Frank when he gets back to try and solve the puzzle.'

'No. Don't discuss it with anyone. Just let it go.'

I could see that I'd pushed it as far as I could and if I continued Manton would lose his rag. I folded my tent and left. It was all very unsettling; somebody knew what was going on but they weren't telling. The day to day work continued, mainly with the Royal Mail and new contracts came in on a regular basis, some for two or three years of research in a specific area. But to quote Marcellus, something was rotten in the state of Denmark.

There seemed to be a real lack of leadership and planning. It truly felt like a government department with work flowing through being dealt with the staffers while the Mandarins wandered about searching for purpose and direction. The Bureau was what it was designed for but as there seemed no scope to move outside the original remit, the scope for innovation was severely limited.

The time had come for the second and final instalment in payment for the sale of the practice. I had kept in touch by popping in from time to time but Alan was usually out and his secretary made me feel as welcome as a turd in a swimming pool. In fairness he had not contacted me once for advice or information and seemed to have everything under full control. I telephoned and he suggested we meet on Saturday morning at nine to finalise the deal. While having lunch with Max on the Friday, I mentioned the planned meeting.

'I don't think Alan is happy with the practice.'

'Really, that's news to me. What's the problem?'

'There are a lot of very small clients and it's often difficult to extract an economic fee. I think but that's just my feeling.'

I festered for a couple of hours and finally decided that if there was a real problem I would simply offer Alan his money back and take the business over. All well and good but where would the cash come from? Finishing the house was a drain and a couple of new projects were hoovering up resources at a scary rate. I phoned the bank and explained the position.

'Look Peter, it's late Friday afternoon so there's nothing we can draw up today. You've been a client for a long time and never given us a moment's concern. If you need to, simply write a cheque for what's required and we can sort out any formalities next week. We will back your decision 100% and honour the cheque without question.'

What a magic moment – just like the Count of Monte Cristo – unlimited credit. So I approached the meeting ready for a fight followed by a grand gesture, all completely unnecessarily. Max had totally got the wrong gist of the situation.

I went through the client list, knocking out a couple of problem cases and adjusting a fee here and there. Alan concurred, wrote out a cheque according to the formula agreed and we were done. He was a gentleman of the old school. No problems were mentioned and we were finished in less than fifteen minutes

Even with these monies things were tight and I was reluctant to borrow more from the bank even though their door was open. I decided to sell the Aston Martin.

It was running well but a couple of incidents had reminded me that it could be a deep money pit. The first was when it needed an oil change. In the spirit of keeping a reasonable level of normality between me and the guys working at the house and the bunch of nutters running the garage opposite, I asked them to carry out an oil change. The first difficulty was that they didn't understand the fly-off handbrake, the second was they were incompetent.

When I went to take the car out I noticed a small oil stain on the garage floor and on getting down with a torch the reason was obvious. They had over tightened the sump plug which had resulted in the alloy sump splitting corner to corner and droplets of oil escaping. So it was down to John Somers for a brand new sump that together with fitting, hit me with a bill for £1,250. Plus all the time and expense of taking and collecting.

The second event was on the M2 when I pulled out into the third lane only to discover a large lump of metal on the road directly ahead. With a car on the inside and the barrier on the outside there was no option in that split second other than to try and drive over it between the wheel and the engine. That worked except it ripped off the exhaust which bounced off the road, damaging the floor pan. Back to John sounding like a Lancaster bomber and a bill of £1,500.

Putting a quality car up for sale attracts not only the dreamers but the crazies as well. The first call was a very posh voice enquiring as to the mileage.

'78,000 miles.'

'Oh, that is far too much.'

'The car is ten years old and priced accordingly.'

'I want something under 10,000 miles.'

'Impossible.'

'I'm looking for a bargain.'

'Ain't we all.'

The second call, another toff.

'Does the upholstery have contrasting stitching?'

'No.'

'Oh, I'm not interested then.'

The third caller had a lovely Scottish brogue.

'I am phoning from Aberdeen about the Aston. I know nothing about cars but my husband has asked me to call you.'

'Is he there?'

'Yes.'

'Well, can you put him on?'

'Oh no, I can't. He's reading his paper and I can't disturb him.'

I pictured this geezer sitting in his kilt and sporran with a morning malt in his fist, looking for other stupid errands for his wife to run. She sounded a great girl, so I gave her a few details and chatted generally for quite a long time. It broke up her morning and ran his telephone bill up to boot.

The next call was from a young man asking to see the car. He arrived about an hour later with wife and child in a Rover Vitesse. He told me that he was a mechanic and had worked on many Aston Martins and other high-end cars. According to him, his Vitesse was viewed as a poor man's Aston Martin. Who by?!

After a walk around the car I took the trio on a test drive and on the return journey he asked if he could take the wheel. I was reluctant but with his assurances that he was 'the man' we changed places. Once again the handbrake proved to be his downfall as he had no idea whatsoever on how to release the fly-off. I instructed him and we drove back in silence with all his claims exposed as a big fat lie. Once back, he shuffled off without a word, climbed into his poor man's Aston and departed. You have to deal with a lot of turkeys before you soar with the eagles.

I've saved the best to last. A few guys called for details and some asked for an address but the only one that showed arrived the next Saturday lunchtime. Smart suit and with uniformed son in tow, we looked over my vehicle and in due course set off to show how it drove. As this bloke seemed a real prospect I took the car up to the North Circular and let it rip. During the exercise he talked and talked about Astons, namedropping just about everybody who had been involved since 1914 and all the trivia about the marque that anyone could possibly know. He asked if we could take the car to show his wife and we ended up in a mews off Exhibition Road, Knightsbridge, pulling up outside a fantastic house. His wife was suitably impressed and off we went again on the M4 way past Heathrow and back.

I left them with the promise of a firm offer and as the jaunt had taken up over four hours and used a tank of fuel, I believed him. No call was received. Two weeks later I was engaged on the Saturday car washing routine, when who should I spy but my man with the great suit and schoolboy son heading my way.

'Afternoon, come to make an offer?'

'Oh no, my son and I were at a loss with what do this afternoon. So I thought we could come over and you could take us out in the Aston again. We so enjoyed the ride we had two weeks ago.'

'Look, I'm not going to swear in front of your boy but you've got more front than Woolworths. What do you think this is – Free Aston Experience Time – I'm trying to sell a car. Go away and don't come back.'

'You're a very rude man.'

'You don't know the half of it.'

They left but this was just an example of the entitlement most of the upper classes believe they have. We plebs are here on earth for them to use, their amusement and our time is of no value. When we bite back they are truly surprised and upset. Clearly the world, their world, is going to the dogs. Finally, I sold it to an amateur trader who was collecting in anticipation of a market boom.

A creative shop called Cousins Advertising asked me to take care of their finances and the partners Jon (creative) and Caroline (administration) were two of the most agreeable folk you could wish to meet. Based in Drury Lane over an upmarket laundry, I found myself in a small office on the top floor adjacent to the studio. It was a great place to work with a positive mojo from top to bottom and Caroline was a great organiser, so the paperwork that came my way was faultless. It only needed two or three hours a week and I made it my Friday morning job.

The end of 1989 would bring my fiftieth birthday. The house was finally finished and had turned out well, so I decided to throw a party for friends, clients and a few of the guys who had worked on the house. A friend of Marion's provided the catering and I got in a good stock of booze. I asked a couple of South London lads to man the door as some of the local goons were of criminal bent and I really didn't want gate crashers. About eighty people turned up and all went well.

When Manton left he said to me: 'I didn't expect a house like this'. What did he think, that I lived in a cave or something? It finished off the year with me on a high. Better, and worse, was to come.

I moved into 1990 with a solid client roll that provided a good living, with no staff worries as I had none. The garaging was in demand and with the Aston gone another space could be let out. There were a couple of projects on the go and my recent exchange with the bank assured me that I had their backing if needed.

On my travels I had bumped into a Japanese lady and one evening I received a call. We arranged to meet at my favourite Italian restaurant on Wardour Street on the Saturday evening. To my horror I awoke that same morning to discover that I had lost my voice but with no telephone number I had no choice but to front it out.

Haruyo arrived spot on time and a difficult evening got under way. I had taken some photographs of the house and she had brought some shots of her paintings so we muddled through. She called me the following week and I suggested a fine restaurant in Highgate for 7.30 on Saturday. When she hadn't shown by eight, I was thinking the worst but then she called to tell me she couldn't find the place. Eventually she arrived and all went as it should.

A few more dates followed and it was becoming fairly obvious that this could be a long term commitment. But that hadn't changed my attitude to going through a ceremony and signing worthless bits of paper. One experience of all that was enough for my lifetime.

Meanwhile, Chris Pearson had found me more work that frankly, I only half-heartedly took on board. Maslin Rees Fitton was a fairly new start up advertising agency and they had a couple of rooms in a converted warehouse in Lambeth. They had set up the business with £25k investment each and then promptly spent £25k each on a company car. Typical for the industry. They had an impressive client list and the accounts were computerized, so a couple of visits per week should suffice. Another new job was with Hardman Advertising in the Strand but when it moved to London Bridge I passed it over to Richard to run.

MRF was unusual in that all three partners had their wives working on the premises. Larry Rees allowed his wife Jenny King free space to run Can-Can, an events production company; David Maslin had his wife Lyn Middlehurst as joint creative director and Brian Fittton's spouse Sara had desk space to operate her motivation business.

For some unknown reason I shared a corner with David and Lyn and I'm sure that my keyboard noise was an irritant when they were seeking creative inspiration. The business was profitable largely due to a very low base overhead, paying a rental that covered all premises costs, so it surprised me when they announced a move to Chelsea Harbour. That was a very new upmarket development on the River Thames comprising shops, restaurants, offices and a hotel together with some very fancy apartments. The first week we were there a hotel guest couldn't pay his bill and killed himself by jumping out of a window.

It wasn't a good move, being without a car at the time, but I was persuaded.

Brian's role was somewhat ambiguous. On paper he was in charge of finance and media but in reality he left the numbers to me and there was very little media buying. As he had time on his hands, I would have thought that chasing new business would have been an obvious area to pick up. But at the end of the day, management was none of my business as I was just a service provider.

The transport problem was solved when Brian offered to sell me his Austin Metro, which proved to be an excellent little car. I found it suited me to drive over to be in the office by 7.30, check the mail when it arrived and be done and on my way by eleven. It was totally flexible and the only important factor was to make a daily appearance.

There was an underground car park that was reasonable. Wishing to save money, one girl made the mistake of parking outside the complex. On returning to her Ford Escort one fateful afternoon she found it up on bricks, all four wheels having been stolen. Her father turned out, recovered the car and new wheels were sourced. But she'd learned nothing and parked it outside the safe area again, from where it was stolen, new wheels and all.

By now, I had been a bachelor for a long time and there was little doubt that it suited me. I had time to myself when I wanted it, company on tap to dine, go to theatres or even on holiday with when I chose to. But there is something sad about an old bachelor, creeping about the town and trying to look like Jack the Lad when it hurt to even cough and spit. I saw an elderly guy regularly moving around Covent Garden who must have been eighty plus, whose Dowager's Hump was well disguised by some brilliant tailoring. He invariably had a high maintenance woman on the arm, more often two, and although I admired his spirit, it wasn't the greatest of looks.

Of course I had missed out on the normal family thing but that was just too bad. There is no point dwelling on which was the best path and in fact I have known plenty who have lived married and bachelor lives simultaneously, causing grief all over the place.

I had a dinner with Tina and explained what was in my mind. Our relationship had lasted longer than many marriages and although it was strange to many, the fact was that it had suited both of us. It had worked but we both knew that if we had tried to change it to a cohabiting setup, the wheels would have fallen off. She was totally accepting that I was moving into a new situation and took it in her stride.

1990 continued without drama until September when DMSB took on a couple of salesmen, Carl and Henry. The first I knew of their arrival was when I was introduced to them and Frank passed me their employment details for processing. I don't know whose idea it was, or how they were intending to sell and to whom but I kept out of politics and paid the matter little attention.

One Monday morning I had dropped into the Bureau at about eleven when my phone rang with a woman on the line.

'Am I speaking to the firm's accountant?'

'Yes you are.'

'Good, I am calling from Jaguar finance and I must have a cheque for eight thousand pounds immediately.'

'Are you having a laugh, why would I send you a cheque for anything? We haven't bought any Jaguars.'

'Yes you have. Two of your directors each bought a Jaguar on Saturday, signed leases and took the cars.'

'What are their names?'

When she told me I couldn't believe it.

'They are not directors and don't have the authority to sign anything. They're just a couple of salesmen and you let them drive off. I think you had better call the police and report two stolen cars.'

'You must send me the money.'

'Not a chance. Send me the paperwork and I'll take it up with the CEO.'

'I can't send you any paperwork. It's confidential.'

'Well, then you have a problem. A Mexican standoff if you like but it's your problem to solve. Can't help you lady, I've got to go.'

I hung up and a few moments later Manton marched past on his way the boardroom. I followed.

'It appears Carl and Henry have promoted themselves to directors and bought a Jaguar each on the company. I've had a woman on the phone demanding I pay for them.'

'Pay her.'

'What the hell is going on? They're just a couple of staffers and they have signed agreements as directors which is fraud.'

'Sort it out, it's under control.'

From where I stood it was very much out of control. I did nothing and a few days later I received copies of the agreements. Where Carl and Henry were with their new Jaguars, I knew not. Frank was also out of the office and nobody would talk to me about what was going on. Even Jo wouldn't have a social drink with me. Everyone was buttoned up.

A message arrived from Manton that Frank had resigned, was to be paid up to date plus a year's salary tax free plus the company BMW. Generosity knew no bounds. Out of courtesy I dropped a line to Frank to tell him the car insurance ran out at the end of the year and the policy would not be renewed.

In due course Manton instructed me to pay Carl and Henry their wages up to date, plus three months tax free in lieu of notice. I made damn sure that all the paperwork was signed by him as I could see a real need for bulletproof arse covering.

I met with my friends in the south and made arrangements for the Jaguars to be repossessed by force if necessary. Manton wouldn't have a bar of it, informing me that the two miscreants had promised to drop the cars back to the dealers. A bill for twenty grand arrived for breach of lease and again I was told to pay up.

This was crazy. Jaguar finance would have been laughed out of court at their sloppiness in accepting those guys at face value and letting them drive two high value cars off the forecourt without a check or a cheque. There wasn't an ounce of business sense here: we had just thrown eighty thousand out of the door with nothing to show for it.

Manton then told us that he had asked the firm's auditors to prepare a report on the Bureau's finances and a cheque for £6,500 was to be paid in advance. That was no problem for Richard and I. Accordingly we sent an up to date set of detailed figures showing that we were hugely solvent and that the next annual stipend of £640,000 was due shortly. All the salesmen's costs were written off of course, as was the report fee. With all that rubbish taken out the Bureau was as healthy as it had ever been. With the Royal Mail solidly behind it, it simply couldn't fail.

Manton phoned and asked me to visit him at home to review the financial report. Why I had to drag over there I didn't know. Why not in the office? It would have been much more convenient. As usual the bloody dog's noses headed in my direction and I had to ask for them to be taken elsewhere.

When he handed me the report, I couldn't believe my eyes. All the stupidities of the past two years were listed as still alive and kicking despite being written off as they happened. The costs of the production of the direct mail manuals and the USA sales were there in black and white as assets to be written off together with the Swiss fair and even the recent fiasco with the short lived salesmen and Frank's golden goodbye.

'Well, what do you think?'

'It's a complete pile of rubbish.'

'No, ignore the numbers. What do you think of the report?'

'Ignore the numbers, what are you talking about? It's literary merit? Who wrote this shite, the Brothers Grimm? Hans Anderson? Enid Blyton? It's a work of fiction. All this stuff they have listed as 'bad' was written off ages ago. They have the latest figures from Richard and me, so why not use those?'

'Well this is what I will present to the board on Friday.'

'Then you'll be presenting a pack of lies and I will be taking this up with the auditors, be sure of that.'

There was no further discussion to be had here. I don't know what Manton was doing but it all had a very bad smell. It made Richard, me and the auditors themselves, look like a bunch of chumps presenting every month and then annually, financial results that hadn't written off all dead losses which was totally incorrect. In fact our approach had been the opposite in that we had got rid of any nonsense out of the books as it arose, fast and furiously. The figures we had supplied to the auditors prior to their report were bang up to the minute and deadly accurate.

On the Friday I made sure that I was in situ to watch the board members parade past. Manton arrived without a word or a glance. An hour later they all filed out. I was in reception when Manton approached.

'Peter, the board have decided to close the Bureau. Because you and Richard are freelance you won't receive any compensation.'

He walked away.

This was too strange for words. Why were we closing a very good business that was not only in great financial shape but had excellent staff dealing with clients' requirements on a professional basis? And why in a short meeting would the board of directors discuss the trivial matter of the part time accountant guys? None of it made sense. Sure we needed a new CEO but that was no big deal.

Early in the following week, I received a list of compensation to be paid. Jo Howard-Brown and Jeanette Hull were to receive a lump sum each, plus would be taking over the core business of DMSB. All the other staff were to be paid to the end of the month plus one month tax free, even a young girl who had been here for only three weeks.

Michael Manton was to be compensated with a year's fee of £15,000 no less and he was freelance. Because Richard and I were freelance we were to get nothing. I wrote to the company's lawyer regarding the ethics of all this and also wrote to the auditors. The lawyer didn't reply but called Manton to tell him that the working classes were revolting.

The auditors called and requested my attendance at a meeting. When I arrived I was ushered into a large room to be greeted by three grinning young men. The only item on the desk between us was my letter with two spelling mistakes highlighted in red pen; a shame they were not so concerned with accuracy in their number crunching.

'We understand that you are not happy with our report.'

'It's a pile of crap and you know it. You have listed financial losses to be written off that have all been dealt with, some as long as two years ago. Not only does it look like I and my colleague were asleep at the wheel but you lot also.'

'The interpretation of finances is not a science and one accountant will take a different view from another as we have here.'

'Bollocks!'

The three were still grinning and, after all why not? They had pocketed six and a half grand for ten minutes 'work'; they had a happy client and apart from this oik making noises everything smelled of easy money.

There was a silence.

'Look, let's get this out of the way,' said a fresh voice. 'We produced the report that Michael Manton told us he wanted. And we did just that. I don't see the problem.'

'The problem is that your report aided and abetted Manton in closing down a perfectly sound company because he decided to. So much for auditor independence. You guys should be bloody ashamed.'

They didn't look ashamed, in fact they looked as smug as could be.

After several intimate evenings in the Soho pubs I felt that I was able to put together what had occurred. Recent events had started with the arrival of Carl and Henry who, after a short few weeks, concluded that they could make a far better fist of running the place than Manton and McGinty. No doubt with an eye on the resources available to provide them with a serious income stream. So they decided to mount a coup d'état.

My understanding of that course of action in business is to convince the investors that those currently in charge are ineffectual and that the conspirators could do a much better job. How you carry this out by leasing two Jaguars, falsely representing yourselves as directors is lost on me.

The coup d'état obviously failed but annoyed Manton enough that he decided that he would close the business regardless of putting decent hardworking staff out of jobs. He couldn't do it without a bent financial report but the auditors happily provided one. He knew that the board would simply nod the decision he had made through the gate on the 'facts' that he laid before them without a word. He had laid the blame for the malaise of the firm on a couple of contractors who would be of course excluded from any compensation.

It was of no account to him that Richard and I were professional people with reputations to uphold or the recent history between us. He was self-opinionated and selfish in the extreme, expected people to automatically accept what he said as kosher. No wonder he got turfed out of his own advertising agency.

My other clients were taking a back seat at this time while I dealt with the fast moving events at the Bureau. Royal Mail paid a quarter of a million pounds into our bank account to ensure all debts and commitments were met. It was totally unnecessary as even with the crystallization of the office lease and the recent excesses, funds were already available to settle everything.

Another Monday morning found me working with the receptionist in getting some letters out when Manton arrived. I called out a cheery good morning but he stormed past, slamming the door of the boardroom with such force I thought it would break.

Peggie's voice piped up behind me.

'Michael is very angry with you for writing to the lawyer. We don't understand the fuss, after all you have been paid.'

I had prepared for the end of a beautiful friendship and here it was. I carried on with the work in hand and when it was done I straightened up and turned to face Mr Manton's woman.

'I'm sorry madam, but I don't know who you are.'

I walked away but after two strides turned and added: 'But I do know what you are.'

It was a shame but she had nailed her colours to Manton's mast and in the game of life a great meal ticket will always beat a great friendship.

Frank phoned.

'Peter, tell me that the BMW insurance is still being paid.'

'Didn't you get my letter, Frank?'

'Yes, I got it but didn't bother to read it.'

'Well, there you go, and no the insurance is not being paid. It's your car, not ours anymore.'

'I can't afford to pay the insurance. It's a white elephant.'

'Frank, you got twenty grand tax free and a twenty grand car. I'm getting nothing and you expect me to worry about your car insurance.'

'I can't be concerned with your problems.'

'My sentiment entirely.'

And hung up.

Then half a dozen very young and excited men arrived bearing black rubbish sacks. They were from the auditors and could not have shown more disrespect if they'd urinated in the corner of the room.

There was no computer stuff as records were all hand written. They gaily threw the books and files into their sacks and went on their way. It was all so rushed that they omitted to pick up the bank account book and bank statements, which I took to a place of safety and waited for a call as to their location, a call that never came. How the accountants managed without them is beyond me.

If the staff were not demoralised enough already, these thoughtless actions ensured that they were now. There was a creditors' meeting and the auditors became the liquidators.

A small party was held at which Manton was presented with a gift. I absented myself as to have gone would have been hypocritical and there would have been a real danger that with a few bevvies under my belt things could have taken a turn for the worse.

I don't know if what had taken place constituted a crime but there had certainly been a conspiracy to mislead the DMSB investors, especially the Post Office. After festering for a while I decided that I just couldn't leave it there and would make every effort to bring this rotting fish out into the public arena. It would cost money that's for sure but if nothing else I would rock a boat or two. I asked a lawyer to send a demand to the liquidators for compensation for Richard and myself of one thousand pounds each. Compared with the largess ladled out to Manton, McGinty and the salesmen they were trivial sums but this was deliberate on my part to make it obvious that I was not after money but making a point.

The liquidators refused and appointed Kingsley Napley to act for them. Through my lawyer I told them they couldn't have that famous firm as they had acted for me when I was CFO at Theatre Projects and also after I had moved on, so think again.

Over the next year the case ground on and I pressed for the matter to get before the court, where I hoped to get the chance give my version of the tale. I heard that the Royal Mail guys were angry that two ex-contractors were holding up the straightforward closing down of DMSB.

Finally the liquidators offered £7,500 in settlement. My costs were already at £9,000 and the lawyer told me that if I refused to accept he would need twenty grand to proceed. In the final analysis, an eventual court hearing might simply decide that the one and only offer had been reasonable and I was simply being vexatious. And that would be an end to it.

To show the lack of care and attention by my lawyer, when he received the £7,500 he sent the lot to Richard. I had to write a letter as if to a three year old telling him Richard was due £1,000 and the balance was for my account which still resulted in a personal loss of £2,500. Not great but at least I had tried and stood up to be counted.

*****

I had been attending Japanese language lessons for some time on a once a week basis with an outfit named MOA, based in swanky offices in the heart of Mayfair. The costs were very reasonable and I was sure we pupils were being subsidised by somebody. The groups were small, usually six or seven students but looking back I think their approach was not best suited to my needs. We spent much time trying to learn the three alphabets, which I think would have been fine if our plan was to migrate there. But what I needed was everyday conversation and not the ability to read the Tokyo newspapers. More often than not I sat next to a woman with a dolls shop inside the Cumberland Hotel. Her needs were to be able to communicate with customers at the simplest of levels and that wasn't happening here either

The curriculum was taking us towards a set of official examinations in language efficiency that were not on my agenda for sure. As with all these courses people came and went. The worst I can remember was a young Chinese guy who sprawled in his chair, yawned and scratched and had to be told by the teacher to remove his back to front baseball cap. When asked to introduce himself he told us that he was the son of the founder of the Wagamama chain of Japanese cafés and that he had been sent. He took no part in the proceedings and did not return. One evening a week they held lessons for Japanese who planned to become language teachers and I often attended as a guinea pig which could be fun.

*****

A new face arrived at Maslin Rees Fitton. The first I knew of it was when Sean Irwin walked into the room, introduced himself and took over an empty desk. It seemed that his recruitment was largely Larry's doing and that the others had gone along for the ride.

I was surprised that he started off at the full partner's salary level but without a car. Brian told me that he had been CEO at Tavistock Advertising, part of Allen Brady Marsh and was bringing several clients with him. The hard fact was that he brought not a single client through the doors and although he was a genial bloke I couldn't work out exactly what he had brought to the party. All I do know is that he shadowed Larry as if they were joined at the hip, which on one spectacular occasion evoked a very harsh reaction from a client.

One morning Sean told me that he was very worried about the firm's accounts. It puzzled me as the monthly figures were not due for a few days and I had no idea what the hell he was talking about.

'What accounts? I haven't produced any.'

'I went through your waste bin yesterday and found this computer printout. It shows us that we're in a very dangerous position.'

"What are you doing, going through the rubbish? What you found was just a routine print to check balances. It's not adjusted for the end of month stuff, mainly because there's no work in progress calculation. I produce a monthly report for Larry and you should ask him to share that with you. And don't go through the rubbish anymore, 'cos that's what it is, rubbish.'

From the look on his face it was clear that he didn't believe a word but stuff him. After that I took cast off paperwork to dispose of at home.

Soon after this he pulled another stunt that for me reduced his credibility to zero. On a Monday morning he asked if I could get him some figures for client billing for a 'meeting on Wednesday'. This was no problem and on Tuesday I gave him the information before lunch.

'Thanks, this will be useful for Friday's meeting.'

'Hold on, you said the meeting was on Wednesday.'

'I told you that to make sure it was done on time.'

'Look mate, I'm 50 not 15. Pull another stunt like that and you'll be doing the accounting yourself.'

As with all small agencies, the loss of even one client would have given them real problems. And the new boss of Malta Tourist Office gave them reason to worry. He'd made it clear that he expected to be wined and dined frequently but none of the partners were willing to pick up the baton. Larry wanted to change the name to Advertising Warfare and decorate the offices accordingly with camouflage. But we were in enough trouble with the landlords already and making the place look like an army surplus shop could have resulted in our lease being torn up.

To my mind, too little thought was being put into new business efforts. Larry organised a selective mailing offering a free of charge brainstorming meeting for prospective customers. For a time we chased up any news of other agencies losing a client but nothing came of any of these schemes. We had no golfers, freemasons or members of gentlemen's clubs on board so those obvious channels were unavailable.

Worst of all, no interest was shown in preparing a budget and it was all fly by the seat of the pants stuff. Profits were being made but employing Sean would eat into that unless he pulled a rabbit out of his hat and if we did lose Malta TO or anyone else then the near future could be a struggle. Worst of all the partners seemed to be going in different directions with a serious lack of communication between them. It did not bode well.

I kept to my rule to stay out of the office politics but had spent social time with Brian and Sara. As the firm divided into two camps, it seemed I would be lumped into the anti-Larry and Sean faction, whereas I regarded myself as simply providing a service, no different to the cleaners.

Lynn and David took the first move, announcing that they were leaving to set up shop in Brewer Street and by agreement, taking with them Rotary Watches. When they asked if I would look after their finances, I told them I'd happy to do so. Brian quickly followed who took nothing apart from a promise to handle any Rotary media buying.

I could see the writing writ large on the wall, so I called Harrison Willis, my old agency from back in the day to ascertain the situation in the current freelance market. I carefully outlined the circumstances: a very part-time job, the agency polarised into factions and the fact that I might, repeat might be looking for a few hours contract work to fill up my week.

'How old are you?'

'52.'

'Oh Jesus, we've got nothing for you. Go home and put your feet up, you're finished.'

'So you don't even want to see my CV?'

'Waste of time, you're too old for anything.'

The next morning Sean came to see me.

'Are you looking for work?'

'I've been putting feelers out. Why do you ask?'

'Yesterday afternoon I got a call from Harrison Willis who told me that they had several suitable candidates to fill our accountant vacancy. When I asked them where they got their information they told me that they knew everything that was happening in the accounting world. And then couriered a pile of CVs over to me. What's going on?'

'It's simple, Sean. I can see the possibility of you and Larry deciding that I am friendly with Brian, David and Lynn and wanting me gone. I just made an initial enquiry about the contract market. No big deal, just covering my bases.'

'There is no plan to make any changes in our arrangements.'

'Thank you.'

What happened to professional integrity?

I telephoned Harrison Willis and they denied everything including sending any CVs to Sean, even though I had the stuff in front of me.

*****

During all this time I kept in regular touch with brother Jeffery by phone once a week and a visit once a month. His health was not good having returned from Burma with malaria which had a habit of recurring. He also suffered with sciatica and from the effects of smoking thin roll-ups from dawn to dusk, all of which was compounded by living in a damp cold house, much like camping indoors. I had tried to sell him on the benefits of moving to a village in Italy with a better climate and a lower cost of living but it all fell on deaf ears.

He claimed that he was independent but that was nonsense. The nearest shop was a long walk down the hill and back. His neighbour was a fussy, dreary man named Jack Horner but amazingly did Jeff's shopping at the local Tesco once a week and generally helped him out as situations arose.

Anita considered me tantamount to a pagan so I wrote her off, simple as that. Freda made occasional contact but since I had insisted on no further calls from her drunken husband that had fallen away.

Karen came over to see her dad at least once a year. The girl was born in Streatham and spoke normal English yet insisted on talking like an Italian waiter, bloody ridiculous! I took this up with her but apparently she thought it all perfectly normal. When she arrived I would put in an appearance and take everybody to a good lunch but when she brought her husband it all turned into a trial.

This massive geezer insisted on meat at all meals, even breakfast. He wouldn't eat anything that he had not seen walking, flying or growing in the ground. When I took this pinhead to a French restaurant, he scraped every vestige of the beautiful sauce from his meat, complaining loudly throughout in Italian that this garbage wasn't his style of cooking. I tried to be civil, to be there and to be generous but it was hard going and in fact was not to last.

A call came from Jack that Jeff had fallen ill, had been taken to Croydon Hospital but was now back in the house. I drove down with Haruyo and found him in a shocking state; he should never have been sent home. He said Karen was coming over and asked if I could meet her at Heathrow.

I had a business to run, projects to monitor and a life to lead but it seemed I was expected to accommodate every need. I drove to the airport and to my horror found she had brought the man mountain complete with a pile of luggage. As I was driving a Mini Cooper, it was a miracle that we all squashed in including the bags. I dropped them off but a few days later was pressed into taking husband back to Heathrow. Karen had written on a large piece of cardboard and hung the following sign around his neck:

ITALIAN

NO ENGLISH

GO MILAN

PLEASE HELP

Karen had in fact called the airline and asked that her husband be looked after by the folk who tend for unaccompanied children but they had refused. Still it was worth the effort to watch the golem shuffle into the airport concourse with his cardboard label swinging in the breeze. Where's the camera when you need one?

Jeff was soon back in hospital and I judged that his end was near. Freda had arrived to keep Karen company, sans the drunkard praise be. Every trip was an expense for them as a taxi had to be called from South Croydon station and the fare was in effect double bubble. I called my friend Michael who was between jobs and lived in the next borough and asked him if he could help them out. He agreed and I told the two women that he could assist them by driving them locally. Of course they jumped at the opportunity and soon Michael was running them all over the place

It was twenty years later that I discovered that these two had not paid him a penny piece for his trouble, not even paid for a tank of petrol. When he enquired about a set of crappy dining chairs, Karen charged him top dollar. What happened to their common sense, let alone their gratitude? How could they call a man they didn't know time after time for help assuming that his service was free and gratis? Or did they? If they thought at all, perhaps they assumed that good old Uncle Peter would pick up the tab?

So every day I would finish work, pick up Haruyo and fight through the rush hour traffic to get down to Croydon Hospital to visit my brother. At the weekend we might go over to the house to find Karen pulling loose bricks out of the wall in her search for money. There was never an offer of refreshments or a sensitive word. I tracked down the lawyer who held Jeff's Will which was recovered from deep storage. Anita, Freda and I were to get £ 300 each and everything else left to Karen. Fair enough.

I asked one of the nurses what treatment was available but she explained that he was already too far gone. Everything was shutting down and after a couple of weeks she tipped me that the end was bleeding nigh. At five in the morning I got a call from Karen to say that he had kicked the bucket and asked me to come over straight away. I couldn't understand the rush as he wasn't going anywhere but off we went. I helped organize the funeral, the flowers, all sorts of stuff that needed doing.

The day arrived for the cremation and in order to have a bit of a crowd, I asked a few close friends to show their faces even though they had never met the man. We arrived at the house well ahead of the undertakers coming to chauffer us to the crematorium and Karen greeted us with some news.

'I've sold all the furniture. I know some of it was yours but I sold it anyway.'

Two items I noticed parked with the loot ready to be shipped back to Cortina were Jeff's rocking horse and Anita's dolls house. I had paid for both of these to be beautifully restored and she knew it but possession was ten tenths of the law in Karen's world.

My brother's only request was for his ashes to be taken to Cortina and scattered over a meadow behind the house. Not a difficult task. My dear friend Jane brought her father back from Australia in her hand luggage with a stopover in Singapore no less.

As we drove to the service Karen told me she had contacted the Italian Ministry of Heath, Customs and Excise and God knows who else. She had been informed that dead people could not be taken into Italy in any shape or form. What crap! All she needed to do was just put the urn or box or whatever in her suitcase. If she was caught, I don't think anyone would be bothered with a pile of ash. She'd asked the funeral guys to dispose of my brother's remains. It wasn't much to ask but she couldn't be bothered to deal with the task properly and with respect.

Everything went off okay. Haruyo and I stood to one side afterwards, watching the pressing of the flesh.

'I want you to take a real good look at this lot,' nodding towards Karen and Freda, ''cos you're never going to see any of them again.'

A week after the cremation, Anita flew in from Melbourne to stay at the house while the sale was being completed. Karen phoned to invite me over and I refused. Then she called me again.

'Peter, you know that my dad left you, Anita and Freda £300 each?'

'Yes, and you get one hundred and ten thousand.'

Jeff had lived like a pauper to put that together.

'Well, I thought that if the three of you give up the money to my son Stefano, it would be a nice memory of his grandfather.'

'You must be bloody joking! If your son wants to remember his grandfather then hang his bleeding picture on the wall.'

I hung up. As an accountant I'd witnessed avarice at its worst and oodles of it but this was egregious. A few days later I received a letter from Freda. It seems that while the three witches of Endor were being driven around by Michael, the only topic of conversation had been my bad conduct, (all in front of my friend) and she'd felt 'unable to offer a word in your defence'.

I really think we were dealing with a time warp and they were in another dimension. I was there running myself ragged and digging deep into my pocket and this was bad behaviour. It was long past the time to disengage. I wrote to Freda to explain that however hard I had tried to keep a connection it hadn't worked. Would she explain to Karen and Anita that I was estranging myself from family and wanted no further contact whatsoever. There is an old cliché that family is the most important thing in life but I think that depends on the actual mob you are born into. Mine had been dysfunctional at best, unhinged at its worst and failed to drop into the 'most important' category.

I did hear about Karen's son's bad accident. Stefano was a professional rock climber and a leading light of the Cortina curling club. At the season's opening ceremony in 2010, he and two other guys were to descend from the ceiling of the arena carrying the tools of their trade, to wit a curling stone and two brushes. The brushes arrived safely but Stefano with the very heavy stone in his backpack wasn't so lucky. He lost his grip and fell 20 metres to the ground landing on the stone. It was a miracle he wasn't killed. He was in hospital for eight months, but I have no idea as to how well he recovered.

Anita and Freda both died when they reached 85, no doubt cursing the black sheep of the family with their last breaths.

The lawyer had carried out a crackerjack job selling the house and assembling Jeff's small estate. He called me to say that my niece was unhappy with his account and I assured him that if any difficulties arose I would back him one hundred per cent. I guessed from the very beginning that one debt would cause a problem and I was spot on.

I think the reception area can tell you a lot about a firm. The finest that I've experienced belongs to a large firm of international solicitors based in Kensington. It boasted a marble floor, beautiful furnishings and to top it all off not only two beautiful ladies behind the jump but twins to boot, a real class act. When you walked in you knew you were among the best in the business.

Over the years my brother had made a little money producing cartoons. At one time he was published by one of the national newspapers under the pen name Buz but for some years his only customer was BPIF based in Bedford Row. He created three works for their magazine for the princely sum of twenty-five pounds. I doubted if that even covered the card and ink but that was his concern not mine. A few times when I visited he had a set ready to post and as I lived only a block away I would deliver by hand. Their reception area was the exact opposite of the one described above, it was brown, dark and dreary and the two old women at the counter were the rudest you could not wish to meet. I would enter with a cheery 'Good morning, how are we all today? I have a package for ....' They would neither speak or turn their heads, let alone make eye contact but one would point at the counter top and that was it. As a representation of the outfit, the whole thing stank.

Well they owed for one set of cartoons and I had a copy of the magazine with the drawings signed J Roy. The solicitor told me that when he'd applied for the cash they denied that they owed the money, had never heard of Jeffery Roy and would the lawyer trouble them no more. I knew it! I wrote them possibly the sharpest missive ever, setting out all of the above and accused them of trying to profit from a dead man's work who had served them well and enclosed a photocopy of the magazine. The response was immediate, saying that they'd been very upset by my words, but they paid up. If they learned anything about how to present a face to the world then it was a cheap lesson. Somehow, I doubt they'd learned anything.

Down at Chelsea harbour, MRF continued. It was a fee based operation and also sub-let spaces to several one-man bands, so the profit was a reliable commodity. The clients might not have been blue chip but they were very stable businesses and cash flow took very little time and trouble.

One exception was Larry's cousin, who when chased for money always claimed that the invoices hadn't arrived. It got to the point that I hand delivered a complete set myself and yet when I phoned the same old excuse was rolled out. I don't like it when someone pisses down my back and tells me it's raining so I asked the court to serve a winding-up order and as a result they were out of business in double quick time. We didn't get paid but it wasn't very much.

Larry had started a long running battle with the landlords as he'd discovered that many tenants coming in were getting a first year rent free which we hadn't been offered, so I was instructed to withhold the payment of the rent. I set up a separate bank account to transfer what was due every quarter, so that when the matter was resolved funds would be available.

Motoring through King's Cross I was hit from behind. The Metro was drivable but as luck would have it some middle management had left and I was given the job disposing of the company cars. I bought a white MG Metro for myself and sold the others. The insurance paid in full for my original Metro and I sold it to Charlie's mum for a knock down price of £500 and spread the luck. It needed a couple of hundred spent on fixing the back but even then it was half price.

On a Sunday morning I heard a knock on the door and looking out of the window there was my old Metro and a man I knew of, but had never met. Charlie's dad had died a few years ago and his mum had taken up with Eddie, the meanest man in the world I was told. I opened the door and with a watermelon grin, he introduced himself.

'What do you want? A refund?'

'Oh no, did you know this car has a Pioneer sound system? It's the best you can get?'

'Of course I knew, so what?'

'Well, I pulled it out and sold it for £500, so I've got a free car.'

'And you drove across London to tell me that. I sold it to Charlie cheap because I got a good deal and he's an old mate. Frankly I don't know you from a bar of soap.'

'I'm surprised you didn't take it out before you sold it.'

'Do I look like a bloke who pulls radios out of cars? I don't want to be rude but you are an idiot – go away.'

And the door was shut.

At the end of 1991 I decided to throw another party. By this time the Metro had been part exchanged for a brand new Rover Mini in British Racing Green. Haruyo and I drove over to Calais to fill it to the gills with champagne. Her Japanese friends helped with the food preparation and about sixty people turned up and all went well.

*****

Max told me that Bob Price had closed his business and that the top two floors of Tudor House were vacant. Also that Alan Brison had moved to his own office one block away, so Max was on his own in the whole building. The landlord had shown up and he hadn't made up his mind what he would do with the building. He'd offered Max free usage if he would act as the caretaker of the place until further notice, which suited my old mate down to the ground.

A few months before, I had taken on a job that I didn't want or need. One of MRF's suppliers was a jobbing printer based just outside Chelsea Harbour. I decided to knock it into shape and pass it on to Richard.

It was not a difficult job in itself but the owner was a weird cove and his access to the computer resulted in minor problems with the accounting software from time to time. He had gone on holiday to the West Indies for Christmas and had paid out the staff wages just before he left. All the cheques bounced leaving a trail of difficulty and hardship.

When the shop reopened after New Year I was told that he'd marched into the premises big, saying that his holiday had been wonderful and that he'd maxed out his credit card. Only then did he realise that a reception committee was awaiting him. Many of the female staffers had their husbands with them and he was surrounded by a threatening mob demanding money. He was forced to go to the bank accompanied by a couple of large lads and arrange an overdraft, returning with cash to pacify the ugly crowd.

Soon after this he managed to wipe all the accounting records off the system. I spent a Saturday with a freelancer repairing the damage and quit. Richard did take it on but it was a difficult place to travel to on public transport, so he may not have lasted and we never spoke of it.

The Institute of Chartered Accountants were bringing in new requirements for members to attend courses to ensure that their professional education was up to date which was totally understandable. That was fine when applied to large firms who could easily arrange for members to attend but it was difficult for one-man bands to comply. Therefore I didn't carry out any audit work and little taxation. My aim was to retire early and I'd chosen Madeira as my preferred destination. Accordingly Haruyo and I were making regular visits to the island.

Max had a major client and he asked an old friend of ours to carry out the year-end audit. He kept the accounts with the help of Linda who was the most accurate bookkeeper you could ever find. They would prepare the accounts and the firm's manager Mr Patel would audit. Over a couple of years, Mr Patel embedded himself into the company more and more, making monthly visits to go through the company's progress with the directors. The business was making a ton of money and I guess that was the attraction.

This went well for some time until Patel started to produce monthly accounts that bore no resemblance to the true figures. Max challenged this but in the end Linda walked away being unable to reconcile with what was happening and finally Max threw in the towel. Some accountants bend the rules, others stamp their muddy boots all over them. All a strange business.

Marion had asked me to take over one of her clients, a solicitor who I will call Mr X for reasons that will become obvious. I was surprised at her giving up income but her reasons were twofold: he wanted to computerise the accounting and time recording records. She didn't want to take on the task but more importantly, she just couldn't work with him as he was difficult in the extreme or so she said.

Now I always considered that I could get on with just about anybody and the computer systems packages offered by Sage and the like were straightforward and should hold no fears. I dropped in to see him and he baulked at my price but agreed to it as he was in no position to put up a fight. I totally failed to pick up on the warning bells ringing.

I was to find that he was another of those charmers who would turn into a real nasty piece of work at the slightest annoyance. I was based in my own office in the attic and Marion joined me on my first visit to show me the ropes. After half an hour she had had enough and legged it.

Marion had done a first class job and it was an easy task to get everything digital. The time keeping side which I had never come across before performed beautifully and the secretary worked with me to ensure a trouble free visit.

However, I soon discovered that if Mr X could avoid paying a bill he would and being in the legal profession, knew every trick in the book to dodge the column. Additionally, if a mistake had been made, there was no quiet word in the shell like. Instead his modus operandi was to happily scream and shout at the offender in front of anyone who happened to be around.

Confident that I could perform well enough to avoid his tantrums, I turned up, carried out my tasks and departed. I met with his accountant, we hit it off and all seemed well apart from having to deal with suppliers he was dudding from time to time.

I had also met with MRF's accountant and we hadn't hit it off. A grotty little man with a handshake as cold as death, he didn't like me and the feeling was reciprocal. A couple of weeks after the meeting he wrote to Larry Rees offering to replace me with a Nigerian gent who was about to launch his firm's new visiting accountant service. It could be that he would get the chance.

On a Sunday morning a few weeks later I received a call from a woman whom I knew by name but had never met, to tell me that Marion had died and could her daughter Karen come around to my house for a couple of hours. I agreed but Karen never arrived. I assumed that in the stress of it all she had meant that Marion's elderly mother had died. But it was Marion who was only about 38, who had suffered a massive heart attack and slipped off this mortal coil. I couldn't claim to be surprised as the three generations lived in a state of constant warfare and to say that Karen was difficult would be the understatement of the year.

The funeral was a ragged affair. Marion never spoke of the man but Karen's father turned up. All I knew of him was that he'd burned his own house down for the insurance money.

A by-product of all this was that I took on another client I didn't want or need. Elizabeth from the Marketing Office called and was desperate for help. Marion had looked after her finances and had told her that if anything happened to her to contact me. Thanks Marion. I made a visit and it looked small potatoes with manual bookkeeping, a staff of only five and as the clients were mainly in tourism or entertainment a few tickets would be coming my way, so I agreed. I didn't get a desk allocated but a tray where all the accounting stuff accumulated during the week and I would take it to a spare space on my visit.

It turned out to be a decent enough billet. One staff member was a professional singer and was easy on the ear although a little too much West Side Story for my liking. Elizabeth was, I soon found out, difficult to deal with at times and untrusting enough to go over my work and I guess the others when I wasn't there. However, she chose to work from home on most days and that suited everyone.

The legal firm was a soul-destroying place as there was none of the usual social interaction that I think is normal in the workplace. Occasionally the secretary and I were the first to arrive and we could have a chat but that seemed to be the extent of it. On most visits I would spend a few hours bringing everything up to date and leave without saying a word to anyone that I thought was unnatural. One of my tasks was to produce a summary of photocopier usage that frankly I resented as being outside my remit. Sorry to say, I didn't keep a copy of the work which would bite me hard down the road. One month I knocked it out, left it on the secretary's desk, then she lost it so I had to do it all again. And when you do a crap job a second time, mistakes slip through.

I brought some cheques down to the secretary for signature just at the moment when Mr X had spotted an error in the photocopy tally. He kicked off in front of the other legal eagles and made a mountain out of it and there was no way I would drop the secretary in the clag so I had to take it on the chin in bloody public. That was the end of it for me. A couple of weeks later I put my letter of resignation on his desk; four weeks and I was off.

At the end of the third week he wrote me a letter to say that he had not found a replacement so I would HAVE to continue until he did. My letter in response politely informed him that I had given him a date and that was that. As far as I was concerned, it was set in stone and if there was no successor in the wings then tough titty.

I came in on my last day to find another missive telling me that a guy would be starting next Monday and could I spare an hour to show him the ropes. It seemed churlish to refuse so I decided to give a free hour to hand over. The secretary was very nice, kind enough to express her appreciation of my friendly personality and her pleasure working with me, all of which cheered me up no end.

On Monday I was there at nine and a strange Quasimodo like figure named Ben arrived at half past. I handed over my set of keys and went through the system with him, showing him the location of all the files. I gave him a schedule of the monthly activities that I'd prepared and even took him to the tea making area in the basement. But I didn't make any introductions as he could do that himself. After an hour I wished him luck and left. An hour later my mobile rang: it was Ben.

'Where's the wages book?'

'Top left hand drawer of the desk.'

That was the pattern for the next five days.

That same afternoon I fielded two more calls.

'Where are the purchase invoices?'

'To the right of you. Bottom shelf, labelled Purchase Invoices.'

And: 'Who do I call to get help with the computer system?'

'Business card on the desk.'

Tuesday, Wednesday and Thursday saw an average of four similar inane enquiries but on Friday it finally stopped. But by that time I was having serious concerns over the wellbeing of the well-oiled system I'd left behind. Of course it was no longer my concern but it would have been a shame to see yet another phoney ruin a fine working situation. However unlike Upwards, there would be no return of the prodigal son to sort things out.

I sent in my final account and received a letter to the effect that it would not be paid as I had, it was claimed, made a total mess of the last month's accounting and Ben had had to redo everything. I was furious. The man was supposed to be a brilliant lawyer and here he was with a stupid and lazy excuse to dodge paying a legitimate debt. What a real piece of work?

I had some very bad thoughts at the time and I could easily have turned those into a reality. Instead I simply went over to the local courthouse and served a writ. I received a prompt reaction in a letter accusing me of blackmail which I thought that was a bit rum. After a couple of months without any action from the court, underpinned by a lack of confidence in getting a sensible hearing, I offered to settle for half. I also took the opportunity of letting him know exactly what I thought of him and his bad habit of making suppliers walk over hot coals to get paid what they were due and wished him an unhappy life.

I had the lowest possible opinion of Ben who seemed to have turned my five hours a week into a full time job. It wouldn't have surprised me if he was prepared to lie in court at the behest of his paymaster. My ploy was in part that if my offer was refused, the court would lean in my favour. But a cheque did arrive. I doubled it and send the total to charity, letting Mr X have a copy of the receipt.

Jo Howard-Brown was making a real success of the son of DMSB and had three personable young men working with her. Manton who was Chairman, decided that he would mentor these guys whether they liked it or not and would attend for a couple of hours a month to do so.

After a while the lads told Jo that they found Manton's words of wisdom a waste of time and they wouldn't put up with it anymore. Poor Jo, what a job to have to tell the bastard that he was considered out of date and that his advice was of no value. It must have been a bitter pill for such a self-important pompous ass to take that from a mere girl.

I saw Manton just one more time. Jo's lovely mother had died and I was invited to the service at Golders Green. When we arrived, Lord and Lady Rough Diamond were to the fore and Manton being Jewish, was of course wearing his kippah. Well, I'm not Jewish so don't own a kippah and wore the only hat I possessed, a black fedora that I thought fitted the bill rather than borrow a cap. Perish the thought!

Manton fixed his death ray stare on me throughout the service. He really was a gold plated bastard. When he fell off his perch in 2013, I offered the media an obituary drawn from my personal experience but it was declined. I wonder why?

I sold the house in Northington Street. I received a good price, maybe not good enough but I made a decent profit. A couple of other projects wound down and I could start to lay firm plans to be out of the game by 60 and move to warmer climes. We moved to a rental in Muswell Hill and started to look around for one last house to flip before the big move.

Jo and Jeanette had been busy finding premises for their new business Direct Mail Information Service (DMIS) later to become HBH Limited. They were to enjoy the support of the Royal Mail by the continuation of their work at DMSB but with no annual fee. Manton was to be the Chairman and they asked me to handle the finance. I accepted on condition that I would never have anything to do with the Mantons. They agreed.

The girls knew how to throw a party and their Christmas do became a hot ticket. Richard and I were always invited but so were the enemy and I needed to keep a sharp lookout to ensure that I didn't bump into them.

After all this chaos, my favourite client Cousins fell off the tracks. I had made my usual visit and all seemed as normal until Jon appeared in my office followed by a large geezer who he introduced as a management consultant. He in turn introduced a highly pimpled young bloke who would be available to help me with any problems. I must admit that I was wrong footed by their arrival, forgot their names instantly and couldn't think for the life of me why Jon would employ a time and motion man in a creative shop. And the cost of this service was £2,000 per day – a fantastic sum at that time.

The first thing Mr MC did was sell Jon a time recording diary where every hour was broken down into six minute segments that was ideal for a lawyer or other professional type but bonkers in this business. A large job had just been completed for British Telecom that had taken three months but it had been invoiced out; Caroline had checked that it was approved and on the next cheque run. All was well as it always was and she made my job a walk in the park.

On my next visit Caroline was gone. Mr MC had produced a report that the three month job had endangered the business. Complete crap but I guess he had to justify his fee. I was horrified and resigned. Jon asked me to change my mind but I had my say and that was that. He found a replacement quickly.

I was told that Jon and Caroline's relationship recovered quickly and I was very happy to hear that news. Mr MC or whatever his name was, was an idiot, a rich idiot and an irresponsible one to boot.

Right from its creation attempts were made to convert a Mini into a soft top. The amateur attempts often ended in disaster turning a fine little car into a skip on wheels but the professionals made a better fist of it with proper strengthening modifications to compensate for the removal of the roof.

But the people building the class jobs had to factor in wages and the many specially designed parts that made the final result expensive. Crayford was a firm that produced special editions of factory made cars for discerning clients over many years. In their early days they were contracted to make 57 convertible Wolseley Hornet Minis as prizes in a Heinz competition. It was a big ask as they had no industrial premises but ran the business from a house garage. But they completed the order and I believe some forty of these cars still survive today.

I spotted in a motoring magazine that in 1991 Rover commissioned the German company Lamm Autohous to build 75 prototype Mini convertibles. Looking at the pictures, they got it just right: huge wheel extensions housing super wide wheels and tyres and although the hood when lowered sat on the back of the car like an old-fashioned pram it did have a tonneau cover to tidy it up. New they were around twelve grand, about double the price of a standard car but in my opinion worth every penny.

I found one for sale with John Cooper Garages and did the deal. It was a wonderful little car and attracted more interest than the Astons ever did. We did the rounds with the various Mini meets and shows.

Early in 1995 Larry arranged a meeting with the landlords to sort out the disagreements over the lease. He had a fair point in that MRF had paid a full market rent from day one whereas new tenants were still moving in with a year rent free and financial help in fitting out. He told me that the auditor was coming over to join us. Oh joy.

On the arranged day, Larry approached with the auditor in tow and I handed over a set of the accounts year to date.

'What's this?' asked the auditor.

'Up to date figures, spot on,' I replied.

'Do you really have a quarter of a million in the bank?'

'Of course. This is advertising and that's how it should be.'

'I can't use this. This is fucking useless.'

With that he takes out paper and pen and designs his own balance sheet.

'Right, we'll call this bank balance an overdraft. Now that improves everything. This is something I can use.'

'You're going to show a completely fraudulent document to the landlords to support your case?'

'Creative accounting.'

With that he turned and walked off. Larry started to follow but then looked back.

'Aren't you coming with us?'

'Not in a million years. I don't want any association with what you guys are about to do.'

In twenty minutes they returned, grinning like a couple of Cheshire cats.

'That was easy.' said the auditor. 'It's been agreed that Larry will pay them thirty grand from his personal funds and MRF will start paying full rental from the next quarter date.'

'That's very generous of you Larry, I didn't know you had thirty grand.'

'Of course he hasn't. You pay the money into his account from the firm and he passes a cheque to them.'

'So not only did you two produce bent figures to show that the agency is in trouble when it isn't, you told a big fat lie to secure a deal.'

'None of that fucking matters. It's a great piece of negotiation.'

'What happens if they want their pen pushers to run the rule over MRF before they finalise and quickly find your figures are inaccurate?'

'I'll tell them you gave me the figures.'

Again he walked away with Larry following. Luckily he left his paperwork which I parcelled up and attached to mine. They're still sitting in deep storage with my lawyers together with my Statutory Declaration. I decided that I just didn't want to be around this lot any more. I would work to the year end a couple of months away and quit.

There was no doubt that the two stooges believed they'd done a grand job working over the landlords and many would agree. However I just cannot accept that you go into a meeting with the intent to win your case, not by sound argument but by presenting falsified accounts and telling lies. If that makes me a dinosaur in this cutthroat world then so be it.

In this instance I think the property owners were so aggravated by the whole business that would have agreed to almost anything to be rid of the problem. In any event the settlement allowed the cash I had put aside for rent to be released into the firm's cash flow and drop profit through to the bottom line of the annual accounts.

In due course I slipped a note onto Larry's desk to the effect that my last day would be Saturday 1 April when I would produce the annual accounts to 31 March and that would be an end to it. Larry didn't respond and Sean said nothing, so I guess that they would be making plans to replace me. With the savings in rent the accounts showed a solid profit but I couldn't envisage this mob having a long-term future. I was right and in a couple of years it was gone.

I have always believed that a person has the intrinsic right to accept that the accounting put before him or her is as accurate as it can possible be and that the figures don't come from the land of make believe. Otherwise how can commerce function? What occurred at MRF must have been a crime as by cheating and lying they gained a financial advantage. That can't be just a matter of ethics alone. Although it left a hole in my client list, I was well out of it for sure.

Marketing Office could never be described as a happy place but the five hours a week it brought me was not demanding. Then Elizabeth took on a contract from the London Tourist Board that brought £1,500 a month into the business and gave me an inordinate amount of paperwork. In no time at all my hours doubled and I even put in a few Saturday mornings at no charge to keep on top of it all.

It all came to a head on Friday 2 June. I walked in at nine to a silent office, even our songstress was mute. No 'Luck be a Lady' or

'I wanna be in America' for us that morning. I found a hot desk and settled in. Elizabeth called and told a staffer that she would be working from home that day as she felt under the weather. That was the first of maybe twelve calls that morning. But none for me. Apart from the deadly quiet that was a normal set of circumstances.

On top of my in-tray was a page torn from an exercise book. It was obvious she'd been checking my work yet again as she had spotted errors that took up both sides. These were mainly cancelled cheques which she claimed had not been cancelled but they had. Where we differed was that she thought the correction should be made by crossing out the original entry whereas I made the change contemporaneously and cross referenced which was a much tidier method. Before slugging through the list I looked at the last line of her missive with astonishment: it informed me that she had found 'another Marion' to take over the accounts and that I could, in effect, sling my hook. No phone call, no quiet word, just a scribbled note.

My first thought was to walk out I reminded myself that I was a professional and so worked on as if nothing had happened. Of course everybody knew and were watching, only to be disappointed that there was nothing to see. I pushed through bringing everything up to date and making sure Marion's double would take over a crackerjack set of records. I finished at 2pm and I was hungry. I rose and headed for the door, dropping my keys on a desk and calling out 'nice working with ya'all'. And I was gone, for a late curry lunch.

I wrote to Elizabeth suggesting that she took a course of lessons in good manners. She could have called me at home, suggested we step out for a cup of coffee or whatever. But to give out serious news on a torn out bit of paper was crass to say the least. I reminded her that she had begged me to help her out when I neither needed or wanted the bloody job and had put in a chunk of pro bono time to cope with the mountain of LTB paperwork.

In addition I pointed out that that she really needed to trust people as to go over my efforts (and those of others) just wasted our time. The list she had provided of errors had all been dealt with but had swallowed an hour to simply check this and make out a report. I was going to sign off with the wish that the fleas of a thousand camels infest her nether regions but had second thoughts on that as it was unbecoming and let it go.

Following so closely after MRF, the loss of MO left a hole in my income and gave me rather more free time than I would have liked. It was just over two weeks later when I received a call in the evening from Anne Wilson who I hadn't seen for some five years. Her boyfriend was a director of a full service ad agency and they needed financial help. The fickle finger of fate. The very next day I was flying to Madeira for a few days but was able to arrange an interview for 29 June, the day after I returned.

Our trips to Madeira were largely spent looking at the real estate situation and generally driving around looking at possible locations for our home. We were making some useful contacts and were very positive about the whole proposition.

When I arrived at Barnett Williams Partnership on Bloomsbury Way in Holborn, the three directors Bob Barnett, Kevin Williams and Ian McArthur were there to meet me.

They explained that the ad agency part was managed by Bob and Ian while Kevin looked after events, conferences, product launches and the like. In fact the business was far more complicated than that as I was to later discover. The current financial controller was leaving for two reasons. He was over sixty-seven and refused to undertake the computerisation of the accounting records which surprised me as the systems available were very straightforward and even bulletproof.

They in turn went through my track record in advertising and Ian got into the detail of which computer system I preferred. I was used to Pegasus but he insisted on Sage but that was no big deal for me. They offered a solid annual fee and were happy for me to attend hours that suited me which would enable me to cover other clients. What they wanted was to modernise the bookkeeping and receive financial reporting that would simply keep them informed, a luxury that had not been available up to now.

It was agreed that I would start on Wednesday 6 September which would give me a few weeks until Len the current incumbent left on 29 September. That suited me down to the ground as I had a couple of trips planned.

We had only been home a few days when our Mini was stolen in the night. I walked around to the police station that was only a block away to find they were only open from 9am to 5pm. This struck me as strange in that most crimes are committed at night but I guess it suited them. The insurers sent an assessor around and we were paid out in full.

A few days later I spotted an advertisement for a Rover Mini in red in Cambridgeshire and drove up on the next Sunday to a large industrial estate. The seller told me he had bought a job lot of trade-ins, mostly Fords and Vauxhalls and was out of his comfort zone with the Mini. Nevertheless we did a deal and I arranged to take delivery the following week.

I was still attending the MOA Japanese lessons each Wednesday afternoon although uncertain as to how helpful it was to me in getting to grips with the language. It was announced that there would be an intensive course in Japan at a cost of £2,000 to include flights, accommodation, meals and lessons, leaving on 11 July. It seemed too good an opportunity to miss.

The plan was for me to go on ahead to the course with Haruyo catching up at the end. Then both travel to the island of Shikoku together for a few days holiday then back to Tokyo. I would fly home leaving H to spend time with family and friends.

I caught the ANA flight at 6pm out of Heathrow arriving in Narita at 1.40pm the next day. Then bought a ticket to Central Tokyo where I found the Shinkansen line to Atami, arriving late in the afternoon. Taking a taxi to MOA, I was amazed by the sheer quality of the hotel and was even more puzzled at the cheapness of the package deal.

When I arrived the teachers were there to greet their students many of whom had already come. It was a truly international crowd: American, Canadian, French, Italian, New Zealand and a couple from the UK setup. There were about two dozen in all which were split into three groups. After checking in, I went up to my room which was very spacious and well appointed, making a point on my way to the pre-dinner meeting to seek out the pool and spa which were breathtaking. This was to be a very happy and productive few days, no doubt.

There seemed to be no restaurant in the hotel and it was explained that we would be taking our meals at the MOA facility a few minutes walk away. The food served was all produced by natural farming and was full of vital energy and flavour and at that stage a warning bell went off in my head.

Before we set out to eat, the teachers handed a file to each student with the request that we read it later and bring a short report to the first lesson in the morning. It was the history of MOA, its teachings and culture. Effectively it was a religion and there lay the answer to all my questions. Our course was subsidised by the believers and in return we were expected to participate in some way.

I handed my file back.

'Not interested mate.'

'It is a requirement.'

'Not for me it isn't. I'm here for a language course, period.'

I was certain that a teacher would have to ghost my report. When the chief honchos of this mob requested a written reaction from twenty-four students that is what they must have. Twenty-three and an explanation would not cut the mustard but deliver a great loss of face to all concerned.

The Japanese are known for their politeness, much of which in my opinion comes from the crowded conditions in which they live and work. Frankly the miniscule apartments with very little privacy would result in a high homicide rate in any other country. I never thought that I would take to the bowing but it has a charm when meeting a stranger in the street. But it can be oppressive in a business structure where the bowing depth depends on the ranking of the people present.

Of course, rudeness and rough language do exist. You only have to watch one Yakusa (gangster) movie to see the other side of the picture and I guess the tough workers such as fishermen, construction, military and the like can be colourful. As a visitor I had never engaged with any of these and didn't expect to. As I mentioned the lessons with MOA in London were strictly by rote and realistically I had advanced very little. I had picked a small book '*Outrageous Japanese – slang, curses and epithets*' by Jack Seward and learned some short phrases just for the fun of it but never really expecting to need them. But just in case, I had a little ammunition.

What I had found on my travels in Nihon was that I could make myself understood by using the vocabulary that I knew. However native speakers were unaware of the level of my ability and simply spoke in everyday language which usually lost me totally.

We were taken over to what resembled a prison canteen, the only difference I could see was that the plastic furniture was not bolted to the floor. There was no cry of irasshai mashita (welcome) to greet us as we entered which is mandatory in any Japanese eatery, big or small, top end or red lantern. Joining the queue for food we shuffled towards the famous home grown organic offerings that strongly resembled a second rate dog's breakfast. I am sure that a vegan would have been in raptures at the sight and smell, but my stomach shouted at me 'what are you doing to me' and threatened revolt.

I could see no salad or soup, not even miso. The dishes all appeared to be vegetables in liquid but it had been a long day so I selected two choices and was about to load up when a guy in chef's whites started screaming at me while waving a large kitchen knife.

I was utterly wrong footed but quickly realised that I would be no equal in a slanging match. However there was no question of meekly walking away.

As far as I could understand there were two star dishes amongst the spread and I had taken both which was not permitted. While he raved, I put my tray down, folded my arms and waited for him to finish, pulling together a sentence from my rude Japanese book.

Finally he stopped. I took a deep breath and, dropping my voice down a couple of octaves I spoke.

'Kisama kutabare o baka.'

Roughly translated it means "drop dead you big fool". The key word kisama is the lowest word for 'you' that I can find and tells the person so addressed that he is inferior to you in every way. I doubt the sentence was good grammatically but it is language never used by a normal Japanese to anyone. To be used by a big-nosed foreigner would be unheard of and the effect was electric.

There was a brief silence while my new friend and his staff took on board what I'd said. The shock wave was palpable and open mouths were the order of the day. My fellow students had no idea of what I'd said but were well aware that it wasn't very nice. A flustered teacher appeared at my elbow asking what on earth was happening.

'This bastard needs a lesson in manners. I'm not being shouted at by this inaka mono.' (Rustic person.)

From the reactions of the kitchen staff, I am sure that his

behaviour was part of the daily grind for them. I blame reality TV for showing top chefs swearing, cursing and throwing stuff about. The teacher set about calming the situation down. I walked off to a plastic table, sat down on plastic chair and did the best I could to get the stuff down my throat.

The chef got his revenge within the hour. When I reached my hotel room my long suffering stomach just gave out and I was empty again. An hour in the spa pool on my own was wonderful and some energy bars washed down with a couple of Asahi beers from the vending machine completed my first day.

Waking very early the next morning I decided to have breakfast first, then put in a couple of hours of study before the lessons began. The cafeteria was almost empty with just a handful of diners and not a staffer to be seen. There was no full English or Continental and the offerings appeared to be very similar to the past evening's fare. I made up a small plate, sat and ate. As per my previous visit, I only just made it back to my room before it all left me. I was exhausted. If I wanted a rapid weight loss course I was definitely in the right place.

The lessons started at nine but after being told that the first hour would be a group discussion on MOA, I left and returned at ten. I had been placed in the middle group but so was the American who was so far advanced that I couldn't understand why he was even here and why he wasn't in the top class.

To my absolute horror, the pattern of the teaching simply picked up where we had left it in London. No roleplaying, no total immersion, no inventiveness, just taking turns to read out loud from the prepared materials. The yawning gaps between the students' varying ability was obvious and for me, extremely embarrassing. It seemed apparent that the teachers were on a jolly with full pay, free air tickets, full lodgings and board. This opinion was reinforced when it was announced that the following day would be a museum visit without lessons.

I skipped lunch and at six I took myself down the hill into town. Finding a small restaurant I loaded up on gyoza, yakitori, rice and miso, all washed down by two large ice cold Sapporos and the die was cast. Over the next weekend there was going to be a Matsuri (festival) and many teams were in the streets practising their stuff. One group had a tiny girl about five or six on a drum and she had fallen fast asleep but was still playing. Great, real life at last.

Picking up some iron rations from the convenience store, I made my way up the hill to the hotel, then spent an hour in the pool before bed. In my entire stay only once did I share the pool with anyone, a Japanese guy and his young daughter. What a waste of a superb facility.

Friday started with a visit to the farm that produced the vegetables for the cafeteria, that I can safely say no one wanted to see. The MOA museum was impressive but there was an overlay of preaching to the non-believers. A one point we were asked to look at the view through a certain window that was described by the teacher as paradise. When our American asked in excellent Japanese where the line of massive electricity pylons walking through the middle of the scene fitted into this vision, he was ignored.

At the end of the day, we were informed that on Saturday we would be mingling with the MOA community and enjoy a home stay. We were told to pack an overnight bag, take our suitcases down to a storage unit and vacate our rooms by 10am. The rooms were needed by followers that night. We did as we were told but not without a great deal of grumbling.

The venue was a fair distance away and we arrived at a meeting place around 6pm. Our hosts comprised about thirty people of all ages who had made a great effort in laying out a handsome selection of home-made food but it was a long evening. Around 9pm the New Zealand guy and I were introduced to two women who were to drive us to our lodgings and at 10pm we headed off.

It was past midnight when we arrived and we were surprised that the ladies drove off. We were welcomed into the house by an elderly couple and their son. They too had food and drink ready for us but we struggled with our limited Japanese to make conversation before having the traditional bath and bed. In the morning they had made their version of a European breakfast that was really kind and charming. To finish it all off the older man drove us two hours to a railway station where we could catch a train to Atami. I don't think we took anything away from the experience, except an anger in me that the religion had asked so much of their followers just to make a few rooms available for their leaders.

One of the London students was an Irish lady in her late sixties. Her son had married a Japanese girl and lived in Tokyo. All she wanted was to learn some basic stuff to make her daughter-in-law feel a bit more comfortable around her. From her name I knew she was a Roman Candle and I could see that she was getting quite distressed at the way things were working out. Back at the hotel I told her that in my wanderings around the town I had found a tiny Catholic church not two blocks away and asked if she would she like me to show her. It was Sunday so it was open and the Lord be praised, had an English speaking priest. Later she told me that it had been a wonderful experience and restored her spirits.

After leaving my friend, my intention was to drop down to my favourite restaurant for lunch and then head off to see the Matsuri. When I arrived on the sea front to find a spot I found myself surrounded by my course colleagues, together with an equal number of handmaidens from the hotel. You saw these youngsters all over the place doing small jobs like cleaning, arranging flowers or running errands. I don't know whether they were paid or volunteers. This outing was organised so I can only guess that they were there to help us keep out of trouble but I slipped away to be with the locals until dinner called.

Monday and Tuesday passed without any drama but the lessons were tedious in the extreme, so I missed a few due to 'ill health'. I contacted Haruyo from a call box to let her know what I had sleepwalked into so that when she arrived on Wednesday there would no shock or horror. That was the day when the mutiny took place.

Our teacher announced that as Thursday was our last day he would be going to Atami castle. We would be required to find him to show we were capable of travelling in Japan.

'We are here,' said the American.

'What do you mean?'

'In order to be here, we travelled on our own from Narita airport. Therefore we do not have to demonstrate to you or anyone else that we are capable of travelling in Japan. As far as I am concerned, you will be here to teach us.'

In Japan teachers expect their students to do as they are told and talking back is unheard of. I pushed my seat back and added my bit.

'I agree. Enough of this trip has been wasted with farms, museums, homestays; stuff we didn't sign up for and have been of very little use.'

There was a murmur of agreement. At the last lesson of the day we were all informed that there would be a meeting at 5pm on Thursday when a senior member of MOA was coming to address our concerns. I had spent so much time running solo that I hadn't realised that my fellow students had kicked up a stink about the way the course had been run, having to give up our rooms for a night, the food and other aspects that I knew nothing about.

The last day's teaching was derisory; everyone had lost interest and it showed. The meeting took place, a litany of complaints rolled out and the guy did his best to make peace but when lawyers were mentioned in the mix, it reached a dark place. It was closed down by a strange turn of events. The Kiwi who had zero Japanese, piped up in English that he had had a great time, learned so much and wanted to thank all those concerned in providing this wonderful experience from the bottom of his heart. Where this jovial jellyfish had been I don't know. Was he nobbled? Maybe.

Early on Friday 21 July we checked out and made our way to the island of Shikoku. A wonderful ten days followed with great onsen, terrific food, more Matsuri, plenty of castles and lovely people. My highlights were time spent at the famous Dogo Onsen in Matsuyama which is Japan's oldest hot spring and was the model for the bathhouse in Miyazaki's 'Spirited Away'. And the almost deserted roads in the mountains which were wonderful. Then it was back to Tokyo and a flight to UK on 2 August, leaving H to spend time with family and friends.

In due course I wrote to MOA to inform them that they would not be seeing me again. No surprise there. One of the trainee teachers took me on for a hour each Saturday with the emphasis on conversation which is what I needed, not studying for examinations that I had no plans of sitting.

12 BARNETT WILLIAMS PARTNERSHIP

'I think a compliment ought to always precede a complaint, where one is possible, because it softens resentment and insures the complaint a courteous and gentle reception.'

Mark Twain

Barnett Williams Partnership occupied the top floor of 24-28 Bloomsbury Way in Holborn while the rest of the building was taken up by the landlord, a major advertising agency.

Unfortunately the centre of the space was filled up with the lift, a staircase, an exit to the roof, washrooms and storage which restricted the usable space to four corridors with rooms off them. Reception was next to the lift, behind which lived the agency run by Bob and Ian with some five staffers. The next corner held offices for the events side with Kevin, Judith and Lisa. Then there was a run of small rooms let out to various freelance operatives and one of those would be mine. A design shop occupied the third corner run by one Fitzwilliams who on introduction I judged to be somewhat unhinged and a miserable sod at all times. I was told by one of his two crew that this was because his wife was earning more than he did. What surprised me was not the money bit but that he had a wife.

The last corner brought the bad news. It was a typesetting/print outfit called Amber run by yet another morose geezer with a couple of helpers and this pile of crap, which it turned out to be, was jointly owned by Fitzwilliams and BWP. The accounting naturally fell into the lap of BWP's bookkeeping department, so here we go again with the NGA and a mountain of small sales invoices to deal with. Happy days.

I briefly met my predecessor who offered a soft handshake, a few words and he was gone. Amazingly he was the double of Mr Lewis, my boss at Pall Mall Safe Deposit, not only in looks but with the same strange habit of being in perpetual motion. Constantly on the move, clutching bits of paper and appearing to the world that that he believed his errands were of life or death importance. The big difference was that Mr Lewis had a huge building to prowl complete with two basements, whereas at BWP the four short corridors could be gently walked in around three minutes maximum.

Len had an assistant called David, a young man with clubfeet. He was a nice enough fellow with a better knowledge of computers than me but seemed devoid of any ambition and content with his lot.

My early assessment was that one person could run the whole thing with or without a computer and for two it would be a cakewalk. Len told me that the workload had been so great previously that Bob's two daughters had been brought in during the summer holidays to bring everything up to date and at the year end the books went to the auditor to sort out. In a word, nobody had a clue where the businesses were heading at any time. I also discovered that it had become the practice of some of Amber's suppliers to ask Len for a payment on account even if they were not owed anything. And he would comply!

I had made it a rule never to criticize those who went before but in this case I would make an exception.

Later I was to discover that Len not only enjoyed a very good salary from BWP but he paid himself another wage from Amber and the petty cash funded a first class season ticket. So this poor excuse for an accountant had hewn himself a remuneration package at the level of the directors/owners and created nothing but chaos. The sole reason that the business never suffered from regular financial uproar was that Bob had negotiated a deal with a major client that they paid their media accounts four months in advance. As a result, BWP enjoyed a permanent six-figure interest free loan. After a few days, Len did offer me his help if I needed it. I politely declined.

Ian had already installed the computer system, which was a great help and meant that over the next four weeks I could set up the various accounts in preparation for the new financial year. Then I piled into wading through the books to knock them into shape, produce some year end results and have new balances to get our Sage system on the road. There were some unhappy suppliers when I went after the extra payments on account that they had wheedled out of Amber. But they all put their hands up and fell into line without a word.

Len organised his leaving do much as he lived his life. He chose the grottiest pub in the area and reserved the upstairs room. It was a pay bar but the food was laid on and free. And so it should have been: a range of sandwiches complete with all the makers' fingerprints was about as pathetic as it could have been. If you can't put on a proper spread, then don't do it at all. At last he was gone and we could get down to running the place properly.

Bob's daughters had returned to University and I had hoped that David would step up to the plate but was sadly disappointed. He did what he was given to do but showed no curiosity about the other aspects of our work. I found him a pay rise but that didn't light a fire under him either so I resigned myself to accepting him as being of very limited use.

As with most ad agencies, everything was straightforward, the staff very personable and with time to look after my other clients, I was in the right place. The mob at the other end of the corridor were a miserable bunch but I had little reason to make contact. And since David was carrying out the routine stuff on Amber, that left me with BWP.

This agency punched above its weight. For a small outfit it had some major players among its clients. Of course the problem was that the loss of just one client would have a dramatic effect on the business. Bob Barnett was a keen golfer and always on the lookout for new customers at the club but none appeared during my tenure. There was often mention of a small car manufacturer but again, nothing ever materialized.

For me things could not have worked out any better. BWP provided a solid base with an excellent stipend and with flexible hours so that my handful of clients could be serviced comfortably. Property renovation continued but at a gentler pace; Haruyo had an excellent and reliable building crew on hand which took much of the strain out of the work.

When we reached the end of 1995 we took a two-week break on Madeira which convinced us that the island was definitely the place to be.

So in 1996 we made two property purchases. A semi-detached house in Abbots Gardens in East Finchley came up for sale so we took a look. It was like walking into a time warp. The last decorations had probably been carried out, I guessed, around the mid-thirties. What little work that had been carried out in the place was detrimental, such as taking out the original fireplaces. The rear garden was a dump and the fences made with old broken doors that I imagine had been pulled from skips. We later discovered that the neighbour, a merchant banker, had offered to replace the whole fence at his cost but was knocked back. In fact this suited us very well. The renovation project was perfect for us and the timing was spot on. A cash offer was made and it was ours. On Madeira we had taken a leap of faith: we bought a plot of land, hired an architect and got introduced to a builder. My long held aim to retire before sixty was looking very real. We could knock our 'new' house into shape and get our retirement house built at the same time. Almost too simple, but what could go wrong?

The year turned out to be routine with a capital R, with enough work bringing in enough reward to meet the bills. The only downside was the commute. Having lived for so long firstly in Maida Vale and then Holborn, the journey from North London took up a great deal of time and energy. It was made easier by early starts and finishes and on occasion by using the car but still a pain.

In March 1997 we went to Madeira for a week. All went well but at Funchal airport waiting for our return flight on the Sunday I really didn't feel too good and on Monday morning something was definitely out of sync. My plan was to drop into Jo's company and knock out the VAT return on the way to BWP. To my horror I found it almost impossible to work out the sums and a half hour job took two hours. I was still there struggling when the troops arrived. When I tried to speak I stuttered and it was impossible to make myself understood. I went on to BWP where my problems continued and after a short while I took a taxi home. I thought that I must have had a stroke.

A medical merry-go-round followed. First my doctor, then a specialist, then hospital for scans and back to the specialist who announced that it wasn't a stroke but that I had banged my head which I denied. I was diagnosed as having sustained a subdural haematoma for which the only treatment was to rest and was told it would clear in a few weeks. The medics were right: in four weeks I was back to work. Then I remembered that just before the flight to Madeira I'd stood up under a low beam and hit my head hard. It was thought that the pressurised air on the plane had caused the problem to manifest itself. I confess it was scary at the time.

A meeting was called by Fitzwilliams who joined Bob and I in the boardroom together with Allen, Amber's manager. Allen opened the meeting by informing us that he was tired of working for 'The Man' and was taking the business, lock, stock and barrel away and opening up on his own. It was a fait accompli. He had the premises, the staff of two had agreed to join him and the clients frankly didn't give a monkey's toss as long as the work got done.

It was no loss for me apart for the loss of rent from the two small offices. I started to open up a discussion as to how we could retain a connection but Fitzwilliams went ballistic. He screamed at Allen for his treachery and lack of gratitude for all he had done for him. This was all going to hell in a basket and I left the scene. The next day Allen and his lads had gone.

This left me with an assistant who was essentially redundant. BWP's accounts could be run by one person part-time and without Amber's paperwork there was nothing for David to do. I had thought that my days as a hatchet man were all behind me. I was wrong.

Kevin quickly solved the vacant space situation. One of his major clients was looking for a couple of rooms to put their IT department and they moved in in quick time. But due to the nature of their business, they installed miles of electrical cables and trunking. Accordingly I asked Kevin to get a cast iron contract signed to fit a separate electricity meter. Plus when they moved out, they would pay all restoration costs otherwise our landlord would be sending the bill to BWP.

The situation with David was more difficult. For almost twenty years I had run my business solo and frankly lost the stomach for throwing folk out on their ear. In addition he was a raspberry ripple and finding a new slot would be no easy task for him. He was a decent bloke but if he had any aims and dreams they were not in the career arena. However something did come up to provide a reprieve.

One of BWP's suppliers based in Covent Garden asked me for help with their accounting. So it was arranged that David and I would visit every Wednesday to take care of business, the income arising flowing to BWP. It was my plan, and forlorn hope as it turned out, for David in due course to run it without me but that point seemed unreachable.

Bob asked for a meeting.

'Peter, the Board got together yesterday and it was agreed to ask you to become a Director of BWP. Would you do that?'

I was taken aback. This was something I really didn't want to take on.

'I am sorry Bob, that really is a great thing to be asked and if I was ten years younger I would jump at the chance. But I'm closing in on sixty and planning to retire before I hit that marker. It's no secret that I'm having a house built on Madeira and that it's not a holiday home. I'm moving there. I have plans in place to arrange for a replacement.'

'Not David I hope! When you were sick I realised how clueless he is.'

'No, not David. Sorry Bob, my plans really are laid.'

It was a shame. Another bloke might have agreed and just kept quiet but these guys had been decent to me and deserved the truth. I was sorry I couldn't pick the time and place, but it was out in the open and I was content with that.

My old friend Max had cancer and was booked into Kingston Hospital. What a shock to the system. His office was in Victoria House which, as luck would have it, was one block from BWP. So with the agreement of the directors, I took over the running of his practice until Max had recovered and felt well enough to return to work. This would involve taking a long lunch, plus weekend time but there was a first class part-time secretary who proved an immense help. Of course, with existing clients plus a couple of visits minimum to the hospital every week, life resulted in being crazy busy. But I didn't consider that I had any option; a mate of almost forty years means a lot in my books.

Max survived the operation and discharged himself on Christmas Eve 1997 when he spotted extra beds being set up to accommodate the surge of wounded expected over the holiday period from booze fuelled fighting and other excesses. It took a couple of months before he felt ready to take back the reins and then we moved the whole operation to his house in order that he be spared the commute.

It was not long after I embarked on the additional undertaking that I noticed David being on the missing list at odd times. I soon realised that he was actually taking advantage of my absence to go for a wander and spotted him from the sandwich shop around noon heading towards the British Museum and then trolling back into our office at 3pm.

'What time did you go for lunch?' I asked.

'Just before you got back.'

He must have thought I'd come up on the down train. How could he know when I got back if he wasn't here? I carried out a couple of checks and sure enough, a two and a half hour lunch break had become his norm. After trying to keep his job open and looking out for him, I was as mad as a skunk. With Kevin as my witness I fired him on the premise that since Amber had folded there wasn't work for one man let alone two. A decent payout was made and I gave him the Wednesday job that would provide about half of his BWP salary. I considered that generous especially when he'd been taking such bleeding liberties.

Then Bob went down with cancer but his was inoperable; he worked on for a few weeks and then stopped coming in. Very sad – he was a lovely bloke.

Another disaster struck: we lost a major client. There was nothing we could do about it and it was nobodies fault. The business simply got taken over and the buyer was happy with their ad agency. It punched a big hole in the gross income and the bottom line.

A meeting was set up for Richard Graham to meet Kevin to take over when I retired, which turned out to be in September 1998. I dropped a terrific deal into Richard's lap in the shape of a fixed monthly fee for a twenty hour weekly attendance, which would give him free time to cover his other clients. The only proviso was that he needed to show his face every day.

Since Max was not wanting any new work, I fell back on Cartwrights to take on most of my other clients and a Chalk Farm accountant to become auditor to BWP. All bases were covered.

Kevin's major customer held several events, conferences and get-togethers every year and their preferred location was at a Stakis hotel in Kent. Our arrangement was simple: we would pay 10% deposit and the balance of 90% seven days from the finish of the event after deduction of our 8% commission. We had received the deposit invoice for an upcoming conference and paid it immediately. Job done. Then an invoice arrived for the same event requiring one hundred per cent payment straight away. I phoned Stakis credit control in Glasgow and explained the situation. Their response came as a surprise.

'We take all our credit decisions based on a Dun and Bradstreet credit report and they recommend no credit granted to your business.'

'Look, all D and B do is look at the accounts filed with Companies House. No one from D and B has approached me for information.'

'I'm not interested. They say no credit and that's the end of it. You are required to pay in full up front or no conference. Makes no difference to me.'

'Hold on, we are an ad agency and don't need big capital assets backed by shedloads of finance. Our profits go to the individuals who make up the business. Over the past five years we have spent millions with you and paid on time, every time.'

'Not interested. Your past activities are irrelevant.'

'Can I speak to your manager?'

'He's not here. He's on a training course.'

'If all you refer to is D and B reports, what the hell is he being trained for? A half-witted monkey could do his job. You say we must pay 100%? What about our commission?'

'Do you get a commission from us?'

'You don't know?'

I was over all this. I could not risk the client's conference, so I sent a cheque by courier with a copy of everything to the Stakis CEO by fax. Two years later the hotel group were taken over by Hilton Hotels and I hope they fired the credit department en masse.

As my personal R Day approached, the Inland Revenue decided to become a nuisance. At the beginning of the year a tax inspector had arrived without an appointment demanding to see Bob and clearly on a fishing expedition. The inspector had noticed that directors' cars were all claimed to be doing a serious business mileage and the personal tax charge to the users were therefore minimized. It was a stupid error of judgement by an advisor. A check of the total mileage from the service records proved his claims and a bill for forty grand arrived. Belatedly, I took up the cause and with some smoke and mirrors cut the cost in half.

Then came another attack in the shape of a fistful of six years' assessments for seventy-five grand each. Now here is some really boring pen-pusher stuff. If an appeal is made against a tax assessment it usually goes in front of Commissioners who are just local business people who are unpaid and the tax mob always prevails. In my experience they are a waste of time but the Special Commissioners are a very different kettle of fish. They are appointed by a government department, are paid and do not nod everything through the gate. So where did my stack of appeals go to? I knew that the taxman would not like that one bit.

What he was trying to do was tax the payments in advance for advertising that we enjoyed, at the time the monies were actually received. There is an internationally recognised tome, GAAP (generally accepted accounting principles) and this confirmed what I had known all my working life that media, whether it is TV, radio, print or whatever is taxed when the media is actually published. So, I submitted a long 'snow job' missive, together with a mountain of data and drew attention to the silliness of his actions. Firstly, the pre-payments were around £250k at any one time and he had slapped tax on at 30%, hence £75k. But the £250k is the gross and our net profit at 2.5% would be just £6,250, with tax at 30% of £1,875.

Secondly, there would not be six years of this small sum. If you took profits back from year two into year one, then year three back to year two would replace what you had left for year one and whether it was six years or a hundred, it would still be a one off shot. He didn't understand a word and told me that his position was unchanged. There was a real danger of this nonsense knocking my retirement plans out of sync, so I wrote to the chief tax honcho to try and find some common sense. And it worked.

Officially, I stopped work on 4th September although I worked over the weekend to get the year end accounts completed. BWP had organised an in-house lunch and I threw an evening bash at the local Thai restaurant for friends and clients.

On the 8th of the month, we were on a flight to Madeira. But that's another story.

My connection to BWP didn't end there. The following year Kevin asked me to meet him to discuss the finances which were good, very good and sent a ticket and a fee. How could I refuse? It was good to see the gang again and after our business was done, I asked how Richard was getting on.

'He's gone.'

'What happened? It was a great chance for him.'

'Yes, I know but he was never here before lunch. One day I told him I needed to see him urgently and he told me he would be in the next day after lunch.'

'And was he?'

'Yes, at 6.30pm! When I tackled him on how ridiculously late he was, he simply shrugged and replied, "Well, it is after lunch, isn't it?" So I fired him for being disrespectful and insolent. I was not going to put up with that.'

There really are some people you just can't help. I know he had a slot at the Imperial War Museum for five quid an hour so I guess he preferred that. Real Ale wins.

A few months later BWP relocated to Jockeys Fields in Holborn, but without Judith who set up her own events business in Brighton. In London again, I dropped by but could get no answer to the doorbell and could see empty desks with computers in situ, much like the Mary Celeste. I rang the business on the first floor and was told that one day they were there and the following day they were gone. I found out later that Kevin and Ian had gone their separate ways but never the reason why and why overnight. Still, I was glad that I left before the break-up and wasn't dragged into the politics of it all.

Afterword

Every country in the world has a class system, some based on birth, others on wealth. In England in the 1950s there were five distinct groups: aristocrats, upper, middle (sometimes split into upper and lower), working and lower classes.

The lower consisted of the long-term unemployed, the homeless and the general unfortunates of life. Today a couple of additional classes have been identified but back then it had remained unchanged since Victorian times.

My mob were working class, although we were often on the cusp of sliding down into the degradation that is the lot of the lowest class, due to my father's inability to hold down a job in the long term. Wherever we lived the kids were much the same. We were rough knockabouts, playing games in the street, rummaging through bombsites and treating school as a place to go to during the day with only a minority really interested in serious learning. Few households had a TV or took in a daily newspaper and we didn't even own a radio. On those rare visits to the cinema, the Newsreel would offer a glimpse of the world outside our grimy cocoon.

My first experience of the boys from the higher ranks was during my four months of suffering at Haberdashers' Aske's Hatcham Boys Grammar School. The only lads I recognised were the handful of scholarship winners like myself. The vast majority were from the upper middle or upper class and they were different. It was not just because they came from homes with indoor plumbing, where their parents had cars and mothers that actually drove. They had an adultness about them and a worldly bearing in the way they conducted themselves. To have a decent roof over their heads, new clothes to wear, a father with a secure profession bringing in an income to cover all aspects of life was a given. I didn't realise it back then but I was to set myself the task of bridging the gap.

My path to qualification was a long one with many obstacles to overcome and some of my own making. It is a highly respected title to hold and I took it seriously. I believed that anyone looking at accounting information you had produced had the inalienable right to accept it as the most accurate that was possible, without bias or prejudice and not dreamed up to deceive and distract.

I also believe that the majority of my fellow members hold the same core principles. But I have also met too many who on the necessity to protect fee income will put aside honesty. They simply knock out a result suitable for the occasion and to quote, 'make the client happy'. If you know the true financial situation, however desperate, you are in a position to make informed decisions and hopefully take the steps that will bring improvements to the business.

If that Scaramouche Pilbrow thought for one moment that paying a wage would entitle him to use my qualification and reputation to do his bidding he was very much mistaken. To corrupt the 1976/77 figures by including imaginary profits from Iran in applying for a bank overdraft to give us time was, in my view, a foolish and dangerous plan. All he would get from me was my A-game, which would help turn a basket case unto a success story in less than four years.

But that was the way Pilbrow ran the business, from crisis to crisis. In his book he admitted that when he appointed Tony Field as CFO he hoped he would provide six months' breathing space: 'we need that credibility'.

Despite the many failures in business where the auditors were at least in part to blame and all the time and effort addressing the subject, the problem of being paid by the very organisation you are auditing is insoluble. In the early 2000s we had Enron, Lehman, Madoff, Saytam, Carillon and Ted Baker, to name but a few. In some cases the auditor was in collusion or turning a blind eye, simply not up to the task or even asleep at the wheel. In one notorious case the auditor was in a sexual relationship with the client CEO with plenty of pillow talk.

Accountancy produced a good living and opened many doors. I met a great many good people but of course a share of the bad and the mad. But they're the ones you tend to remember best, sorry to say.

In January 2024, as we were preparing to go to print, I received the news that my nemesis Pilbrow had died on 6th December 2023 aged 90. This had generated a feeding frenzy amongst the trade media with much of the saccharine excess simply lifted from biographies that were already on the web written by the man himself. It was to be expected of course but nothing could wipe out my memories of the man's treachery and mendacity.

One writer expressed his joy at receiving a letter signed 'Love Richard' and believed this was a genuine emotion. I got one of those too – two days before I was sacked!

My personal reaction was complete indifference. My persistent sorrow and regret was ever meeting the bloody awful man in the first place. In 1977 Theatre Projects was on the very edge of a financial precipice caused by the utterly bonkers commitment to the Iran project. By 1981 TP was on the first rung of the Stock Exchange ladder but within two years Pilbrow had taken it back to the edge of an even higher precipice. Despite several further injections of new capital, the agony of liquidation was dragged out to 1988 and all described as 'reorganisation'.

Also by Peter Roy

Madeira: the Floating Dungheap

A natural sequel to his autobiography, it tells the tale of Peter's retirement to Madeira with Haruyo and how it all went so wrong. A tale that spans the five rollercoaster years that the pair spent trying to escape from the island.

www.ingramcontent.com/pod-product-compliance
Ingram Content Group UK Ltd.
Pitfield, Milton Keynes, MK11 3LW, UK
UKHW042225281224
453045UK00002B/93